Heart Knocks

from Strayed to Straight

B. Lou Guckian

Independently Published
United States

B. Lou Guckian, Publisher
San Antonio, Texas, United States

Copyright © 2024 by B. Lou Guckian. All rights reserved.
U.S. Library of Congress Copyright Office Registration No. TXu 2-438-630
Library of Congress Control Number: 2025922591

All rights reserved, including the right of reproduction in whole or in part in any form by any method. No portion of this book may be reproduced, stored in or introduced into a retrieval system, or transmitted, in any form, or by any means—artificial intelligence, electronic, mechanical, photocopying, recording, or otherwise, including existing methods and those not yet developed—except for brief quotations in printed reviews, without prior permission of the author.

Professional headshot photos: Robert Burton. Personal photos: B. Lou Guckian. All photos wholly owned by B. Lou Guckian who reserves all rights.

Paperback ISBN: 979-8-9933560-0-6
Hardback ISBN: 979-8-9933560-1-3
eBook ISBN: 979-8-9933560-2-0

Strayed...

On such a night, long past midnight, a man accompanied me to my one-room flat where the predictable happened. When our deed was done, I lay on my side with my back to him, motionless, under the sheets and naked, curled snug into myself like an embryo and braced on one edge of the capacious king-size brass bed that had been my husband's and mine. A different man was there now, by my invitation and submission, naked, too. Glass-eyed, the both of us, from drinking straight whiskey and swallowing pills without names. Quiet tears spilled onto my pillow. I sensed his smirking; I was not what he had expected. All I had wanted was affection. Without a word, he dressed and left. And I knew I would not see him a second time. So I anguished there, alone, with only my scalding shame.

Dedicated to Mama and Daddy, without equal.
Thank you for your bravery, honesty, devotion and selfless forbearance.
For giving me someone to look up to and forward to becoming.
For loving each other and me when I was insolent and unlovable.
For praying me out of hell.
And to my Big Brother whose resilience taught me to "keep moving forward."

Why I Wrote This Book

I wrote this book for the benefit of you who read it and to God's gracious glory.

It tells what happened in my in-between years, the ones sandwiched by childhood and emergence from the disturbance I was for a very long time. It tells of multiple spiritual deaths; my spirit died each time I suffered a blow. I identify them all and how I live now despite and in light of spiritual death. This book also answers questions about why someone, why I, ventured down the perilous paths I have taken, and uncovers fascinating and enlightening outcomes that hopefully inspire you to steer clear of similar self-destruction yourselves or if already on a self-destroying course to turn from it.

I urge you to read this story all the way through, even the ugly unsettling parts. Keep reading through my mother's mental illness; teenage sexual exploitation; rebellion and disappearance; a deceptive abusive addicted spouse; divorce in my 20s; alcohol abuse and promiscuity; abusive lovers; terrifying threats by fire and guns; a 14-year crossing into and out of lesbianism; and deeply painful family tragedies, dysfunctions and betrayals. I tell of my slow bloody journey from self-inflicted and learned self-hatred, self-destruction, guilt and shame to a wholly altered life, one defined by the willingness to pursue God's will. In the end, as I reveal, no matter what our upbringing, wholesome or wretched or something in-between, we each have a spirit given by our Creator and what we do with it is a matter of choice. Even the most horrid experience as terrible as it is leaves us with a choice as to what we will do with it and after it. When I stopped looking outside myself for causes of bad breaks and bad temper, I took hold of something supernatural and powerful and things shifted in my favor.

Because life is a continuum, like a river, and intermingles with itself in a constant spin, I tell my story in linear time but also in serpentine fragments, those back and forth segues, because our past becomes our future and our future fades into our past. Both are recognizable and relevant. Time, as life, is at once concrete, elusive, eternal. So I tell my life story inhaling and exhaling through shifting whispers of time.

Despite parts of my story irritating some who may deny certain events ever happened or insist a predisposition to a particular even unsavory way of life is unchangeable, those who know me contend I am the quintessential example of the contrary. Also, while childhood influences may manifest in adulthood, analyzing implications of genetics or the psychology of environmental influence is not within scope of my book. I only describe my risky and risque life, which was tripped up and frighteningly ugly at times, for years at a stretch, but which now is changed, so much so, people who have known me long have observed my "transformation." I am recognizably different. Tangibly, I have returned to the humble virtues of youth and grown up anew.

If we cannot be authentic first and foremost with ourselves, and so with each other, then what is the worth and substance in human life? If we are not an honest lot, then all human life is an empty facade void of worth. There is dignity, daring, sparkle and splendor in truth.

Acknowledgements

Thank you, first and foremost, to my Creator, God, for giving me the words and a publisher. To Sacred Scripture, God's own hand, for conviction, affirmation and wisdom. To my parents, for being the loving, living manifestation of God on Earth; your exemplary lives saved mine and made it, at long last, worth your generous gifts of love, time and patience.

Thank you, Patrick Lynn, my elder brother by eight years and the eldest, without whom the foundational story of our parents' early lives as experienced by you would have been impossible for me to tell with all accuracy. Your love of history and the written word fed this book with firsthand remembrances in the details of our family's past. You spent hours talking with me about events I could not recall or did not know. Thank you, Big Brother, particularly for the anecdotal account of Daddy's firsthand encounters on the European front during World War II (WWII), and the humorous segues a human man, our father, had to grasp in-between recurring rounds of inhuman slaughter on the battlefront to survive it.

Thanks to my eldest sister Jo Ann and my Aunt Cathy for facts about Mama's illness and its immediate aftermath in the form of your recollections I was too young to understand or later remember. Thank you, Aunt Cathy, for your faith in God and me.

A few depictions of my parents and our family are in small part snippets from pro-bono articles I published prior to writing this book. These are "Daughter Fondly Recollects Father's Finest Legacy—Himself" published by the Gonzales Inquirer June 18, 2004; and "Through Tough Times of Every Sort, Daddy Never Gave Up" published by the San Antonio Express-News June 20, 2004.

Portions of chapters entitled "Daddy's Sick, Hell is Real" and "Daddy's in the Ground and I Climbed In" contain details gleaned from my master's thesis, "Elder Abuse: More Is Expected Unless Society and Newspapers Intervene," published December 2005; and my related pro-bono article, "Daddy Suffered in Silence—Are You Next?" published by The National Consumer Voice for Quality Long-Term Care September 2009 and reprinted in the Spotlight on Recovery 10th Anniversary Fall 2011 issue.

I relied on online research, with sources including Encyclopedia Britannica and Wikipedia and others, for fact-checks and accurate descriptions of parts of my parents' stories related to times and circumstances they lived through before I was born as well as for other data checkups.

I refer to the Holy Bible (New King James Version or NKJV used interchangeably with Scripture) and various books of the fellowship of recovery, including "Alcoholics Anonymous, The Story of How Many Thousands of Men and Women Have Recovered From Alcoholism, Fourth Edition" published by Alcoholics Anonymous World Services Inc., endearingly referred to as the "Big Book of AA," or more briefly, the "Big Book"; and "One Day at a Time in Al-Anon" or ODAT, and "Courage to Change," the successor to the ODAT, both published by Al-Anon Family Group Headquarters Inc., World Service Office for Al-Anon and Alateen.

No words are sufficiently eloquent to express my eternal gratitude to those dear ones instrumental in walking patiently alongside me through the slow, grueling process of recovering myself, particularly Edwin, Jim, Milena and Robert, Connie, Judith, Caye, and David and Mary Frances. A special thanks to my multifaceted friend Robert Burton for trusted friendship, commissioned photography, and faith in God. You helped me envision emotional well-being when mine was murky.

I express my deepest gratitude to Jim for dedicating every Saturday for an entire year to guide me through the toughest earliest times of my awakening; to Caye, who after years of battling illness never lost her smile or faith in God and who I count among my most inspirational friends; to David, for teaching me I could restart a troubling day at any time; to Mary Frances, for standing by me through some of the darkest and joyous times; to Milena, my beloved friend, you are my Nurse Nightingale, without whom my whole world would be much less bright; to Connie, for sanctifying my spirit with frequent exchanges of gratitude in the happy ups and lonely downs of daily living; to Lorraine, a true Texas woman, your humor, strength and poise while surviving the unthinkable reminds me how vital is our faith in God and ourselves; and to Dana and Terry for your friendship, love and encouragement in a resurrected camaraderie after having skipped past 5 decades since high school graduation without contact.

I extend deepest thanks to Phineas (Phin), for being an unwavering source of abiding light along my journey and introduction to Don, a gifted licensed counselor who became my voice of reason, whose insights on the nature and credence of dreams are noted herein. Don, your patient guidance lifted my morale and helped me evolve. To Brenda, my childhood neighbor who by no accident re-appeared in my adulthood when I needed a lifesaver; without your kind understanding and wise direction, I would not have taken that very first step away from a bottom-dwelling subsistence into a changed life. To Sober Indian Riders, for your unique and cherished friendship; I will not forget any one of you.

Most appreciatively, to relatives, dearest of friends and fellowship of faith-filled others near and far, you know who you are, who have come and gone, or stayed; thank you for gifting me with unconditional love and lasting hope. Deep love goes to my dozens of nieces, nephews, and grand-nieces and nephews for the joy you've given your childless auntie.

And with utmost appreciation to those entrusted ones who poured over this work in its earliest stage in advance of publishing, for your candid critique and contributions for the benefit of readers to come: most especially Lynn, your thorough and truthful review improved this book considerably, and Don, Milena, Lorraine, Deborah, and Connie, you have the eye of a hawk, as well as those anonymous others who contributed to the betterment of this book. Thank you.

All events in this book are true. Some names have been changed. Most of those in the fellowship of recovery are void of surnames, in line with the principle of anonymity, except where the individual granted permission.

A final proviso. I have pardoned myself and everyone who caused harm in my life through cruel words or ruinous acts however levied. And unless I tell of the damage done, I cannot then tell of how I was impacted by it or most importantly how I overcame it, which is my story. This book is not intended a finger-pointing to the grossest wrongs but an enlightened accounting of what I have surmounted and the means by which I have done it. To that end, every individual and event mentioned herein holds earnest purpose: In the telling of the truth, hearts may be healed and lives revived.

Chapters

The River
Daddy's Honor
Mama's Breakdown (First Spiritual Death)
My Charmed Childhood
The Diary
First Kiss, Cigarettes and Motorcycles
At the Drive-in (Second Spiritual Death)
Runaway (Third Spiritual Death)
Married to a Stranger
Stoned and Scared (Fourth Spiritual Death)
Denial is a Liar
Split (Fifth Spiritual Death)
Bad Behavior and the Unpriestly Priest (Sixth Spiritual Death)
O'er the Sea
Fresh Starts
DWI: Living Through Roger's Dying (Seventh Spiritual Death)
Gunpoint (Eighth Spiritual Death)
Don't Save Me, I'm Drowning
A Big Car and A Virgin
Burning Building (Ninth Spiritual Death)
Out and Up
Front Page News Against All Odds
Me and Daddy: A Dream Come True Tale
The Duplicitous Face of Abuse (Tenth Spiritual Death)
Daddy's Sick, Hell is Real (Eleventh Spiritual Death)
Daddy's In the Ground and I Climbed In
The End to Abuse: A New Beginning (Twelfth Spiritual Death)
The "R" Word
Epiphany
My Mother, My Judge, My Friend
An Inside Job
Mentors of the Spiritual Kind
In Step

From Strayed to Straight (First Spiritual Awakening)
FishHook
Indigenous People, Native Spirit (Second Spiritual Awakening)
Of Bliss and Sorrow
Sober Indian Riders: The Ride of My Life
This White Light (Third Spiritual Awakening)
Red Spirit and Me
Kelly's Gone to Golden Pond
Mama Died and Grief Stayed Long
Angels and Ghosts
4,000 Miles
Lynn
Debbie
Confident Humility in Self-Validity
Divine Accounting
Down River

The River

My favorite place is alongside a murmuring river, any river. I suppose it is because I am perplexed by time and space that comes and goes like a river flows. When alongside an experience, it is as if it is everything and all. But once it goes, like a river flows, it vanishes somewhere. Where does all that everything go?

All I know is, no longer am I the infant in a crib in diapers who learned determination early. A bone specialist bolted my ankles together with a silver steel brace I wore 24/7 for six months to straighten my legs (I presume I was pigeon-toed), like a female Forrest Gump. Mama took pleasure in sweet appreciation of my determined learning to flip myself over in the crib to then pull myself up to stand, all with a wide baby's smile.

Neither am I a child of 4 anymore, nor a young woman of 30 or maturing woman of 50, but all my past years, live. In present tense. All of "them" are "me." Does all that life, all that space and time, accumulate into some mysterious universal collection of energy somewhere, to then become one shared stream of energy or light disbursed in bits, here and there, in various forms? Will I recognize it when I see it? Is this what memories are? Do other people see and hear what I do? Is it all waiting for me somewhere like a game of hide and seek? Will I find what has passed if I chase it, down river? Will I remember this day, once I go, down river?

And what of dreams, sometimes vivid and other times obscure; sometimes bizarre or otherwise honeyed, of which sensations from the latter linger indefinitely. Do dreams have meaning? Why do some recur while others do not? Why do we not remember some while others leave stubborn scars on our psyche? Don explains dreams are the means by which the subconscious mind makes sense of occurrences and circumstances and thus informs our conscious mind. Yet, some dreams are merely "a bunch of stuff," he says. And sometimes, no clarity comes at all. But some dreams answer questions we ask of the subconscious, that power within, God, or Spirit. These sincere supplications can deliver either with clarity or symbolism solutions to perplexing situations in which we find ourselves. Sometimes, I have asked a question outright and the answer has come into my mind swiftly. And sometimes, there is no answer at all.

Our dreams are ours. The symbolism, validity, credence or interpretation belongs wholly to the individual dreaming. I learned from Don to keep a pen and notebook on my nightstand, so on occasions when I awaken from a meaningful dream, I immediately switch on the light and record it. And then return to sleep.

I am astonished at how time and I have created a cross-stitch of experiences that form on the finished side of the fabric of my life a pleasing picture. But on the underside are knotted threads and frayed ends hidden from view. Sometimes I'm astounded at the twists in life. And sometimes I'm disgusted by the choices I have made. And I wrestle with If Only. If only I had not put myself in those places, with those people. If only I had not lived so thoughtlessly, dangerously, impulsively. Were my destructive choices pre-destined with some higher purpose in mind? I could have been killed. Jailed. Shot. Stabbed. Beaten. Drowned. Kidnapped. Worse. But I was not. Why not? Why are some? Why not others? Why am I still alive but my younger brother is not? Or the woman on that horrid dismal night who crashed her Ford Bronco into a parked 18-wheeler; gone, too. Will I see them again someday, down river?

My memory is somewhat sketchy before the age of 8 but I distinctly remember the river that summer. Mama was at an institution in Victoria and Daddy was working in San Antonio where we lived. My youngest brother and three sisters and I were at my Aunt Marie and Uncle James' home in the country in Cuero, an historic Texas town along the Chisholm Trail where gunfights ensued, so stories go. The old house was spacious in my childhood memory, with scratched worn wooden floors and airy rooms. The bedroom where all us kids slept had a wood-framed unscreened window that opened with some effort and early one morning a cow stuck its head inside it. When we awoke at its mooing, we found my 5-year-old cousin had wet the bed, again, and the sheets were cold because of it.

Nearby was the Guadalupe River where in the afternoons we played in the mossy rippling waters that were ankle-deep in some places, knee-deep in others, and waist-high and swimmable in still others. To say I swam is untrue. Mama nearly drowned in the river as a child and so kept us away from the inner parts of rivers, lakes and the waves of the ocean. Only tiptoeing into the water's edge or going in barely ankle-deep was familiar.

But that summer, with Mama away and us with our cousins, we played freely in the river. I did not linger only in the shallowest parts. I let the river wash around me and then carry me along for a short distance, a few yards or so, gliding along with the current like a human sailboat. As I write this, I can see my littler self in a Sears-catalog one-piece black bathing suit, my long hair soaked and sticking to my freckled face and my skin glistening in the sunshine.

I remember the smoothness of the stones on my bare feet, legs and hands when I sat down in the shallows. And the delight of it on a hot day. Not only toes, feet and ankles like when Mama was nearby but all of me. Submerged in the water, I felt the push and pull of life in that river. It was both soothing and powerful. It had the power to sweep me away if I let it. I knew something about power at 8. My legs pressed hard and sure against the force of the river's downstream current as I stood and walked through it in its opposite direction upstream. Here, in the river, while safest in the shallowest parts, I imagined I was master over the mighty water while being nearer the middle of it. And I have been lured by the river ever since.

A typical child with average intelligence cannot intellectualize the essence of creation, or her oneness with it, or that which created it and her. But her spirit knows that essence is alive, that the hypnotic lure we call life keeps pulling each of us forward, through space and time, like a river going someplace, always going someplace, never still too long. It is like when I am outside in a dark, noiseless midnight, looking heavenward and feeling a tug, no longer an observer but inside the sprawling sky, the moon, the stars. And I wonder, is this what makes the river flow, and the moon glow, and the wind blow, and the wolf howl, and the grass grow tall and sweet, and a human being who is born to become 10 and 20 and 80 and 100 years old?

For decades, I was swept along blindly in a living nonexistence, a submissive rider on the downstream current of life, often pitched about and injured by its turbulence. But today, I choose whether to drift with the current or plunge head first to swim strong upriver in the opposite direction.

So I return often to the river to walk reverently along its banks and listen to its rippling speech, and to the tempo of time in front and above and in all that surrounds me. I am bound by it, and in it, and it in me, profoundly aware of its intimate reach into my heart.

The river's lure, the moon's hypnotic pull, the assuring stars, the bond with another human being, with all creation, these and more all are bits and pieces of the same… thing. I am subdued by all that whispers to me, while on the inside, I am coursing like a river.

"And it shall be that every living thing that moves, wherever the rivers go, will live" (Ezekiel 47:9 NKJV).

Daddy's Honor

I suppose like most adults I cannot recall my life at 4, but I am told two unalterable events occurred that year. One was an accident. We had a swing set in the backyard that had two swings plus a slide on one side and a tall crossbar on the other side from which we hung and swayed like monkeys. Apparently, I was swinging one day and fell off onto the ground, hard, breaking my collarbone. I remember the swing set but not the fall. The other event transformed our family forever.

It was 1959. Our big family lived in a little house at 244 Charcliff in southeast San Antonio, Texas. It was the second home my young parents purchased, after outgrowing the first one they bought in Highland Hills thanks to the G.I. Bill. Eight of us occupied the 900-square-foot one-story house: Mama, Daddy, my two brothers, three sisters and me. The front room served as the girls' bedroom, the boys shared one small bedroom, and my parents had a room. Our one tiny bathroom had a sink, bathtub and commode and a small window overlooking the backyard. I remember Daddy in his white tee-shirt and khaki slacks shaving at the sink while we three youngest girls took a bath together. I imagine our shared baths were a function of savings, both of water and time. A tiny kitchen with a window over the basin faced the street, and a cozy living room had been formed by a section of closed-in carport.

We were fortunate to own an electric wringer washing machine and hung everything on the clothesline in the backyard to dry. The backyard was encased by a chain link fence with honeysuckle vines engulfing the stretch along the alley with fragrant blossoms all spring and summer long. We kids used to pull out the skinny threads from the blossoms and lick droplets of sweet nectar at their tips. How we rushed to climb onto the thick honeysuckle to sit on top in time for the garbage truck to make its way through the alley, because sometimes the garbage men gave us paperback comics. When Mama spied them, she told us promptly to throw those "dirty" books in the garbage can, wash our hands, and never take anything from the garbage men again! We didn't understand her deep anxiety over germs.

So when I was 4 and Mama was 33 she had a "nervous breakdown" that marked the start of lasting consequences and end of life as we knew it.

It is important to pause here to tell of key events in my parents' histories that led up to that despairing day in 1959. I cannot tell my story without first telling crucial parts of theirs, because who they were formed who I was and would become, a realization that took me one-half of my lifetime to understand.

Mama and Daddy were born in 1926 and 1923, respectively. They were raised during the Great Depression and fought WWII against fascism, enduring the largest combined-forces war in human history. Their entire generation lived with courage, maturity and wisdom, working hard from an early age at home on the farm through an international economic depression, and sacrificing at home and abroad during WWII's crushing threats to liberty. This is why they are called the Greatest Generation and this is why they must be remembered for their honor and life lessons to us all. The Greatest Generation passed onto their children, the Baby Boomers, undisputable qualities of perseverance, bravery and faith in God. They had little, wasted nothing and shared all they had.

When I grew up, respect was taught and practiced. We did not call my parents by any name except "Mama" and "Daddy." The only exception was "Mother," a formal term my father used with his mother and my brothers used often with Mama. Anything else was considered disrespectful.

My parents were God-fearing, protective and providing people, as were their parents and grandparents. I never knew them to lie or cheat. In one way, I lived childhood in a bubble, protected from that which could hurt me and completely trusting. But in another way, hurtful things were happening all around me. And inside me. As I have matured, I have come to believe the sweet innocence of childhood is divinely ordained. We learn, soon enough as adults, about the ugly in the world in which we must learn to live, or die. We learn there are many ways to live. And many ways to die even while living.

One-half of my beginning was Daddy. Eugene Patrick Guckian, invariably Eugene, Gene or Pat, was born into a family persuaded toward the Baptist faith on his mother's side. He had one younger brother, George Edward, and three sisters: Helen Joyce, Dorothy and Doris Marie. His grandfather, William Guckian, immigrated to America from Ireland in the early 1880s to escape ruling British oppression. Many immigrants entered through Ellis Island, New York, but others, as with the Guckians, arrived at Galveston. Employment prospects teemed in Texas supplied by the Southern Pacific Railroad in Lockhart, where they settled.

Daddy's parents, William Patrick "Willie" and Alta (Mercer) Guckian, were farmers in Lockhart where my father was born. I remember fondly Grandpa and Grandma on their rare visit one summer. When we little ones heard the faint approaching ice cream truck's distinctive, tinkling xylophonic melody, Grandpa reached into his baggy pants pocket jingling with coins, handed us each a nickel, and told us to get a penny from Mama so we could buy an ice cream.

The Guckians moved to Gonzales when Daddy was 1 year old to help Alta's daddy, Milford "Papa" Mercer, work his place. Papa Mercer owned a 640-acre ranch that spanned into Luling, complete with cattle, crops and oil wells. He drove an automobile, a sign of affluency in the early 1900s during the Great Depression when one quarter of the working population was jobless. Daddy's family lived on Papa's land in a small house built for them, along with families of hired help who had small houses of their own. Daddy told how sometimes on Saturday nights, after a week of hard work and supper, all the families gathered on the porch of the main house to play music, sing and dance.

Papa kept a line of mason jars filled with hard rock candy and Scotch whiskey on the kitchen windowsill. First thing every morning, Papa poured some of that mixture into an empty mason jar or tall glass, squeezed fresh lemon juice into it, filled it with cool water, and drank it down. I do not remember Papa Mercer but Lynn has fond remembrances of him and the Mercer's place in the country. At the back of their house was a sleeping porch with an iron bedstead and mattress where Lynn slept during visits. Between the house and barn was a sulfur water tank with a windmill and into that tank the undersized catfish from the river would go. By the time Lynn was old enough to know what a catfish was, he accompanied Papa to the tank where Papa with a handful of maize fed the fish. He'd whistle and up they'd come, some of them huge.

Lynn remembers Papa standing on the front porch of the main house telling him to watch the giant red ants in the yard. He'd say, "See that one? Watch him." And then he'd spit tobacco juice and it swallowed the ant. Papa kept a laying hen on the front porch so he was guaranteed a fresh egg nearly every morning. Behind the house was a chicken coop. One day, when Lynn went to collect eggs, he found a glass egg and asked Papa why he kept it in the coop. Papa explained it was there for the chicken snakes; they have a saw bone in the back of their throats used to open egg shells, but if they swallow a glass egg, it shatters and kills them.

One memory of the old Mercer camp house I do recall albeit vaguely because I was very young, but Lynn made many a visit there to fish with Daddy and other relatives. Down by the river, called the bottom, there was a camp house built on stilts that decades later was washed away by a flood. It was built in 1944 when Mama and Daddy married and the whole family gathered to raise it. It changed over time and even wound up with screened windows instead of shutters, air-conditioning and indoor plumbing. The Mercers, Guckians and other kin enjoyed retreats there when they'd fish, hunt and gather at the table. There were cans stuck in the rafters with fishing poles in them for folks to fish with, complete with hook, line, sinker and bobber. "The Camp House" is a very fond family memory.

Daddy's boyhood evolved around chores, including plowing fields with a heavy manual plow fastened to a mule, picking cotton, hoeing corn fields and carrying firewood; a one-room schoolhouse; community picnics where he helped his daddy barbecue; and vast open spaces where he fished, swam and rode horses. When he and George Edward played cowboys and Indians, they rode horses buck-naked sometimes. Daddy had a pinto stallion and on it one day he rode. Upon returning home in front of the gate, he saw beneath it a large muddy puddle. As he leaned from the saddle to open the gate, the pinto evidently did not want to walk through the mud, and bucked, pitching Daddy off and into the muddy water.

He hated plowing but despised picking cotton more. When he was 10, they'd all go to the fields to pick. He filled his sack with scarcely enough cotton for a pillow and napped beneath a tall stalk, until his daddy found him and gave him a whipping. As soon as Grandpa was gone, he'd lie down again and go back to sleep.

In the summertime, Daddy and his three sisters and brother rode down from their farmhouse in a horse-drawn wagon with their mother and daddy to the river to bathe. As Daddy told it, he and his brother "fell off anywhere along that river and swam clear to the bottom like ducks." Daddy loved to fish and was raised to respect and know wildlife. Mama once told how Daddy could hear a bird singing in the distance and without ever seeing it tell you what it was.

It was along the banks of the Guadalupe River near Papa Mercer's place where Daddy first made at the age of 12 what later became his tasty barbecue sauce. He set out to fish one day when Grandma gave him bread and fixings for sauce to take along to eat. The then young Eugene cooked the red gravy in a tin can over an open fire on that riverbank. Daddy said sometimes on weekends they loaded the family and camping supplies in a wagon and headed to the river to camp. Sleeping on tarps in open air, he said there surely were snakes all around but they never bothered them.

One day, as he and another boy walked to school, a dog followed. Daddy ran back home to retrieve some high-life, a liquid used to repel dogs or put on spines of work animals to get them moving, and poured it all over the trailing hound. When they got to the schoolhouse, the dog still in tow, they entered as did the dog behind them. Soon after, it commenced discharging diarrhea all over the place inside and outside. I never learned whether Daddy was punished for that, but I'm certain Grandpa heard about it. I did hear that Daddy and the other boy involved had to scrub the schoolhouse clean.

As a boy, Daddy had a rat terrier that hated rattlesnakes. It seemed to have been born to kill them. One day, the dog was barking vehemently at a wood pile from which a large rattler emerged and bit it. The little dog swelled to the size of a football and ran away. For three days, he was missing. Then, one day, a scratching was heard on the back door and there stood the happy hound, perfectly well.

When in my 40s, I accompanied Daddy and Mama on drives through Palmetto State Park, near Gonzales where they grew up. The San Marcos River runs through it. We drove past the pavilion and campgrounds to fish from a low-lying concrete bridge at a spot along the river where Daddy as a boy of 12 pulled a girl from the water before she drowned. On a different Sunday as we exited the park, we pulled over to admire the overlook of sprawling, red granite hills. Taking in the panorama, Daddy commented with evident fond remembrance, "Me and George Edward used to crawl all over these rocks when we were kids."

Daddy turned 16 in 1939. That year, WWII began in Europe, so he decided to quit school and enlist in the Texas State Guard. His unit one year later was mobilized to federal service as part of the 36th (Alamo) Division, 141st Infantry Regiment, U.S. Army. At 18, he trained in the Louisiana maneuvers with 400,000 men in the largest war games of its kind up to then. Before deployment, Daddy was home one day when he and Grandpa went outside to work. In the 1940s, tractors required hand-cranking to start. When Daddy spun the flywheel to start the John Deere tractor, it rapidly spit fire on Daddy and set him ablaze, immediately igniting his cotton shirt, snapped up the front and cuffed at the wrists. Consumed in flames, he struck out running from the barn toward the water trough, with Grandpa chasing after him. When he tackled Daddy, the shirt peeled away readily and his burnt skin with it. For several weeks, Daddy recovered in a hospital from third-degree burns over 75 percent of his body.

By 1942, at the age of 19, Daddy had risen to Sergeant and trained in Florida and Massachusetts prior to embarking for the Torch landings in North Africa on Nov. 8, 1942, as part of the spearhead (lead unit to hit the beach and as a result absorb high casualties). It was the first land engagement of German and Italian forces by the U.S. Army. Daddy survived it unharmed. Deployed to the French Morocco, Daddy fought across North Africa, and following the surrender of the Afrika Korps and Italian forces began amphibious training in preparation for Operation Husky, the invasion of Sicily, which occurred July 9-10, 1943, from Tunisia. Once Sicily fell, Daddy, again, was in the spearhead on Sept. 9, 1943, this time for Operation Avalanche. There, Allied forces invaded the Italian mainland at Salerno on the southwestern coast of Italy.

Daddy didn't talk much about Salerno, likely because of its ferocity and bloodshed that occurred there. History calls it "Bloody Salerno" for the savagery that took place. Even the Germans paid tribute to the 141st Infantry for its bravery, tenacity and military dominance during the battle. Daddy again survived. In 1998, he and Mama saw "Saving Private Ryan" when the film premiered in theaters. Daddy wept quietly at the opening scene. While the movie depicted the Normandy Landing in France, Daddy said the Salerno Landing in Italy was precisely like that.

As the fight made its way up the Italian peninsula, on Jan. 12, 1944, Daddy turned 21 in a foxhole in a cemetery on a mountainside near Naples. That's where he buried a cache of German weapons covered in grease (cosmoline) and wrapped in a shelter half (one-half of a pup tent). He planned to retrieve it but never did. For all we know, it's still there. When Lynn was in Naples in 1981 and '82, he tried to find the location but had no luck. He surmises some Italian probably got a surprise when digging a grave in that cemetery or it was never found and remains there today.

Daddy subsequently fought through Naples to the Rapido River and Monte Casino. By June 4, 1944 (2 days before the Normandy Landing in France), he had seen combat in numerous spearheads and suffered shrapnel injuries and was pulled from the Front with sufficient accumulated points to be sent home. During WWII, for a soldier to return home, he had to have accumulated a certain number of points accounting for time in service, number of times in combat, and/or face-to-face combat in various theaters/battle areas.

He sailed from Italy on the troopship Brazil, which arrived (we believe) in New York, and then took a train to Texas where he and Mama were married in August 1944. Sergeant Guckian was transferred to Maxwell Field (now Maxwell Air Force Base), Alabama, where Mama joined him and where they remained until he was mustered out following VE Day or Victory in Europe Day when in May 1945 Nazi Germany surrendered. VJ Day or Victory over Japan Day followed that August when Japan surrendered. This ended WWII and ushered in what would be called the Baby Boomer generation, as U.S. soldiers returned home.

Like soldiers of Daddy's generation who survived WWII, he rarely spoke of battlefield experiences, saying only, "war is hell." But he did share a few stories with me and even more with Lynn. Here I recount a few to depict the man my father was, who at a young age dutifully and unflinchingly confronted the shocking, unimaginable horrors of war abroad, and in so doing, kept the rest of us from it. One story has to do with "no man's land." Daddy commanded a platoon of 14 men assigned to areas of cease-fire in the middle of a bloody battle zone where each side carried in gurneys to collect bodies and body parts of fallen comrades. Another concerns the doctor Daddy served with who delivered him at birth. He was in a tent performing a surgery when their camp came under mortar fire. A piece of shrapnel shaped like a needle pierced the doctor's heart, killing him and dropping him instantly to the ground.

Most stories Daddy shared with Lynn were on the lighter side. Despite the revolting horror he witnessed repeatedly, Daddy held onto his wit. He said he knew he was going to heaven because he already had been through hell.

While on patrol in North Africa with his squad in the half-track (a truck with steering tires in front and tank tracks where dual axles would have been), they were strafed (shelled) by an ME-109 (German front-line fighter plane). The gunner in Daddy's squad manned the .50 caliber machine gun mount and apparently killed the pilot as the plane continued straight and level into a mountain and exploded. The gunner kept firing until pried from the gun. One night, following a lengthy patrol, Daddy climbed into a duce-and-a-half (two-and-a-half-ton truck) and fell asleep. When he awoke, he could see daylight through the canopy. Turns out, the encampment had been attacked from the air and he slept through it all—in a truck full of ammunition.

While in North Africa, he and his squad were traveling down a road in the half-track when they came upon an Arab in a donkey cart. They honked, yelled and did everything possible to get his attention to move off the road to no avail. Daddy wasn't about to drive off the road as either side had not been cleared of mines. So, he let the Arab get a way up in front of him and then proceeded to drive over Arab, donkey, cart and all. The old man and donkey were not hurt; both were smashed in the sand. But the cart was demolished.

While bivouacked in Tunisia doing amphibious training, he took a DUKW (fondly called a Duck), an amphibious version of the duce-and-a-half, and a case of hand grenades out into the Mediterranean Sea to fish. The grenades stunned or killed the fish, which he scooped up and took back to camp to fry. This same camp was running short of toilet paper. One of Daddy's relatives or friends was a B-24 bomber pilot who said he'd take care of it. Days later, air raid sirens went off as a plane flew in at low altitude. It was the B-24 bomber pilot who "bombed" the camp with a case of toilet paper with rolls streaming down from the bomb bay.

This is one of my favorites Daddy told Lynn. He was in the thick of the fight at Monte Casino. One evening after his squad had set up their gun emplacement (they towed a 37-milimeter anti-tank gun behind the half-track), Daddy went to check on the British unit on their flank. When he arrived, the Brits were starting a fire to brew tea and invited him to stay for a cup. He asked if they did not know that the Germans had 88-milimeter guns on the mountain and would fire on them if they started a fire. The Brits replied, "Jerry can't hit what he shoots at" and proceeded to start their fire. At that time, Daddy figured discretion was the better part of valor and took off for his own emplacement.

About that time, the 88's opened up and continued until the fire at the Brit emplacement went out. Daddy went back to check on them, finding shell holes all around the position and the Brits cheerfully telling him, "See, Yank. We told you Jerry can't hit what he shoots at!" Now comes a second part to this story. In 1985, Lynn and his wife Judy vacationed in Tenerife, Azores. He sported a moustache then, as did Daddy in 1944. At dinner one night, an older Brit called out to Lynn saying, "By God, Pat, you haven't changed since Casino!" It was the Brit from Monte Casino who had invited Daddy to tea.

While in Tunisia training for the Sicilian campaign, Gen. George S. Patton was inspecting the troops and came upon Daddy's squad with a half-track towing a 37-milimeter anti-tank gun. The General sat down behind the gun and told Daddy to give him a firing order. Daddy advised the General he might want to move back a bit from the sight on the gun, but Gen. Patton said, "I know what I'm doing. Give me a g******** firing order, Sergeant!" So, Daddy did and Gen. Patton fired the gun. The recoil knocked him backwards on his butt, when he looked up and said, "By God, Sergeant, you were right!"

The 141st was a mechanized infantry outfit but it used mules to move equipment, arms and ammo. While ascending a mountain with pack mules, Daddy's unit came under German artillery fire, at which point he said he'd walked behind enough mules plowing and wasn't about to get killed because of one. He pushed his mule over the side and down the mountain. The firing stopped after that.

When back in the States at Maxwell Field, Daddy transferred to the Army Air Corps Military Police. He completed military service Sep. 30, 1945 at 22, receiving decorations and awards for service to America during WWII during the European Campaign. He was awarded the Bronze Star Medal, American Defense Medal and Combat Infantryman's Badge, the latter two of which he was most proud. Once home, he would raise a brood of kids with my mother, attain his General Educational Development (GED) degree, attend business college, become a founding member of St. Benedict Catholic Church and school, retire from federal civilian service and be named Sir Knight Guckian with the Fourth Degree Knights of Columbus. The Knights' principles embodied my father's: charity, unity, fraternity, patriotism, integrity, professionalism, excellence, respect.

His moral standard in life was personified by perpetual service, sacrifice, humility, generosity and honor. Daddy never spoke of his achievements. He lived them.

After all he endured and would, Daddy was a sober husband and father, good to my mother and us kids, faithful and stern. He handled whatever came his way. And even rediscovered his sense of humor, laughter and joy in living. Again and again. I published an article about my father in the Gonzales Inquirer on Father's Day 2004. After reading it, he looked long at me and fell silent. I asked, "Don't you like it?" Daddy replied, humbly: "It sounds like you really think something of me."

My father was a tough, strong gentleman of muscle and fortitude, and dually, a man of sensitive mirth possessed by an endearing natural humility. He was a man of few words, except when detailing a cherished story, which often fluctuated between coarse candor and charming humor, and had an undeniable imposing presence everyone acknowledged and respected. And I mean, everyone. Daddy was to be feared as God is feared. Not as in Almighty but in reverent awe.

Mama's Breakdown

First Spiritual Death

Mama, Margaret Elenora "Margie" Brzozowski, was born in Ganado, Texas and like Daddy was raised in the country. While a child, Mama moved with her parents Tedo and Floy (Kridler) Brzozowski and three younger brothers, Donald, Billy Joe and Charles, to Gonzales where Grandpa farmed as a sharecropper. Also like Daddy, Mama picked cotton, fed chickens, and was educated in a one-room school where all ages learned together.

Unlike my father's upbringing defined by dutiful work lightened by leisure and humor, Mama was raised in fervent rectitude; she was held to her mama's stringent standards for housekeeping and personal conduct. Grandma Floy was a tall robust woman, stately and witty. Born in 1907 the eldest of two daughters among seven children, Grandma was the one who as a girl left her bed in the wee hours to bake yeast bread and cook breakfast for the family before everyone else arose to eat and tackle chores. She grew up with no electricity or indoor plumbing.

Aunt Cathy, who Grandma dubbed Cat, told me Mama's girlhood room in their tiny unpainted wood home on the farm was off-limits to her brothers. She did not want them to disturb its clean order. As the only daughter, she was pampered by her daddy and held to high ideals by her mama. Mama's standard for cleanliness was concretely consistent and paramount with few exceptions. When she graduated high school, she received a new watch. One day, when she went to use the outhouse, the clasp on the watch broke and into the pit it fell. And in the pit is where it stayed. Mama gave no thought to its contaminated retrieval from the mucky hollow!

Like other young women, she was excited to take a job in town, excited about dating, excited about the prospect of marriage and a family of her own. At 17, Margie worked in a bakery in Gonzales. One day, a local young man asked her on a date and she accepted. Shortly after, a handsome uniformed Eugene walked into the bakery accompanied by her Uncle Carol and Eugene's sister, Dorothy, who asked her to go with them to a dance that happened to be on the same evening as her date with the other boy. Margie said yes. When she told Grandma Floy what had happened, and that she was not going to the dance with Eugene because of her promise to the other boy, her mama told her, "Yes you are!" And, so, she was ready when Eugene came calling. The young couple married soon afterward in a civil ceremony Aug. 19, 1944, and a week later at St. James Catholic Church in Gonzales. When Lynn was born, a doting daddy brought his wife peach gladiolas. Throughout Mama's life, Grandma Floy reminded her often of the unusually decent husband she had in Daddy, unlike most, and she was lucky to have him.

As my father endured horrors of war, my mother survived another kind that subtly yet progressively culminated over time, as unrelated but troubling events piled up and dispensed the final blow. In the end, there was no coup de grace for my mother, only suffering for a very long time. Unlike Daddy's resolute resurgence from the numbing, gruesome scars of combat, Mama was unable to resolve her torment. Even Daddy's unwavering love could not fix it.

Her first trouble happened when she was 9 and nearly drowned. Their farm was near the San Marcos River and into it her brothers flung her one day. As she struggled, screaming, Grandpa came running and brought her out. I do not know what penalty he delivered to my then-young uncles, but I'm sure it was severe. After that, Mama feared deep water and banned us kids even into our teenage years from it except at ankle-deep.

Her second torment occurred at 18 about a year after she and Daddy married and before their move to San Antonio in January 1946. Their first child was stillborn. Awful as that was, it was not the entire tragedy. At the time, they lived in Alabama where Daddy was stationed at Maxwell Field and Mama's unborn child stopped moving. The practice of medicine was not in the mid-1940s what it is today. There were no attentive birthing centers resembling the mother's home bedroom or nurses busying themselves in making a mother-to-be comfortable and safe. She was placed at the base hospital in a solitary room and left unaided to scream and cry out through excruciating labor till finally she delivered the lifeless infant. Daddy, on duty at the time, was notified and hurried to her side. Mama later recounted afterward she saw a small black figure lying still on a table next to her bed and asked if the baby was a boy, to which the doctor replied yes. Decades later, in recollecting that dreadful day, Mama and Daddy wished they would have given their son a name, baptized him and buried him properly. They deeply regretted having agreed in their grief with hospital staff who said they would take care of it.

Mama often mourned her stillborn son and thought of his going unbaptized with no name. Whenever we took a drive and spotted a discarded bag or bundle on the side of the road, Mama insisted Daddy stop to make sure it was not a baby. "Go see what that is." And Daddy did. We never found a baby. Only after Daddy investigated was Mama satisfied.

Grief can deaden our senses or heighten them. Dread can lodge inside us temporarily or for life. And grief and dread can take on lives of their own inside a person. I believe Mama harbored a haunting fear after her near-drowning as a child that later was compounded by the catastrophic conditions of her first childbirth. She may have feared losing future babies but had them anyway and miscarried early in another pregnancy. When carrying her youngest, Roger Paul, she was prescribed weekly injections to treat anemia to carry him full-term. Jo Ann, 8 at the time, recollects walking with Mama two blocks from home to see a neighbor who was a nurse to get the shots. Roger was born in 1958.

By late 1959, Mama had given birth to six "stairstep" children. Like steps, our ages were close. Roger Paul was a baby in diapers; Deborah Jean or "Debbie" was 3; I, Betty Lou or "Lou Lou" was 4; Mary Kathryn was 6; Jo Ann was 9; and Lynn was 12. Mama was a full-time mother and homemaker; Daddy was an Army veteran employed at a military base.

Life soon delivered the pivotal blow. In 1959, we kids contracted a pinworm infection. Pinworm is a parasite spread person-to-person that then required treatment for many weeks. All of us took prescribed medicine daily, and the doctor told Mama she must rigorously wash in boiling water all dishes, cookware, clothing, bedding, towels and washcloths every day, and bathe us all twice each day. Bear in mind, there were no disposable diapers, automatic dishwashers or clothes dryers. Once the clothes, diapers, sheets and towels were washed, they had to be hung on the clothesline in the backyard to dry. Imagine the enormity of relentless around-the-clock labor required to care for eight people, including six children, one in cloth diapers. This was Mama's lot every day, for weeks, aside from preparing meals morning, noon and night, and cleaning house. And we did not have pinworm once. We had it twice.

My beloved Chatty Cathy doll did not escape germ warfare. She had brownish-copper hair, blue eyes and freckles, and a string on her back below her neck that when pulled made her talk through a screened opening on her chest. She said, "Please carry me" and "Let's play house" and even cried and laughed. But one day, Chatty Cathy went missing, along with other toys belonging to my siblings. Evidently, anything we had touched while treated for pinworm that could not be laundered and sterilized had to be thrown out. That was a hard pill for us to swallow.

At the peak of the pinworm malaise, my mother finally collapsed. On this day, all of us were home except Daddy who was working and Lynn who was on his paper route. Mama was in the kitchen cooking peas and washing Roger's glass baby bottles. When Jo Ann complained of having peas for supper, Mama became frantic, bashing a bottle against the hard basin and hollering, "Alight! Alright!" severely gashing her hand. I was 4 and do not recall that day, but the subtle sure disconnect between my mother and me came without warning and without welcome and marked my first spiritual death. Doctors said Mama would never regain use of her hand but over time she regained its use completely. The injury on the inside was altogether different. On the inside, something severed.

What came next was a sequence of events our family did not sit down at the supper table and discuss. But we did live it. We littlest kids did not hear about all the problems around it while growing up. But the eldest two bore the brunt. All I knew was "Mama had a nervous breakdown." And even that was beyond grasp at 4.

In the late 1950s, nervous breakdown was the term for Mama's condition and personality change. Diagnoses or treatments of postpartum depression, or worse, postpartum psychosis, did not exist yet. As she turned increasingly agitated, nervous and obsessed with scrupulous cleaning and destroying germs, over ensuing years Mama fell prey to a protracted series of cruel, archaic medical and psychiatric methods. Meanwhile, Daddy agonized alongside her, not knowing what else to do or where else to turn, despite the gut-wrenchingly inhumane practices of the time.

As a result, my mother suffered her own private hell while Daddy subsisted incessantly in bewilderment, heartbreak and despondency but with a fierce fortitude. All the while he worked at his job and sometimes extras, maintained our homestead, attended business college at night to move forward in station to better manage mounting monetary demands, and kept himself sane, and his children and wife safe and provided for. Through it all, he is the one who with the fortitude of a lion and fidelity of a saint held our family, and himself, together. It is with no small amount of grace that he and Mama had help from close relatives, neighbors and friends along the way. Mama's struggle was no secret to everyone who knew us. But it seemed almost obscure as Daddy strove to keep our lives structured.

None of us are sure about the exact chronology of Mama's bitter journey through the anguish of mental illness over 12 years, but I will try to describe what happened. Prior to Mama's collapse, my parents were fit adults in their 30s. Mama had taken excellent care of herself, children, husband and home. She was devoted to housekeeping and child-rearing and enjoyed gardening in her bare feet. Our home was clean and safe, and we were loved, well fed and clothed. As a rule, we all got regular medical checkups.

As Mama took prescribed drugs hypothesized to help her, she gained weight. Some pills brought her "down" while others brought her back "up," and a side-effect was weight gain. So off we went, with Mama driving herself and me to Montgomery Ward or Sears to shop for dresses that fit. From the racks she selected dozens we carried to the fitting room. One by one, she tried on each dress, usually without success, and I returned them to hangers. And so it went till all had been put on trial. Sometimes, we came home with nary a one. In truth, I hated those trips. As a self-absorbed child, I did not realize Mama must have been terribly frustrated with her weight, ill-fitting clothes and what she saw in the mirror and her own mind. And the pills she took did not help her get better. She must have felt powerless and often was nervous and sometimes screamed.

Mama was strict about housecleaning and got progressively so. We cleaned and disinfected precisely as instructed, and if we did not, then she made us redo the task, whether washing dishes, mopping floors, dusting furniture or folding towels.

When the pills proved ineffective, doctors next prescribed electroconvulsive, or electroshock, therapy dispensed at the State Hospital not far from our home. I do not remember how often or for how long Mama suffered them but Aunt Cathy who was 13 at the time recalls they were administered every weekday for at least a month. She described the treatments as the barbaric beating up of Mama's body, leaving her a zombie unable to do anything afterward. Aunt Cathy said Mama adored her grandmother, Grandma Josie or "Jo," and was devastated when she died. Grandma Jo used to say,

"Little kids, little problems. Big kids, big problems." My aunt surmises Grandma Floy's perfectionism was innately in Mama as a girl, who later took it to its extreme as a mother of six amid the pinworm outbreak only to find she could not keep up.

When premiered in 1938, shock therapy was used to treat severe depression. Still in use in the 1950s and simply put, electrodes were placed on the temples of a patient through which electricity passed. This reportedly caused the patient to convulse and lose consciousness, and the lingering after-effect was memory loss that ranged from slight forgetfulness to extreme confusion lasting indefinitely. I don't know whether Mama suffered shock treatments without anesthesia, but when first introduced, patients were awake when electricity was bolted to the brain and suffered full-body seizures until losing consciousness.

On treatment days, while the rest of us attended school, Daddy dropped off Roger at Grandma Floy's, drove Mama to the hospital for treatment, and then went to work. Grandpa Tedo picked up Mama after her appointments and then drove her to their house to sleep a while before taking her home. When Grandpa brought Mama home, he escorted her to the bedroom to lie down, amid a house abuzz with kids barely home from school, loud and hungry. I vividly recall one such afternoon. It lives perpetually in my memory but I have forgiven Grandpa. After he helped Mama to her bedroom to lie down as usual, he headed down the hall to where we kids were playing and fussing. Removing his thick black leather belt from the loops of his slacks, he grabbed me by one arm, accused me angrily of being a smart mouth and the cause of a squabble, and whipped me so hard his belt left welts on my legs and me in gulping sobs. I did not understand then as a child how deeply grieved and troubled he was about his only daughter, my Mama, or what I had done that warranted Grandpa's wrath.

I remember, especially early on, Mama's sporadic behavior vacillated from docile and comfortably familiar to hysterical and irrational. We had a long, aqua blue Formica dining table with shiny aluminum trim and eight chairs to match. To be clear, I am unsure whether I witnessed it myself or heard the story. From what others tell me, a childhood memory can be experienced by several individuals who later in life each may recall it differently. The table was set for a meal, complete with Melmac dinner plates and silverware. Melmac was popular then because it was plastic, durable, virtually indestructible and affordable. Something caused Mama to become agitated. Abruptly in a wild frenzy, she sent all the dishes and silverware flying from the table onto the floor with one long swipe of her arm and hand as she screamed. Daddy tackled her to the floor in the adjoining living room onto the braided rope rug, and held onto both her wrists to stop her from swinging and hitting until she was calm.

I reflect on that day with a heavy bottomless sorrow and compassion for Mama and Daddy. The alarming hopeless tragedy of Mama losing herself and Daddy losing her seems worse than if death had come. I do not wish death to anyone. I only make a comparison. When someone dies, the agony is over and mourning begins. But with mental illness, there is no deliverance, no escape, no apparent end. Only intermittent reprieves. And the only thing Mama and Daddy knew to do, was to keep hoping, trying, believing, that somehow, someday, she would get well. They had grown up in a time when people worked hard, had little and were grateful for the little they had, and took life in stride.

Throughout these disturbing times, Jo Ann, then only a girl who carried adult obligations, remembers Daddy leaving the house numerous times after supper with his cigarettes, lighter and car keys. He drove two blocks and circled back to the corner where he sat in the dark smoking. Whenever he left on these short runs, she fearfully followed him outside and stood in the front yard watching, until she saw the car complete the loop and stop at the corner; only then did she go back inside and to bed. Lynn recalls one night when he was 15 Daddy took him along for a drive, needing to clear his head of what was happening at home and the numbing realization he could do nothing to make Mama well. So Daddy drove and talked, and cried, and cried out, while his eldest son sat and listened.

One midnight, stirred from sleep, I left bed to peek down the hall to the living room where Daddy sat smoking in the dark. All I could see in the shadows was the fiery tip of his cigarette. Worry must have kept him awake countless nights. He surely held himself together with cigarettes, grit and God.

Without a doubt, the barbaric practice of shock treatment broke my father and grandparents' hearts. All I knew was Mama was weak and sleepy and I never will know all she endured. But leaving the situation alone without trying to help her was out of the question. So there was no recourse but for Daddy to trust doctors who kept saying they could continue to try. Still, shock treatments did not cure Mama. In fact, she worsened. That marked the end of her visits to the State Hospital but not the end to her torment.

Mama next was admitted to a hospital in Victoria that treated patients with mental conditions. While she was there, the shock treatments may have continued, but neither I nor my siblings recall for sure. One time, Daddy drove all six of us kids in our white and red Ford station wagon to visit her. Our station wagon had red exterior trim and red interior seats and was clean as a whistle after Daddy washed it in the driveway on Saturdays. We picked her up at the hospital and drove to a park where we had a picnic and took pictures. Mama was 36 then and three years into her illness and thus-far failed treatment. A poignant snapshot Daddy took that day captured the penetrating toll exacted on Mama, observable in her emotionless beautiful face and the instinctive clinging of her children to an unintentionally absent mama. We littlest kids had no comprehension of the cruel reality of my parents' circumstances. I will never know the depth of my mother's despondency after years of failed attempts to return to a healthy frame of mind, to return to herself, to Daddy, and to us kids.

It was while in Victoria, so we were told, she was diagnosed with a tumor in her uterus for which she underwent a hysterectomy. In truth, I have wondered, although I have never uttered this to anyone till now, whether a tumor was the medical fact or doctors suggested a hysterectomy was to Mama's benefit; for without another childbirth and its after-effects, her mental health may improve.

That summer, while Daddy worked and cared for us and Mama continued treatment in Victoria, we kids sometimes stayed with my Aunt Marie and Uncle James and our cousins at their home in the country in Cuero. I cannot recall how often we stayed there, how long Mama was at the hospital, or how much time would pass before it became clear that neither the medicine nor the doctors in Victoria could cure my mother.

After she came home, years passed as Mama showed scant sign of improvement. At that despondent impasse, in 1967, when I was 12 and Mama was 41, when all other options available at the time failed, the final barbarous recourse was proposed. Although he never spoke of it, Daddy faced making an agonizing and frightening decision. The doctors recommended Mama undergo a controversial procedure called a frontal lobotomy at a hospital in Galveston that specialized in that type of brain surgery used in the treatment of neurological disease. A frontal lobotomy had its dangers. It could permanently alter Mama's personality and life, as the frontal lobes of the brain situated directly behind the forehead govern decision-making, physical moving, speaking and temperament.

Mama underwent the lobotomy. The surgeon drilled two holes each about the size of a matchhead into the front of her skull at the forehead, through which the supposed damaged brain tissue was extracted, thereby putatively removing memories of tragic events believed to cause her agitation and cure her.

One Friday in mid-April, Daddy drove us kids to the seaside Boulevard Motel in Galveston near the hospital. Our room on the second floor at the top of a metal stairwell had a window air-conditioner we enjoyed as cold as it could blow, linoleum tile floors and large windows. In my memory's eye, that building was void of color except for ashen hues. Drab floors. Dull walls. I've wondered whether it was in reality gray or my mind painted it a lifeless color. I do not remember anything about Mama or the hospital on that visit, only that we kids stayed at the motel and went swimming while Daddy visited her. And then, on Sunday, we drove home.

Five days later, Daddy brought Mama home, finally, once and for all. I watched from inside through our large living room windows when they arrived. Helping Mama from the car, he put his arm around her waist and escorted her up the sidewalk and into our house. She wore a wedge-shaped scarf that covered a portion of her forehead and a short-sleeve dress that may have been a pale green or blue and white. I cannot recall whether she smiled or spoke, or Daddy either. I cannot recall whether I went to her, hugged her, or whether she hugged me. I only remember the scarf pulled down on her forehead and Daddy helping her inside.

Gradually, Mama improved and much of her memory began to return. But there were lasting outcomes. After the shock treatments and lobotomy, Mama suffered migraines for most of the rest of her life. She became a bit calmer but not always. It took years to fully regain herself. There still were plenty of periods of strain, for her, for Daddy, for us. But some of those times were just... life. She professed later it was not the surgery, psychiatry or treatments that cured her. My mother was baptized as an infant and raised a Catholic. She was devout. Throughout treatments and hospital stays, she did not go to church or attend Mass at all for stretches of time. She declared it only was when she returned to Mass and Confession her mental health improved, which she attributed to the grace of God.

Mama's breakdown altered all our lives. Even when obscure or nameless, the ever-present undercurrent of a subtle yet powerful dynamic manifesting within each of us was influencing who we were then and who we would become. In our future selves and in the lives we ultimately would choose is where the weight and pull of this influence would reveal itself.

Through thick and thin, my parents gave of themselves. To our family. To America during WWII. To each other for more than 6 decades. To God and church. To their grandchildren and great-grandchildren. To their aunts and uncles, brothers and sisters, in-laws and elders. To our neighborhood and school. To neighboring widows and widowers and countless others struck with grief or hardship. My parents' lives taught me being alive means there will come unforeseen unwelcome tragedies, thankfully sprinkled in-between with snippets of welcome delight, even the occasional thrill. And the best anyone can do is survive the trials and hope for the next reprieve. The most fortunate among us not only survive the intolerable but live past survival to a productive and reasonably happy and healthy existence.

Some, however, get stuck in tragedy perpetually, or until, if and when, as in my mother's case, the people who care about us most, including ourselves, never relinquish the determination to outdistance the turmoil. In my case, the pandemonium that would define my life for a very long time was just beginning.

My Charmed Childhood

Despite Mama's breakdown, my childhood was charmed. The ill-fated seed planted in my soul at 4 would take years to bud.

On the surface, our life looked and was typical for a family of eight in the early 1960s. Both my parents kept our home life as close to normal as was humanly possible given circumstances. And they did so for not hours or weeks or even months but years. They did so even with a brood of kids' needs and behaviors increasingly influenced by the sheer act of growing up and progressive exposure to the outside world that had its own set of influences. Looking back, I admit, and not without any small measure of gratitude, I was for the most part unaware of the trauma inside my parents' daily lives and our family, especially since most of the time it did not look like it because of Mama and Daddy's dauntless devotion to each other and us.

Mama despite her illness and Daddy in the heavy midst of his dutiful perpetual oversight and care of Mama, and us, his job, our home and everything else in the whole wide world that was his and his alone to carry, kept our home life structured and steady. I still had parents, brothers, sisters, a home, food, clothes, neighbors and friends. We still went to school with our paper-sack lunches with our names written on them and our Sears & Roebuck denim-covered notebooks. We arrived on time and were expected to complete our homework and make good grades. We still learned penmanship writing with No. 2 pencils in a ruled Big Chief tablet. We still dressed up and attended church reverently on Sundays. We still celebrated holidays and holy days. We kept living life day after day as the weeks, months and years slinked by.

We Guckians were a steadfast clan. I'm sure our steady foundation helped keep our family as balanced as it could be through the early toughest times. We held to one home address after moving into our new house on Dysart; attended one church and one school; and had one analog phone number that Southwestern Bell initiated as Edison 3-1358, shortened to ED3-1358 and finally switched to 333-1358. I remember when home phones shared a circuit called a party line, where we could hear other peoples' conversations and had to wait, unless an emergency, for them to end a call before placing ours.

My parents still were people deserving of trust and respect. My mother was a genuine lady. Her illness did not change her character. She did not use profanity or smoke or drink alcohol. She dressed attractively and was clean and neat. She kept an immaculate house, an ethic passed on to the rest of us, including my brothers. We wore fresh clothes in fine condition, including hand-me-downs. Our clothes may not have been expensive or fancy but they were laundered and tidy. My mother stayed home attending to us, the house and budget, and everything quantifiable went like clockwork in our household.

My father was physically strong and mentally sharp with a tough facade tempered by an unpretentious, kind and witty disposition. Mama's illness exacted harsh tolls, but Daddy's character remained intact. One of my favorite memories is of Daddy getting ready to leave for work each morning in his ironed shirt, tie and sport jacket, clean-shaven and smelling of Old Spice, carrying his paper-sack lunch and wearing a white gold Bulova watch Lynn bought for him in Panama in 1966. Daddy wore that watch every day of his life. He'd kiss Mama and us bye every morning. And every evening after work, he'd come straight home to help make supper and take care of us all. It is for that reason most I love and respect him so.

Many men would have quit when the going got too tough. But my father stayed. He was true to my mother and their wedding vows; throughout their life together they kissed and hugged and on occasion danced in the dining room. After working all day, Daddy came home to pick up and carry his obligations there. And he did it all over again the next day and the next and the next. Daddy did smoke cigarettes nearly nonstop and was quiet until he was affronted, when his temper erupted in volcanic justice. That made Daddy a fierce and authoritative force to be revered and not wrestled with.

But he also liked to laugh, be outdoors, keep the yard pretty, barbecue and fish. He fried fresh catfish he caught and cleaned, and pork chops and steaks and chicken, and cooked bubbling pots of chili and stew and barbecue sauce. His cooking filled our house with familiar aromas and our stomachs with hearty food. And he made biscuits, and sliced tomatoes and onions with precision, and filled tall tea glasses with stacked cubes of ice. And he washed dishes and cleaned countertops. Throughout Mama's illness, Daddy was our family's stronghold; without him, we would have collapsed.

Most memories of my earliest years are tender ones. I am sure much of that is because Mama and Daddy did not allow themselves, their marriage or our family to descend into self-pity. There was no time for regret. They were staunch in the truest sense of the human spirit despite relentless realities and threats of debilitating circumstances that would weaken many people before breaking them.

I still played house with wooden blocks. Blue ones were milk. Red ones were juice. Yellow ones were butter. Roger played the role of milkman or postman. He walked up the short hallway from his room to mine that I shared with Debbie, pretending it a city block, knocked and announced himself, and delivered either my dairy or the day's mail. I was the merry homemaker. It was customary to offer him something to drink when he knocked, using toy dishes I'd gotten for a birthday or Christmas present. And then we sat on the edge of the bed, pretending it a table or couch, sipping imaginary tea or coffee and chatting away about nothing like we had seen our parents, grandparents, aunts and uncles and neighbors do.

Saturdays still were chore days. Daddy kept the exterior of our house clean and painted, car washed, and yard mowed, edged and watered. Jo Ann recalls Daddy getting down on his hands and knees with scissors to clip wayward grass runners from an otherwise perfectly edged lawn; his lush green grass was the envy of the neighborhood. The inside of our house was Mama's realm. After breakfast, she enslaved us kids to do a thorough housecleaning and disinfecting. We girls split chores among us four and got 25 cents allowance every two weeks. I remember climbing a yellow metal stool snugly situated next to the kitchen sink to wash dishes.

On Saturday nights after my bath, Mama rolled my long, shampooed hair in pin curls or pink foam rollers for church the next day. Easter Sunday was a special dress-up day for Mass. Mama outfitted us girls in frilly skirts with full petticoats, hats and shiny patent leather shoes paired with thin, white, fold-down ankle socks. Easter mornings we awoke to filled Easter baskets sitting in a row on the couch in the living room. After Mass, once Mama and Daddy had hidden brightly colored candy eggs in the yard, we had an Easter egg hunt. I think of those eggs whenever I see similarly tinted purple, yellow or turquoise cars; they look good enough to eat.

Our brand-new house on Dysart was three blocks from the tiny house on Charcliff, which we outgrew. It was in a budding neighborhood of families called Eastwood Village, complete with lots of kids and a wide-open field beyond our backyard to run, play and pretend in. My parents likely thanked their lucky stars for the outdoor space we had to carouse in. A single-story with four bedrooms, two bathrooms, linoleum floors, and huge yards in front and back, our home was not fancy but it was safe, comfortable and clean. Mama and Daddy's bedroom was off-limits; a place furnished simply and revered. You would not want to get caught in there unless on an assigned mission, such as when cleaning house, and your chore was to dust and vacuum their bedroom.

At first, our windows had no screens and often we slept with them wide open. The nights were quiet except for the occasional bark of a distant dog or faraway accelerating whirr of a motorcycle or car. I savored the aromatic invitations of night, beckoning with a breeze through the open glass. I will remember that feeling always and the soothing glow of moonlight on the grass.

In those days, our car sat unlocked in the driveway. There was no need for locks. Neighborhoods were safe places to live and bring up children, even after dark. Sometimes, till we were caught, we piled into the car when I for one pretended to drive, steering the wheel this way and that. I remember what my Great Aunt Bea used to say about driving. She'd ask us, "Do you know what the colored traffic lights mean?" We'd shake our heads no and then she'd continue, "Red light, stop. Green light, go. Yellow light, go like hell to beat the red light!" And we'd all laugh.

Sometimes following a passing afternoon rain when the sun shone bright again, and sheets and towels were drying in the sun, we'd sneak a sheet or towel from the clothesline and run down the block waving it over our heads to join other kids from our neighborhood. We squealed and stomped our way through the water puddles that sat irresistibly in shallow valleys at the street corner.

Summer was the absolute best time of all and never changed no matter my parents' endurances. No school for three whole months, although I liked school. Going barefoot. Wearing shorts. Eating watermelon and playing in the water with the hose on hot afternoons. Playing outside even after dark with the Bredas, Verettes, Vogels, Martinezes, Pilands and other kids on our block. Lying in the soft, sweet-smelling grass in the front yard after Daddy mowed while watching the clouds float by, and seeing and hearing the infrequent wavering sound and appearance of a Cessna humming its way above and across it all. Little did I know I would fly a Cessna one day. Even now, past spans of time, I am transported instantly back there whenever I hear a small aircraft aloft or a gas-fueled mower humming or smell the sweet scent of freshly cut grass.

Sometimes, Daddy bought a big green speckled watermelon and let cool water from the hose run over it a bit before setting it atop our picnic table in the backyard. There, he sliced it in long red ample strips dotted with black seeds. We each got one, dusted it with salt and ate it, spitting seeds everywhere and making a juicy mess, which was a good excuse for hosing down us and the table. My uncles and Grandpa Tedo teased us, saying if we swallowed seeds, ate a little dirt and drank water, watermelons would grow out of our belly buttons.

We still played "Bonanza" in the backyard with the Bredas and Vogels with us girls wearing quilts fastened around our middles with clothespins as pioneer dresses, and the boys playing cowboys and Indians, setting the picnic table and benches on their sides to make a cabin or fort. We played Tag, Kiss Chase and Roll Chase in our front yard, and Murder in the Dark and Hide and Seek at everyone's houses, and Red Rover, Simon Says, Marbles and Red Light-Green Light. We rode our Radio Flyer wagons with one bent leg inside and the other propelling our carts up and down our block, where traffic was infrequent and slow with familiar cars driven by neighbors we knew. We mastered Hula Hoop and Hopscotch and baked mud pies on the curb in the sun.

In the summer, we sometimes walked a few blocks to the W.W. White Elementary School for "Recreation," where kids from all over the neighborhood gathered to play games and drink soda water. Back then, I could buy a 12-ounce RC cola in a glass bottle for 10 cents from a machine. Inside the auditorium were a large stage, and tables, chairs and board games. Outside were workshops for making art with popsicle sticks and pictures with macaroni glued onto paper plates.

Sometimes, Mama gave my sisters, little brother and me large brown paper grocery sacks stuffed with her dresses and Daddy's jackets and slacks to carry to the dry cleaners next door to the elementary school. I started out wearing shoes but after rounding the first corner slipped them off and carried them, jumping quick from the steaming asphalt into cool green grass and back again onto hot pavement, like human popcorn. On those tiny trips made enormous by a child's imagination, I darted behind a corner of the bank or church, hiding from a colossal monster looming as high as the sky and after me. And then, minutes later, as quickly as it came, the giant faded as my mind returned to the trek and task at hand when I rejoined the others in stride.

If we had earned 25 cents allowance apiece, then after dropping off the dry cleaning we'd rush into the Winn's store to ogle and buy candy. You could buy plenty with a few cents back then. Jawbreakers. Lik-M-Aid. Green apple sticks and red cinnamon fire sticks. Red candy lipstick in gold foil. Sweet Tarts. Long thin taffy dyed red, purple, green and orange, striped white and wrapped in wax paper. Chewy cinnamon Hot Tamales. Multicolored round nickel-size candy disks in a roll and candy necklaces. Chocolate, strawberry and banana bon bons with coconut filling. Peanut patties, a favorite of Daddy's. And bubble gum.

On one end of the same small shopping center was Henry Schloss's barber shop where I took my little brother to get his hair cut for $1. At the opposite end was Model Market grocery store, where Daddy worked part-time sometimes and from where I stole a torn bag of Brach's chocolate-covered raisins. When Mama and Daddy found out, Daddy drove me to the store and made me apologize and return the half-eaten bag of candy. I never stole again.

Christmas still was special and one stands out. Daddy brought home a tall, fragrant Christmas tree and erected it on a stand in our living room. He and Mama adorned it with shiny ornaments made of glass and strands of multicolored lightbulbs one-and-one-half-inches long apiece. They screwed the bulbs into a strand of sockets and wrapped the whole thing around the tree, after which we kids hung twinkling silver slivers of tinsel called icicles. At its top sat an ornament larger than the rest in the shape of a star with a round starshaped concave middle and a long hollow tail at the bottom for sitting steadily and reverently at the treetop's highest vertical limb.

I don't recall having gifts to open every year. I do remember when Grandma Alta Guckian and Aunt Dorothy and Uncle Carol visited, we unwrapped Avon soap on a rope or spray foam bath soap we painted the tub tile with. Aunt Cathy said one Christmas when Mama and Daddy had no money to buy us gifts, Daddy took our old dolls to Grandma Floy, who washed them and made them all new clothes, and those refurbished dolls became our Christmas presents that year.

We still honored religious traditions. When I was 6, I made my First Communion. I wore a delicate white dress with puffy petticoats, a white veil, white socks and white patent leather shoes. I felt like an angelic princess. Even at 6, I recognized the Benedictine nuns who taught us in school were strict but

I admired them. During recess or after school until the third grade, I sauntered about sometimes with my brown uniform sweater wrapped around my head like the nun's habit headdress, pretending one day I, too, would be a sister. They all looked alike at a distance but each nun was different. Some were pious. Others were mavericks. Still others were downright mean.

My first-grade teacher, Sister Lucy, was a doll, literally. She was young, petite, pretty and soft-spoken. Quite the opposite, Sister Scholastica was up in years, stout and rough. When my schoolmate Randall, who had a long Polish last name and big ears, misbehaved, Sister Scholastica advanced toward him with her stealthy ominous presence, grabbed hold of one of his ears and shook it while scolding him. By the time she let go, Randall's ear looked like fried red bologna. Sister Scholastica was one scary nun. She liked to pop us on the palm of our hands with a hard wooden ruler when we misbehaved. How it stung.

My third-grade teacher, Sister Albert, was a young, plump, robust nun who was both kind and stern. She put little bars of soap in our classmate, John's, mouth when he talked back, instructing him to leave it there till she said he could spit it out. And then there was the school principal, Sister Thecla. She was lean and stood absolutely straight, with a skeletal face, a hard mouth always tightened shut and beady eyes. She stood on the sidewalk and watched us file by with her arms crossed beneath her black apron, rocking on her sinister black pumps filled with her sinister black stocking feet. I cannot recall ever seeing her smile.

Sometimes we attended Mass during the school day when the nuns marched us single-file with our mouths closed and hands folded piously as in prayer from our classrooms to the church. Up the steps and inside we went to waiting wooden pews with padded kneelers and carved pockets stuffed with Catholic missals and hymn books. The church smelled of incense and Old English furniture polish. It had stained glass windows all around, and ornate brass candelabras on the altar topped with tall, thin, white candles. We wore uniforms of checkered brown and white cotton fabric sewn into short-sleeve blouses, skirts and matching belts, solid brown beanies and sweaters, all tailor-made at Threadgill's. My skirts and petticoats size husky marked by an X on the label Mama thought sweet because she said being chubby (I didn't know I was chubby) made me cute. I wore brown oxfords with laces and thin white folded ankle socks. But I wanted to look like Liz instead. She wore an A-lined uniform and brown penny loafers that made her look modern, polished and grownup. Next to Liz, I felt frumpy in my skirt and oxfords.

When little kids like me in second grade kept playing during recess rather than going to the bathroom before class recommenced, accidents happened. One afternoon, after filing back into the schoolroom, as I stood in line to turn in my paper to Miss Maxine who sat at her desk receiving each of us in turn, I wet my pants. No one knew, but I was devastated. By the time I reached Miss Maxine, I began to whimper, shyly handed her my paper, whispered my dilemma, and was excused to go to the bathroom where I dried my underpants with toilet paper.

Evidently, my shame evaporated quickly, along with any compassion I might have mustered for another kid in that predicament, because on another day, I noticed my classmate Michael, who sat to my right, putting sheets of notebook paper one at a time on the seat of his desk beneath his rump while we took a test. Michael had wet his pants, too, and was attempting to slyly soak it up. But his khaki trousers revealed the watermarked truth. I made fun of Michael later and told our friends and caused him shame, the kind of ridicule and fun-poking little kids inflict on each other. Decades later, as I write this, I regret that. I also find it humorous that a tendency like wetting our pants in the second grade is a problem we outgrow, but eventually it revisits us in adulthood if we live long enough. Instead of wetting our pants in class as little kids, we likely will be wetting our pants in other places as we enter our 80s, when our bodies' degeneration accelerates and incontinence arrives. Better to learn and practice compassionate discretion while young.

I wonder if all little sisters cling to and idolize their big brothers. By the time I'd turned 8 and entered third grade, Lynn joined the U.S. Navy Reserves, left home after high school and never looked back. Before he went away, I awakened early one twilight to help him roll a scarf he wore with his dress blues uniform beneath its square Sailor collar as he readied to report downtown. And one afternoon, he played ball with me in the backyard wearing his white bell-bottom trousers and undershirt. Then, abruptly it seemed, he was gone. Looking back, my brother was around when Daddy was not. My father was busy with multiple jobs, night school, Mama's illness and taking care of things around our house, which all rendered Daddy stretched far too thin to pay much attention to each of us, other than to discipline. It was not his fault. So when

Lynn left, I lost something precious: his time and attention. And when he left, my little brother, Roger, was overjoyed, because he gained a bedroom all to himself.

And here I share two amusing anecdotes to do with underwear.

At St. Benedict, physical education occupied morning recess and did not involve changing clothes. When the bell signaled, we all spilled from our classrooms onto the parking lot in front of the church where the teachers led us in jumping jacks and toe-touches. We girls always wore uniformed skirts. I was terrified the boys behind me would see my underwear when I bent over, so I bent my knees during stretches to keep my skirt from rising. My mother refused to let me wear shorts under my skirt like some girls did. My modesty soon was forgotten, though, when the teachers set up a record player with huge speakers atop the front step of the church, and we all danced to the Jerk, Twist and Polka to round out recess.

The second underwear tale involves the neighbors across the street where a family with two daughters about the ages of myself and my younger sister lived. They were rich I thought because they had a Jungle Jim in their backyard and a violin. The eldest did not wear underwear, as became evident one day as she sat in her open screenless bedroom window wearing baggy shorts with her legs propped up and crossed while her younger sister played the violin. I remember the Jungle Jim as clearly, because one day as we hung and swung and pulled up and down on the bars like chimps, my right front tooth slammed into a steel bar, chipping a small piece of it. To this day, my smile is marked by the missing bit of tooth.

Throughout childhood and Mama's illness, my parents did their best to keep us interested in school, church and fun activities they could afford but we could not afford much. When I was in third grade, Mama and Daddy offered me piano lessons provided by Sister Michael. I joined the Brownies and especially enjoyed the time we made food trays for our mothers for Mother's Day from aluminum record albums stripped of vinyl with glued appliques of fruit on them.

I believe being a middle child and one left wanting for my mother and father's affections impacted me from a very young age. At times I was timid while other times outgoing when I fed on the attention of strangers. The Parent Teacher Club (PTC), for example, of St. Benedict hosted a kids' talent show one evening, during which I performed "I'm A Little Tea Pot." I was terrified and excited all at once but performed the whole skit and enjoyed the applause. One Saturday afternoon, Daddy drove us to the grand opening of McCreless Mall. With my hair in pink foam rollers and me wearing pink baggy shorts, as the band played and sang, Daddy hoisted me up onto a raised platform across from the band and I danced to the lively music in front of the gathering crowd. I enjoyed the attention.

Sports and I did not get along too well, however. I attempted softball and liked to bat and run, but when playing outfield I failed at catching the ball or quickly knowing what to do with it. In fact, the coach told me one day that I should try a different sport. In retrospect, I believe that teacher should not have said that to me. After her words, I abandoned team sports altogether. My team aptitude dissolved.

But then I discovered tether ball and in it found I could play a sport, have fun and compete by relying solely on myself—a budding maverick—and that appealed to me. No coach or team required. No disparaging critique. No rules to remember. Only me, the ball and my own determination. The tether ball was tied to a long rope fastened to the top of a tall steel pole anchored with concrete inside a ground-hugging rubber tire. All it required was two kids competing to outdo the other one with hard strong fast pounding of the ball sending it wrapping around the pole till it could wrap no more. I mastered the game and challenged boys and girls alike to a round. By self-proclamation, I was Tether Ball Champ!

Tether ball was one-on-one and I liked it that way. Throughout grade school, I also found I liked to spend time with one best friend at a time, until I switched to someone new. Not until high school was I part of a regular group of friends and even then my group participations were few. This self-sufficient subsistence would reappear and even demarcate my life, throughout my life.

We still went to Grandma Floy's for dinner after church on Sundays. When I was a kid, dinner was the midday meal and supper was eaten in the evening. Because Daddy secured a job for Grandpa Tedo at Kelly Air Force Base, Grandma and Grandpa were so grateful, they had us over for dinner nearly every Sunday for years. They always seemed happy to see us, and didn't seem to mind the fuss and work of feeding our hungry army. Meals always included a main course, dessert and iced tea, all homemade from scratch.

Grandma Floy's house had a pleasant familiar aroma of oiled wood furniture polished to a sheen and fresh yeast bread. On a given Sunday, she baked a tall layered white cake with coconut icing, Grandpa's favorite, and chocolate and coconut cream pies in tin pie plates with fluted edges. She often baked sweet kolaches with pineapple, prune and cheese in the centers, and coffeecakes with sugary cottage-cheese filling and tops dusted with cinnamon and sugar. She varyingly served slow-cooked pinto beans seasoned with garlic; fried chicken, steak or pork chops; and baked yeast rolls. She carefully patted softened butter onto the tops of each roll after rising, placing them touching "side by each," before popping them into the oven to brown. Before the meal, she covered the dining table with a white tablecloth and put out stemmed tea glasses for the adults, silverware and China dishes. Grandma's kitchen was her culinary domain; she spent lots of time in there. It was chockfull of pots and pans, including the pink Club aluminum Dutch oven in which she cooked her beans, and all sorts of foodstuffs. Her kitchen had a generous double white porcelain sink beneath a window where we girls washed dishes once everybody had finished eating.

It was simple fare by some standards but to us it was mouthwatering cuisine. Back then, there were no ready-made teabags; she strained boiled tea leaves into a large clear glass pitcher and filled it with tap water, measured in sugar, cut a lemon in two, and squeezed and dropped both halves into the pitcher. Once all the tea had been drunk, we kids squabbled over who got to eat the sugary lemon halves at the bottom. Grandma Floy blessed our young lives more than she or we may ever know. Everything she did was with artful precision and a flair that looked effortless and fun.

While the adults lingered at the table sipping coffee and talking, we kids played outside before landing on the living room rug at evening's onset to watch TV shows like "Maverick" and "Bonanza" till it was time to go home. One June evening in 1969 when I was 14, everybody crowded in front of the TV to watch an exclusive broadcast delivered by Walter Cronkite showing Apollo 11 with Neil Armstrong and Edwin "Buzz" Aldrin walking on the moon.

In front of my grandparents' 1940s pier-and-beam bungalow on Highland Boulevard was an ample covered porch with stoic columns and a screened front door. And in back, a detached garage sat at the end of the unpaved driveway.

It had a musty woody odor I remember fondly. The spacious backyard was dotted with giant leafy pecan trees occupied by katydids that called from their concealed perches on hot afternoons. In the one bathroom was a large, oval clawfoot cast iron and porcelain bathtub and a small gas heater Grandma had to strike a match to light. Great Grandma Jo dipped snuff and spit into an emptied blue Noxzema jar that sat in the bathroom windowsill.

Grandma kept her house immaculate. Sometimes I stayed with her. She gave me small chores to do when she cleaned house, which was daily. After supper and baths, we donned nightgowns, housecoats and house shoes and strolled up the boulevard in the breezy evening air, saying hello to neighbors sitting on their porches. In the near distance was a white church steeple with a purple cross shining bright. At bedtime, she made me a cozy pallet on the floor next to her clothes closet; her bedroom always was icy cold from the window air-conditioner. While Grandpa worked nights, Grandma lay in bed reading the newspaper and I lay on my pallet watching her read. My memories of Grandpa who passed away at 89 mostly are jolly and Grandma Floy who lived to nearly 94 never said a cross word or spanked me. Mama told me later with regularity Grandma was her best friend.

Despite Mama's illness, the 1960s were stimulating times for a young girl like me. A month before my ninth birthday in 1964, the Beatles came from Liverpool to America, when l watched John Lennon, Paul McCartney, George Harrison and Ringo Starr perform for the first time on TV on "The Ed Sullivan Show." All the girls in the audience screamed, cried or fainted while we joined in the flurry in front of the set, twisting to the songs and music. When I consider the Beatles' style of music at that time in American music history, when rock and roll was deemed immoral by many, I credit my parents then in their late 30s/early 40s with having an open mind and sense of fun even in the midst of their troubles.

One evening, I was in Roger's room watching the Beatles on "The Ed Sullivan Show" on our small black-and-white TV, riding the arm of a chair that had wide wooden arms and red cushions. I lost my balance and hit the floor hard. The next thing I knew, Daddy was rushing me to the hospital and I came home with a cast on my broken left arm. For weeks afterward, I reveled in attention from kids at school who gathered around me to sign my plaster-of-paris trophy.

Time with Daddy no matter how it was spent was wonderful time for me, watching him down a glass of cold iced tea after working in the yard on a hot day or when he made biscuits and homemade syrup for breakfast. Throughout my adolescence, western movies were popular and aired on TV after the nightly news ended on Friday and Saturday nights. Daddy sat relaxed in his chair in our living room, while I lay on the braided rug, propped on my elbows at his feet, as the melodious introduction and visual sensation of a mountainous or desert image found us both silently rapt. I looked forward to those western movie nights, watching the likes of Audie Murphy, John Wayne, Jimmy Stewart, Gregory Peck and Randolph Scott. I liked westerns so much, I got a Bat Masterson coloring book for my birthday one year.

Cowboy characters in movies even sounded and behaved like Daddy. Maybe because my father and western movie stars then were raised on farms and ranches and shared the same lingo and mannerisms as his. To this day, I watch old westerns repeatedly without getting bored. They are a palliative balm to a troubled heart or an otherwise preoccupied mind. It is not only the movies into which I'm drawn, with their wide panoramas; cross-country cattle drives; whinnying, nickering and snorting horses; late-night campfires; shootouts; and romance. I re-live fond memories with Daddy.

To their credit even amid my mother's struggle, my parents made sure we saw a medical specialist, not a general medical doctor, when we needed one. Whenever I was sick, which was recurringly until my tonsillectomy in my early teens, Mama kept me home from school and cared for me. In bed with strep throat once, Mama brought me warm black coffee in a grownup's cup to sip and soothe my sore throat, and afterward I fell into a slumber listening to the hum of her vacuum. When I was 12, I had Scarlet Fever when my tongue turned black and white spots from the fever appeared on my front teeth. Thankfully, in time, my tongue returned to its normal pink hue and those spots disappeared. What stayed even until now is the soothing sound of a vacuum and tender memories of Mama it evokes.

We had everything material we needed and it was understood there was little money for extras. When whining for something, Daddy cooly reminded us there was no money tree outside. I remember my parents buying several half-gallons of milk and loaves of sliced white bread on sale and storing them in the tall freezer in our dining room. They kept a small Tupperware container they called a kitty on a high shelf in the kitchen into which they dropped extra change for a rainy day. Sometimes, Daddy gathered us little ones into the station wagon and drove to Salado Creek, not far from our house, to fish. It was fun to sit in the back seat facing the road as he drove. I have wondered about those fishing jaunts, whether Daddy took us fishing to get away from every day cares for a short while or because we needed the food.

Store-bought sweets were rare at the Guckian house. Occasionally, Daddy stopped at Montgomery Ward on his way home from work, likely on a payday, to buy a giant shiny Navy-blue paper sack full of smaller white paper bags stuffed with confections. Daddy used to say a little sugar brings out the flavor of food. But sugary soda and candy were rarities in our home. So on those infrequent dessert nights, we all sat around the supper table after eating a plate of beans and cornbread, and instead of eating Jell-O, binged on maple nut candy, jelly beans, candy-coated peanuts, sugared gummy orange slices Daddy liked, chocolate-covered almonds and pecans, chocolate and caramel turtles, peanut-butter bars and bon bons.

Throughout elementary school, we carried paper-sack lunches nearly every day. Mama or Daddy handwrote each name on each sack with a pencil. There were no dollars to expend on cafeteria lunches, except for a pint of milk, which cost 2 cents, and on rare occasion, chocolate milk for a penny more. Occasionally, we were treated to a hot lunch. As a child, I disliked meat and devised clever ways to avoid it. One time, when we were treated to the infrequent cafeteria lunch, a round meat patty was part of the meal served on a pale green hard plastic tray that had small cutout sections for each item. The Benedictine nuns all clad in head-to-toe flowing black armor stood by the trash can policing our trays to ensure we ate all the contents. When they were not looking, I stuffed the entire meat patty inside my emptied milk carton and crushed it flat to remove all doubt whatsoever or threat of questioning as to whether that carton indeed was empty. I employed a similar tactic at home. One evening at supper we had fatty roast. I filled my mouth with meat from my plate and promptly excused myself to go to the toilet, where I spit it out and flushed it down. No one was the wiser.

Halloween was grand fun when I was young and Mama's illness did not diminish it! Kids in hoards walked neighborhood streets after dark, climbing trees, shouting, laughing, and filling large brown paper grocery sacks with candy booty, homemade popcorn balls, candy apples and bottles of Pommac soda. Before we were old enough to trick-or-treat on our own, Daddy drove slow through the streets in our station wagon stopping regularly so us littlest kids could hop out, run to a door, ring the bell or knock and shout, "trick or treat!"

How my parents funded our private elementary school education at St. Benedict, especially in light of Mama's medical bills, is beyond me. All six of us kids attended parochial school through the eighth grade, at which time we attended Sam Houston High School from where all six graduated. And my parents tithed. They belonged to and participated in the PTC, and the men's and women's clubs of the church. Mama was an active member of the Catholic Daughters of the Americas and my father belonged to the Knights of Columbus. My mother hosted bunco parties at our house with the ladies of the church and neighbors, while my father played cards with the Knights and participated in charitable activities. They were regular volunteers and contributors to the annual church picnics. Mama and Daddy also were helpful neighbors and spent time with our relatives, especially the elders and widows. My great aunts and uncles visited us, too, dressed to the nines. My uncles were sharp in suits and hats, and my aunts donned dresses, high-heels and gloves, with handbags decorating their forearms. And they all drove gargantuan automobiles of the 1950s and early '60s.

As a child, the times I cried seem few matched to merry recollections, but indeed there were tears, and in a fit of tears one afternoon, I had a child's epiphany. It was a mild South Texas summer's day. We had moved that April into our new house. I was crying after a squabble between me and my siblings and I got blamed. I hurried out the back door, darted around the corner of the monstrous square frame of our water cooler that protruded portentously onto the cement porch as it hung outside the dining room window like a sleeping dinosaur, and sat down on the bench of our kid-size picnic table. The little table sat like a secret, squashed tight in a corner where the house met the water cooler on the edge of the porch.

The water cooler had a boggy smell like day-old rain, which I liked. Its exterior sides were packed thick with yellow straw held in on all sides by a latticework of skinny metal bands. It incessantly dripped tiny waterfalls of moisture that formed lilliputian puddles on the porch.

That day, I slid my bare feet across the cool cement beneath the table as I sat down on the bench and cried. And I cried and cried. I cried so hard, I gasped for breath in-between sobs while shaking my head No, my long stringy reddish-brown hair dangling around my freckled face. In-between sucks of air, I said to no one in a whisper, "It's not my fault, it's not my fault," and a voice inside replied, "Nobody cares." My tears tasted salty on my lips. Although young, not yet old enough to reason things out, I inherently knew. I had no name for this knowing, but I knew there was something inside me that hurt and made me cry, and nobody understood or seemed to care. There was no one to put a reassuring, comforting arm around me, dry my tears, say it was alright, offer me a caring smile or word. I sat alone like an unseen shadow looking into nowhere across the backyard, feeling invisible and real at once. And then, as swiftly as when they had begun, my tears stopped. And so it seemed to go with me for a long time; feeling unnoticed and guilty of believed blame would linger and influence my behavior that commanded unproductive attention, along with futile tears of inevitable disappointment.

Despite family life remaining seemingly unchanged on the surface, changes that did happen sometimes obviously and sometimes obscurely produced hidden impressions on the inside that at the time went unrecognized. Only till much later or in some cases, never, did those feelings and their effects see light.

We still were held, and increasingly so, to rigid housework rituals, strict standards of behavior and precise schedules, all of which understandable in a household of eight people. The fight against germs prevailed and escalated.

After and throughout Mama's illness, cleanliness was an urgent priority as germs became the archenemy and disinfectants became absolute staples. Saturday morning house cleanings were the rule. Beds were stripped, sheets were washed and dried and beds were remade. Every room and every item in every room was meticulously dusted. Floors were swept or vacuumed and mopped. Countless buckets of mop water were dumped into the backyard lawn and refilled with the garden hose for another round. Bathrooms were disinfected till shiny and the sterile scent of Pine-O-Pine permeated the air. Clothes were washed, dried, folded or hung, and put away in closets and drawers. The ironing came later. Shoes for work, school and church were carried outside to the sidewalk, cleaned, polished and shined, with particular attention given to Daddy's and Mama's shoes, and then returned to their respective closets. And finally, all the rags and remnants used to clean the house were washed in the washing machine in hot soapy water, rinsed twice, dried, folded and stored in the linen closet on the bottom shelf until the next Saturday's housecleaning.

"Wash your hands" became Mama's ready recognizable refrain. After we used the toilet. After we came in from play. After we had touched something "dirty." Before we sat down to a meal. Mama herself washed her hands up to her elbows with bar soap regularly, transforming her milky flesh to flakey and frail. Still, we washed our hands. And the washing spilled over to other things. If a clean cloth or item of clothing made an accidental unfortunate fall to the floor while being folded, it was pitched in the dirty clothes bin for another washing before it could be used or worn. Our floors were spotless, but in Mama's mind, they were dirty. Paradoxically, water had nearly drowned Mama as a child but water had become her deliverer.

Funny, decades later, when Mama was in her mid-80s, I treated her on Mother's Day to breakfast at a restaurant we liked. After ordering, she said she needed to go to the ladies room. After waiting a while outside the stall I finally peeked in. And there I found my formerly germ-obsessed mama sitting on the toilet, bending over to pick up scraps of toilet paper from the floor. And it struck me; Mama finally had forgotten her dread of germs.

Without knowing, I knew, I counted on Mama and Daddy. I trusted them amid and perhaps in light of the chaos. They were my parents. That alone was everything. What they said was etched in stone. There was no talking back and stiff consequences for it. After them, came God. And Texas. While still very young, I began to appreciate my birthright as a Guckian and Texan. Mama and Daddy grew up in Gonzales and Luling, legendary for barbecue, oil and the first gunshots triggered for Texas independence. I mean no disrespect to anyone whose bloodline is not of Texan ancestry. Wherever born and of whatever ancestry, honor it. But being Texan is not about learning to dance the "Cotton-Eyed Joe," or wearing Wranglers, Stetsons or Lucchese boots. It's about bloodline and a straightforward manner bred by birthright. Texans are tenacious, loyal, resourceful and devoted to our generational heritage. We have inherited the fortitude of our forefathers, those industrious assiduous people of Texas.

Uncle Don, Mama's brother, was the last succeeding sheriff of Gonzales County. He was the quintessential stiff-necked sheriff, straight as starch but fair and well-liked. He served 10 years when he and Aunt Delo and their two sons lived on the first floor of the county jailhouse and my aunt cooked for the prisoners every day. Now a museum, the jailhouse was built in 1885 of concrete and steel to jail up to 200 prisoners. Above the first floor are three more floors of iron cells, its walls blanketed with long-gone convicts' scribblings and an indoor gallows reputed as one of the last used in Texas. The jail Uncle Don held charge over once held the likes of violent outlaw John Wesley Hardin.

My parents, grandparents and other relatives settled in or were born in Gonzales, Luling, Lockhart and outlying areas of Texas. They were and are the lawmen, ranchers, farmers, railroad workers, businessmen and oilmen whose hardships and hard labor formed, and preserve, the state of Texas and who I am. I can see a town, field, river or building and sense my ancestors there, and remember. We Texans are warm and hospitable yet stick to our convictions amid opposing opinion. We are a Christian and military society. We are proud of our entrenched Texas roots and American nationality, evidenced by wide display of Texan and American flags on our homes, vehicles, clothing and hats. My home town is home to the Alamo, where a few hundred Texans and Texas patriots resisted several thousand Mexican troops for 13 days during the Texas Revolution, spearheading formation of the sovereign Republic of Texas 10 years before we entered the Union. Our speech resounds, our manner echoes, and our blood pulses with an inimitable Texan character and creed.

Mama's misfortune did not change my heritage. I learned by my parents' example that my birthrights were respected and grounds for pride. I was 8 in 1963 when President John F. Kennedy was assassinated. That day, Miss Maxine turned on the TV in our classroom to watch the disturbing report. I lay down my head on folded arms on my desk and wept, along with others. It was a solemn, confusing time for us little ones. I never had heard of anyone getting shot, much less the President, who we learned to hold in exceptionally high regard.

I found out something else the year I turned 11. I discovered I was not a little girl anymore. It happened in a bathroom stall at school and scared me. Having returned to the classroom and whispered to my teacher what I'd discovered, she sent me home where I found Mama in her and Daddy's bedroom. As we sat together on their bed, she explained to me, in a gentle, caring, nondescript yet understandable manner, the natural role of menstruation in making babies. And, with a certain unintimidating finesse only a mother knows, she told how she and my daddy made us. Upon hearing the latter and thereby repulsed upon hearing, I exclaimed, "Ew! You let HIM do that to YOU?!" Mama tolerated my surprise with a tender smile. I didn't realize it but I was having my first grownup conversation with my mother.

As Mama's slow road back to herself and us naturally eased Daddy's frame of mind, I regrettably became a trying trial to both my parents. Only God knew the trouble brewing for them, this time in the form of my impending pubescent mischief.

The Diary

Shortly before I turned 12, my best friend Dominique, who lived two doors down and had the thickest, blackest, longest, curliest hair I had ever seen and whose mama was French and whose daddy was in the military serving in Vietnam, gave me a diary for my birthday. It was sky blue with gold-colored embossed letters that spelled "Five Year Diary" on the padded faux-leather cover.

From a big family of eight on a little budget, I had never seen anything so splendid, unless that one Christmas when I got a bottle of Avon peach-scented lotion from my Grandma Guckian and Aunt Dorothy, or the light blue nightgown and robe I sauntered around in that made me feel rich and elegant.

Inside my shiny new diary were white ruled pages with gold-tipped edges, like the Bible that sat admired and untouched on the coffee table in our living room. Sometimes I wonder if Dominique remembers the birthday gift a lifetime ago, or if she knows I have become a writer, or after all these years that my little blue diary is one of my most cherished keepsakes. Every time I touch the cover or slick pages, I think of her and the bygone innocence of childhood.

In my diary, I scratched brief entries during much of my 12th year when it was new. I earmarked every birthday of family and friends; remembering and celebrating birthdays no matter how old or young was an important and recurring event of our lives growing up and remains a mainstay in mine still. I wrote about visits to the dentist, mine and my family members. I wrote about the boys my girlfriends and I chased during recess at school. I wrote about meeting Danny Kaye at a UNICEF fundraiser and after shaking his hand vowed I'd never wash mine again. But as I turned 13, my notations diminished and then abruptly ended. Pubescence and the thrill of high school with new friends and interests left my little diary behind along with my girlish purity.

The teenager subtly emerged from the little girl and with her the onset of a faintly maturing vocabulary, and a growing preoccupation with personal appearance, clothes, the opposite sex and new doings outside home.

First Kiss, Cigarettes and Motorcycles

I kissed my first boy when I was 8 and I kissed him smack dab on the lips. He was 6 and the most handsome boy in our neighborhood. A tiny Tom Hanks with blue eyes and curly brown hair, Todd lived next door with his sister and parents.

On this summer's day, some kids on our block converged in our front yard to play Kiss Chase. In the game, instead of tagging somebody "it," you caught and kissed them on the lips. I tagged Todd, we fell to the ground and kissed. But it was Daryl who introduced me to my first French kiss.

It happened the same year Mama came home from the hospital after the lobotomy. I was in seventh grade with a longing to graduate eighth grade and become a high schooler. Daryl was a freshman and smelled of boy. Taller than Daddy and stocky, with blonde unkempt hair and a freckled face, he had a wide smile filled with teeth crowded into his mouth like white chalk pressed into a box. Daryl lived on the corner on the second block of our street. He was the one who first ushered me toward my teenage escapades with all the tingling titillation that comes with being in-between a 12-year-old girl and a budding teen. Adolescence had arrived with impenitent intensity, dragging my childhood illusions with it.

That afternoon, we were dallying, flirting, outside our house where no one could see us, hidden on a narrow strip of grass flanked by the neighbor's fence and our garage. I stood on the backyard side of the 3-foot-high chain-link gate and on the opposite side loomed Daryl. Our tete-a-tete paused followed by silence when he leaned over the gate and put his mouth on mine and with it, his tongue. The kiss was warm and I welcomed it and that marked the start of a newfound appetite. It seemed seconds later Mama called me for supper. Daryl went home, I went inside, and I was different.

I began taking heightened notice of things I had not noticed before. I began to feel insecure about my looks—the shape of my body, my weight, my hair, my facial features and blemishes, my teeth, how I looked in my clothes, the hair on my legs and arms. I thought endlessly about these things. Coincidentally, my behavior began to shift, no longer the instantly obedient little girl following directions but an independent thinker who decided whether and when I obeyed.

Shiny lip gloss tinted varyingly pink, rose or peach was on my person in a pocket or purse around-the-clock. I looked forward to being allowed to shave my legs at 13. A schoolmate named Janice had thick blonde hair on her arms, which she shaved, and where she had shaved there grew a short, light, uniformly even beginning of sprouting new hair. I had inherited my father's hairy gene where my arms were concerned, because I had what I considered too much of it for a girl and it was not blonde but brown. Mama however had skin of pale white, soft and hairless without blemish. Even so, I did not mimic Janice. It was decades before I did anything about the hair on my arms and I cannot recall anyone mentioning it. But in my mind, it was ugly and unfeminine. I never asked her, but perhaps Janice felt the same about her stubborn short strands of arm hair.

The long saga of sickness I had been prone to as a child disappeared by age 12 after a tonsillectomy and it was then I smoked my first cigarette. Daddy may have been an influence; he smoked for as long as I can remember, first those he rolled himself and later the ready-rolled packs of filtered Marlboro. On my walk to school one morning, which took me behind Lone Oak Mall where the new Thrift-Tex, which was the Texas-based H-E-B grocery store's earliest try at a discount store, was built, I found an unopened pack of Lark cigarettes sealed in cellophane. Back then, a pack of cigarettes cost 25 cents and kids could buy them. Daddy sometimes sent us to the store to buy his. I picked up the abandoned pack and carried it to school where I handed out the ready-rolled treats to kids during recess. Two brothers, Raul and Saul, refused one, stating we didn't know what might be in them, even though the package had been sealed when found. That thought had not crossed my mind. I stumbled upon the pack of Larks, and instantly was eager to smoke and share them with no thought to consequence.

My 12th year also marked a time when I quit certain things. The Montgomery's had a piano and there was one in the W.W. White Elementary School auditorium where we played in summer. I liked to bang the keys so Mama and Daddy let me take lessons. But since we had no piano and I had to practice during recess at school while other kids played, I had second thoughts. My decision became clear when it came time for me to play a solo during a concert held for the parents; I froze at the thought and quit one day in April before Mama came home from the Galveston hospital. I wrote in my diary I quit because I was bored but that was untrue. I didn't quit because of boredom or missing recess. I quit because I was afraid of playing poorly and feeling embarrassed. And maybe, I was afraid of something else—of my parents attending the recital. Mama was disappointed I had stopped. I also joined the Girl Scouts but because we couldn't afford summer camp, I quit the Scouts, too, one month after quitting piano lessons.

I was growing up. And so was my defiance. I had a pair of tight, flesh-colored short-shorts that zipped up one side and from a distance looked like I wore none. Daddy made me take them off every time he saw me in them. But I liked the shocking effect of those shorts on people. I liked raising eyebrows. Daddy took notice of my attitude, which little did I realize burdened him. I suppose he saw a rising rebellion in me. Sometimes he called me smart mouth. By the time I turned 13, graduated eighth grade and entered high school, I craved to be clear of the rigors and rituals of household rules and duties in exchange for the excitement and spontaneous liberty I imagined existed in the outside world. The dissenting filly in me was stirring.

Between my 12th and 13th birthdays, Sister Michael asked me to a retreat at the Benedictine Convent in Boerne and I went. Or truer, perhaps, Mama and Daddy made sure I went. I suppose the cloistered weekend was intended to corral my rising rebellion. But all I would remember of it was the sight of Sister Michael without her religious habit at bedtime. She had cropped hair and wore a red plaid flannel robe. There were girls at the convent I did not know. Apparently, they had been sent there by their parents for reform. One spoke of smoking cigarettes and marijuana. Another showed us scars on her wrists where she had cut herself. I have wondered what became of them, whether they lived happy lives or had lives like mine that went afoul.

As a fledgling freshman, I handwrote an essay on ruled notebook paper that detailed my heart's desires, at a tender time in my life when I knew little but thought I was full-grown and ready to play the part. I fantasized about falling in love, getting married, keeping a home of my own and having children. Paradoxically, at the same time I yearned to be free of home as I knew it, I hungered for my own home to look exactly like it. I took for granted all men were decent men, husbands and fathers like Daddy, and all women were caring, devoted mothers and homemakers like Mama. I was becoming a woman yet still held to the musings of a dreamy girl. I began to listen less to my parents and more to the mustering call of my impatient heart.

During my freshman and sophomore years from 1969 to 1971, I wore block-heel platform pumps and short trendy mini-skirts that barely covered my rear and revealed ample muscular thighs. I teased and Aquanet-sprayed my long hair till it was voluminous and lofty. I went nowhere without thick makeup to cover juvenile imperfections on my face. My friend Paula and I, with our big hair, big heels and big thighs, were sent home from school one day, not without a small amount of glee on our part, because our skirts were too short. They were so short, in fact, that when we sat down at our desks the boys in front of us all turned around to gawk. But we didn't care. We welcomed their ogling even amid our trifling well-hidden modesty.

I think back on Daddy especially, having four daughters all teenaged at once, and wonder how he made it through those worrisome years and our foolish antics. He was a caring, protective, godly father. Later, as we grew older with careers or families of our own, Mama smiled at having four grown daughters all in some phase of menopause at the same time.

One night, Mama and Daddy and us kids were in the living room watching TV when abruptly there came a thud and voices from the rooftop. "What… the… hell?" Daddy said, rising from his recliner to investigate. Telling us all to stay put, he walked through the front door outside into the front yard to look up to see obviously drunken boys we knew from school on the roof. Upon seeing Daddy, they asked, "Can Mary and Betty come outside?" With the blunt imposing composure of Marshall Rooster Cogburn, Daddy directed them to get down and get gone. I didn't hear Daddy's unreserved threat, but it must have been stiff because they disappeared in a wink and never returned.

The night enchanted me like the consuming allure of mythological sirens. Night air smelled fragrantly different, felt rousingly different, sounded intriguingly different than did day. Under camouflage of night, the ordinary turned exotic and stimulating. I often have wondered whether all teens perceive life as I did—in vibrant animation. We knew a boy named Steve who liked Mary and his friend Doug who liked me and both rode motorcycles. I still remember the bewitching trance of hearing those bikes approaching in the summer's slow unmoving night. We never rode with them; Mama and Daddy had none of it. But inside, I rode.

Children and young teenagers cannot read between the lines. At whatever unfathomable price my parents paid, we kids were shielded from the ugly in the world and felt secure in a set routine at home that was predictable, which made us feel safe. I perceived my home life from the eyes of a pensive girl watching sweet naive movies on TV, when TV aired only three stations and delivered the likes of "Ozzie and Harriet" and "Father Knows Best." I imagined being a grownup, living exactly like those TV characters, but not really. Not as tame. Full-blown rebellion was right around the corner.

At the Drive-in

Second Spiritual Death

By 15, I was coming home drunk. And that was only the enigmatic beginning. When I think about my 15th year, when I was hungry for 21, I reflect with a shudder. A lingering twinge of troubling certainty tells me I put myself and my parents mercilessly through hell, as if they each and together had not enough hell already. I dealt them harm, even at times when they did not know what I had done. I know they have forgiven me, for this and more, and perhaps I have forgiven myself. But what I did and the pain I caused myself and them has forever scarred me, and I cannot dismiss it or deny it or wipe it clean as if it never happened. It happened.

Like some 15-year-olds, I was a precarious minefield. Not a girl anymore and not a woman yet. Daddy used to say, "You think you're grown with a piece hanging off." That free-floating in-between condition where I had little-to-no emotional maturity to consider or care about my behavior or consequences of it. Ironically, I often was obedient and respectful. But inside me was a growing storm. I had a wild side brewing. A need. And little bits of it were beginning to spill out like water seeping through a cracking dam.

I was straddling sensible and stormy. If I could liken my mindset at 15 to something tangible, it would be the exhilarating ride on the swing at the playground at St. Benedict I loved so much as a little girl. When the bell rang recess, I flew outside to the towering swing set, jumped into the waiting hanging seat, and pushed my uniformed frame frontward and backward propelling the swing higher and higher, till it could soar no more. And when it was nearly straight up in the air, I stopped pushing, afraid it would encircle the swing set with me in it. And in that brief, in-between, titillating short span of space, while the swing was suspended in the air nearly perpendicular to the ground and before it swung toward the earth again, the swing and I sat in a most enjoyable millisecond of thrilling excitement. That is where I lived perpetually at 15. In the in-between thrill.

Day to day was a steady stream of in-betweens, not lived with a defined start and stop but in perpetual motion of always going somewhere. It was in this airy flippancy in which I lived, responsible and irresponsible in parallel, connecting my in-betweens one after the other like railcars on a train. Always going somewhere into something or someone without much thought, except for a brief rationalization or attention to dutiful tasks expected of me at home and school. Only much later in life have I reflected, and laughed and cried, at the absurdity and danger of my teenage behavior. At 15, I of course did not know this.

Still, I made above-average grades throughout high school. I enjoyed Stenography, which later proved the starting foundation of a future profession, and Home Economics where I learned to sew and expand cooking and baking skills I picked up at home. Mama and Daddy were forever in the kitchen; it seemed before one meal was over another began. I became so adept at sewing I made my own prom dresses. I attended Mass weekly and confessed to lying and cussing. I did my chores. I was a model daughter in this regard. But there was another side to me far from ideal. I was allowed to go to parties and ease into dating but when Mama and Daddy asked, "Is there going to be beer there?" my answer was a lie every time. There would be alcohol. And I would drink it.

Mama had recovered three years by then. She was not well but on the very long road to regaining herself and self-control. I however was uncontrollable. One day, we were in my bedroom. I don't recall what we argued about, but I told Mama I hated her, and at that, she delivered a hard flat-palmed slap to my face. And I slapped her back. She was dumbfounded and deeply hurt. I was nervous but still nervy and dared her to slap me again. She did not. I may never forgive myself for having done such a horrendous thing to my mother. I do not recall ever hearing anything more about it, not even from Daddy. There was no penance except my lingering guilt.

At 15, I learned to dance to country music. I wore skin-tight hip-hugging denim pants, Roger's cowboy boots and a Stetson Silverbelly with a curled narrow brim. I was allowed to go to dancehalls, including the famed Golden Stallion, with Jo Ann. It was "the" place to go to hear and dance to live emerging country artists. When the Stallion closed for the night, we crowded into the adjoining smokey Conastoga Club to hear intimate live performances by the likes of country legend Johnny Bush. There were other dancehalls, too, in the country, including Lubianski's in St. Hedwig, and others in Mesquite and Poth. Back then, legal-age patrons carried liquor inside and bought setups of ice and soda in plastic cups. I learned to dance the "Two-Step," "Cotton-Eyed Joe," and "Waltz" in those places.

One night, I rode with my sister and her date to a dance in the country and there met some boys I knew from school. My friends and I piled into a '57 Chevy and proceeded to down Jim Beam and 7 Up and make out. On the way home, Jo Ann and her beau stopped at the Pig Stand on Rigsby Avenue for an early morning bite. I was drunk, with mascaraed racoon eyes and an unchecked mouth. A police officer who was a friend of my sister's happened to be at the cafe. When she stopped to say hello, I poked his chest and said something foolish. I cannot remember what I spewed, but I learned later he told my sister threateningly she better get me off him and take me home. There were times at home after nights like this my bed spun, causing me to make multiple trips to the toilet to throw up. I'm sure my parents heard, dismayed, and prayed.

The late '60s and early '70s covered an historic era in my life that was marked by the Vietnam War and Woodstock, a time when subcultures were influenced by psychedelic drugs. It was a time when "acid" or "LSD" themes were pronounced in art, paisley patterns, peace signs, lava lamps, and Volkswagen Beetles and vans. As I inched toward 16, I embraced the trendy hippie fashion and its bold imprudence that embodied my attitude as it did my clothing, or lack thereof. Teenage girls like me and young women everywhere began to go braless.

On the outside, I looked daring but on the inside I doubted I measured up to imagined perceptions of me by others, to characters on TV and in movies, to my friends, to strangers. My outsides exhumed confident arrogance but my insides trembled with insecurity. I hid it well and plunged headfirst anyway. Like the swing.

I met my first dangerous man at 15. I discovered despite my charmed upbringing it was danger I was after. Scott was a senior at Sam Houston and a year older than his classmates. I had numerous acquaintances in high school but few close friends. Some were studious. Some were cheerleaders who dated athletes. Some were in the Rodeo Club. And some like me were members of the Better Business Leaders. Some held no notoriety or ambition whatsoever but mustered at the Bull Ring in-between classes to smoke and rouse. Scott was part of this group. He and his brother were friends with kids I had known at St. Benedict who now attended Sam Houston. In my thinking, this was the "cool" crowd. They did not make stellar grades or hold high aspirations. Not in the least. Their highest ambition was fun.

One afternoon I rode in a car with Scott and these gregarious cronies who drove the streets of Dellcrest, a neighborhood a bit more affluent than ours, and hurled raw eggs at cars parked at the curbs. I began dating Scott and only him. He taught me to drive his blue-green and white standard-shift Chevy and gave me a sweetheart ring and we made out often. Some of his friends asked me why I was with him, saying I was too pretty for him. Scott lived on the "other side of the tracks" in an impoverished neighborhood. His house was miniscule and plain and his parents held blue-collar jobs. His father worked at a cement plant where everyone called him Tom Cat; his mother worked as a waitress, dyed her hair black and chain-smoked unfiltered Camels.

Their sparsely furnished house had bare linoleum floors and a single tiny bathroom. In the backyard sat a shabby mobile home that served as the three boys' bedrooms, while his parents and little sister had rooms in the house. Scott's parents worked nights, making this the perfect place for teenagers like us to gather, smoke and drink beer, unescorted. It was a breeding ground for trouble. Even when his parents were home, they said nothing about our beer-drinking or cigarette-smoking. They, too, smoked and drank, often until inebriation. But I thought them cool, unlike Mama and Daddy, who I considered strict.

There were other kids in Scott's neighborhood whose parents both worked outside the home. On occasion, a bunch of us skipped school to collect at one of their houses to do what teenagers do. On one such afternoon, a boy named Bill was flirting with me and tried to kiss me. No, I said, threatening to cut his face with a razor blade sitting on a nearby table. But he persisted, and so, I reached for the blade, and ran it smoothly and quickly down the length of his cheek. It was not a deep or serious cut, a scratch really, but I cut him, drawing blood. He could not believe I had done it. Reflecting, neither can I.

The razor incident was not the first time I exhibited an impulsive blazon of disregard. When I was 8, I caught a horny toad. Our neighborhood was not fully developed yet, with houses springing up around ours, and beyond our alley sprawled open field. Back then, we saw horny toads daily. One day, I caught one, pinned it stomach-up on an empty Cheer laundry detergent box with a few of Mama's safety pins and proceeded to dissect the little unsuspecting critter's abdomen from neck to toenail, simply to see what its insides looked like. In my defense, we were studying frogs in science class at the time.

On another day, I spotted an orange cat walking across our yard. I called it to me sweetly, Here kitty, kitty. But as soon as it stood in front of me, looking up at me with trusting eyes, I punt-kicked the cat like a football. That cat squealed loud and darted fast away. I don't recall ever seeing it again. I do not even step on an ant or a doodle bug now, but when I was a girl, I did those shocking acts to animals. And to people on occasion, as with the razor blade.

Throughout my childhood, drive-in movie theaters were popular. You could sit in a lawn chair on the ground or in the bed of a pickup truck or inside a car and watch movies on a huge screen the size of a wide two-story building. It was bigger than life, unencumbered and exciting, watching movies after dark in the open air. The Towne Twin Drive-In was complete with restrooms and a snack bar with burgers, ice cream and soda, and was the place to be for dating teens. During intermission of a double-feature, we scurried to the restroom and snack bar and then settled back into our movie-watching comforts for the second show. But one night was unlike all the other nights at the drive-in. As I mentioned, the kids I befriended were free-spirited ones, mostly from the other side of the tracks, who drank and smoked, and, as I discovered, broke moral bounds. One night at the drive-in, I happened upon two dating sophomores having oral sex in the front seat of a car. We called girls who engaged in this behavior sluts.

So, on this particular night, Scott and I were in the front seat of his Chevy. It was an exciting time of discovery and escapade. Toward the end of the second feature, near midnight when many cars had left the theater, he gestured for me to slip down to the floorboard as he sat on the seat and unzipped his jeans. I at once felt a dichotomous trust in him combined with cavalier daring mixed with trepidation at uncharted territory. I went along; after all, I trusted him, and other girls I knew were doing the same thing.

But I was repulsed by it. Yet I said nothing. Despite my feelings that told me otherwise, I clung to the idea that we loved each other and this was normal behavior. After the act, he held me and we drifted into sleep until at 2 a.m. we were startled awake by a security guard who told us it was time to go home. And now I, officially, was a slut, too, although I did not label myself as such.

I must pause here to state the obvious, which I did not consider then either. Legally speaking, Scott was 19, an adult, and I was 15, a minor, and what he had initiated was immoral and illegal.

Admittedly, I felt deeply ashamed yet concurrently convinced we should marry. This obviously was a defect in my thinking, for without thinking, I thought by default marriage was a foregone conclusion. After all, where there is "love" and "intimacy" surely marriage follows. Naturally, I had it backwards, twisting and distorting what I had learned better at home. I did not learn about sexual immorality at home. My parents exemplified a proper relationship that taught me sexual intimacy was sacred and came after, not before, the religious and civil commitment to matrimonial vows; it was reserved for a married man and woman who loved each other within the bounds of wedlock.

My teenaged mind did not identify what had happened in the front seat as being what it was: Abuse, illegal, immoral. I sped past all that without reflection and rushed headlong into plans to wed. Like most girls I knew, I had bigger-than-life dreams brightly colored by fairytales and no clue of the often-hard reality of daily living in adulthood. My generation married immediately after graduating high school emulating our parents' examples, hurrying to live life as adults on our own.

Neither was this the first time nor would it be the last, far from it, I would fall numb and keep going mindlessly in the same misguided direction anyway, chasing after danger.

Runaway

Third Spiritual Death

I've always said, my high school years were my happiest. But let me restate. Those years were not my happiest. Despite my parents' best efforts and my attention to duties at home, scholastic goals, and ideas about and worthy expectations for my future, my high school years were unbridled. In truth, what I craved in the midst of instability was stability, not confusion, which I courted. I went looking for stability in inane recklessness, which made what I truly wanted impossible to attain.

I was nearly 16 when Scott gave me his high school senior ring to wear to show the world we were one, and soon afterward in the wee hours of a summer's night I snuck out my bedroom window to run away with him, with full intent to head to Mexico to marry. While his friend Dan helped Mary out of her bedroom window that faced the backyard, Scott helped me out of mine, which was next to my parents' room and faced our neighbor's garage. As I climbed into the night, I whispered to Debbie not to tell. We were as quiet as church mice, or so we thought, until the neighbor stirred awake, grabbed her pistol thinking us burglars and crept outside toward us. But we lit out running faster than she was creeping and tore for the corner near the alley where Scott's brother was waiting in his Chevy.

My heart pounded in my chest as my mind raced with the exhilaration of running away. The night air was sweet and naughty and penetrated every cell of me. I gave no thought to anyone or anything else, not to my sister back home who I left with the secret, not to my parents who would worry themselves sick once they saw us gone not knowing where we went or with whom or when and whether we would return, not to the pain we were causing people who loved us. There was no one and nothing but us and Mexico.

The first place we drove to was Scott's house, a mere 2 miles away, which was empty except for his younger siblings. We all sat in the front yard drinking beer and smoking cigarettes, keeping watch for my father. We decided to sleep a while and then leave at dawn. While Mary and Dan made out in the living room, I went with Scott to his parents' bedroom. It was my first encounter with sexual intercourse. I thought I was prepared, getting ready to have an adult experience I had imagined for a while. It would be a storybook occasion and joyful. But it was not splendid or happy. It was painful, nearly over before it began and left me in tears. There was no tenderness. No romance. No purity. There was no love as I imagined love to be. Yet, I numbly accepted it as the way it was and was supposed to be. I accepted the disappointment and the barren vacuum inside my heart.

As the sun rose on this first day of newfound freedom, we excitedly headed not south to Mexico but northeast to his aunt and uncle's farm. They were pleasantly surprised we had come to visit and wondered why. We lied, telling them we wanted to take a drive and visit them. They served us breakfast with fresh scrambled guinea eggs, homemade biscuits with jam and orange juice. It was a cheery morning despite our arrival on false pretenses. But soon there came a call from Scott's mother who said Daddy had phoned her and she was calling on the chance we were there. Daddy had threatened to have police dispatch a statewide All-Points Bulletin on Scott with charges of kidnap and rape if Mary and I were not returned home pronto. Thus, our plans for Mexico were curbed and the road returned us home instead.

I never will forget the pain that shown on Mama and Daddy's faces when we got home. Scott gallantly dropped us at the curb and sped away, and we walked inside where quickly we saw through the back screened door Mama and Daddy sitting in lawn chairs. When they heard us stirring inside, they stood and walked slowly toward us. My mother was pale from strain and said nothing. My father, sternly quiet, too, until he spoke and kept it short: "You'll never know what you've done to your mother." Knife. Jab. To the stomach. There was no punishment. Only his words. And that was penance enough.

I know now Daddy was as sick with worry as Mama. But he was not a man to parade his pain. He was our provider and protector, he loved my mother, and he loved us. We were his world. And that is a sin I may never fully forgive myself for committing. The anguish for hours-on-end I caused my parents who only loved me and did their level best to give me everything good. Still, it was not good enough for a reckless maverick like me. A lot had happened in less than 24 hours. But a lot more was coming.

Married to a Stranger

Never. That's when I will forget what my mother told me. She and Daddy in perfect unity sat me down for a heart-to-heart soon after learning of my plan to wed the man who had stolen me under the cover of night. Mama said, "Betty Lou, we're no better than anyone else, but we are different."

My mind refused to hear what she said. My head was wrapped around an idea it would not let go of, and nothing my caring parents could say or do would change it. Mama and Daddy loved me and cared about my future. They wanted me to understand the family I planned to marry into was nothing like ours. My husband-to-be's upbringing was extremely different than mine had been. We were the quintessential polar opposites in every way, except one. Apparently, Scott and I both had a taste for recklessness.

My parents were right, of course. After all, Scott's parents were the ones who had known I, a minor, had run away from home with their adult son and said nothing to anyone until threatened by my father. Their way of life was a world removed from the nurturing commitment embodied in Mama and Daddy and reflected in our rearing. I did not perceive then Scott was the child of alcoholic parents whose families were infested with the disease or that he may have been a budding addict himself. Yet, nothing my parents said to me sunk in. I could not hear their worried words. All I could hear was my own voice saying what I wanted.

From my parent's commitment to each other and us, I still believed all men and women to be upright husbands and fathers, wives and mothers. I still thought without thinking, as the naive impulsive girl I was, that everyone's life looked exactly like theirs, while contradictorily disregarding my betrothed's visibly questionable character, upbringing and relatives. There was a blockage in my brain like a steel door slammed shut on every ugly detail about him, and a strong conviction that told me I loved him, was in love with him, and he was the guy for me. Of course, I had nothing to base that on except my distorted view of physical intimacy, which I labeled love, and love meant marriage, and marriage was for life.

Scott was the only boy I dated. I was 16. Once again, the intimacy we had consummated, albeit immoral and dull, along with my Catholicism played a strong role in my believing marriage to him was fixed and imminent, although

I did not think of it in such legalistic terms. I was a wistful girl. Not a woman. I saw only the excitement of change and the times he treated me with tenderness, which were few, perhaps even feigned.

My junior and senior high school years followed with limited escapade. In springtime in 1972 when I turned 17, Scott and I attended my junior-senior prom and it was then our engagement was set. He presented me with a modest white-gold engagement ring set with tiny diamonds. About this time, he also enlisted in the U.S. Naval Reserves and after he graduated high school soon left for basic training in Mississippi. The rest of that year I continued my studies, worked nearly full-time at Thrift-Tex, planned my wedding and stayed close to home. And then at Christmas, Scott flew home on a short holiday leave.

Throughout 1973, my senior year, because my grades were above average and I had completed nearly all required academic credits to graduate, I attended classes mornings only and worked afternoons and Saturdays saving money for my wedding. I continued corresponding with Scott long-distance while looking forward to my graduation and wedding. We mailed each other snapshots, including some of me in seductive poses, which I suspect he shared with his peers, and wrote letters professing undying love and a much-anticipated reunion.

There was no extended courtship. In March 1973, I turned 18, and at once placed the engagement and wedding announcement in the newspaper. Also in March, Scott returned home from basic training. Daddy drove me to the airport to meet him. A startling and disturbing thing happened when Scott dove into the back seat where I sat, scooched over next to me and kissed me. My feelings of amore were missing. I felt differently about him. The seductive quality of the anticipation I had experienced for months was gone. Being with him now, kissing him, left me hollow. I had grown out of it and didn't know it, till that instant. And I was afraid, confused and sad. All I had planned and hoped for was fading fast.

I never told a soul about my feelings that day. I told myself it was cold feet. That my dreams and plans were solid. That it was normal to lose some feeling when someone you love is away for a long time. That he was "the one." And I allowed myself to slip back into believing and acting as if I was in love with him.

I daydreamed about married life over the next few months. We set the date. Reserved the church and reception hall. Ordered invitations and Thank You cards. Got excited. Told everyone. As the wedding date loomed, my sister-in-law Lois and Jo Ann held wedding showers for me in April. I had inherited my Great Aunt Bea's cedar chest, which became my trousseau, into which I collected cherished belongings, including an heirloom linen tablecloth and napkins that had been my Great Aunt Pearl's and embroidered pillow cases that were Aunt Bea's. I fantasized about my honeymoon, for which I bought a sheer pink nightgown and robe fringed in lace.

In early May, I handmade a halter-style, ankle-length, bright orange dress patterned in paisley and wore it to my senior prom, escorted by my betrothed. Later that month, with my family cheering me on, I graduated high school with joyful tears to the grand march of "Pomp and Circumstance." And then spent much of that night, into the wee hours in fact, making out with Scott in his makeshift bedroom in the backyard trailer. I was 18, an adult, and knew I could do whatever I pleased.

With high school behind me, I wasted no time in selecting an empire-waist wedding gown of white organza draped over taffeta dotted with Venetian lace and a floor-length mantilla veil. I bought a white satin heart-shaped wedding ring pillow with white ribbons affixed on top with which to tie our wedding bands, and a wedding book where I would preserve accounts of the matrimonial gifts, photos of the momentous occasion, guest list and other remembrances. We made plans to rent a tiny furnished flat at the Fairdale Apartments on Rittiman Road, near the railroad tracks, as our first home together. I was spellbound by the image of married life based on my parents and grandparents' devotion to their vows, an impression blended with reaffirming happily-ever-after married couples from lovable television shows I had grown up watching. An ideal picture, to be sure, to which I clung, believing beyond questioning a man and woman who fell in love naturally wed and stayed true forever. I interwove myself into all those worthy images, ignoring the dangerous prospect the man and life I imagined may not manifest similarly. In short, I denied a voice inside that told me something was terribly wrong.

But here I will pause and confess. Perhaps there were other reasons, reasons I did not realize or talk about at the time, why I was with Scott and why I would marry him. Perhaps I was itching to get out of the house, to do as I pleased, and marrying him was my way out. Perhaps because I could not face the embarrassment of cancelling the engagement and wedding after shouting about it from the rooftops, despite inklings my feelings had changed, which I ignored. He was my distraction and became my escape. Right or wrong, I would take it. I did not contemplate this then, but looking back, I believe all of this was true.

My wedding hinged on a shoestring budget. Requests were made and accepted by Mary as maid of honor joined by five bridesmaids, including three school chums, Debbie and Scott's sister. Their gowns were tailored in pastel yellow, complimented by sheer floppy hats and happy daisy bouquets. Scott's friends and brother filled in as best man and five groomsmen. Roger would usher, joined by Scott's youngest brother, while my neighbor's kids filled in as ringbearer and flower girl. The ceremony would commence at St. Benedict on a Saturday evening in July followed by a reception at the picturesque Lone Star Pavilion. It was situated in Hemisfair Plaza, flanked by the Tower of the Americas and scenic San Antonio River. Daddy agreed to barbecue and Jo Ann offered to bake the wedding cakes. Mine was a traditional multi-tiered white confection with a small plastic husband-and-wife toy topper in tux and gown; and for the groom, a German Chocolate sheet cake. A friend agreed to play records for the dance.

Once voicing a concern Mama sometimes repeated herself, but Daddy never shook a finger in my face, even when I was dead wrong. In the case of my impending matrimonial mistake, upon recognizing my resolve to go through with it, they did their utmost to support my decision. They participated and tried to be happy for me, likely all the while praying their way through every advancing minute. At the church the day of the nuptials, the photographer asked Daddy to place a penny in my shoe for good luck and he obliged with a smile, as did Mama in a snap of her looking affectionately at me while holding the lace edges of my veil. Smiles on their faces did not reveal the frowning concern for me lurking in their hearts and the choice I was making in determined ignorance and defiance.

As the church filled with formally dressed well-wishers who excitedly exchanged hellos before taking their seats, as the wedding party mustered at the back of the church into proper processional order, as the organ piped the "Wedding March," and as Daddy escorted me in harmony with the pulse of

Mendelssohn's masterpiece to the altar, I hesitated. A sudden wave of anxiety swelled up in my middle, as I told Daddy I was nervous and whispered this question, "Does everyone feel this way before taking their vows?" He met my panicked reservation instantly: "Betty Lou, you do not have to go through with this, if you are not sure."

But, I went, anyway. I went to the altar with apprehension and my apprehensive father, anyway. I went through with the vows, anyway. I detached from my parents to attach my disquieted self to this freckled-face boy in a white tuxedo. I went before God, the priest and everybody else with hesitation in my heart and stubborn resolve in my head. As we knelt, the man-child spoke the oaths inferred upon him by the priest, and as he spoke these high mighty pledges, my gaze pointed with soft laser sharpness upon him and his words, saying telepathically across the intimate air between us, "Please understand, I'm going to hold you to it." This 18-year-old starry-eyed child, for whom her parents had held high hopes, married the 21-year-old below-average boy from the wrong side of the tracks.

With it done, we strode from the church beaming. Our reception was naturally cheery with 120 relatives and friends visiting and well-wishing. We ate wedding cake and drank champagne. We danced. We opened gifts and cards enclosing money. We saved the white plastic husband-and-wife toy topper to look at when we were 80 and remember. As was customary, we took home the top tier of the cake for good luck, to freeze and then thaw and eat on our first anniversary. Toward the party's end, I tossed my bouquet to a waiting assembly of women and girls. My husband removed my garter from my thigh and threw it to a gathering body of boys and men. And when the party was over, we newlyweds drove home to our tiny Fairdale flat, No. 60, near the tracks.

There was no honeymoon, only a short trip planned to the South Texas coast the next day. We could not afford more. I did not mind. Imaginings of how perfectly my wedding night would go played in my mind like the music of sweet violin to my ears, as perfect as my wedding gown. I would don the new pink negligee. We would kiss and make champagne toasts while what we had just done would sink in. We would let it. There would be romance. The night would be passed in an unhurried pace, in our little place, with its low-pile low-budget emerald green carpet. Sharing love and hope, with no thought of tomorrows.

When we arrived at the Fairdale, still in our wedding clothes, the first thing Scott did was roll and light a joint. He inhaled it deeply. We drank champagne. Unfulfilling sex trailed and was nothing to remember with reverence, certainly not the passionate climactic moment I had imagined as a new bride. And then we fell asleep. And that was all. This scene was destined to replay with repellent regularity.

I reflect a great deal now on my lifespan so far. Many people whose lives have not turned out anywhere near how they had hoped because they made too many mistakes or even one grave error say it is all for the best and they have no regrets, for without pitfalls and pain, they would not be who they have become, as if a life dashed of dreams serves higher purpose. And indeed I suppose it may, and a new dream may surface and manifest after the missteps, but not for all. And what of that? Maybe, just maybe, without all the damage done by ourselves or others to our treasured dreams, we would be much happier, much healthier, much wealthier.

As for me, yes, I do have regrets. I do allow myself to wonder at times what my life would have been had I chosen not to take those vows I took at 18 with a man-child who, frankly, was not, as my parents dutifully edified, on par with my upbringing or aspirations. Regret, though, is an empty bag. Life cannot be re-lived. It can, however, be revived. It can be lived differently, after and in light of mistakes. It is possible, even probable, life can be lived better than, less pained than, less damaged than the self-inflicted woundedness we do to ourselves by making wrong choices and suffering their ill-fated consequences. We can be healed of all that. We can improve our thinking and therefore our being and lot in life. We do not, I do not, have to live perpetually beneath a diadem of shadowed sorrow based on wrong moves. And so, to that end, I accept what choices I've made, and their outcomes, and where I am today. Whether, or not, my rambunctious reckonings have rendered my life, at long last, less happy, less healthy or less wealthy, I accept the regret. I live alongside it but not in it.

At 18 years young, I thought I knew everything and no one could tell me anything. When and how did I become so worldly, so all-knowing, so infinitely wise at such a young age? Alas, I was none of that. I was incautious. My principled want for a loving marriage, home and children was valid and good. But marriage to an unprincipled man would not deliver it.

I did not know this person, not really, to whom I had blindly pledged and entrusted my life for all time. I am certain he had shown me repeatedly who he was, in fact, since our first meeting three years earlier, but my naive denying brain didn't register truth's legitimacy, didn't listen to recurring insistent whispers; no, neither my brain nor my heart would allow it. My heart denied the validity of raw reality; and I lived by my heart, bulged with abstract pride. I saw him only through the idealistic lens of a child's illusion that seduced me into believing I was starting the picture-perfect life with the picture-perfect husband, despite all conveyances that showed me otherwise. Despite the illicit immorality he introduced me to. Despite the absence of any feeling of love for him that day when Daddy and I picked him up at the airport. Despite the warning that churned in my gut on my wedding day. Now, the sordid certainty was beginning to come into focus already on this the first night of our marriage. And soon enough I'd learn there was much more I didn't know.

Stoned and Scared

Fourth Spiritual Death

At the start of our marriage, I took birth control pills until we were ready to have children, but the pills caused me debilitating migraines so I stopped. On a whim, I cut my long hair very short and then saved my foot-long locks in a plastic bag and grieved the loss of my strands for months. Scott's employment as a welder was spotty so I worked as a bookkeeping clerk at a local bank and applied for federal civil service employment at Daddy's prompting. After six months at the Fairdale, Scott and I moved to a larger apartment at the Southcross Villas. We excitedly filled it with furniture bought on credit: a king-size brass bed and dresser; dining set; and a couch, coffee table and end table. The new furniture and new apartment ushered in new hope.

By December of our first wedded year, I had obtained full-time employment in civil service at the same locale as Daddy, securing health insurance benefits for myself and Scott. One afternoon, I returned home to find him and his friends smoking marijuana. At my confused surprise, Scott said they had gotten off work early, but he lied; he had not worked at all that day or for the entire week, I learned. Soon after, he was hospitalized with a Hepatitis C diagnosis. It seems unconscionable now, but I did not question the source of his illness or wonder whether dirty needles were the culprit.

I still was a girl who saw myself as a woman living the life I had dreamed about. I subsisted in the habit of denying the truth while blind to my denial. I saw but denied my husband's affinity with addiction. I saw but denied my life was built around and focused on his behavior and decisions. I saw but denied my circumstances that illustrated our marital lot was solely about barely getting by and purely led by him. In my heart, I held to romantic illusions of a happy marriage to a loving man, home and family of our own. I told myself that's what I had or could have with him. But that was a lie I told myself repeatedly and I was unhappy. My marriage was an empty existence. My husband was not loving but selfish and self-centered. And so far, there were no inklings of children or the security of a stable home. Scott's persona began to change and with it his eyes turned wild and empty.

Scott followed work to wherever it led and naturally I followed him. Within a span of four years, from 1973 to 1977, we lived in six cities in two states. One year into my federal job, I resigned to relocate with my husband when his work ended in San Antonio and we moved to Baytown. There, we lived a while with his like-minded cousins. I supposed the energy bill went unpaid because we took cold shallow baths. As work waned, Scott took a part-time job mowing commercial lots and stacking cut brush in a huge pile for burning. I naturally wanted to help, so off I went to Walmart to buy a white cotton shirt to wear with jeans one day to his mowing site. There, he left me alone to tend the brush fire. I had never tended a bonfire before. Hours went by before he returned. I was frantic. My mind was as sprayed with confusing thoughts as was my shirt with holes from flying cinders. To where had he gone? How could he leave me alone like that? He was delayed, he said upon returning. Here I was, abandoned, bewildered and heartsick, yet still willing, still believing, still clinging to us.

After Baytown, we moved to Louisianna, where we lived in a motel several months and befriended other couples who worked for the same construction company as Scott. We next headed back to Texas, to Kingsville, where Scott's drug habit escalated; I didn't question the names or types. One night, he and friends boiled something down to a liquid in a spoon, cooled it, sucked it into syringes and injected it into each other's arms. Not long after that, my high school senior ring and some record albums went missing. No doubt, they had been pawned.

When the work ended yet again we found ourselves rambling, this time on a move to Smithville, where we lived briefly with his accommodating grandmother. While Scott scrambled for work, I decided to return to San Antonio to stay with Mama and Daddy until he was set, immediately securing a part-time job as a typist with a temporary employment agency. But two months later I quit to rejoin Scott who had found a job and an apartment in La Grange. A month after arriving there, I got a job as a cashier at the H-E-B grocery store about a mile's walk from our apartment and kept the job for the next eight months. Off I'd go in my little gold-colored uniform to my little part-time job, exactly like when I was in high school.

We did not have a marriage except on paper. There was no meaningful intimacy. How could there be when people are anesthetized by substances or situations that remove the capacity to feel or be accountable. I cannot recall a single fond memory of lovemaking. Only the disappointing phantom of it. It was not what I wanted but I went along with it. I even tried to excel at being the person Scott apparently expected me to be: a silent observer of his destructive mischiefs. I was accommodating. Strove to fit in. But the person I was becoming was a distant version of my former self. I was a stranger to me. And a shadow of him.

All this time, my ideal image of marriage fought for survival as I acted out the role of dutiful wife, making a homey nest wherever we landed. I existed every day in anxiety, fear and frustration, but no one knew it, not even me. This is what denial looks like. I became increasingly uneasy, though, with our way of living, all the while trying to maintain some semblance of the life I had idealized before exchanging vows at St. Benedict. I cooked breakfast for Scott before he left for work and packed a hardy lunch. I cooked supper every night. I placed thin linen cloths filled with shredded potato on his closed eyes to soothe them from welder's flash. I baked. I cleaned. I laundered. I even sewed him a western shirt with intricate yokes and snaps.

Our only friends were drug addicts and dealers. Getting high was usual and daily and I went along, to a point. It started in the morning and ended at bed time. Scott's manner toward me became even less loving and more emotionally detached. All the while I kept putting up the Christmas tree, baking cookies, celebrating birthdays and going to church. I supposed if I pretended everything was alright, it would be, like when I was a little girl and hid under the bed when scared. I pretended away what scared me by closing my eyes believing no boogie man could see or hurt me if I could not see him. But the boogie man was staring me in the face.

I was 22, married and childless. I wanted to pay our bills and pay them on time, have roots, a home, kids. Oh, how I wanted a child. I wanted my husband to be reliable. But after four years, I had nothing I wanted.

One evening, Scott introduced me to a couple our age. She had given up drugs and alcohol while pregnant and now was home from the hospital after giving birth to their first child. They invited us over presumably to meet the new arrival. We all tiptoed into the nursery to where the baby slept in his crib. We then walked to the living room, where all three—the two new parents and Scott—exposed an upper arm, tied it tight around with a rubbery band, and injected some form of drug into each other's veins. The new mother said with obvious glee, "I've been thinking about this for nine months!"

Scott prodded me to join them, saying, "Come on, try it, you'll love it!" My response was as flat as my heart felt at that instant: "No. I don't want that." And I walked away, feeling afraid and nauseous. I first stepped back into the nursery where the newborn slumbered. As I peered down upon that unwary infant, I shed silent tears for the child as much as myself and then tiptoed away to sit alone in the den on a small sofa. I was deeply grieved. And I thought, this is not my life. This is not what I want. I was disgusted by the scene I had witnessed in the living room and the new mother's words. Two young parents whose thrill was not their first child but whatever drug they were injecting into their bodies. I said nothing. But I could not ignore what I had seen and heard. It made me sick to my stomach.

An ever-deepening darkness began gnawing at my insides. One night in April, I told Scott I wanted to see a doctor in San Antonio about why I was not conceiving. I'll pause here briefly. It is vividly clear to me now only in retrospect how deeply embedded in crushing denial I was. No matter what I saw, felt or heard, I still wanted a child and marriage with a man who scared and nauseated me.

As we stood in the walk-in closet in our bedroom and I began to pack, an argument started about my trip and escalated. Scott pushed me against the wall, tightened his hands around my throat, told me angrily he could not give me what I wanted and he was not the person I wanted him to be. And then, he let go and I collapsed to the floor and wept. But he drove me to San Antonio, dropped me at my parents' home and returned to La Grange. I remember vividly the fertility test and how deserted I felt that day when the doctor performed a Hysterosalpingogram. I remember thinking, here I am, utterly alone, without my husband, and he is home, doing drugs, seemingly without care for me whatsoever, or for what I want or for our marriage. Conflicting thoughts and emotions stirred altogether. I was tangled up inside. Nothing made sense. And still, I hoped.

The test revealed I was ovulating albeit irregularly and was capable of pregnancy. That night, I phoned Scott. Surprisingly, he agreed to come to San Antonio and be tested as well. After the test, he returned home to La Grange but I stayed. The following day, the doctor phoned me with the test results and

I shared the news with my parents. I did not know how Scott would take the negative news but I phoned him. Predicably the call went badly when I repeated what the doctor had said of Scott, "He could not get a fly pregnant." Two days later, I got a letter from Scott demanding divorce.

Years later, I would view his letter as good news. But at the time, it crushed me. His words sent me reeling but prodded me into action. Daddy rented a U-Haul, and he, Jo Ann, Debbie and I drove together to La Grange to collect my things. As we drove into town, we spotted a young blonde woman driving the fire-engine red Ford short-bed truck that belonged to Scott and me. We motioned for her to pull over and she did. Springing from the U-Haul, I ran toward her screaming and demanded she get out of my truck. Quickly, the sheriff arrived, telling us he knew Scott, and if I didn't back off, he'd handcuff me and take me to jail. Reticently, I climbed back into the U-Haul and we drove on to the apartment.

Upon walking inside, I found the gold-colored cast aluminum Dutch oven I had purchased for our kitchen sitting on a cold stove with mold inside it. As I washed and dried the pot and the four of us packed and loaded boxes and furniture into the U-Haul, Scott arrived alone. He declared to us all he was keeping the truck and stereo and said nothing of the blonde.

It is difficult to describe my mental and emotional state at that moment in time. Both my head and heart were spiraling out of control from anything resembling rational. I felt detached from myself. I could not fathom what I was seeing and doing was real. Yet, it was real. My feet were on the ground. My family was with me. I was inside a wicked dream and wanted to wake up to find it untrue. While I stood in the kitchen packing my world into cardboard boxes and sobbing uncontrollably, Debbie turned to me and said matter-of-factly, "I know you're getting a divorce, but he's my friend and I'm still gonna be friends with him." My heart was breaking, my mind was splintering, and I could not comprehend why it was urgent my sister speak those words to me when clearly I was in torment.

With my family buzzing about, Scott and I hugged and cried and through his tears and mine he told me again he could not be the man I wanted him to be. And then, he left. Leaving me at once with the cold truth of his leaving and the denial of it at war within me.

Denial is a Liar

I believe many, maybe most, people live in denial… of something harmful. Denial is an insidious cancer. It corrupts a soul, devouring mind and heart. Denial is a tyrant. It crushes our God-given spirit and darkens the sparkle and wonder in living. Denial is a liar. It told me who I was with and what I was doing was who and what I was supposed to have and want. Denial is deadly. It destroys the one in denial. Denial is unstoppable unless confronted. And left unconfronted brings death.

I have learned all about denial and its companion, spiritual death. Death to one's spirit can happen abruptly through a tragedy, such as the sudden death of a loved one, cruel betrayal, an armed holdup or rape. These kinds of awful events we live through but our souls are terrorized by them. Or, spiritual death can happen subtly, such as through seductive lure into substance abuse or immoral acts. However it happens, spiritual death occurs when the human spirit suffers noxious injury and does not recover. Denial takes over, seeping the damage done deep into the innermost part of a person and leaving the injury unacknowledged. And when the injury is denied and unresolved, it gets buried but lives, randomly rearing its hideous head and exacting tolls—in our perspective, choices, behaviors and relationships.

Each time we deny the trauma that causes spiritual death, our spirit dies a little bit more until ultimately it perishes altogether. Spiritually dead, we either become void of human emotion sacrificing feelings to robotic reactions, or, we become bitter and destructive to ourselves and others. In my case, each deadly blow to my spirit cut away a piece of my soul without my awareness yet with my inattentive consent. So, I anguished. Some people end their anguish in suicide. Some become addicted to destructive people, places or things. In the case of my dysfunctional marriage, I chose distracted addiction to a destructive person and situation until forced from it.

I lived in emotional pain, converse to what I instinctively knew was right and good. I allowed myself to agonize, as if the angst I felt was OK. As if I was supposed to welcome sadness, pain and fear while doing the thing that damaged me—the very thing that made me sickly acceptable to those inflicting and practicing the destructive damage. Denial was the cornerstone and perpetuator of my suffering.

Split

Fifth Spiritual Death

The two years trailing our separation hinged on the sick back-and-forth bargain I made with madness brought about by an extended and indolent farewell.

I have pondered, since my parents and grandparents married for life, why it is that four of my siblings and I divorced and the sixth came close. The answer, of course, is obvious. It comes down to this: the choices we make and those we avoid. Despite all I had been through, despite knowing separating from Scott and our looming divorce was justified and imminent, still I clung to our fading marriage, as if worth keeping. And I was ashamed. Ashamed of failure, as if the fault was entirely mine. What I had in reality without labeling it was addiction. Addiction to suffering from a sick gut-wrenching craving for the addict. Like in the cartoons, an angel sat on one shoulder and a devil perched on the other. The angel in me desired goodness, stability and love, and whispered it was not available with Scott. The devil—a bottomless abysmal hunger—told me what I desired could be fulfilled with him. But ultimately, with the end of my marriage came the end of all the hope, time and effort I had put into it, and the end of me as I had once known myself.

As I wrestled with the vexing turmoil swirling inside me, I still found the wherewithal to sort through a tough new single life. While living with my parents, I set about looking for employment and bought my first car, a new white 1979 Toyota Corolla hardtop sedan. It cost $3,000, the loan for which I secured with Daddy as cosigner. That little car was my first liberating acquisition, a 2-door, 1.8 liter, 4-speed's worth of independence. Yet, I cried incessantly. I cried in bed, in the shower, at supper. I cried while driving. I cried my way through most days and I cried myself to sleep most nights. But I kept moving forward, no matter how muddy and messy I was. The one saving grace was I was not alone on this trail of tears. Mama and Daddy were there, endlessly supportive and patient. They became my best friends in spite of myself. Fortunate for me although not so lucky for them, I often spent time with them at times when I was not easy to be with. I was a hardworking go-getter one minute and a traipsing tornado the next. No telling what went through my parents' minds or to what their worried conversations turned.

I drank and smoked. It seemed old cronies from high school began spilling back into my life and most of them were no better for me than my soon-to-be ex. I was caught in a crossfire of troubled emotions that came out of me in raging bursts, which I torpedoed onto people I loved and sometimes coworkers. I had a nasty mouth at times, as profane as I was angry. And I was angry because I was deeply hurt and scared and had no idea what to do with the confounding snarl of feelings that entangled me. Grief-stricken, I drowned any surviving self-esteem by swimming in self-pity and lament, and worst of all, plunged myself into a steady torrent of drunkenness and promiscuity. When not actively engaged in emotional self-desolation, I took small steps to forge a new life. I was committed to standing on my own as a single woman and seemingly as committed to destroying myself.

I did seek help, however. There lived a priest at the St. Benedict rectory. I went to see him one day, to ask for guidance, to find a way to soothe my grief, to know more of what God might have in mind for me as I muddled through mayhem. He welcomed me into his office and offered me a seat. We talked. I wept. When our time had lapsed and I stood to leave, he hugged me close, pressed me into him and kissed me. At the time, I was so befuddled and unaware of what abuse looked like in all its foul disguises, that even though I felt strange at his advance I also did not shrink from it. In retrospect, this priest's vexing behavior was insulting and sinister; yet, I said nothing. I dried my tears. I smiled. He smiled. I left.

A short time later, a guy I barely knew arrived one night to pick me up for a date. Daddy answered the doorbell's ring, told him I'd be out in a minute, and left him standing on the porch. As I readied to go, Daddy shook and lowered his head, dismayed, and said, "I never thought I'd see the day when I'd answer the door to find a man here to see my daughter who was going through a divorce." My father knew, from my failed marriage and failed judgment then as now, confirmed by the looks of this caller, I was doomed for more of what had landed me here so far. Daddy was right. I no sooner dislodged from an injurious marriage before picking up another man and then another and another. These so-called men were Bad Boys in men's bodies. They were sordid, each of them, stuck in their own boyish sewers. And there was I, blindly attracted to who and what they were: Trouble.

Within a few weeks, I obtained a clerical job with a department store's district office and moved to an apartment nearby. My boss was a gentle family man. I told him one day I was going through a divorce and sometimes cried without notice. With compassion, he told me any time I needed to cry, I can excuse myself and that was fine. While in that job, I constantly was on the scout for others that paid more, eager to improve my circumstances. After six months, I quit to take a temporary job as a transcriptionist for an insurance company. I remained there four months while also working as a waitress part-time at a restaurant. I next landed full-time employment with a liquor distributor as a computer terminal operator. It was the highest-paying job I'd held so far and I kept it three years.

The culture there was a flawless fit. Nearing the end of each work day, the general manager's secretary, a tall colorful divorced lady who chain-smoked and wore a poufy black wig and full knee-length swing skirts, high heels and bright lipstick, served me the alcoholic drink of my choice as I keypunched. The company held monthly meetings for its salespeople who converged at our office from across the region. I indulged in the drinking, during meetings and afterward. Eventually, I was gifted with gallons of drink mixes and liquor to take home. I could not have been more satisfied with this arrangement as my alcohol habit escalated. Dually, I enrolled in basic courses at San Antonio College and scored As and Bs.

On the surface, I was carving out a single life professionally, financially and academically, despite my emotional shakiness and immorality, attested to by alcohol abuse, promiscuity and sick clinging to Scott. One night, I had an unpropitious attack of painful withdrawal—that inexorable agony that twisted my gut caused by division from the addict to whom I was addicted—when I begged Roger to drive me 110 miles to La Grange to see Scott. Roger sat in his car two hours on a cold winter's night while I entered the apartment that once was Scott's and mine and there consummated my compulsion. Maybe this had to happen. It was nothing more than a vile romp. And it left me with more than rug burns on my knees. It brought to my heart and brain for the first time since we'd parted the strong conviction it most certainly was over. And then Roger drove me home.

Scott had not let go yet either. I received a letter from him some months later. He still was a rambling construction worker living with a coworker in

Arkansas. He first wrote, "the pot here is good," but in the next lines declared he didn't do drugs anymore and had not written any bad checks. In closing, he signed it, "My love always." It occurred to me while I was making strides in rebuilding my life, he still was stuck in menial jobs and wrote in a teenager's scribble not a man's hand. This is the same individual who 18 months earlier told me he was not the man I wanted him to be and left me packing my belongings in a U-Haul.

Any observer of the wobbly swinging door that was us could readily see the noxious nature of our lingering split. We were finished. And we were not finished yet. Sometimes he visited San Antonio to spend time with friends and when he did I spent time with him. But it was I who filed for divorce in the fall of 1979. It was a simple procedure nailed down by a 1-page decree, given Scott and I did not share property or children. For a meager $100, a liquor salesman with whom I worked who drove an outdated Corvett and studied the law agreed to help obtain my divorce through the law firm with which he was associated. With him I engaged in an immoral act on a dark night while under the influence of alcohol, an act for which I later realized I had unconsciously traded a piece of my soul for the discounted legal fee. Once the divorce was executed, I discarded my former married last name and took up again my legal maiden name. At the impressionable age of 24, when many women were wives and mothers with growing families, I already had married and divorced.

By July of 1980, I had saved enough money for a road trip. Jo Ann and I drove together to visit Mary in Colorado and Debbie in Nevada, both married then to military men. We took turns at the wheel of my little Corolla through arid North Texas and New Mexico, the breathtaking mountains of Colorado, and the dusty deserts of Utah, Nevada and Arizona. It was like driving a lawnmower, chugging along with no air-conditioning, but that trip remains a fun memory in an otherwise disparaging season.

On the first leg of it, we drove nonstop to Colorado Springs, pausing briefly for food and rest. On the night we wound through rising mountains, we pulled over to take in a cloudless midnight sky and stars so bright we sensed we could touch them. On the trek from there to Nevada, we traversed the deserts of southern Utah. As afternoon came, we grew dangerously weary and stopped at a roadside rest area with covered concrete picnic tables. Jo Ann reposed on the tabletop with her pistol while I sprawled on the bench.

Miraculously, oblivious to our surroundings while asleep, we awoke in safety and refreshed.

It was another two years before I annulled my broken marriage. As a Catholic then, I knew annulment was mandatory if I wanted to wed again in the Catholic church in the future. So, in December 1981, I went before the appointed Ecclesiastical Tribunal of ominously holier-than-thou clergymen, all bumptiously adorned in sinuous black cassocks topped with white unadulterated clerical collars, and thereby and to them justified my split marriage, at which point they smugly granted me annulment and even put it in writing, thus wiping clean and righteously renewing my eternal soul for the immaculate sum of $200. And there was I, 26 years young, nearly 27, settling for a mere $300 total the dissolution of the past eight years as if they never were.

Bad Behavior and the Unpriestly Priest

Sixth Spiritual Death

As the late '70s gave way to the early '80s, I still drank and often till drunk. Though my alcohol habit slacked, I would linger in this sorry state for nine years, from the age of 23 when I first separated from Scott till I turned 32. As shameless as was my double-standard, self-degrading ravages of living in an inebriated state countless nights and weekends was not nearly as deadly as the waste I dumped into my soul. And with it I carried, like a second skin, the soul-rotting ghosts of guilt and shame.

At times I was prone to blackouts. Some call it alcohol-induced temporary amnesia. I walked, talked and laughed but did not know the next morning what had taken place the night before. I remember twice, once on a public street in New Orleans and once on the dancefloor at a club near home, I fell down, stood back up, and kept walking or dancing as if nothing had happened. When drinking like that, it was easy to engage in promiscuous behavior that by the next day was forgotten, except for sketchy recollections of it. As with my mental blackout, so were bits of my soul, blackened. I do recall a dirty, roach-ridden, thinly carpeted floor in someone's nasty apartment, and sleeping with a man in a motel room where his buddy slept with another in the bed next to ours.

However they began, my nights out nearly always ended the same. I wanted to meet someone. To have fun. To be liked. To be treated with kind regard. Home alone was not where I found it. I went out with friends or accepted a date, typically with a man I met someplace before, knew from my past, or was introduced to by a friend but did not know well or at all. Or I went to a bar alone and drank myself into oblivion. And wound up in bed.

On such a night, long past midnight, a man accompanied me to my one-room flat where the predictable happened. When our deed was done, I lay on my side with my back to him, motionless, under the sheets and naked, curled snug into myself like an embryo and braced on one edge of the capacious king-size brass bed that had been my husband's and mine. A different man was there now, by my invitation and submission, naked, too. Glass-eyed, the both of us, from drinking straight whiskey and swallowing pills without names. Quiet tears spilled onto my pillow. I sensed his smirking; I was not what he had expected. All I had wanted was affection. Without a word, he dressed and left. And I knew I would not see him a second time. So I anguished there, alone, with only my scalding shame.

Looking back at this murky time, I realize I could have been hurt in a terrible way and not recall it. Perhaps I was. But for the grace of God go I.

I was a different person by day when sober. I kept at it, working hard on an undefined career and academics I labeled loosely "communication." The drinking and sexing were fill-ins for whatever else I chased after in the name of fulfillment, or perhaps, rescue. In November of 1981, I resigned after three years with the liquor distributor to return to federal civilian service, accepting a ground-floor administrative job with advancement potential. Early the next year, Daddy retired and I continued in federal employment and would, until 1988, making the job and employer the first in my life to which I was loyal for more than a few scant months or years' stretch. I excelled in academics and work. I worked steadily at my post, advancing incrementally while learning I was smart and capable. And I discovered my sharp fascination with the written word and its persuasive power.

I made new friends along the way. Friends who exemplified the same prudence and scruples my parents and other adults in my clan likewise lived by. My new friends were professional, educated and prosperous. They showed me I could do as they had done, that I could attain what I wanted with hard work and due diligence. Most had families. I wanted what they had. I had no clue how to get it.

In same measure, in efforts to improve my living conditions, I moved out of my little flat and into an efficiency on the far north side of San Antonio. While my work life stabilized and my education continued, my personal life was far from stable. I vacated the tiny efficiency at the end of its lease when a girlfriend from high school, also single, invited me to share a downstairs two-bedroom apartment. I'll confess here that I moved nearly every time my existing lease came up for renewal, at least a dozen times in 10 years. While living with the high school chum, we frequented Burgandy Woods, a discotheque well-known for happy hours and fun times. One evening, dressed to the nines in skirts, heels and nylons, we danced and drank the night away and thereby became acquainted with two like-minded men we invited home at closing time.

At discovering our place was near the pool, they suggested we skinny dip. We all lost no time in stripping ourselves, grabbing bath towels and springing out the door toward the waiting water, hooting and hollering along our run. The moonlit sky was clear and the night otherwise quiet at the very late hour, with the silence broken only by us and then by residents who soon appeared in the surrounding apartment windows and balconies. Obviously rocked awake by the drunk naked rascals in the swimming pool, they yelled down to shut up and go home. We climbed out and ran for home. I cannot recall what happened next, but I believe with fair certainty unabashed sex ensued. We never saw those men again, or at least, we did not know them if we did and I could not tell you their names. But make note of this for future reference: No one left us money.

I am ashamed to admit it, but there were times when I drank too much and drove. And there were countless reckless instances when I was sober and drove dangerously fast. I always was in a hurry, unflinching and unthinking. On the highway, if traffic slowed too much to my liking, I drove around it on the emergency shoulder. I sped everywhere, with my car windows down and radio blaring full-blast. I was the most important person on the road. I deserved to be noticed, to be first, to be ahead of the rest. One night, I heard Mary was paying Mama and Daddy a visit from Germany. Sober, I raced from my apartment on the north side to my parents' home on the southeast side, taking a curvy exit lane too fast. Afraid I could not navigate the curve at high speed, I hit the brakes hard, throwing my car into a spin like a top and then bounced to a stop, the car rocking from side to side.

After exiting the highway, I drove off the road into the grass. As I sat in my buckled-in seat and calmed myself, I thought, I could have rolled over, been killed, hit another car and hurt or killed other people. I admonished myself, thanked my lucky stars and drove on, not breathing a word of it to anyone. I wish I could say my reckless driving stopped after that frightening night, but it did not.

My friendship with my roommate fizzled and I next moved in with a woman I did not know to share a two-bedroom apartment. I soon knew this roommate was in fact and in practice a hooker. One night, after returning home alone from a neighborhood saloon, I arrived to find her there with a tall, hefty man in a cowboy hat, boots and Wranglers. Given it was the middle of the workweek, I said good night and went to bed. The next morning, as I headed to the kitchen for coffee, I saw the pair already was up. As she stood by the dining table in pajamas, with her dyed blonde shoulder-length hair in a crumpled frizzle and racoon eyes and him dressed to leave, he pulled a wallet from his jeans pocket, handed her cash and left. It was soon after this eye-popping revelation I relocated yet again.

As I reflect now on the roommate's Johns and my payless promiscuity, I realize the two are not that different. Both are immoral. Both kill the spirit. With or without the barter for dollars.

This time, I leased a first-floor one-bedroom apartment near the South Texas Medical Center, which I switched six months later for an upstairs flat at the complex next door. By this time in 1985 I was 30. I was employed in civil service earning a satisfying salary with excellent insurance benefits and a growing pension. I had bought a new car, a sporty gunmetal blue, two-door Chrysler Laser with automatic transmission and bucket seats. But all that was not enough. Life felt slow and I felt restless. Despite advances in my job and commendations for my work, a rising disquiet and boredom in what I considered mundane repetitiveness in my workday convinced me there was more and I must find it. I stayed put but took a part-time job as a front desk clerk with a small guesthouse in the medical center near home. It catered to families of patients in area hospitals, university students and medical professionals, and offered a fresh change of pace and extra cash.

To counterbalance my restlessness, I joined a gym and began working out five days a week. I bought a 10-speed bicycle and rode it often. I took up jogging, weight training and high-impact aerobics, once completing a three-hour aerobathon for charity in which I garnered first place for the most donations. I made new friends and let go of some old ones. But I still drank, just not as much or often. Despite my drinking escapades, I lived an otherwise disciplined regimen that made me feel productive and accomplished. Weekends were an especially disciplined time. Whenever my part-time job did not require it on Saturday mornings, I took a long walk, run or ride on my bicycle, followed by a spic-and-span cleaning of my apartment. After showering, I shopped for groceries at a health food store and once home again sat down to a hearty lunch. I discovered the craft of macrame and from a tutorial in a book crafted a large decorative owl made of jute and colored wooden beads, which I hung proudly in my living room. But come sundown, I had a drink before heading out, sometimes alone, sometimes with friends, to a dance club to party and close it down.

Reverent Sundays spent at church and Grandma's had taken their place in the past. I still attended Mass some Sundays but was inconsistent with the practice. I stopped the ritual of Confession. I did not pray much. I did not read the Bible. Mama and Daddy had given me a large, ornate New American Bible and a brass bookmark with my name engraved on it for Christmas in 1976, but while I glanced in its direction, the holy book sat unopened most of the time.

It is odd to think of myself as two unalike people in one body but I was, based on the way I lived. There was the me who was the woman I was born to be, the one who was responsible. And there was the facade of me who turned into something and someone altogether different while drunk. I was professional, athletic and studious. I was a woman headed somewhere. And I was a drunk, without realizing it or calling myself by that name. I lived with a desperate need to fill a deepening emptiness and loneliness that never left me alone except when I was busy doing something. I chased after men and once we were through, I kept chasing them until I was irreversibly crushed completely by their contempt.

I did not acknowledge it but I held a secret conviction I was not and never would be enough. I continued to work hard, play hard and fill up on alcohol and sex, all the while stubbornly believing it would get me the life and love I wanted. After a few drinks, I was brave, beautiful and desirable, and sex was love, and my soul died a bit more each time I buried my true self.

I became even more prone to emotional storms, which I exacted onto people. When my damaged insides were triggered by an unintending or innocent word or action, I lashed out with a mean mouth or a firm word or tears or all of that, cutting the person to shreds. These seemingly irascible reactions to people and situations started rearing their ugly heads soon after my separation and only worsened with time. They took on a life of their own. My family, friends and coworkers must have cared about me because they tolerated my aggressive outbursts often without imposing justifiable judgment.

A case in point of my out-of-bound behavior happened while living with Mama and Daddy early after my separation from Scott. Our family had gathered for an Easter barbecue. I could not stop being sad even in the midst of fun and family. I did not let them help me. I lashed out telling everyone they did not understand. Finally, I blurted out "F*** you!" to all of them, and stormed out and up the street. I felt justified, dead wrong, and intensely confused all at once. My head hurt as much as my heart.

My walk was blurred with tears the 3 blocks to St. Benedict. Reaching the rectory's back door, which was made of clear glass, I rang the doorbell. No one came. I rang a second time and then a third. Finally, the father appeared from a darkened hallway walking slowly toward me. This was the same priest with whom I'd sought comfort shortly after leaving Scott. Despite my throbbing sobs, he did not open the door but spoke through it, informing me matter-of-factly through the glass he could not speak with me right then because he had a dinner appointment. And then with no sign of compassion on his blank face or another word, he turned and walked away. I stood there with my angst as I watched the back of his black cassock until it disappeared down the dark hallway and I could see it no more.

Crushed by his frigid indifference, I was doubly disparaged that a priest, this particular priest, turned his back on me in obvious light of my torment, considering I had grown up in that parish and he knew my family. He knew my parents were founding members and financial donors to the church and school. And he knew my marriage had ended. The perplexing pain of all that was unbearable. I also believed my family did not understand what I was going through because none of them yet had been through it. Now, even this so-called holy man turned away, offering me only his backside. It was as hurtful as it was baffling.

I sat outside on the curb a while. In disbelief. And then I stood, walked across the parking lot and turned east on Lord Road. I kept walking till I came to a park at the end of the street. I wandered across the grass to a picnic table, sat on top of it, as close to heaven as I could get, and raised my eyes and tears and cracked voice to God. I cried out loud in deserted desperation to Him, "Where are You in all this? Why are You not helping me? Please, please, PLEASE help me!" My words were as anguishing as the constrictions in my stomach. I sat there on that picnic table a long, long time, until the weeping and heaving subsided. It was precisely like when I was 8, that day I sat at the petite picnic table on our back porch next to the water cooler and cried about being blamed and feeling no one cared.

Why is it a woman, who was raised in a loving home with God-fearing, married, well-meaning parents, and plenty of other wholesome role models in her grandparents, aunts and uncles, likewise loving and caring, binds herself to situations, to calloused individuals, to people void of moral character, only to get beaten up emotionally and mentally and sometimes physically, over and over, again and again and yet, go back for more? I didn't know it yet, but the reason I went back for more, the reason for my dysfunction, was me. The trouble was not with everyone else. I was the problem.

I did not intend to be the problem. I did not know I was. My soul was turbulent, disordered, unsettled. My spirit was dying. And I was emotionally slipping. Not just because of circumstances that led me there so far. But because this thing called harmony, peace, was not achievable for me. Not as long as I continued getting drunk and degrading myself. Not as long as, when sober, I filled myself up with things. Not as long as I did not look at the root of my misery. Anger often accompanies misery, you know. When I was drunk, I was amicable. But when I was sober, anger and pain gushed out of my mouth because I was miserable. And I was afraid. Afraid no one would love me. Afraid I would be alone. Always. I was 30 already and that seemed old to me, a woman who wanted children. When not preoccupied with work, working out or succumbing to the beguiling wiles of a man, when idle, I could not tolerate occupying still space with nothing in it but me.

My personal life was a monumental mess and I was detached from my innermost self, but my professional life was budding, and with it, a newfound confidence that either had been there all along undeveloped or it came about as I tried to rebuild. Either way, I was financially able to take a real vacation. In 1986, I put hard-earned savings into a well-deserved excursion. To Europe I would go, to visit Mary, who lived then in a town not far from London. It would be a grand adventure! I secured my passport and set plans astir to fly away for three weeks in June.

O'er the Sea

After 14 hours of trans-Atlantic travel counting flight time and airfield connections, I landed at London Heathrow International Airport, unnerved at first by the big-gun-carrying airport police but too thrilled to be concerned. Immediately connecting with Mary and her husband and collecting my luggage, we drove 80 miles to the air base where they were stationed, and there I showered and changed. Then, we set off on a remarkable road trip.

We drove through lush, wooded Camelot countryside and toured medieval castles. At Belvoir Castle, we attended a renaissance festival, watched a jousting game and delighted at period-costumed musicians. Never before had I seen 18th century Baroque art and architecture, sculptures, ceiling murals and ornamental artifacts that adorned the magnificent Blenheim Palace near Woodstock. The Gardens of Blenheim residing within the estate's 2,100 acres were elaborately landscaped with stone walls, graceful water fountains, manicured hedges and walkways and an abundance of flourishing flowers, and on the periphery, wooded forests. Everywhere I looked was picturesque, romantic and inspiring.

The next day we explored London in a frenzy, riding the sparkling underground Tube and top tiers of red double-decker buses. I stepped inside an iconic red telephone booth, savored fish and chips sprinkled with vinegar and wrapped in newspaper, and sipped cream tea served with freshly baked crumpets and jam. At Buckingham Palace, I posed with a crisply uniformed British Bobbie in front of the palace's vibrant rose garden, and beyond it, the eye-catching Queen Victoria Memorial. I beheld Big Ben and the Houses of Parliament, and toured the solemn sepultures and effigies of British monarchs and their regal relatives who since the 11th century have rested within Westminster Abbey. From a shaded sidewalk in Trafalgar Square, I watched a ceremonial march of English constables welcoming the German Chancellor.

I was photographed at the London Bridge and Tower of London flanked by shutter-friendly Beefeaters. These ceremonial guards of the fortress were royally clad in elegant 18th century red and deep purple uniforms of tunic, knee-breeches, stockings and flat hats to match. Inside the towers I saw surprising vestiges of children's armor and other relics, was awestruck by the golden winged Lion of St. Mark, and gasped at exhibitions in the Guiness Book of

World Records Museum. Each day opened a mollifying new world to every aspect of me: pleasing delights to my eyes, a consoling solace to my heart, a rosy hope to my mind, and a long-overdue buoyancy to my spirit. It seemed impossible anything else beyond what I already had experienced could occur. But more was due.

The next day, we boarded a ferry that sailed from the famed White Cliffs of Dover coastline bound for Belgium. Disembarking, we drove to Namur to tour the Citadel, an historic fortress situated atop a stone mountain that towers above the Meuse River Valley. The air that day at the fortress's pinnacle was as chilly as the impression emitted by cold black cannons and gray stone walls, and combined with the stunning panorama of the valley below created a stimulating setting. We descended into the Citadel's dungeon and there saw an original guillotine and rock prison cells that delivered shivers as I imagined how it must have been for a convicted victim of primitive torture.

Our first night's lodging was a quaint inn carved from stone with arched doorways. The second night we slept in a Swiss-style chalet in the hills. From Belgium we drove through scenic Luxembourg to Orenhofen, Germany, our key destination. There lived Frau Heinz, my sister's friend. Arriving at her home and adjoining pub, the Gasthaus Grumbach, we found Frau Heinz and her enormous German Shepherd, Heikel, waiting in the open door of the pub. We drank Bitburger Pils and apple schnapps in the cheery Gasthaus with Frau Heinz, her son Walter, his family and neighborhood patrons who were intrigued with Americans and my Texas drawl.

For a very long time, except for my parents' abiding love, I had not experienced the immediate or genuine kindness as with Frau Heinz and her family. She relinquished her bedroom to me as her guest. I was astounded at the loving gesture of this woman in her 60s, to give up the comfort of her bed to me. Her bedroom was at the end of a tall narrow stairwell aside a modest bathroom. It was sparsely furnished with only a sturdy wooden-framed twin-size bed topped by a feather mattress and an adequate wardrobe. At night, as we slept, Heikel kept watch, his muffled footsteps audible as he paced the stairwell. Mornings we awoke to strong coffee and cream, and a table amply set with freshly baked German Bauernbrot bread deliciously crusty on the outside and soft on the inside, fresh butter, cheese and homemade jams. By the time we had eaten and tidied the kitchen, Frau Heinz already was preparing for the noonday meal, marinating a large pork loin. I was a queen attended by servants. I will remember her thoughtfulness always.

Orenhofen is a tiny town in south central Germany with everything within walking distance. The weather was chilly when I strolled one day to the local grocer. I browsed the small shop to find it quaintly more enjoyable and interesting than the large overstocked grocery store chains of America. I returned to the Gasthaus to find Frau Heinz out back on her knees in her garden, harvesting fresh vegetables for the afternoon meal.

One morning, we all piled into two cars for a most memorable excursion. Trier, the oldest city in Germany, was our first stop 18 miles south of Orenhofen. I saw the Black Tower of Trier, or Porta Nigra, constructed as a city gate and named in the Middle Ages for its darkly hued sandstone. I beheld medieval and Baroque architecture, and the oldest church in Germany, the grand Trier Cathedral, or Trier Dom, which contains some of the world's most venerated artifacts of Jesus Christ, including shackles used on Him and a stake removed from His cross. Locked gates made of gold enshrine and protect what is believed to be Christ's tunic, or Holy Robe. I saw the Trier Coliseum and Amphitheatre, alive with imaginings of helmeted Roman gladiators in vicious contests with each other, wild beasts and ill-fated prisoners.

From Trier we headed to Bernkastel some 30 miles north along the Mosel River, a region famous for its wine by the same name. Bernkastel is neatly posed at the water's edge from where lush knolls slope gracefully above and around it. After a sightseeing stroll through town, the Heinz's escorted our troupe to Winemaster Grumbach's wine cellar, where he tapped kegs of aging Reisling and Mosel for our tasting. We then hiked up into his vineyard where we met robust German women of varying ages dressed in soiled cotton dresses and ankle high boots concluding their day in the fields sipping wine.

It seemed no time at all before we found ourselves yet again at the Belgium coastline boarding a ferry that returned us to the White Cliffs. Yet, Mary had more in mind before my flight home. Once returned to England, the next day we set out for Warwick Castle, which sits atop a cliff above the River Avon. Touted the most famous of all castles in England, the imposing 3-story motte-and-bailey stronghold was constructed in the 10th century to defend against invaders. The castle was built on a high mound called a motte, surrounded by a bailey, or enclosed yard. We took an exhilarating walk to the rook's highest point and looked out over the tree-topped countryside from 60 feet up. We meandered through the castle to see paintings, silver period tableware, armor and wax figures posed in everyday activities before descending into the dungeon, where from the ceiling hung body shackles in which people historically were perched and left to die.

From there, we segued to Bourton-on-the-Water located within the Cotswolds, named for its golden Cotswold stone, and designated to my good fortune an "Area of Outstanding Natural Beauty." It was a calming spot, where village streets were bejeweled by verdant landscapes fed by the River Windrush that winds through the settlement. In quiet admiration, I strolled along the riverwalk canopied with willows, and across enchanting arched stone bridges, gazing about at neat rows of longstanding stone houses and inviting cafes situated dreamily aside the river's edge. The tiny hamlet offered a gentle divergence from castles and dungeons. From there, we drove past Avebury toward Marlborough and along the way discovered the Cotswold Woolen Weavers in the town of Filkins. This generations-old weaving mill sits inside an 18th century barn, and outside, sheep meander about. Not only did we watch the looms in action, we browsed the mill shop where an impressive array of colorful throws, garments, hats and rugs made from the wool were sold. I treated myself to a scarf, and for Daddy, a beret.

Our final stop of the day was especially captivating. After yet another pleasing drive through gorgeous green countryside, we came to Marlborough, where there we saw Merlin the Magician's grave atop a tree-covered hill. And from there, on we went to the prehistoric circle of Stonehenge that stands curiously in the middle of an otherwise sparse Salisbury Plain. Though its primitive creators did not document its origin, Stonehenge is said to be a ritual site dating back to 2,800 B.C. Standing before it felt inexplicably unearthly, in proximity to its mammoth trilithons that stand like giants, weigh dozens of tons, and are aligned with seasonal risings and settings of the sun.

All too soon, my remarkable adventure came to a close. But I was changed because of it. Before this trip to Europe, never before had I been kissed by the wonder that held my wide-eyed attention at every turn. I had not realized when I left Texas three weeks prior that this intercontinental trek would be the penetrating balm so craved by my troubled spirit that whispered to me now everything was going to be OK. That I was going to be OK.

Fresh Starts

Five months after returning from Europe revived and hopeful, I looked death in the face. It lurked around Roger's hospital bed like a dim shadow for days. Then one afternoon, the shadow was gone. And so was my brother. I must tell his story because it intertwines with mine and once I begin I will not stop until I tell it all. Not telling it would be like severing a limb; I would not be whole and neither would be my story. I loved Roger Paul. He was my friend and a man I admired almost as much as my father. He was with me in the lowest of times when no one else was and I hope he felt the same of me.

The Texas summer of 1958 delivered with its mid-August heat a newborn baby to the Guckians. Arriving on the 18th day, the child was the second son of six offspring and youngest. His name was Roger Paul. He had electric blue eyes, thick sandy-blonde hair and a fetching smile sure to charm. If the adage was true about the size of a baby's feet indicating future height, then Roger was sure to grow tall. Even as a child, he seemed an old soul who embodied the persona of a wiser individual than his years suggested. As a youth, he often visited the elder widows in our neighborhood to while away the hours chatting. He was, however and after all, a little boy, prone to mischief. After Lynn left for the Navy when Roger was 6, my little brother was left to grow up with four older sisters who alternately bullied, babied or spoiled him. Sometimes he was obliging. Sometimes not.

He sometimes displayed a rough temper during squabbles with us girls, inherent in a big family. One time, he pitched a fork at Debbie, stabbing her in the leg, and on another day hurled a croquet mallet from where he stood in the backyard at Mary who was inside the house, breaking the window but missing her. Roger had a tender side, too. He fancied the guitar, and taking lessons while a boy discovered he was a natural with it. Everyone liked him. By the age of 10, his friendly charm and wit had become endearing trademarks.

Roger's best friends were two brothers, Randy and Ricky, who one night, when Roger was 12, dared him to climb the lamp pole at the corner of Holmgreen Road and W.W. White and crow like a rooster. He did, of course, and from then on claimed the moniker Rooster.

By the time he graduated high school, Roger reached a slim 6 foot 2 inches. He leased an apartment, bought his first car, a 1962 Dodge, and worked as a welder, aiming to buy his own rig one day and was saving money for it. Compared to his high school cronies, Roger already had succeeded in building a productive life with a bright future. He was proficient with the guitar and played the acoustic on occasion but preferred his electric. He played "Stormy Monday" for me one time. Seated on the edge of his bed, as he lightly touched the strings and strummed the old blues tune, his head hung low and draped over the guitar, he whispered the lyrics, "Well, they call it stormy Monday… but Tuesday's just as bad…" I sat in pleasing silence, watching his face flinch in reflex to the bluesy notes he played.

By the time he entered his 20s, Roger was mischievous to a fault when carousing with his pals but had become a gentleman, sensitive and gentle with Mama and Daddy and our grandparents. I saw in him my father. One night after midnight, he appeared at my apartment carrying a single red rose. He gave it to me and told me a girl had stood him up. So we walked to the pool and sat under the stars and talked of life, love and loneliness.

Life changed dramatically in early 1978 when Roger met the sister of a fellow welder. Her name was Cathy. Soon thereafter Roger announced his impending fatherhood and consummated marriage to her. I cried at the news because she was a cohort of my ex-husband. Yet, Roger was committed to caring for her and the unborn child. Jason Paul Guckian was born in October that year and baptized at St. Benedict, as was his father before him.

But the dream Roger held for his fledgling family unraveled quickly, dashed by a turbulent truth. He found himself living with a stranger previously hidden within the facade of the woman he had married, a woman who now unveiled her unfaithfulness as a wife, unfitness as a mother and dependency on drugs. When the baby was 2, after dropping Roger at work, she took his car and their son and fled. Cloaked in lies, the marriage disintegrated into divorce and with it went Jason, awarded by the court to his mother. I watched helplessly as Roger's sanity splintered and hinged between despondency and incomprehension at the thought of losing touch with the son he loved and lived for. His regular visits with Jason were short and sometimes spent with me. When together, they sparkled.

Living apart from Jason most of the time, Roger became uncharacteristically lost in the foreign and frightful world in which he now lived. He succumbed to depressing anxiety and sought refuge in dangerous compulsions. As he descended, his troubles went unresolved and his temper roared. There were times when his wit turned more cutting than funny and many an apology he made because of it. In a short span of time, he lost everything. My parents, Jo Ann and I each took a turn taking him in but our help was not the kind he needed and his stays did not last. One night, I asked him to leave after a crowd of shifty characters he called friends overtook my home. The next day, Roger spit-shined my apartment, repaired a hole in the wall into which he had plunged his fist and left me a tender note. On one side of the paper, Roger penned "Betty Lou," and on the other side he wrote: "Lou, I fixed the wall and cleaned up the place. Thanks a lot for all you've done in the past three months. This was your home and I hope I didn't make it too unpleasant for you. If there is anything I can do for you just let me know and I'll try my best to help. Love you, Lou. Rog."

Roger never intended to upset anyone. He suffered unceasing heartache and anguish, and did not know how to relieve his misery or regain himself or the life he had begun to build. But inside him was a spark of who he once was and that was enough to carry him to a recruiter one day when he enlisted in the U.S. Navy. He viewed military service as a way to recover himself and provide medical care for his son and allotments for child-support payments. Seaman Roger P. Guckian was assigned to a U.S. naval base in Japan where there he befriended a band of fun-loving seamen, The Boys. They all had monikers; of course, his was Rooster.

After his tour of duty, a healthier Roger returned home to Texas to rebuild his life. Jason was 4 by then, living with his aunt and uncle, and looked even more like his daddy. Sometimes, father and son spent a night or a weekend with me or Mama and Daddy. They played on the living room rug like a lion and cub and read books together. They slept peacefully in the security of each other's company and awoke in a playful frame of mind. I watched them some mornings share cereal at breakfast, with mops of uncombed hair and sleep in their eyes, and the warmth of their affection emanating love like sunshine through a window.

On a Sunday night in early October of 1983, Roger and I left the company of our parents after a dinner at St. Benedict for a local country and western dance club. We stood next to the dancefloor, watching the crowd swing and scoot. Roger's lean chiseled face enhanced his handsome, mustached smile, an attractive accompaniment to his blue eyes. He was a tall muscular frame of a man, typically standing heads above most people, with thick brown wavy hair, the sort a woman likes to run her fingers through. He was comfortably dressed in his favorite attire: blue jeans and boots. The six young women surrounding him evidenced his charismatic, unassuming manner coupled with a cool, alluring confidence. But Roger's eyes were fixed on another female he saw standing across the room.

When the DJ played "Cotton-Eyed Joe," she walked toward him. She was Texas pretty, tall and shapely, with cropped hair that framed a freckled nose and cheeks, and round hazel eyes that held whispers of blue and brown. They had caught glimpses of each other a very long hour ago, but it was she who took the initiative. Roger held to a harmless mask and air of cocky coyness barely hiding the boyish insecurity that settled inside him.

Risking rejection in front of the other women and despite her thunderous heartbeats, which she was certain could be heard by everyone in the noisy, smoke-filled club, she asked, "Would you like to dance?" Roger's smile went wide at the question, his lip a bit crooked on one side as it tended to do when he felt especially clever or unguarded. He liked her looks and her soft sincere voice but privately struggled with a kindling swelling fear, the residue of a painful past. Roger looked at me and asked, "Whadaya think, Lou?" Before I could speak, he said, grinning, "Aw, hell, why not?" And with that, took her hand and escorted her onto the dancefloor, smiles fixed on both their faces.

She was an independent sort, having struck out on her own at an early age, changing her given name from Karen to Kelly as she went. His ear-to-ear smile captivated her. They danced and talked. He showed her a picture of Jason, proudly sharing his name, as he eased the photo from its sacred place inside his wallet. He spoke negligibly about his son, though; it hurt too much. Kelly secretly wished Roger would not do what other guys did: Ask for a ride home. She knew after that question the next would be as disappointing, the one about staying the night. But she also knew he had arrived with me and I had left already. When Roger walked Kelly to her car, he gave her an awkward brush of a good-night kiss on her cheek and asked for her telephone number. She happily complied and then drove away, remembering the neatly folded red bandana in his rear pocket, relieved he hadn't asked for a ride.

That night, Roger walked from the club several miles to Mama and Daddy's house, where he was staying while getting back on his feet. He thought of Kelly with every step. Mama and Daddy awoke when he arrived and Roger excitedly told them, "I met a girl!" He was floating on air. Mama readily saw Roger was happier than she had seen him in years. The next day, Roger called Kelly to set a date for lunch that Friday. After lunch, before dropping her at work, they set a second date for later that night. An hour later, Kelly received a small plant with a note, "Thank you, from Rog." That night, when he took her home, she kissed him, stepped inside, and Roger left. Roger told Mama and Daddy, again, "She is special."

At the time, Roger drove delivery trucks to El Paso for the San Antonio-based department store Joske's. He enjoyed time alone on the road, just him and his rosary. Over dinner one night, Roger asked Kelly to accompany him on a routine road trip and she agreed. On the return trip home, they passed through a tiny town called Valentine and light-heartedly spoke of marriage, saying they'd marry in Valentine next trip. And then it came. Roger fumbled through his first "I love you." The couple sat quietly, elated, for an eternal moment, reflecting on the weighty words sweetly spoken, their hearts beating in rhythm with the hum of the truck's huge engine as it roared down the highway. As each minute passed in awkward hush, their excitement grew. By the time they arrived home, they were engaged. To mark it, they had their left ears pierced, each wearing a rhinestone stud.

The wedding did not take place in Valentine, however. It happened over Kelly's lunch hour on Nov. 4, 1983, four weeks after their first hello. Roger bought a modest ring, and he and Kelly wed in a civil ceremony at the Bexar County Courthouse, vowing to love, cherish and take care of each other for the rest of time. They told no one, yet. Following the ceremony and snapshots outside, the newlyweds bid farewell in a sudden downpour as Roger delivered Kelly back to her workplace and he drove away to prepare for a drive to El Paso that night. While on the road, in the coming weeks and months, they both listened to an all-night radio station, KWKH in Shreveport, where the DJ became familiar with Roger and Kelly by playing their songs. Kelly told me she told Roger each time before he left on a trip, "Be careful. Be happy."

When we learned of the marriage, we learned Kelly, indeed, was special. Amid the undercurrent of uncertainty during their first months together, their life as a couple was like a free-flowing river, as emotions were shared, fears were exposed and eased, faith and trust were renewed, and insecurities were bathed in a confident and loyal light. The transition was gradual but obvious. Two independent people became one. Roger, as Kelly told, no longer awakened from fitful sleep with clenched fists but rested peacefully aside her with one hand snuggled beneath her.

He worked nights while she built a home-based business, so daytime hibernating became a pleasing pastime. They ceremoniously closed blinds, disconnected the telephone and talked the day away, catching up on two lives that had gone unshared. They were tardy one time for Christmas dinner at Mama and Daddy's by six hours, which they attributed to their hibernation habit. During these seclusions, Roger spoke devotedly of family, how Daddy was his best friend, and how important it was for him to prove to us he was a changed person worthy of our love and respect. He spoke seriously and regularly of dying, never expecting to live past 25, given the hard life he had lived so young. He told Kelly on regular occasion with explicit instruction he wanted to be buried in his jeans and boots with no crying but a party. He told me, tongue in cheek, when he died he wanted to be propped up in his coffin looking at everyone with a grin on his face. And then he laughed, his unmistakable, unreserved, resonant, infectious laugh.

Roger wanted no one to shed tears for him. But he cried. He cried about our parents and grandparents, not wanting to live to see them die and insisting he would not attend their funerals. He cried about wanting to raise his son and teach him about the perils of drugs. He cried he had ever met Cathy, the destructive force that all but took his life, but he loved their son. He cried over arguments. And he would not speak of Mama's illness.

In the beginning, Roger struggled with old habits as problems resurfaced through his former friends' influence. But he realized it jeopardized his marriage and broke those ties. Roger and Kelly spent cherished time with Jason. They fished. Played tennis. Had water pistol fights. It was the stuff of memories in-the-making. Kelly talked warmly of them growing old, imagining their golden years akin to Henry Fonda and Kathryn Hepburn's characters in "On Golden Pond." Nearing their first anniversary, they bought a home on a street named Prairie Sun in a subdivision off Foster Road called Sunrise. It was a cozy, three-bedroom single-story with a room for Jason.

The first night in their new nest, they nestled by the fireplace. They told each other with delightful surprise they were "real people, with a house, a mortgage, neighbors, two dogs named Frisbie and Tiffany and a cat named Spike, and had moved into a new world together."

Roger brought flowers home to Kelly often. He appreciated the simplest things, like a new rake or aluminum measuring tape. All the kids on the block called him Uncle Roger. He spent time fishing with Daddy and in meaningful talks with Mama. Occasionally, he and Kelly invited them over for a fish fry, which he cooked in a home-made deep-fryer he welded.

One night, he and Kelly went dancing where there Roger saw a heavyset girl standing alone in the corner and he asked her to dance. No one put him up to it. He did it because he wanted to shine a little sunlight into her life. Roger was like Daddy in that way. Both father and son shared a certain humble confidence, a particular compassion for people. They did not fight to be right. They chose to be content, bearing the same gleam in their eyes and slight grin that said: I know better, but I'm going to let you have it your way. When Roger was low, he looked to lift someone else. When a situation was hard, he made jokes to ease it. When the last thing he wanted to do was laugh, he gave laughter to others. When he had lost it all, he gave his heart and humor. I often was a grateful recipient.

Increasingly, Roger was intrigued by the computer he and Kelly had received as a Christmas gift from her parents, and contemplated taking vocational courses and obtaining an office job. Their 1978 Pontiac Firebird Trans Am devoured cash with endless maintenance but a new car was on the horizon. This was happy news to Kelly. She had not mentioned it, but she had had premonitions over the past six months of the Trans Am being in a collision.

DWI: Living Through Roger's Dying

Seventh Spiritual Death

Roger yearned to raise Jason full-time, realizing with stinging truth this deeply held longing would take time to attain. For the first time in a long time, he thought of the future with hope. And I hoped with him.

On the afternoon of Friday, Dec. 19, 1986, I was at Roger and Kelly's where I washed my Chrysler Laser in their driveway. Afterward, Roger said coyly, "I know how to dry that car real fast, Lou; let me take it for a spin." I cannot explain it, why I replied as I did, but I told him, No. I have suffered enormous guilt for that No. My No would loom heavy in days to come. Also that day, I snapped a picture of him standing in his driveway. Unknown to us at the time, that photo would become one of the last likenesses of him.

Christmas Day was joyful for Roger, Kelly and Jason, who was 8. For the first time, they shared the holiday. They contemplated spending it at the beach, but Roger knew it would disappoint the Guckian clan if they didn't attend the traditional Christmas Day dinner. So they remained in San Antonio. That morning at 8 o'clock, Roger phoned in high spirits to wish me Merry Christmas. At our family's gathering, Kelly gave him an apron with "Rooster" printed on it. It was such fun watching Jason open his gifts. He especially liked the Rambo hand puppet his Aunt Mary had sent from England, and he and his daddy sat on the floor playing with it, giving the rest of us chances to capture precious moments on film. The photos later revealed a profound longing in Roger's eyes as he watched his son play.

In the early evening on Christmas Day, Roger drove Kelly and Jason home, declaring it a perfect day. Although he knew he had to drive Jason back to his ex-wife's soon, he would do so reluctantly, and think of the day he would have his son with him always. Leaving Kelly home to nap, daddy and son buckled into the Trans Am, kissed her bye, backed out of the driveway, and soon headed north on Foster Road toward Universal City, where Jason's mother lived. Cathy was adamant Roger return Jason to her by 6 o'clock sharp. It was 5:45 p.m. After they drove away, Kelly lingered outside chatting with a neighbor when soon they heard sirens nearby as they said good night. She went inside to have her nap before Roger returned.

The Trans Am had scarcely pulled onto Foster Road, one-half mile from Roger and Kelly's driveway. It was crawling along slowly out of the neighborhood and onto the roadway. Jason was playing with his Rambo puppet and chattering away. Roger was looking forward to at least having the leisurely drive with his son, to talk and laugh before dropping him off, again. Father and son simultaneously saw the titanic 1982 Oldsmobile Regency 4-door sedan bearing down on them fast. We later learned the Olds was speeding at 75 miles per hour, compared to Roger's Trans Am, which was inching along at the posted 35 mile-per-hour speed limit. Foster Road then was a narrow two-way stretch flanked by ditches that ran parallel to developing neighborhoods. There was no time to react and nowhere to go to avoid the onrushing car. In a flash, father and son had time only to dart looks into each other's eyes as Jason screamed, "Daddy, no!" and Roger outstretched his right arm across his son.

Eye witnesses at the scene called 911. They told us later what they saw. The Olds crashed head-on into the Trans Am, rocketing the two cars into the air 15 or 20 feet on impact. Both cars swirled madly in mid-air and then crashed hard to the ground, throwing the Trans Am's two doors wide open on their hinges. The entire front of the Trans Am was crushed, its former long silver hood pressed into the front seat. Rushing to see if they could help, they saw both Roger and Jason were still wearing their seatbelts.

Sparks were popping in both cars, which made them afraid a fire might erupt. Roger's head had impacted the steering wheel with such force the wheel was bent over the dashboard. He could not get out or be moved. They could not help him. He was pinned in on all sides. His face from the nose up was utterly shattered; it was obvious he was bleeding into his throat and likely into his lungs. They heard gurgling, as Roger threw his head back in effort to breathe; he was kicking his legs, raising his arms over his head, as if to clench and scream, but he could not.

Roger did not lose consciousness until Jason was removed from the wreckage. Bystanders unbuckled the boy's seatbelt and carefully lifted and carried him onto the ground. We later learned Jason had suffered broken bones, severe lacerations to his face, a concussion, shock and hysteria. But he was able to give witnesses his mother's name and phone number. He kept calling for "Daddy." A local sheriff soon topped the hill and ambulances arrived in minutes. These were the sirens Kelly heard shortly after Roger and Jason had left home. One ambulance hurried Jason to the downtown Baptist Hospital where a neurosurgeon, who later became a family name, attended to his injuries, while other emergency workers at the scene tried to stop the bleeding in Roger's face. It took at least 30 minutes to extract Roger from the twisted wreckage using the Jaws of Life, when then he was airlifted to the Brooke Army Medical Center (BAMC) Trauma Unit at Fort Sam Houston. Witnesses said when they opened the door to the Olds it reeked of alcohol and beer was everywhere. The driver was dead but his passenger, a young man, survived. Police verified the Mexican national in his mid-20s who drove the Olds was unlicensed and driving while intoxicated (DWI).

Kelly sleepily awakened to answer the ringing phone. It was me calling to reminisce about the perfect Christmas Day it had been, especially for Roger and Jason. She realized after looking at the clock it had been more than two hours since Roger had left. It was nearly 8:30 p.m. He should have been home long ago. Rising panic swelled inside her, and as she told me of it, our conversation was cut short by another call. It was Mama and Daddy. They said Jason's mom, Cathy, had called to see how Roger and Jason were doing. None of us knew till then what had occurred.

We all rushed to BAMC but could not see Roger until he was out of surgery. My mother seemed a rock. My father, terribly scared. Kelly's parents, Gil and Joyce, hurried from Georgia. Daddy phoned Debbie in South Dakota. The Navy at Daddy's request contacted Lynn who was active duty. My parents delayed notifying Mary in England who was pregnant till they knew Roger's prognosis.

After four surgeons jointly performed the epic operation, we were granted permission early the following dawn to see Roger, two-by-two and only for a minute. Before we did, they primed us: He could die at any time, it was a miracle he was alive at all, his brain was severely bruised and swelling, he had lost a great deal of blood, and his face held more than 100 stitches. Heavily sedated with massive doses of morphine plus paralyzing drugs to keep him immobile, Roger was not in a coma. Beneath a heavy medicinal veil, he was aware of what was happening to him. Kelly and Daddy were first to push past the double-doors to the Intensive Care Unit (ICU). Next went Mama and Jo Ann. All four came out in shock and speechless. Then, it was my turn. When Daddy had exited the ICU, his eyes squared with mine and he spoke, "Are you sure you want to see him? He does not look like your brother, Betty Lou." And then his voice broke and he could not say more.

Jo Ann took my hand and held it tight as we walked together ever so slowly. Upon entering the ICU, I immediately saw Roger ahead of us and crumpled as my knees collapsed. His appearance was… terrible and gruesome. It was the kind of thing your eyes behold that makes you want to scream out loud but you cannot. No sound comes out at all. All there is, is utter horror. We gathered ourselves and resumed our measured clasped pace toward him. Daddy was right. There were no words or imaginings that ever could have prepared me for the nightmare taking hold of my senses and my brother. After my mind screamed in silence No! No! No! it emptied, failed me, as my knees had done. Unrelenting tremors shook my body, like a chill deep inside, and stayed for days.

Roger lay on a raised bed in nearly a seated position. His head was the size of an inflated beachball and bandaged; eyes were closed, nose and mouth were enlarged from swelling and stretched cruelly across an outspread face that once was handsome and engaging. His arms and hands, swollen also, rested at his sides. A soft tear fell from a closed eye and rested on his cheek. As I stood next to the bed at his left, I cupped his hand into mine to reassure and comfort him, but suddenly he lurched his head forward and tried to wave his arms about, as if trying to get up and go. Immediately the nurses gently returned him to his original position. I was afraid I had hurt him with the caress of his hand but the nurses reassured me his response was not to pain but a natural impulse. I believe Roger wanted to break out of that condition, to get free of that bed, that hospital, and all the tubes in him, and go home. He was not supposed to be there. He was supposed to be with Kelly. This could not be real. But it was real.

Roger surely must have been terribly scared. And deeply angry. All I wanted to do was hold him and tell him everything was going to be alright. We all had to be careful, though, not to stimulate him much or his brain pressure would rise. The nurses said when Kelly walked into ICU, Roger knew the sound of her footsteps, which caused his brain pressure to climb, but when she touched him, it lowered again. One time, I held his hand and told him I loved him, that he was going to be OK and Jason was OK. At Jason's name, he threw my hand aside, kicked and flung his arms about, and lunged his head from side to side. A nurse hurried with morphine and he relaxed. I think he still was trying to get out of that car and to Jason.

That day, Dec. 26, at 10 a.m., doctors informed us the next seven days were the most critical, and the longer he lived, the better his chances. I still do not know from where the wherewithal came that allowed me to drive to the airport for Lynn. We all camped out in a waiting room reserved for our family, each day hearing doctors tell us of progress, of some glimmer of hope.

Roger had undergone a tracheotomy at the scene of the wreck and was on a respirator so the oxygen to his brain could be controlled thereby controlling swelling of his brain. He received computerized axial tomography (CAT) scans constantly. After the first operation, there was another ahead. One doctor told us they had to remove a blood clot accounting for a few teaspoon-size portions of bruised brain tissue from the left side of his brain that controlled Roger's ability to speak and move, and if he survived, then he would have to relearn everything, like an infant. It was the last thing they wanted to do because it would be exceptionally hard on Roger but they had no choice, they said. OK, we agreed, we all were going to help him through that. After the surgery, doctors reported Roger now had an 80-percent chance of survival with the chances increasing because removing the clot decreased pressure on his brain and indicated bruising was not as damaging as originally suspected.

My brother was medically paralyzed but responsive. He clenched his fist or squeezed a hand or cried a tear. When Kelly was with him, his head turned toward her, and once, his left eye opened to see her. Because his brain was awfully bruised on the left side, his right side was immovable and his right eye was damaged. Before he underwent the second brain surgery, Daddy had been with him. He held Roger's hand and told him, "Son, this is your Daddy. You'll have to get well so we can try our new fishing rods." Tears rolled down Roger's left cheek at his words. He heard. He knew. He shed tears with Daddy. But he could not speak and could barely open his one uninjured eye.

Within a few days, his head and face returned to normal and the swelling in his brain stabilized. But all was not normal. Normal brain pressure is measured at a range of 10 to 14, but Roger's was "phenomenal" when he first arrived at BAMC and now it varied between 16 and 40. We believed this good news signaling recovery. Paralyzing and pain medicines steadied his brain pressure.

In those critical first days, I rallied my workmates requesting donations of blood for Roger. Cards and letters began to flood in to my family's mailboxes telling us of concerns and prayers for Roger and us. Roger's lifelong friend, Randy, came to the hospital every day. He was there for us if we needed anything, a soda or coffee, quarters for the phone. The eye witnesses who had told us about the wreck came to see Roger and commented how good he looked, compared to then. Continually, friends or extended family streamed in and out to be with us in the waiting room. They brought us food and drinks, blankets and pillows. They prayed with us. There were Christians, Catholics, Jews, Muslims, Pentecostals, Lutherans and Baptists. We said rosaries together. Priests and ministers prayed over Roger. We were overcome by kindness.

Nearing the anticipated seventh critical day, Roger was diagnosed with peritonitis, the swelling of tissue that lines the abdomen and stomach that is caused by infection. Apparently, his bowels had backed up, his intestine had ruptured, he had ulcers eating through his stomach lining, and poison from all that had released into his bloodstream. Mama and Daddy now summoned my sisters in South Dakota and England home.

I never will understand why this happened. Why something was not done to prevent peritonitis. After all, this was an experienced trauma unit, the one to which critical head trauma patients were transported from across the entire county. Despite doctors' amazement he was alive upon arrival, we were told he had a strong chance of survival and chances were improving. But now, on Day Seven, we learned he was poisoned. Had they not monitored for such a thing? Were they negligent?

On New Year's Eve, Roger went into a final surgery. During this seven-hour procedure, doctors opened his abdomen to remove the poison. But Roger's body could not withstand it. His body could not handle the initial trauma plus three major surgeries in seven days plus the blood-poisoning problem. His brain swelled so much from irreparable stress, doctors detached the brain pressure monitor as the final figure showed 162. The left side of his brain had swollen over into the right side and then down into the brain stem. There was no operation or medicine to administer. There was nothing more to do. Twelve hours spent, two neurosurgeons declared Roger brain dead, reduced his chances to 1 percent, and halved the heart stimulant that kept his heart beating. He still was on a respirator and covered with an ice blanket.

One doctor said due to his injuries Roger should have been dead on arrival, but his heart was exceptionally strong and his obvious resolve kept him alive. But now, his will's bidding no longer a match for all stacked up against him, only machines and drugs kept him breathing and his once-resilient heart beating. Following brain death, all his otherwise healthy organs that beforehand functioned normally all began to fail. Only his heart continued to beat because of administered medicine instructing it to do so. I knew my brother was no longer present. Kelly knew it, too. But Mama refused to accept it. She kept prayerful vigilance. Faithful somehow her son would resurrect. He was her baby, after all.

On Jan. 3, 1987, Kelly and my parents had to decide something no one, certainly no young wife, no parent, should ever have to settle. Kelly knew Roger did not want to exist solely by functions of machinery; now even that was beyond reach. Against everything in her that ached for their life as one, she signed the papers, with my parents' accord, releasing him from life-supporting equipment and medicines.

Again, we filed in, this time for final farewells. Roger lay flat as if asleep on the hospital bed in a different, smaller room after everything artificial had been stopped and removed. His eyes were closed; he was… so… very… still. I held him. I kissed him, so many times. I whispered I love you's and that I always would love him and keep his spirit alive in my heart and recollections with those of us who knew him and those who did not have the privilege. I remembered the last time Roger had kissed me goodbye. It was Christmas Day when the family gathered and before that, the Friday before Christmas on Dec. 19 at his and Kelly's home. I caressed his hand once more and leaned in and kissed his right cheek. As I kissed him, a bit of scab from his cheek came off on my upper lip. A tiny piece of my remaining brother, I thought. And instantly I felt his presence in the air around me. I knew he was gone. And I knew he was there. And somehow I knew he always would be.

On Jan. 4, Roger's heart rate reached 18 when he was declared legally deceased. My baby brother had died. But I knew God greeted him Jan. 3. The extra 24 hours were merely technical and legal minutes, inconsequential to the fact.

Roger was only 28 years old. He was a young, strong, smart man who should have had a lengthy life. A life with Kelly. And with Jason. Of making love with his wife. Of watching his son grow up, graduate from college, marry and have children of his own. Of having more children and grandchildren. Of having more talks with Mama and more fishing with Daddy. Of working and playing. Of cutting grass and frying fish. Of washing the car in the driveway. Of taking vocational courses, and learning, growing and discovering. Of laughing and talking and crying and remembering. Of growing old. I cannot imagine ever witnessing anything as gruesome as what happened to my brother, or the unspeakable, indescribable, horrifying aftermath it left and laid indelibly upon the hearts and memories of Jason and Kelly, Mama and Daddy, me, my siblings, and countless others who knew and loved him. I will not, cannot, forget.

Was this devastation inflicted by a drunk driver the pre-ordained method God knew far in advance would happen yet allowed it to enact Roger's end on Earth, the pivotal occasion that sent my brother out of the physical and into the eternal? Why did God allow a tragic exit for a good man loved by so many, someone who already had had his fair share of tragedy? Why, oh why, does God allow horror to befall, to devastate, good people? It is a rhetorical empty question. No one can answer it. Only the mind of God knows the answer. But I could not help but wonder.

When Roger perished, each one of us handled his passing differently. Mama said, "No child is supposed to die before his parents." She did not weep for a long time and even when she finally did it was not hysterical. She wondered why not, "What's wrong with me?" But in time she understood her tearless grief likely was due to the lobotomy and shock treatments that had dulled her senses years before. But she certainly grieved. Daddy did weep, a man who wept only in the most desperate of circumstances. I suppose the time he cried before this time was when Mama was sick long ago. Daddy said Roger was even more than his son; he was his friend. He would miss him greatly. He would miss him every time he went fishing. Every time he laughed. Every time he woke up in the morning and took a breath.

As for me, I believed no promise of God from then on. I could not understand why God allowed such horror to happen. I fumbled with the faith I had grown up learning to have in my Maker; it left me. My father survived several bloody battles in his 20s during the war and his youngest son lost his life in a senseless car wreck in his 20s. The adage, "only the good die young," can be said of Roger. But my father also was good and he lived a long life. Both my brother and father faced terror and pain, so why did God let one live through some miracle of grace yet take the other, reserving the miracle? I would ponder and struggle with that unanswered question for decades. For years, I could not string lights or decorate a Christmas tree; it seemed pointless, to spread symbols of joy when there was none in me.

Jason was released from the hospital Jan. 1, a few days before Roger passed away, into his biological mother's custody. Jason only 8 at the time had survived the wreck but with repercussions. Not only had he witnessed his father's terrible head trauma at the scene, but Jason had suffered a concussion, had been covered in battery acid and motor oil, had a broken kneecap and severe gash in his right leg, had broken his left wrist and hand, and had sustained several cuts on his face, right ear and head that required stiches. A muscle in his left eye was torn and inoperable and left doctors unsure as to whether it would repair itself. But he was alive.

On Jan. 6, Mama, Daddy, Kelly and I visited him to tell him his Daddy had died. He cried unconsolably. He and his mother attended the rosary and funeral. In coming months, my parents, Kelly and I consulted attorneys about the prospect of one of us taking custody of Jason but were advised the effort was useless. As ill-fit for motherhood as Cathy had been and remained, she was after all Jason's birth mother and the law ensured Jason remained with her until adulthood.

We held Roger's funeral on the seventh day in January at St. Benedict where he had been baptized as an infant. Two limousines collected our family at Mama and Daddy's and drove us to the church. Along the way, we found ourselves reminiscing, in laughter one minute and somber the next. Inside the church, as the pall bearers carried his casket on the long walk to the alter in front, we filed dutifully behind it, with Kelly and I holding hands immediately after it. As I stepped steadily forward, I could not believe my brother was inside that box. We followed it. Adrift. Uncomprehending. Hollow. Disbelieving. Following blankly in step after the pall bearers who flanked the casket.

Roger's life—and death—had touched innumerable people. More than 400 family, relatives and friends, and friends and families of relatives and friends, attended his rosary and funeral. People said later the funeral procession was one of the lengthiest they had ever seen. The Boys sent flowers and two of them came. Old school chums came. Friends and family of each family member came. But we Guckians knew none of them that day. The sea of people who came wanted so desperately to console us but we could not be consoled, for the life that egressed Roger now left us as well. Kelly and Jason were there but wanted to be with him. At the gravesite, Jason cried unrelentingly.

That day, Roger wore jeans and his camel-brown western boots; a red bandana folded neatly in his rear pocket. His strong sensitive hands that once held rosary beads on trips to El Paso held them still.

As the Mass concluded, people filed past our family to take our hands in theirs, look into our eyes and faces, offer gentle embraces, say, "I'm so sorry." I cannot say who they were. I cannot recollect their faces or names. I was not there. Only my body was there. The rest of me went missing. Roger was in the box. I was awake, alive, breathing. But I was not there.

After the burial, the cavalcade of cars snaked from the cemetery like a train toward our family's home on Dysart. Cars crowded the driveway bumper-to-bumper and parked along curbs throughout the neighborhood. People were everywhere, like ants immediately disturbed from a mound. In the front yard. In the backyard. They filled the house and were streaming through it. People brought in boxes and bags and bowls and plates of food. And buckets of iced tea from Bill Miller Bar-B-Q. Out back, children played croquet in the grass. Everyone told tender stories about Roger, and laughed, and cried. Roger had his party, after all. I kept waiting for him to come bouncing through the back door with his usual buoyant panache. But he did not. He would not. He would never again.

And yet, I knew, I would see him again, in person, one day. His spirit was not taken with his body. His spirit lives and our love for him lives as does his love for us. I tried to remind myself to switch my brain's focus from the image in the hospital to the one of him as he was before, an image of light and laughter and love.

Once Kelly's parents returned to Georgia, she receded into arbitrary seclusion. She missed sleeping with Roger, his hand beneath her as they slumbered. She missed his consoling hugs. She missed he liked to work in the yard. Kelly kept their modest house on Prairie Sun and cared for it and the animals. When Frisbie and Spike each died in turn, it was like losing Roger all over again. But when Kelly resurfaced, she did so with a plan in hand supported by a contagious optimism. Everyone who knew her benefited from being in her company. She took a humble job with the Express-News filing photographs in what then was a dingy, dusty, concrete-and-brick warehouse from where each day she went home tired and soiled. But she was earning a living and surviving. She would never remarry and told me why: "I had the best."

When Roger passed, Daddy lost his best friend, his fishing buddy. Neither Daddy nor Mama spoke of his tragic passing much, the hurt was too deep, but we have remembered him in stories, videos, pictures and reverent laughter. It is wounding to think of what happened to him for too long. The shattering emotions and images rush back and only weeping remains, until taking life up again and pressing forward again, without him, just like we did in church with each step we took behind that casket.

Like giving birth or being carried from a burning building or dodging a bullet, you cannot tell anyone else who has not experienced it firsthand what the tragic death of someone you love dearly feels like. You must experience it personally to know what it is. When Roger died, a part of me died with him. I wanted to stop the pain from coming back, over and over and over again. I did not see then how I would survive. I'd awaken from a brief sleep when after a second or two there it came, the deep-down ache that mushroomed from inside my stomach and engulfed and reminded me. I prayed and prayed, begging God for sleep, for the stabbing in my gut to stop, for it not to be real, for tomorrow to come without the brutal, unrelenting torment, without the memory or images imprinted on my brain. But my prayers went unanswered. I woke up with it anyway.

When someone you know well and love dies, unexpectedly and tragically especially, this is what it is like. I knew it was real but I refused it, too. I closed my eyes and tried to wish it away and pray my way out of it, hoping once I opened my eyes life would be what it had been. But never is there a way out of it. No where to run from it. I was stuck with the pain and stuck with the terrible loss that feels like someone reached into my belly and pulled out my guts. And the only thing I could do was keep moving through it. Minute by minute. Hour by hour. Day by day. Tear by tear. Ache by ache. Until one day, I realized, it seemed a bit easier.

Soon after we buried my brother, I wrote a letter to a friend explaining all that had happened. "It's just so awful. Roger's death was senseless. We cannot help but ask, why? But we are trying to have faith, too."

So, part of me was buried with my brother. But the rest of me had to keep breathing, no matter how much it hurt. I cried till I could cry no more. Only six days after Roger's funeral, I underwent a previously scheduled laminectomy—a major spine surgery that in my case was due to severely herniated discs exacerbated by diagnoses of congenital spinal stenosis and degenerative disc disease, abetted by aggressive high-impact exercise that was my habit. I am certain it was nearly impossible for my family even to consider visiting me during my 7-day hospitalization, to be inside another hospital so soon after my brother's suffering and passing, and I did not expect them to. I understood. I did not want to be there either. But they came. Thereafter, I recovered at Mama and Daddy's eight weeks.

I did not know then the spine operation would be only the first in the years ahead. My neurosurgeon, Dr. Swann, also in his early 30s like me at the time, was the doctor who had treated Jason's neurological injuries after the wreck. Coincidentally, Dr. Swann, a Harvard graduate, had recently begun his practice in San Antonio and already had seen two of our Guckian clan. Decades later would show this was no coincidence. It is astonishing, often perplexing, and at times maddening how God orchestrates the crisscross of lives without help from us.

Something unexpected happened when I was in the hospital. I shared a room with another patient who also had undergone spine surgery but by a different surgeon. One afternoon, I awoke from a dream when the woman told me I had been talking in my sleep… to Roger. I remembered immediately what I had seen and said. Roger had appeared to me, as if hovering above and in front of me so I could see him clearly. His hair was longer than it had been the day he left us, as it was when he was younger, and his head was encircled by a warm, pearlescent radiance with a sky-blue background behind him. He wore his signature smile.

With excited surprise, I spoke, "Is that you, Roger? Are you OK?" He just kept smiling. And finally he said, "Yeah, Lou, I'm fine. I just wanted you to know, I'm fine and I'm happy." And then I awoke. Talking to him had felt as real as if he was standing next to me. With fleeting uncertainty, I wondered whether it had been medicinally induced or real. But every cell of my core informed me, then as now, he was there, we were talking, it was real.

One day in late February on the first pleasant sunny day since the funeral and my surgery, I walked outside into Mama and Daddy's backyard. I basked in the day's cordial warmth and thought of Roger. In one spot in the yard were lifeless brown stems protruding from the ground where a rosebush had bloomed in summer. I saw barrenness where before pretty, aromatic flowers of soft, encircling petals had grown. I knew the stems would turn green and the roses would bloom again in spring. They were not dead, only dormant. I thought of Roger, that he would not return in spring.

A swaying Crape Myrtle in a corner of the yard jostled me from reflection. Its wintry leaves of purple and gold playfully waved as soft breezes lifted and twirled them at will, and I saw Roger there. He was like that. Carefree. Colorful. A merry whimsy. Unlike the bare rose bush, this tree had survived winter. Minus only its dormant bright pink blooms and spring-green leaves, it now provided a pleasing focal point tinted with perennial energy in an otherwise barren setting. A smile relaxed on my face as the sun warmed my skin. And I knew Roger was in it, in the breeze, in the sun, in the dancing leaves, in me. I knew he always would be.

That was when I curbed my drinking of alcohol. I did not remove alcohol from my life entirely but stopped using it to self-medicate. I stopped drinking obsessively. I stopped drinking just to drink. I stopped using it as a way to feel strong or attractive or better. I began to view alcohol as the addictive destructive thing it was, and is, when consumed beyond moderation or uncontrollably.

I asked God to help all of us who knew and loved Roger to be strong, and to have faith and courage enough to accept our loss. To learn from it. To cherish the memories that came to an end too soon because of it. To change ourselves and live restored lives because of it. I joined the Bexar County chapter of Mothers Against Drunk Drivers. I wrote a letter to both local major daily newspapers, the Express-News and San Antonio Light, both of which published it, about the horrific irreversible toll and forever-damaged lives inflicted by drunk driving. In it, I told what happened to Roger and Jason, to Kelly, and to our entire family. I called the wreck criminal and violent and a forced end to my brother's life.

I wrote President Reagan, asking drunk drivers be more vigorously dealt with in our courts everywhere. I had to do something to raise the issue of my brother's tragic, untimely, and sudden, senseless death. And the rippling effect onto hundreds of other people thrown into anguish as a result of it. I found it impossible, then and now, to label wrecks caused by drunk drivers "accidents." They are not accidental. They are intentional. If we drink and drive, we do it by choice. And because we do it by choice, the consequences are ours to bear.

For a long time, I thought I saw Roger driving a pickup truck or mowing a yard. Two years after we buried him, I saw a photo of a man in the newspaper who was spinning a lawnmower around, after reaching the end of a row of mowed grass, to head back in the opposite direction, the same way Roger used to do. It seemed Roger could spin a lawnmower with one finger. Also identical, the man in the photo was tall and slim with thick, layered, wavy brown hair cut like Roger's the day he passed. He wore blue jeans, a tee-shirt and boots, exactly like Roger.

For a split-second, I was stunned into believing Roger was alive and that was him! Of course, my senses returned to me quickly. But a lingering wonder has stayed put. I have wondered whether experiences like these are God's way… and Roger's way… of waving hello. I have wondered whether Roger's path in the spiritual world is trailing parallel to mine here in this earthly world. And once in a while, whether in a dream or photograph or passing truck or the wind in a tree, I get a glimpse of him.

Gunpoint

Eighth Spiritual Death

Roger's tragic taking caused me to look hard at myself. I was 32 and knew I never would again have an alcoholic blackout. I would not stumble about in public or at home because of being blitzed. I still went out. I still drank alcohol. I still danced and had fun. But after seeing what I saw and knowing what I knew, I never again drank till obscure inebriation or drove intoxicated. How could I? A drunken man had taken my brother's life. That irresponsible alcoholic piece of me died, too.

Even though I tried repeatedly to grasp, to feel, to believe in the God I'd grown up with, my brother's tragic death weakened my faith. I never accepted the universe and mankind were happenstance. But I could not fathom why the God who created and loved Roger would allow him to suffer horrifically, along with the rest of us. And if God was that... indifferent... if God could love His creation one minute and allow agony the next, then how could I pray to such a God? How could I believe He heard or cared about me when, after all, He did not prevent the wreck or save my brother's life? As God, He could have done both. But God allowed both. God took him. From us. If God did not act on Roger's behalf, then how could I believe God would act on mine? I simply needed to believe, in something.

I finally decided to believe God was with my brother every second of his trauma and did not allow him to feel the pain as we experienced it, watching, trembling and weeping through it. I did not understand what on the surface seemed a double standard of injustice imposed by God but I accepted it was not for me to question the Almighty Creator. Yet, I had an aching need to know why this happened. One minute, I felt a repriving peace, and the next, again took up my questioning. And so it went, again and again. I simply did not know, for sure, about God, or the Bible as God's infallible word, or my life as created, protected and provided by God. I wondered whether parts of Scripture were real and others only stories, and if stories, then what was I to take as God's truth?

Controlling my consumption of alcohol was long overdue and I did not miss getting smashed or the unrelenting guilt and shame that came with it. I did not miss its accessory, mindless immorality, even though that was a behavior I would wean from more slowly than the booze.

After Roger's funeral, and my spine surgery and recovery at Mama and Daddy's, I returned to my apartment and full-time civil service job and part-time job at the guesthouse. I went back to all of it with a growing dissatisfaction. It was then my coworker Sally suggested I get a cat. She must have sensed my building angst and thought a cushy cat would relieve it. Sally hailed from Maryland. She was a tall, pretty, stately figure with pale skin and dark thick shoulder-length hair, as thick as her dialect, and a sense of humor I found refreshing. She was married to a gentle military man, and they had one small son and one extremely large cat. So one Saturday, I met Sally at a pet store, and sure enough, we found the ideal feline for me, a petite female tortoiseshell kitty barely weaned. Sally paid for it and I purchased all the other items I needed and took the kitty home. I named her Priti.

No sooner had I adopted Priti did a fresh work-related adventure surface. A chirpy colonel in his early 40s had grabbed hold of a tasking report from the Pentagon that urged Air Force major commands to innovate to endure deregulation of the government, in full swing at that time. From that report, the colonel created the first Office of Innovation within the Department of Defense. He hired a skeleton crew of military officers to launch and manage it and train others to use and teach innovation. And then he invited military troops and civilian employees to attend presentations to learn more. At the lively open meetings, he called for volunteers to leave their jobs to serve 6-month transient roles with him and I signed on instantly. I thereby became an innovation specialist with new duties and fresh faces. I had no concerns about not being able to return to my old job.

We delivered innovation seminars and conducted creative problem-solving workshops across our major command. We taught people to strategically identify problems and creatively solve them. It was exhilarating to see attendees' faces smile and eyes sparkle as they learned in our workshops to be creative and positive. And I blossomed alongside them. I traveled with the colonel and his extremely interesting, entertaining and hardworking officer entourage to carry the news of innovation to military installations across America, including below-freezing Alaska and tropical Hawaii. As with my trip to Europe, I saw places I had never seen before. I built my presentation, problem-solving and social skills. I learned how to think more positively and creatively. And my self-esteem soared.

As my self-confidence climbed, so did my appetite for a new car. I traded my sporty Chrysler Laser for an even sportier bright red Mitsubishi Conquest TSi hatchback. Stylish and fast, it fit my new attitude, with its turbocharged 5-speed manual transmission, black leather interior and surround-sound stereo.

When the rotating gig concluded, I took with me all I had gained and grown through and reluctantly resumed my former federal job that had been held for me. I found myself unhappy with the status quo after the exhilarating experience with the Office of Innovation. I had uncovered previously unrecognized interests, skills and talents, and the belief I could accomplish anything I set my mind to. I soon resigned from federal employment to take a full-time executive position with the commercial real estate property management firm that ran the small guesthouse where I had worked part-time. It was another risk but a risk worth taking.

My new job and title evolved varyingly from general manager to marketing manager depending on where I was assigned. My first assignment was the most challenging; it required I live and work onsite for eight consecutive months. I was hired as both general manager and marketing manager of a 48-room guesthouse in Lubbock, Texas central to a medical center and university. The inn had been foreclosed and sat dormant when our firm acquired it. Our aim was to refurbish it, hire and train staff to run it, and reopen it with grand fanfare. My primary job was to fill every room and keep them all occupied at a profitable rate.

At the inn, I hired and trained desk clerks, housekeeping and maintenance personnel and night auditors, and cross-trained them all so each would have knowledge of their teammates' importance to the entire team. Front desk clerks didn't like it much, but I made them clean a room in 15 minutes or less to the same standard to which we held housekeeping staff, including perfectly folding the beginning square on a roll of toilet paper. My mother and Grandma Floy's cleaning standards and work ethics came in handy. Eventually, I trained two clerks to assume general and assistant manager positions when I left the inn for my next project.

While there, I played host to international guests, including a ballet troupe from Russia and an artist who painted my portrait. I handled middle-of-the-night upsets like weather-related utility outages and water leaks. Admittedly, the job was extremely stressful and downright hard. But it certainly was not boring and it paid more than any job I'd held so far. One December night it snowed. I was so excited, I climbed into my TSi and took a slow cruise about town with windows down and heater running full blast to look at the snow and Christmas lights. That night, I carried Priti, who had accompanied me to Lubbock, outside and dropped her in the snow where my staff and I made snow angels. Priti didn't like it much. When the weather warmed, I took her on a picnic, but she didn't care for grass either.

After Lubbock's profitable reversal, the firm used it as its prototypical turnaround and shuttled me among other guesthouses situated within similar communities in Arkansas, Missouri and finally Virginia. I partnered with general managers in duplicating the marketing and monetary wins attained in Lubbock. The Virginia Inn in Richmond was an exception. It had 199 guest rooms, a conference center, and a restaurant and bar. Instead of being located within a medical or academic center, this hotel was located along a main interstate and catered to a diverse range of groups such as conventioneers, tourists, and sports teams and fans. Patty Loveless and her band stayed with us when she was getting started in country music and racecar drivers and fans lodged with us during a NASCAR Winston Cup.

One day, my immediate boss, the vice president of marketing, along with the owner and president, my boss's mother, came to Richmond to meet with me. The owner and I sat alone in the restaurant. She told me she was pleased with my work but wanted me to soften my approach with staff. She put it this way: "Lou, you're a hot dog. A torpedo. I give you a target, and you take aim and hit it. And that's good. But remember, there are other people around you, to the left and right of the target, and you have to consider them."

Her warm delivery made taking a tough critique easier and I took it to heart. When managing the Lubbock guesthouse, I had been hard on staff. I had never before held such a high-level job and held myself to extremely high standards. I expected their work to be on par with mine. I accepted nothing less than perfection. When I obviously carried that same lofty expectation and unintentionally harsh manner with me to Richmond, the boss decided it was time to have a chat with me. She knew I was not deliberately severe and I was smart and hardworking. But she also knew, as did I, that I needed to relax my style or otherwise alienate others who also were valuable to the firm.

While living and working at the Virginia Inn in 1989, I welcomed late autumn followed by early winter but with it came a terrible scare. We had enjoyed a sold-out weekend thanks to a national baseball championship held in Richmond and the hotel safe was full of cash. Late Monday morning, I left my room from where I worked and walked toward the hotel lobby to speak with the general manager. I was dressed in a crisp Liz Claiborne two-piece brown-and-beige houndstooth suit jacket and short skirt accessorized with gold jewelry, including the antique cameo ring that had belonged to my Great Aunt Katherine, pearl and gold stud earrings, three gold chain necklaces, a gold bracelet and a gold cross blessed by a priest.

As I entered the lobby, I passed and walked behind the front desk noticing no one on duty, which struck me as odd. It was shortly after checkout time, 11:30 a.m., when someone typically would have stood at the register. I continued toward the manager's office located behind the front desk, but before I made it, I caught sight of a terrifying scene directly ahead.

The manager was on his knees in front of the safe that sat in an opened closet and a man stood behind him with a pistol to his head. My mind could not believe my eyes. As I turned around at hearing muttering behind me, I encountered two men pointing pistols, one at my middle and one at my face, and the one closest to me yelled, "Get in there and lay down!" In a strange reaction at seeing their stern stoic faces and pointed silver guns, I spoke, disbelieving what I saw: "Is this a joke? Are you kidding me?" At my words, one of the gunmen raised his pistol square with my eyes and told me again, "Get in there and lay down!"

As I hurried into the office, I saw the desk clerk and maintenance man face down on the carpet. I clumsily knelt and then lay down between them, face down. With the depth of reality sinking in quick and hard, I burrowed my hands beneath my chest and quickly removed my heirloom cameo and other rings and dropped them inside the neck of my blouse, anticipating theft. Right then, one of the gunmen now behind me told me to get up. I rose to my knees, when he pointed his gun at me and instructed me meanly to take off my necklaces and hand them over. "Please don't take the cross, it's blessed," I pleaded. I never will know why I said that in the face of what I presumed to be a loaded gun.

Naturally, he didn't care it was blessed. He raised the gun to my eyes and told me to take it off. I did. Then he told me to lie back down. I did, face down. And that's when I knew. I was going to die. I prayed a quick prayer asking God's forgiveness. And I waited for the bullet.

Soon, one of the men came to me again with gun aimed and yelled at me to get up. I stood and he prodded me toward the front desk, where he instructed me to open the register. As soon as it opened, he angrily pushed it closed and then yelled at me to open it again. There was nothing in it to steal; all the cash had been placed in the safe. With pointed pistol, he ushered me back into the office and told me to lie down, and I obeyed. A minute later, he returned, demanding this time my car keys. I raised my head from the floor to tell him fearfully I had no car. Just then, the desk clerk said he would give him his car keys. He eased them from his pants pocket and handed them to the gunman, who seized them and fled the room.

We lay on the floor a long time, trembling and too terrified to move or speak. After a while, I cannot say how long, after not hearing or seeing the gunmen, the maintenance man stood, looked out the window and said they were gone. Sure enough, they were indeed, along with the desk clerk's car that had been parked in the lot in clear view of the window. As we all stood, the general manager entered the office from where he had been in the closet by the safe. Without speaking, he and I together raced toward the restaurant, bolted up the stairs, ran straight to the bar, grabbed a bottle of whiskey from the shelf and downed two shots apiece.

After downing the whiskey, we looked blankly at each other and shook our heads. But no words came out of our mouths. I seized the phone on the bar, dialed my boss in San Antonio, and heard these words gush from my mouth without taking a breath: "We were just held up at gunpoint! Get me the f*** out of here! I want to get on a f****** plane, now! I am leaving this f****** hotel!"

I have learned something about me and swearing. When I'm scared, that is to say, when I am highly alarmed, I swear. Profanity spews out of my mouth like hot steam from an overheated radiator. She calmly replied, saying she would have the flight booked right away and I could take time off to relax over the holidays.

We learned later the gunmen had terrorized their way up Interstate 95 robbing hotels and motels, and at the one after ours took a female hostage. I think back to how lucky I was, the only female in the group when they stormed our hotel. Much more could have happened to me than did. State troopers and sharpshooters were dispatched. They ran down the three outlaws, killing one and injuring another, made the capture, and freed the hostage unharmed.

After Christmas, I returned to Virginia to finish the job. My return home afterward marked the end of nearly a 2-year tenure as a traveling executive. I leased a tiny apartment near the medical center but was considering buying my first home. The ongoing savings-and-loan crisis had caused mass institutional failures and home foreclosures abounded, creating a buyers' market. My search for a home commenced. I did not know that the owner of the firm had fallen gravely ill, or that the firm's principal investor had pulled out and there were no management contracts on the horizon.

In February of 1990, shortly before I turned 35, I closed on my first home. It was a condominium built in 1982 valued at $65,000 I bought for $39,000. My monthly mortgage was less than $300. I loved it. It was located in north central San Antonio in an established tree-studded gated community with a walking trail near the Salado Creek and a live oak canopy-covered community pool. My two-bedroom, two-bath, 1,200-square foot upstairs condo had a wood-burning fireplace and balcony, and bedrooms facing a quiet green courtyard. The neighbor directly downstairs was an older lady named Nancy who didn't like me much at first. She told me I walked too hard and was noisy. But when I adopted a German Shepherd-mix puppy, she told me she had raised Shepherds and softened toward me.

The puppy was eight weeks old when I rescued her from the Animal Defense League, which I visited at a friend's suggestion. She thought I might like a second pet to keep my cat company when I worked long hours. So I went to the League to browse kitties. But a puppy caught my eye. I stopped at her pen to take a longer look and when I did she perked up and came to meet me with tail wagging. When the attendant asked if I'd like to hold her, I declined. I knew if I did I would take her home and I was not sure I wanted a dog.

I left that day without the pup. Or a cat. But a week later, I returned, adopted her, and named her Cristi. And my new puppy and kitty got along fine.

I had a new condo, a new puppy, my cat, my sportscar, lots of expensive Liz Claiborne clothes, credit card debt and a job to pay for it all.

My previous nomadic post had transitioned to a local job titled relocation director. My charge was the launch of the firm's new relocation service. I dug into the project. I wrote and published the premier "Apartment Selector Relocation Guide," and presented my sales pitch in person to human resources decision-makers of prominent corporations and universities, three of which were United Services Automobile Association, St. Mary's University and the University of Texas at San Antonio (UTSA). I succeeded in garnering commitments to our new venture and the firm hired two salespeople to secure the anticipated new business.

By June, four months after closing on my condo, the firm I worked for folded. I was given no notice and two weeks' pay. The owner's son, who had served as vice president of operations and was married, walked me out. I will never forget what he said to me. He asked me to have an affair. With clenched teeth and all the scorn I could muster, I said bluntly: "You disgust me." And I climbed into my shiny red TSi and sped away.

Don't Save Me, I'm Drowning

Despite that I was out of work with bills to pay and a puppy whose housetraining was slow, I still lived in an enigmatic idealistic starlit bubble. It seemed nothing could get me down. Perhaps this is a hallmark of being 30-something. My third decade was a cavalier season when boundless vitality catapulted me into ongoing discovery both aimed and aimless. If something I tackled fell through, I simply and quickly looked for a new something.

It was a time in my life when I set and reset lofty goals to work ever harder in pursuing an education and a career I now termed "journalism." I looked the best I ever would, caught the eye of men and dated several. I wanted marriage and kids but pursued a career till they arrived. As far as men went, I learned the ones who attracted me were not the marrying kind.

Where dating was concerned, I'd had trouble with losing self-control in the past and hoped to learn and develop a new way of relating. I compared falling in love playfully to drowning. I didn't want to drown, but I didn't want to be saved either. I wanted someone strong yet kind. Someone who interested me intellectually and attracted me physically. Someone who loved God and would love me forever. I figured the only way to find such a man was date, date, date. And I decided no sex until, if and when it was within the context of commitment, that is, marriage. I thought it a wise plan.

Sometimes I felt like a lone observer, at a time when nearly every woman I knew was busy attending to the man in her life. I, in contrast, sat alone in the comfort of my semi-success after years of hard work and countless mistakes and failures. I had settled into my new home and curled up most weekend nights on my newly upholstered comfy couch watching TV with my pets. I did not feel desperate for a man but I did yearn for one and at the same time knew there was some truth to chasing away good fortune by pursuing too aggressively what I wanted. Divorced and single 11 years, I was lonesome for a man's company and touch.

Compared to other women, I felt like a steel pillar, too strong, too forthright, and I wondered what sort of man could love a woman like me. I believed he would need to be emotionally strong and able to allow for my developed independence.

So I arose each day, drank coffee, prayed, occasionally read Scripture since returning to Mass again, and walked 3 miles. I read Earl Nightingale's "Greatest Discovery" that taught me "Thoughts are things." Christ had said something similar: "Whatever things you ask when you pray, believe that you receive them, and you will have them" (Mark 11:24 NKJV). So I began thinking about and praying for two things: To become a professional writer and marry the man of my dreams, a man committed to marriage, fidelity and raising children. And I journaled.

Journaling, I found, is a lot like confessing. The writings I penned at 35 revealed an emotionally immature and indulgent individual who at the same time was maturing in a professional career. Journaling also revealed my wonder about many things. What was it about men, I wondered, that warped me into impatient and confusing knots of analytical frenzy? Since the age of 15, I still was figuring it out. Women I knew age 19 to 91 were as lost as me. They expressed on increasing occasion their discontent, inability to understand and utter frustration with their men, whether it was a new relationship or lifelong marriage. I supposed maybe that there were no answers to my wonders.

George and I met at the singles group at church. He was the only guy there worth a second glance. He was tall, wore shorts, tee-shirt and deck shoes without socks, and seemed laidback. I believed him insecure, modest perhaps, because he was a bit overweight, but that did not detract from his good looks. I saw him a month later at a party. I told George before I left that night, "Call me, I'm in the book." Lo and behold, he phoned, and when he did, I asked, "George who?" I honestly did not remember him. But I was impressed he'd done a bit of research and made the call.

I invited him over to watch a movie. He almost sat on top of me on the couch the whole time and then gave me my first quick peck on the cheek before leaving. Two weeks later, we had dinner out, after which he gave me a second peck. We had lunch one afternoon, when came the third peck. George was a Certified Public Accountant in his early 30s, a bachelor, and as I learned, a workaholic. But so was I. I liked George. He was kind, clean and polite, and I admired his professional zeal. His family-owned furniture stores for which he kept the books aside from a full-time job with a large corporation. He played sports and cycled. I especially liked he spent Sundays at church and with family.

A week before Christmas, I invited him to dinner. After we ate, we sat by the fireplace, drank wine and kissed. Our first kiss was awkward; I sensed his excitement. Either it had been a while since he had kissed a woman or he was excited about kissing me, but we enjoyed it and before we knew it, it was 3 a.m. After hints from me the hour was late, he left. On Christmas Eve, we attended Mass together and then he dropped me at home and left; he planned to work Christmas Day on his family business's books, preparing for an audit. On New Year's Eve, I invited him to a party at Rose's but nearly an hour after the agreed time, no George.

That night, I met Frank. A colleague of Rose, Frank was 50, divorced, on the rebound from a 2-year relationship with a woman in her 30s, and on the scout for a monogamous girlfriend. I considered it. After all, George often was unavailable and Frank wanted someone to spend time and money on. I thought, if George does not show up, then here's Frank who looked good for a midnight kiss. But George did arrive and I was happy for it. We sipped champagne and kissed at midnight and then drove to my place.

Sitting snugly on the couch, we spoke of seeing other people while still seeing each other. I didn't mind because we were not sexually involved. The more people we spent time with the more we'd know who and what we wanted. After all this talk, I asked him, "Why don't you kiss me?" My perspective was, here we are, why wait, time's wasting. His point of view was, let's build anticipation. I thought him a bit controlling. By 3:40 a.m., I said it was time to go. He alluded to staying, I disagreed, he left.

I didn't hear from George for four weeks. I wondered whether he was seeing other women or immersed in the family business audit. I thought of him often, about the next time I'd see him, of us making eye contact, smiling, hugging, and then, sharing the eventual sensual kiss. Then I remembered I'd felt the same about other men, had those same anticipatory thoughts, and those men proved hurtful and now were history. I wanted to get to know George. But Rose said he was not at my level emotionally and his first concern was career not marriage. Still, I missed him. We had spent Christmas Eve and New Year's Eve together, holidays typically shared with someone special. I decided to be patient.

Meanwhile, I wondered whether Cristi, 4 months then, would ever be housebroken. And I wished either George or Frank would phone. My ego hoped George thought of me and I wondered why he'd not mentioned the sweet letter I'd mailed two weeks prior. Maybe both men wanted only sex. Maybe neither would ever call again. Maybe, maybe, maybe! Why do I have to figure it all out? Which brought me back to… patience. And journaling. I journaled about my feelings so I wouldn't dump them onto the unsuspecting and named my journal "Male Relationships."

One day, stopped at a red light, I noticed the Laredo Jeep to my right and the guy behind the wheel who smiled at me. We rolled down our windows and chatted about something mindless before the light turned green. I turned left and he drove forward. I dropped off the video I'd rented then looked around for the Jeep. As I returned to my car, I saw him, the Jeep guy, walking past the video store. I felt chased and it was a fun feeling. Catching up with me, he offered his phone number and I took it. His name was Steve. He was in his mid-20s, good-looking with a 5 o'clock shadow and tall. He said he was completing an undergraduate degree in marketing with the UTSA. I called him that night when his mother answered and said he'd be home soon. I considered Steve my transition guy from George. But even if not, I wanted to spend time with other men.

Then Mark came along. He was a marketing representative I met at the rehabilitation center where I worked a short time as a staffing coordinator. Younger than I, like Steve, Mark was a handsome blonde and blue-eyed. But I missed George. I liked him and our last time together was especially affectionate. I wondered whether he thought of me the same.

Life was demanding. My new job was hard, I was taking classes four nights a week to earn a bachelor's degree, and Cristi was peeing in the house. I was tired from work and school and frustrated with my dog. I sat down one night and cried. What the hell is George doing! I wondered. I decided to call and left a message. George quickly returned it. His voice sounded good to my ears like fresh brewed coffee smells to my nose. We talked about how busy we both had been and how I hated that word, "busy." I was busy with a new job and school. He was busy with his full-time job and audit and was planning a trip with buddies to New Orleans he likely would cancel due to work. And he said he should have phoned sooner.

We reflected on New Year's Eve and that's when I decided to tell him how special… oh dear, did I say special… it was for me. I told him I'd been spoiled by his attention and selfishly missed it. He said he was not dating anyone and being with me was very comfortable, and as he spoke, I asked myself, what does that mean? And then I told my mind to shut up. Soon after our call, I met Joe, who proposed dinner sometime.

One night, I went alone to a party but wished I was with one of the men I had met. I wanted to call one, George being first choice. I hesitated but also told myself, it's not "me" to wait. So much for my pursuit of patience. Why stifle who I am for the sake of traditionalism? Why wait for the man to call me? But I called no one that night and after a few days crossed George off my list. I was spending too much time thinking about him and to no positive end. Two weeks later, Joe called. On Valentines Day, I found a paper sack on my desk at work with a purple Post It note stuck to it with my name written on it. It was from Joe. Inside was a stuffed racoon and a sweet card that brought a tear. We later spoke of horseback riding in Bandera. I dreamily pictured the two of us galloping carefree along a beautiful blue and sandy shoreline as a gloriously red sun set on the horizon.

I had volunteered to write letters to U.S. soldiers in the Middle East. Robby, a 6-foot-2-inch Italian cowboy-turned-marine from Oklahoma who lifted weights, chewed tobacco, rode horses, and wanted to meet me, wrote me stating I was "the girl for him." He was 23. Bless his heart. I did not respond. We never met.

George called me after a month of silence. It was increasingly obvious Rose was right. He was not on my level. I decided what I wanted—to date one man in an exclusive relationship. George was not that man. I jokingly nicknamed him Mr. Spontaneous. He said he'd call again and I replied, "Yes, you do that, when you can break away from your pencil." Joe called that night. I hoped we would go out soon.

I then met a physical therapist named Rick. Rick was tall and handsome. Every time we passed in the hallway, we flirted. We had one date. I invited him to my place where we watched a movie and then had a nightcap. He was a fine kisser with strong tender hands. But he was a heavy drinker. For a two-hour visit with me at my home, Rick brought a bottle of wine, a bottle of Wild Turkey bourbon and a bottle of Sprite. I decided any man who carries that much alcohol with him when he's only on a two-hour date is likely a problem drinker and I did not care for that. It also became clear that Rick was interested in nothing but a sexual fling. I did not satisfy his interest or see him again and was glad when he transferred to Houston.

George phoned within less than two weeks of his last call. He was enjoying the challenge of his work and looking forward to a trip to Jamaica with his buddies since the New Orleans jaunt had been canceled. He said he was not dating anyone but I told him I was and would continue, even though I'd prefer more time with him. I asked him why he continued calling me since we almost never saw each other and seldom spoke. He replied, "You're a nice person and I enjoy talking with you." I liked his words. And felt the same about him. I also liked going out with other men because the more men I dated the more I knew how I felt about George.

I found myself reflecting on the past four years. Since Roger's tragic death, I had faced multiple stressful major life changes, including spine surgery, three changes of address, a home purchase, failed relationships, unemployment and adoption of a puppy, and my father had suffered a stroke. No wonder I was looking for a soft, safe place to land. Sometimes I felt old and worn.

And I thought a lot about Roger. How he and I told each other our lonely-heart stories in the wee hours. I looked at the small wicker basket sitting next to a purple bowl filled with sympathy cards. There, too, were an Easter palm, a dried red rose I had picked from a bouquet atop his casket that now was brittle, and a small brown stone I swiped from his gravesite. I wondered why I kept those things, but I knew why. It was because we had been a lonely-hearts club of two and we had been friends. I missed my brother. I looked at the stereo and record player that had been his that now was mine and how I wished it could talk. It would tell me about the times Roger spun his records and strummed his guitar to the tunes.

I met another man at work named Bob. It was not that either of us was exceptionally taken with the other. Although I was drawn to his ponytailed black hair and olive skin. It was more my inherent manner of experiencing everything and everyone all the way. There seemed minimal midstream with me. Either I was disinterested or I was consumed. I called it passion. Some called it compulsive or obsessive. Perhaps it was all that. But I had decided I'd much rather feel the highs and lows, the excitement and sadness, than to walk through a lifetime living only on level ground. The latter seemed stiflingly dull.

Bob was unattached and one year younger than I. We often exchanged flirtatious stares or compliments on how attractive we looked that day. I had fantasized about him for weeks so naturally I applauded myself for capturing his gaze. One day he invited me to a party and I invited Rose. When we arrived, Bob was spinning records. His voice was deeply masculine and gentle, the kind that could melt a glacier. He hosted all night so I spent no time with him, but late in the evening, he sauntered over to me, wrapped himself around me, and whispered in my ear, "Did you drink my beer?" It was tantalizing being so close and equally clear he was a tease and took pleasure, or perchance liberation, in it.

Already I had thrown away golden years and did not want to squander more. In my mid-30s with no loving marriage or children, I was afraid I'd never have either.

A Big Car and a Virgin

The year the real estate property management firm closed was a hard year for many. In 1990, the U.S. economy still was in historic downturn, which made finding a job challenging. I made a full-time job of looking for work while receiving unemployment benefits without which I would not have survived. I voluntarily relinquished my TSi, leaving a $4,800 balance on the loan, but my parents bought me a used 4-door Plymouth for $2,000. I was grateful to have the car but also embarrassed to drive that gargantuan lorry, which felt more like chauffeuring myself around in a living room than a car, what with its lengthy upholstered seats and giant four doors. But "beggars cannot be choosers."

I pinched every penny and got groceries at food pantries. I lived on potatoes, beans, cereal and peanut butter. I collected and recycled aluminum cans for cash. Gone were the days of $300 cash layouts for Liz Claiborne suits. I hunkered down and took care of myself, Cristi and Priti, and my condo. I was hammered by two debt-collection agencies, one for the remaining balance due on my auto loan, which I no longer owed since its surrender, and one for outstanding credit card debt.

That year, I discovered my aptitude for research and found out it was illegal for debt collectors to hound me if I was making a minimum monthly payment and a good-faith effort to stay in touch with creditors. I adhered to those rules precisely, pacifying my credit card lender monthly with calls to advise I still was unemployed and would be mailing a $5 payment.

But one collector hounded me concerning the remaining balance on the TSi. In one such harassing call, I advised the caller I knew my legal rights, the Consumer Protection Division of the Attorney General's Office protects me from harassment, and I did not owe the remaining balance on that vehicle, given I had voluntarily relinquished it. I further threatened the caller I would report the agency to the Attorney General if it continued harassing me. The hounding stopped. In the end, the lender auctioned my TSi, recovering the remaining balance due, and I paid off my credit card debt. I continued driving the big Plymouth for two years and repaid my parents for their generous gift.

Fortunately, I also learned from the Texas Workforce Commission the state offered a retraining program that provided educational funds, whereby I could complete my bachelor's degree at the state's expense as long as I met its criteria. I applied and was accepted. The program required I complete at least 9 credit hours per semester, maintain at least a 2.50 grade point average, and reapply every three months till I graduated. In return for my due diligence, the state would pay my tuition, lab fees, cost of books and even the price of fuel used to commute. I enrolled at Southwest Texas State University in San Marcos in 1991 and began studies toward a Bachelor of Arts and Sciences degree.

Some classes were held at the university campus and others in San Antonio. I transferred 39 of the 40 credit hours I had attained with San Antonio College to my bachelor's 128-credit-hour requisite. And through a course called Occupational Education, I attained 24 credit hours by justifying the maximum credit-hour allocation allowed based on my work life. As part of my curriculum, I completed a 3-month internship with Trinity University's Public Relations Department as researcher/writer, for which I wrote and published a guide for roving student editors of the campus newsletter.

It was no small delight when I bought a Smith Corona PWP 5000 Personal Word Processor for schoolwork and creative writing projects. I loved it. About the size of a large breadbox, it was a compact computer, typewriter and printer combo with a display screen plus a keyboard and floppy disk drive.

One night at home after studying late, my vision blurred. I could not read or type another word and was terribly alarmed, afraid I was losing my eyesight. Upon obtaining an eye exam a few days later, I learned I needed eyeglasses. I laughed at myself for conjuring the absolute worst-case scenario but understood my angst. After all, I had been through several tragic ordeals in a short span of time and naturally lived on high-idle, awaiting the next one. I fully understood the idiom, "waiting for the other shoe to drop."

When I turned 36 in 1991, two life-changing events took place. On the work front, I entered an era that reaffirmed I was a writer-in-the-making. That year, I secured a full-time job serving dually as marketing account manager and technical newsletter editor with a company that provided computer peripheral products to commercial clients. I worked there two years while taking 9 or 12 credit hours of undergraduate courses per semester, all of which began to harden my career focus increasingly to that of a communication pro and writer. The second event had nothing whatsoever to do with my professional life.

There are far too many firsts to count in life. Firsts occur perpetually. But there is a monumental first I must tell of because it came as a shocking surprise and had a long-lasting impact for years to come. During my first year of undergraduate studies, I sat in a classroom next to a woman named Carla. She was near my age, taller than me and fit, with cropped jet-black hair, striking blue eyes, smooth porcelain skin, a bit of an aloof attitude, and a captivating smile revealing a slightly discolored front tooth. I took notice. Unexpectedly, I found myself attracted and confused by the fascination but eager to pursue it.

True to my longstanding impulsive modus operandi, I wrote her a brief note and passed it to her in the middle of the instructor's lecture. I wrote I had feelings for her that typically I had for guys, it blew my mind, and I asked whether she felt at all like that about me, that is, attracted. She took the note. Opened it. Read it. Looked at me. Smiled. After class, she asked if I was serious, to which I replied sheepishly yet affirmatively, yes. I told her I was interested in getting to know her. Thus began a most novel and unfamiliar encounter. She was a lesbian. I was not. Or was I?

Christmas was nearly here. I invited Carla to my condo one evening for a holiday meal. After supper, we sat on a large comfy ottoman in front of the warm glow of the fire, sipping champaign. Warm and happy, I felt thrilled to feel attraction for someone again. Soon, we moved to the sofa and talked of kissing. But she was hesitant. A few minutes later, though, we did. It was only a soft kiss, an experimental one, to see if what I thought I wanted was in fact that.

When Carla left, I was unable to label the emotions stirring inside me but my feelings were definitely astir. Not because of a man this time. But a woman. This tingly awareness was exhilarating. A new frontier. A point of entry into a whole new world, one for which I had never before given even so much as a fleeting thought, one foreign and unexpected yet welcome. At the time, I knew no one gay. But I was willing to go wherever this new world led.

Over the next few months, we saw each other often, flirting, laughing, talking and kissing, and nothing more. Carla was not interested in introducing a "virgin" to the lesbian life or dealing with problems that might arise as a result. What's more, she was in the military and soon would leave Texas. I credit her duly for clear-sightedness. I never saw or spoke to her again. But the memory and emotions of my virgin experience and the wonders that came with it remained.

Burning Building

Ninth Spiritual Death

In August 1993, I completed my bachelor's degree, graduating cum laude with my parents attending. I was the first in our clan to attain a 4-year degree.

Soon after, I exchanged the sizeable Plymouth for a small, black Isuzu pickup truck and resigned from the computer peripheral company to take a job with the Express-News. I aimed for work as a journalist. Although I applied as a proofreader, the only job available in the newsroom at the time, a manager phoned to acknowledge receipt of my application. She said my credentials warranted a different and higher-paying position and referred me to a supervisor in the display advertising department. I called him and learned he was developing a prototypical position that, if successful, would pioneer creation of a new department. Although the work was not connected with the newsroom, the salary plus commission and performance bonuses were appealing and the task challenging, so I took the job.

My title was inside sales/display advertising account executive. My job was pitching display advertising in the newspaper over the phone. These were not classified ads. Display ads were a coveted form of high-dollar advertising historically assigned to seasoned advertising account executives who met with clients in person. This had never before been attempted at the paper, to sell expensive large ads to major clients by phone. But there I sat at a corner desk with my phone, within an intimidating and expansive wide-open sales room filled with desks and aggressive spit-shined Bohemian salespeople. One woman dressed in vintage skirts, period hats and high heels, while another wore wigs and thick makeup. Many of the men looked quite standard in suits and shiny leather shoes. These folks chased after and competed for premium newspaper advertising space that garnered lofty commissions. So the race was on. And now, I, too, was in the thick of it.

In less than a year, I had garnered 200 small-business display ad clients, learned to prepare weekly sales forecasts, and coordinated ad design and contracts for time and budget commitments with the art production and billing departments. Together, my boss and I created a new section in the paper called the "Home Improvement Guide" targeting home aftermarket in which small businesses could buy less-expensive space within the context of a full-page ad. The concept took off like lightening. Small businesses flocked to the Guide and leapt at signing a long-term contract.

That first year, I became a respected member of the display advertising team. But I was not content in the job; I aimed to work as a journalist. It was widely known, except to me then, that historically advertising people considered journalists smug and journalists considered advertising types unethical. So like oil and water, the two did not mix. But I was determined. One day, I would be on the other side of that discord. One day, despite traditional attitudes, I would be a journalist.

Two days before Christmas, I was fast asleep in my second-story condo, with Cristi on the floor and Priti next to me. At 3 in the morning, all three of us were jolted awake by loud voices outside. I bolted from bed and looked out the bedroom window onto the courtyard but saw nothing. I scurried to the front door to look through the peep hole but saw not the porchlight gleaming but dense blackness. Suddenly, someone pounded ferociously on my door, yelling, "Everyone out! The building is on fire!"

Gripped in terror and wearing nothing but a tee-shirt and boxers, with Cristi pacing and whining and Priti nowhere in sight, I removed the security chain and unlocked and opened the front door slightly. As soon as I did, a tsunami of thick black smoke poured inside. And nearly as quickly, a figure looking like a spaceman pushed the door all the way open, grabbed me around the waist, lifted me up and tight next to him and carried me quickly down the open stairwell. He let me down gently on my bare feet on the freezing sidewalk. A few feet in front of me were long fierce tongues of flame hungrily licking the cold night air from inside the downstairs condo across from Nancy's and firemen buzzing about.

Stepping carefully around them, their hoses and equipment, I ambled toward the parking lot, where there I spotted Nancy in her blue sedan and Cristi in the back seat. She frantically waved me toward them. I went quickly and clambered into the passenger seat. Poor Nancy sat in distress in her thin light blue nightgown, mumbling something about the fire and shaking her head. Cristi was wide-eyed and antsy, and there was I, too, freezing, barely clothed, in shocked panicked fright. A person's mind cannot grasp such a thing. That I was fast asleep one minute and being carried from a burning building the next was unconscionable. But it was happening. I was bewildered and speechless. I had no control over anything that was happening and no clue as to what had caused the fire or whether it was harming my home. All I could do was shiver and shake my head in dazed disbelief.

It took a while for firefighters to douse the flames and clean up the mess on the sidewalk and stairwell. When they finished, they told me I would have to evacuate my condo until it was cleared of smoke and approved for occupancy again. The fire had not harmed it. I was given only a few minutes to gather what I needed—clothes, personal items, shoes, a coat and my dog (still unable to find my cat)—and then spent the rest of the night at a hotel. I have forgotten parts of that horrid night. But I remember the wake-up call to fire. The flames lapping out of the window below. And the blonde firefighter who after the dust settled removed his head gear, revealing his handsome face. I thanked him profusely for saving me, my "knight in shining armor" for sure. All he said with complete humility and a soothing smile was, "You're welcome."

Apparently, amid the chaos, someone obtained my name and telephone number, because all the right people contacted me, beginning with my insurance company. The agent had filed a claim on my behalf, told me my condo had sustained smoke damage, and I was not to worry about hotel expenses because I would be reimbursed. The agent explained a professional restoration company would clean and clear my condo for reentry within a few days. In the meantime, I slept a few hours at the hotel that night, then took a shower, dressed, left Cristi in her kennel and reported to work by 9:30 a.m., roughly six hours after the fire.

My boss listened with astonishment as I recounted what had happened and then said I should not have come to work. But the ads I had sold to my clients were pending processing that day, a Thursday, for publication on Friday, and I would not be able to rest until I took care of it. I finished my work and then returned to the hotel and slept. I returned to work the following Monday.

When I was able to go home, I was happy to find the restoration company had done a thorough job. I could not smell smoke at all and nothing was damaged. They had cleaned the walls, carpet, floors and furniture. They had taken my clothes to be cleaned and returned them to my closet. They had found Priti hiding in my clothes closet, understandably shaken and withdrawn. Nancy and I later learned the fire had been set by a "John" who took revenge on a hooker who lived in the unit set afire and who was the niece of the man who owned it. The John-turned-arsonist had set the mattress aflame while the hooker was gone and then left, obviously never considering the rest of us in the three adjoining units. It wasn't long after that the woman moved out. Goodness gracious, we had not known she was a prostitute. We did think it odd, however, that she wore a fur coat in summer.

Shortly after the fire, Nancy presented me with a scroll inscribed with "Desiderata," written beautifully in 1927 by the American writer Max Ehrmann and spiritually inspiring. I framed the encouraging words, which graced the wall of my home then as now. Every time I look at the poetry, I remember that ill-fated fire, my escape, and with deep fondness, Nancy.

Aside from work with the newspaper, I continued experimenting with my attraction for women. I did not tell a soul, from the time I met Carla till this point in time, now two years later. I frequented gay bars to dance and meet other women like me and on one such night met a deputy sheriff. I cannot say my experience with her was memorable, but I experienced something with her I would never ever forget. Because she knew of my insatiable curiosity, she offered me the chance to accompany her in her patrol car on a Friday night. Her assigned area of the city was northeast. That quadrant had a bad reputation on Friday nights for crime, which she said was saturated heavily with domestic violence. After instructing me to stay in the car whenever she left the vehicle to approach someone during a call, we hit the road. From 7 p.m. to 5 a.m. I saw some disturbing things.

On one domestic-violence call, she and local police converged at a house from where a woman had frantically phoned for help. Her husband was drunk and threatening her with a butcher knife, as three small kids looked on. I watched from the passenger seat as the deputy sheriff and other cops entered the house, handcuffed the man, escorted him outside and put him inside a patrol car. Meanwhile, a female officer spoke with the woman and her children. Later that night, we answered a call about a high-speed chase on Interstate 10 on the city's northwest side. It was exhilarating and terrifying to speed down the highway while bracing myself with both hands on the dash as lights flashed and sirens screamed. The car we chased finally came to a stop on the shoulder of the highway and the cops subdued the driver, thus ending the scarry pursuit without mishap.

Around 4:30 a.m. we headed southeast on Highway 87 toward China Grove when we came upon an oasis of flashing lights around the scene of a wreck. Ambulances, police cars and a Ford Bronco sat on the side of the road, and ahead of them, an abandoned 18-wheeler. As we passed the Bronco I asked my friend to drive slowly past the open driver-side door where inside were two women, each bent over the other across the front seat. What struck me most then and has remained with me since was their motionless. I could not take my eyes off the two stock-still bodies.

To this day, I do not know why I was held spellbound by the scene of these two now gone from this life forever. I do not remember seeing blood. Perhaps my mind or memory shielded me from it. Perhaps my brain knew that after having seen my brother's head trauma I could not withstand seeing another like it. We learned it was a mother in her early 50s and her daughter in her 30s. They had been driving toward home at about 50 miles per hour along 87, which back then was a paved narrow 2-lane road with scant lighting, when without warning they crashed into the back of a parked unlit semi. The rig sat abandoned in the Bronco's lane without lights or orange cones or any type of cautionary warning indicating it was at a standstill. I later wondered, were the Bronco's headlights on? Had the women been drinking? Were they chatting and not paying attention to the road ahead of them?

I stopped seeing the deputy sheriff but decided to tell my parents I was gay.

Out and Up

I remember the day I told Mama and Daddy. I had waited two years to be sure. I didn't want to hurt them by telling them sooner and then deciding I was not gay after all.

It happened to be springtime when I shared my secret. A new lifestyle for me was in its infancy, a new year was underway and it was spring, when everything was new. So in the early spring of 1994, Mama and I were on one of our walks together in the neighborhood where I grew up and where she and Daddy still lived. After my divorce, I had spent many a weekend with them and we were accustomed to doing things we normally did. Mama had mapped out a mile-and-a-half route, which we followed that day.

As we walked, I mulled over how I would tell her and the words I would use. But all of a sudden, I chirped, "I'm gay." We both stopped short. She looked squarely at me with the beginnings of an uncomfortable smile, as if her lips and mouth were pushed into it against their will. "You're kidding," she said, emphasis on "kidding," as her voice dipped to signal finality. "No, I'm not kidding," I said with a smile, as if she, too, should be glad. Mama was stunned. "Betty Lou! Are you serious?"

Admittedly, I shivered at divulging the skeleton in the closet I had hidden so long. But I was convinced this new me was who I was and wanted to be, and even though I was not entirely comfortable with it, I was living it. So despite any hesitancy and despite any pushback or expressed concerns made to me by my parents or anyone else, I went through with it. Telling my parents, siblings, and a few adult nieces and nephews was the first step in revealing myself. But I did not tell the world or my workplace. I did not confide in friends except a few. I understood not only was there disapproval by the world at-large of this unorthodox lifestyle but there was hatred for those in it. And I believed this marked the start of a lasting distance between my sisters and me, especially the eldest and youngest.

One Sunday afternoon, I visited my parents. They sat me down, together, as they had done before I married 20 years earlier, and softly, lovingly, told me what they thought of my news. Daddy opened. "Betty Lou, we think you are ill and you need help." My response was polite and with a smile I explained I was not ill and knew what I was doing. They quickly realized as they had 20 years before there were no words they could speak I would hear. They did, however, make it clear they would not accept my bringing home a female date. We two would not be welcome as a couple.

I understood their worry. I grew up in a loving home with a mother and father who wed for life and believed in and worshiped the God of the Holy Bible. I believed in God, but I was not ready to take Scripture as literal life instruction. How could I, given my lifestyle? I studied passages in Scripture that spoke of homosexuality and bent the meaning to suit me. And I kept living my life as a gay woman. Deep down inside was a whispered omen that sometimes accompanied decisions I made, but as usual I let the whispers rise and fall, without paying much attention to the hints. I simply swept them neatly aside, I put them away, somewhere even deeper from where they came from, as easily as I put away folded laundry or groceries.

I did agree at my mother's request to meet with a priest who had been at St. Benedict when I attended elementary school. He welcomed me warmly and then we discussed my living a homosexual life. He was tender but firm and told me homosexuality is not God's will for anyone, and that as long as I chose to engage and participate in an intimate sexual relationship with other women I would continue to live in sin. I graciously accepted his counsel but disagreed with it and went about my way. I believed, and do, that God loves everyone straight or gay, but after that meeting, I experienced a small but recognizable question mark in my mind about whether I was living in sin. I didn't like the idea much.

Primarily, I focused on my ad sales job but spent the next year looking for a way to move to the newsroom. Meanwhile, I took advantage of the lucrative perks of working hard at the paper. When I surpassed forecasted sales, I was rewarded with a cash bonus and courtesy tickets to cultural events. Through these stipends, I often enjoyed the San Antonio Symphony and Broadway plays at the historic Majestic Theater in the heart of a bustling downtown. On one such evening during the Christmas holidays, I treated myself and a girlfriend to Handel's Messiah.

Finally, I found a way to leave advertising: by way of the marketing department in research. Research helped ad execs close sales, but it also supported joint projects between marketing and the newsroom. Predictably, employees were hired to staff the new department I had pioneered, which I eagerly left to begin my new post as market research analyst. In my new job, I poured over data, created presentations aimed at helping ad execs and taught them how to use the researched-backed presentations to close deals.

My involvement in advertorials, those short stories promoting a sponsor through ad-aimed editorial, led to a writing assignment. I researched and wrote a story about the Texas Open for the paper's monthly tourism magazine, Fiesta. As part of my research, I took golf lessons to learn the game so my story would be infused with firsthand understanding; I learned to putt and once played nine holes of golf. And I interviewed golf pros at 10 of San Antonio's most beautiful and challenging golf courses. "The Never-ending Story: Year-round Golf in San Antonio" was published with my byline in Fiesta in October 1995. The publishing of that advertorial sparked in me a growing knowing I was meant to be a writer.

Also in 1995, the World Wide Web premiered, evolving the internet from mostly a research tool into a commercial marketing platform, complete with interactive features and imagery. The Express-News and most mainstream mass media jumped on the web bandwagon readily. I served on a companywide 100-person integrated team to coordinate marketing initiatives across the newspaper to launch its website, and collaborated with information technology and marketing staff to create online reader surveys and implement promotional contests for readers. A fortunate and exciting byproduct was engaging with the newsroom.

One afternoon, I attended a luncheon with the paper's editorial staff and sat at a table next to an editor of the Express-News's weekly neighborhood papers, the Suns. The Suns were a collection of five mini neighborhood papers, each one dedicated to a quadrant of the city. As the Suns editor and I chatted, I informed her of my zeal for writing and interest in writing for the paper. In her smug response, she informed me I "would never work in a newsroom without a journalism degree." After resurrecting my flattened ego and eating the chocolate mousse ahead of my salad, I decided beyond a shadow of doubt whatsoever I would prove her wrong.

I worked another two years in the marketing department, all the while remembering the Suns editor's inadvertent dare. Meanwhile, I designed and ordered 500 business cards for a freelance writing enterprise, "Writer for Hire." Printed on white stock with red lettering, the cards displayed a cowgirl in boots and hat drawing a dripping pen from her holster pointed toward a slogan that read, "If it's worth saying, it's worth saying well." On the card, I advertised every conceivable type of communique for which I had attained proficiency or was interested in exploring. These included advertising and marketing copy, business and technical writing, and customer and employee communication. I handed the cards out to everyone I knew and met, soliciting every assignment I could muster.

In May of 1997, I resigned from my full-time post at the paper to make my mark as an independent freelance writer. I was on my way out and up. I said goodbye to the marketing department and marched with business cards tucked in my pocket to the newsroom, where with some consternation I knocked on the open office door of the S.A. Life lifestyles editor. She sat at her desk with eyes fixed on her computer screen and fingers busily tapping a keyboard.

Front Page News Against All Odds

After announcing myself and extending my card, I was invited by the S.A. Life editor to take a seat opposite her desk. She got right down to business, asking pointed questions I answered promptly.

"How can I help you?"

"I worked in advertising and marketing and want to write for the paper."

"Have you written for a newspaper? Have you published anything?"

"I published a piece on the Texas Open in the October 1995 Fiesta."

After chewing on my plea barely a minute, the editor returned her gaze to her computer screen, tapped a few keys and then handed me a paper as it exited her desktop printer. "We get suggestions for articles from our readers all the time," she told me. "Here is one about anthem singers. I'd like you to interview at least six people who sing the anthem acapella at sports events, write an 800-word article and get back to me in two weeks."

Yes ma'am! In handing me that piece of paper, she handed me the chance to prove myself. I now was officially a freelance writer with my first assignment from a newsroom editor. And by the way, I had no journalism degree. And she never asked me whether I did. I assured her I would follow up and left. Only a few minutes after ending my full-time job with the paper I had landed an assignment as a newsroom contributor. I was going to work hard on this story. I would pour 100 percent of myself into it. I was not going to give anything less than all of me. She gave me the gamble I had asked for and I took her trust earnestly.

I headed home to set about the task at hand with blind faith in myself. My research was deep and wide. I uncovered not six but more than a dozen trained singers in San Antonio who ranged in age from 9 to 50 and belted out the anthem acapella at basketball, hockey and baseball games and other popular events. They were hopeful-newcomers-turned-discovered performers, members of church choirs and the military, contemporary Christian singers, professional singers with music careers, and even a pharmaceutical representative who sang the national anthem in front of thousands of sports fans for the sheer thrill of it. And all of them were eager to appear in my article.

When learning my research spanned wider than anticipated, the editor approved the story at 1,200 words versus 800, extended my deadline, and assigned a staff photographer to capture and compliment my feature in pictures. On Friday, July 18, 1997, the Express-News published my story, "For a Song," on the cover of S.A. Life with my byline, accompanied by numerous full-color photographs. What's more, I was paid for it, and the Texas Associated Press picked up the story and published it across the state in other major dailies.

 I was beyond overjoyed and highly encouraged by this triumphant first byline try. I could not help but think back to the dispiriting Suns editor. Not only had I earned a place among the newsroom and ranks of published writers, but the S.A. Life editor and various Suns editors hired me to write additional stories over ensuing months. My long-held and learned belief set afire in me by the spitfire of a colonel in the Office of Innovation, who taught me I could do anything I set my mind to, was armor-plated now. The verve stirring in me was an explosive Roman candle that set off a longing in me for more of everything.

Me and Daddy: A Dream Come True Tale

Throughout 1996 in frequent visits with my parents, our conversations often turned to Daddy's homemade barbecue sauce. Countless people, me among them, insisted he sell it in stores. It was that good. So on a visit one autumn day, I told them I believed in Daddy's sauce and that he should market it to the whole barbecue-sauce-eating world. And then quickly I followed with, "I will help you do it."

The sauce Daddy cooked in a tin can on the riverbank at 12 was the start of a lifelong dream. After the war, when in his 20s, he worked at a barbecue sandwich shop in downtown San Antonio and fancied having one like it. One afternoon, a tall weedy man carrying a guitar came in begging a cup of coffee. Daddy obliged and added a sandwich for the then struggling country singer. A few years later, Porter Wagoner mainlined the Grand Ole Opry. And decades after that, Daddy's dream would come true, too, with me alongside him.

On Oct. 28, 1996, I emailed an H-E-B executive I had met through a colleague asking how to get Daddy's sauce into stores. She suggested I call its headquarters and ask for the category manager who buys that product type. I did and learned of a specialty food buyer by the name of Tidwell. In mid-February 1997, I wrote him a detailed letter introducing Daddy and his sauce and requesting a meeting with us to taste it. A month passed without word, so I began phoning and leaving messages every three weeks.

That spring, as I dove into producing the article that would become "For a Song," I sustained dogged pursuit of Mr. Tidwell month after month. What possessed me to volunteer more time to work hard on something I could not afford taking on was pure faith. Possessed by a strong unwavering belief in my goals and marketing savvy and Daddy's delicious barbecue sauce, I was eager to be both a freelance writer and an entrepreneur of a food manufacturing business. What I did not have, however, was money in the bank. I had no employment income except freelance stipends I would earn with anticipated publication of my hatching work and no health insurance. But I believed Daddy's barbecue sauce was better than anything else available in stores or restaurants.

I did not know what I was taking on. I did not know how to go about getting Daddy's sauce from the kitchen stove to the consuming market or the myriad legal and regulatory steps in-between. But I did know this: I had learned from the Office of Innovation, the real estate property management firm, and the publishing opportunity with the Express-News I was capable, resourceful and tenacious. I had learned fathoms about marketing and market research. I had attained an undergraduate degree that gave me the understanding of the science and art of communication and I was unafraid of hard work.

Throughout May and into June, I hammered out my first article for the Express-News while plunging head-first into the hoped-for public launch of my father's barbecue sauce. Anticipating a meeting with the food buyer, I wondered, where to begin. I remembered the 1939 Academy Award-winning movie, "Wizard of Oz," which we grew up watching on TV. Every fall, we all ran home from playing outside in the coming dusk to flock to TV sets to watch the magical characters come to full-color life. In the scene where after Dorothy's tornado-swept house landed in Munchkin Land, Glenda, the Good Witch, offered Dorothy sound wisdom about beginning her journey to Oz: "It's always best to start at the beginning." And so, Dorothy set out on a daring trek by taking her first step on the yellow-brick road. Simple enough. All I need do, is begin.

As Daddy experimented with a jalapeno-flavored version of his original recipe, I took pictures of him in his barbecue apron and Stetson outside my parents' home for use on the label. Mama and Daddy both wanted "Country Style" on the label as well as the slogan, "A True Texas Sauce." We agreed to call it Daddy's Country Style BBQ Sauce after discourse around "Guck's." I suggested we use Dom Casual font for our trademark name as it complimented the country image we wanted and my parents agreed. I asked a friend in the Express-News art department who freelanced to create for us mock labels for the original and jalapeno flavors using the picture of Daddy I had taken and the brand name we had chosen, all set in front of a red outline of the state of Texas. And I sustained follow-ups with Mr. Tidwell to secure a meeting.

Meanwhile, I researched how to start a food manufacturing business. I ordered the "Guide to Starting Your Business" from the San Antonio Economic Development Department and a "Business Tax Kit" from the Internal Revenue Service. I drafted a business and marketing plan, outlining every conceivable aspect of a new enterprise. Little did I know this legwork would profit me elsewhere later.

Finally, on July 1, Daddy and I met with Mr. Tidwell at H-E-B corporate headquarters. My father wore his iconic apron and Stetson, as shown on the mock labels of his sauces, which I taped to tall, filled mason jars. We carried with us a loaf of fresh bread, paper plates and napkins. Mr. Tidwell took a slice of bread, poured the sauce labeled original onto a plate, sopped his bread in it, ate, smacked his lips and smiled, telling us how tasty it was. Then he excitedly tasted the jalapeno sauce, when his delight shined across his face as he sopped a second helping. I asked, "On a scale of 1 to 10, 10 being best, how do you rate Daddy's sauce?" We were particularly pleased to hear, "At least an 8, especially the jalapeno! It's awesome!"

In the next breath, Mr. Tidwell asked if we could provide the products by September in a quantity enough to test-market the sauces by stocking 11 local stores, including the one near Mama and Daddy's house and the one in Boerne. He said he would select the stores by rankings for highest premium barbecue sauce sales. He asked we stock each store with four facings, that is, two rows each of the original and jalapeno, and keep them stocked throughout the 2-month test. He also suggested we demonstrate the products in all 11 stores during test-marketing to give customers a chance to sample them, and agreed with us that instead of hired promoters we would do the demos ourselves.

Daddy and I were not at all sure about the short-fuse deadline but agreed to it. We left that meeting walking on air and could not wait to get home and tell Mama the news, all the while knowing we had only two months to get organized, and get the products manufactured, bottled, labeled and distributed to the 11 locations. We hadn't even secured the legal company name yet, or the capital or partnership. Once home, we three sat around the small breakfast table and hungrily gabbed about the sauce, wondering what else to include on the label. Together, we wrote a short prefatory note to appear on it along with Daddy's signature: "Around our house, we eat barbecue sauce like gravy. Spoon a big helping onto your plate, pour it over your meat and sop your bread in it. Try it, you'll like it."

Throughout July, my research escalated with phone queries to the Texas Comptroller's Office, Texas Department of Agriculture, Texas Department of Health, U.S. Copyright Office of the Library of Congress in Washington D.C., Uniform Code Council and an insurance company to gather requirements. I met with the local office of the U.S. Small Business Administration (SBA) through which I learned a company named Creative Foodworks may be our needed production partner to manufacture and bottle Daddy's sauce. This small-label producer in San Antonio would take Daddy's homemade recipe from stovetop to a 120-gallon vat and from there bottle and box our products.

There were endless details to attend to. I wrote a Request for Quote to use to query potential printers of our labels. In it, I specified color options scaled from one- to four-color processing, color and type of glossy or non-glossy stock, paper grain direction and weight and other details, including heat-resistance and more.

About this time, Mama and Daddy recruited Jo Ann to contribute capital and manpower to help with distribution, stocking and demos, along with administration. My parents wanted to be directly involved in the recipe and tastings but not in operations, all of which my sister and I would run. Our business meetings commenced. By July 28, I had finalized the business and marketing plan that detailed the official launch and growth of Daddy's Country Style BBQ Sauce.

The plan included initial distribution and sales projections for the 2-month test-market, estimating sales of 20 cases per day and identifying us as the ones to distribute and stock the 11 stores weekly and conduct demos. It identified our company name and logo; partners and percentages of ownership; product identifications; licenses and registrations; identification of competition with labeling and pricing; and identification of our label's graphic artist and label contents, Uniform Product Code (barcode) specifications, legal ingredients and nutritional requirements. It also identified a label printer Jo Ann offered, bottling specifications to distinguish Daddy's from the competition, manufacturing and production data provided by our partnership with Creative Foodworks, and future forecasts for sales projections, along with targeted sales venues such as other grocery store chains, tourist shops, festivals, trade shows and large-scale food companies.

It also detailed advertising ideas including a company website, packaging operations with gift and condiment packets, and sections itemizing operating expenses, working capital assistance (business loan resources), and bookkeeping criteria. It identified optimal seasons for food sales, potential for spoilage, and whether to enter the industrial-size market, such as scaling up to sell gallons of sauce to wholesale customers.

Jo Ann established our P.O. Box, bank account and accounting system, and finalized license paperwork. She and Daddy scaled his original sauce recipe to a gallon size to help expedite our first batch. On July 30, we four partners registered a Doing Business As or DBA with the Bexar County Courthouse, County Clerk's Office, as Daddy's Country Style BBQ Sauce. As we signed that document we witnessed Daddy's dream coming to life.

I then researched and created templates our business may need, including a partnership capital investment agreement, letter of agreement for distributors and promissory note. Finally, on Aug. 12, Daddy, Mama, my sister and I signed a partnership agreement. Each of us funded the venture with a meager capital investment apiece, enough to get started and meet initial projections identified in the business plan. None of us would draw compensation for our work until the business was launched and profitable.

On Aug. 13, my friend the graphics artist began work on formal label artwork. On Aug. 14, I met with the Texas Department of Agriculture, joined its Taste of Texas program on behalf of our business and secured Taste of Texas logo slicks to add to our labels, thus gaining international exposure through the department's global marketing outreach. On Aug. 18, Roger's birthdate, we four partners reviewed the first pass of the formal label artwork when Daddy and Mama added Aug. 19, their wedding anniversary, as the "established" date.

On Aug. 19, Daddy's Country Style BBQ Sauce signed an agreement with Creative Foodworks to manufacture original and jalapeno products to Daddy's terms. On that day, the manufacturer cooked a 20- to 30-gallon taster for Daddy's approval, and once he gave the nod, we placed our order for the first 160 cases. On that same day, I mailed a letter to my remaining three siblings advising of our business venture, inviting them to contribute capital as a loan we would repay with interest and enclosing a promissory note should they wish to join us. None did.

On Aug. 21, with label artwork slicks in hand, Jo Ann engaged a vendor to print labels. Meanwhile, for distribution at demos, I created and printed 200 leaflets in colors that complimented our brand that spotlighted the history behind Daddy's Country Style BBQ Sauce and introduced Daddy. H-E-B anticipated we would sell 20 cases per day during demos, which we would conduct in 3 or 4 of the 11 stores each weekend, accounting for sale of 160 cases in two weeks or less. On Aug. 28, Jo Ann and I began distributing the two sauce labels to the designated 11 stores and stocking shelves for test-marketing, with my nieces pitching in to help with pre-dawn deliveries. We had met the food buyer's deadline!

Throughout September and October, we as a family and partnership conducted onsite product demos in the 11 stores, with Daddy on hand wearing the apron and Stetson as shown on his sauce labels and autographing bottles for shoppers. Jo Ann and I dressed in red aprons to dispense tastings. Customers were smitten by the red gravy and the man on the label standing by as they took a taste, and were eager to pay $2.69, a premium price in 1997, for a bottle of Daddy's premier barbecue sauce.

Daddy may not have fulfilled his initial dream of opening a barbecue sandwich shop, but his barbecue sauce was for sale in H-E-B, the largest grocery store chain in Texas. I reveled in watching my father surrounded by admirers sampling the sauce we had grown up eating. Even men who made their own preferred Daddy's. I never once thought of whether the business would boom, although I took it for granted it would. My gratification came in seeing, and knowing, my father had attained at least part of a lifelong vision; I felt happy at laying the foundation that made it happen. The test-market proved a success and the grocery giant wanted more. Production and distribution continued and grew.

In November, I began contacting wholesale prospects to gauge interest in gallon sizes, starting with Blue Ribbon, a sausage company, and McDonald's. I met with a tourist shop downtown at the highly trafficked corner of Crockett and Blum streets in Alamo Plaza to pitch decorated bottles at a premium price as specialty items. The store seized the idea and soon we partners decorated the bottles for delivery. This win led to my placing additional queries with other well-trafficked specialty shops and cafes, including the popular Guenther House, Guitars and Cadillacs, Williams-Sonoma and others. Daddy's Country Style BBQ Sauce had arrived, a winning hit with a limitless future. But trouble was cooking.

By November's end, five months after Daddy and I had met with Mr. Tidwell, family arguments primarily between my eldest sister and I ensued. She had not taken part in the foundational research or arduous startup work to launch the business and secure critical contacts, particularly with H-E-B, yet increasingly asserted her will, which caused conflicts between us two and among my parents and me. I also grew concerned about what I considered unprofessional behavior, including open use of profanity while demonstrating our products in stores; leaving demos early, which overburdened me; and neglecting to restock some stores for which my sister was accountable. During family business meetings, my sister sometimes used derisive language I found offensive, disrespectful and intolerable. Admittedly, I contributed to the tension. There were times I overreacted to situations I could have handled better. My overreactions had more to do with feeling all the work I had done was unappreciated; I had devoted most of my time over many months to the launch of the barbecue sauce business at a time when I was unemployed and in financial straits.

I could not abide the growing tension in our meetings and inside myself. I felt increasingly distressed about my cherished relationship with my parents because of the arguing and strain. And the stocking efforts in stores had begun to deliver noticeable wear-and-tear to my lower back. I considered leaving the partnership and having no part in its future success. But before taking leave, I wrote a product demo proposal for the H-E-B Demonstrations and Procurement departments that laid the groundwork for Daddy's Country Style BBQ Sauce to partner with sausage manufacturers on in-store product demos from New Year's through Easter. This would continue the momentum we had begun with the test-market and secure at least one local sausage company's commitment. Supplemental to the proposal, I outlined a tentative schedule for the 52 demos across six months in the original 11 stores we had test-marketed.

On Dec. 20, 1997, 14 months after my first outreach to H-E-B, I advised my parents and sister I was divesting myself of the business and why. It was a heartbreaking decision but the right one. I reminded my parents they were in good hands with the business relations I had formed and foundational documentation I had provided, including a comprehensive business and marketing plan. All they and my sister need do was follow the plan, keep in contact with stores, court new customers and stock shelves.

I notified H-E-B and other associates I was leaving the concern to pursue a writing career but ensured them the remaining partners would foster the relations we had established. I took with me the certain knowing I had created a company from scratch, and Daddy and I had effectively marketed his product to food-store giant H-E-B, a major retailer most said was tough if not impossible to penetrate. To my sister's credit, she grew the business over the next few years to the extent Daddy's sauce was in 242-plus H-E-B stores statewide.

In the early 2000s, an unexpected international opportunity surfaced as the Texas Department of Agriculture continued marketing Daddy's sauce. After tasting it, food buyers from the United Kingdom wanted to test his products overseas. Sadly, my sister declined pursuing the prospect on Daddy's behalf, citing other obligations. So, Mama and Daddy turned to me, twice asking I return and help them follow this international lead, but politely and sadly I declined. I knew we could do the work and succeed. But I explained I had attained full-time employment and much-needed income that I was not able or willing to sacrifice, and a loving bond with my parents was most important to me.

By the time the barbecue sauce had enjoyed a 10-year run, the relationships I had pioneered and my sister had fostered trickled, after my father's unexpected illness. Daddy's Country Style BBQ Sauce faded quietly into history. But no one can deny it made a prominent impression while it lived. I believe had the business been pursued without letup, it would have become a million-dollar baby. Even now, as our family keeps Daddy's proprietary sauce recipe under wraps, as we continue to cook it on our stovetops for special occasions or no particular reason except to enjoy it, as we tell the story about how Daddy's sauce was on H-E-B shelves across Texas for 10 years and courted by Europe, people ask even now where they can buy Daddy's tasty barbecue sauce.

Daddy and his barbecue sauce had enjoyed the Big Time. My writing career was promising and on the rise. But my private life was in turmoil.

The Duplicitous Face of Abuse

Tenth Spiritual Death

Sometimes large doses of benign dysfunction mixed with equally large doses of imposed emphatic religion can produce a maverick in a child, a child who can become an equally dysfunctional adult—until, if and when that individual undergoes radical transformation. Or dies.

Lynn said once, "You know what your problem is, Betty Lou? You're an idealist." I didn't know his meaning then and in truth it angered me when he said it. But I realize now an idealist is a deeply sensitive soul who needs the real world to be not as it is but as it should be. And I realize idealism can be fatal; some of the world's most gifted idealists have taken their own lives. For some, this world will never be livable.

In my case, despite conditions telling me otherwise, I saw only what I wanted to see in relationships I picked and suffered through, until finally once and for all I was forced by those same conditions to see what was real, and what I saw was far from ideal. On the one hand, I still craved a loving marriage that would last a lifetime. Back then, I thought marriage to a woman foundationally was the same as marriage to a man. Both were lifelong commitments. I still held to the ideal of marriage my parents had exemplified in theirs. But on the other hand, I chased after would-be partners who were noncommittal, unreliable, selfish, dishonest and emotionally unavailable. Naturally, I did not see them that way, at first, through my idealistic lens.

Going back to the idea that idealism can be fatal, some of the most tumultuous years of my personal life took place when I was between the ages of 41 and 50, when I was in two successive relationships with women in which I was intent on making something ideal out of something sick. The last straw came when the second of these two relationships ended abruptly after my father died. When I found myself the willing victim of spewing hatred and on the fringes of dialing 911 for rescue from domestic violence. When I found myself in counseling with the Battered Women's Shelter. When I found myself teary and scared in a meeting for families and friends of alcoholics. That is when I knew I was ready to climb out of the idealistic hole I had dug myself into. I aimed not to live the next 50 years as I had the first 50.

The first of these two relationships was with Muriel. We met three years after I told my family I was gay. She was an educated professional in an executive job, smart and pretty. I learned later she came from a broken home with an alcoholic father who came from an alcoholic home and a mother who was a domineering force. Although she never spoke of it, I believed, based on vague inferences, that she may have been sexually abused at home when young and carried that cavernous wound secretly inside her. In the end, I would conclude this fueled her incapacity for, and even combatant comportment against, emotional intimacy.

Our years together were a time of duplicity. We attended parties and hosted them. Went dancing and to dinner. Camped, fished and traveled. We even purchased a tract of prime Texas Hill Country acreage one-half mile from the Guadalupe River where we planned to build a home. But we argued and the spats intensified. The primary reason for quarreling was that while I was open with my family about Muriel's place in my life, she kept our relationship a deep secret from her mother. She referred to me as her roommate not partner and kept her distance from me whenever in her mother's company. When I asked about it, she refused to discuss it, telling me one day she would tell her mother. When I explained that her indifference toward me in her mother's presence was hurtful, phony, pretentious, she became incensed and shut herself off in another room.

I believed then as now two people in a relationship ought to talk through problems and come to some agreeable solution both people can live with. I needed to understand her dilemma. To feel included, respected, acknowledged. She refused to talk about it but I begged for it. Muriel's withdrawal was extremely hard for me to endure emotionally and mentally yet my clinging to her even as she withdrew was as painful. And so it went. She withdrew. I pleaded. Repeat.

Despite our troubles, when Muriel purchased a small house and asked me to move in with her, I sold my condo, profiting double what I had paid for it 10 years earlier, and joined her. I rationalized the profit made the sale smart and the move ideal. But all the while, behind a happy facade in public we quarreled behind closed doors and became increasingly emotionally distant. During this time, I found comfort in the occupation of work. I freelanced as Writer for Hire and obtained a full-time job with the energy utility in San Antonio. I was thrilled to be working full-time as a senior writer, crafting all sorts of articles for the company's magazine and contributing to its photography and design. I was invited into executive discussions around communication strategies about company changes affecting more than 4,000 people, and garnered multiple awards for my technical and creative work. I kept happily occupied working, such that my private life did not drag me into dreadful depression, but its harsh reality loitered in the alcoves of my mind begging for attention. There were times Muriel frightened me.

I learned she had been unfaithful. During arguments about it, which had begun to occupy the lion's share of our time together, I pressed her for the truth but she gave none. She often shut down, refusing to talk or as much as look at me. I was in the room with her but alone. During one argument, she opened the door to a small, narrow closet in the bedroom, closed herself inside it and sat on the floor in a curl in the corner. When I opened the door and cajoled her to come out, she came out swinging. When I was able to stop the fisted whirls, I looked into her eyes. And they were black. Hollow. Empty. It was like looking into the eyes of a lifeless mannequin. It reminded me of my ex-husband. And I remembered he, too, had grown up in an alcoholic home. He, too, was emotionally unavailable and unwilling to discuss anything that mattered. He, too, was not a tender or giving partner.

I soon moved out and refunded her part of the land we had purchased, ecstatic to own it outright. I was not able yet to build a house on the property but I frequented the river, taking Cristi along and inviting friends. I often went there for solace and contemplation. To listen to the wind in the tall cypress trees and cedars. To look at the sun's reflection atop the ripples. To feel elusive peace.

I signed a year's lease on a darling tiny house several miles north of where my condo had been. The one-bedroom, one-bath single-story cottage sat on a half-acre surrounded by live oaks, cedars and quiet. Its scuffed hardwood floors creaked. Scorpions appeared now and then and were easy to spot, light crawlers on dark planks. Cristi and Priti liked to sniff at and try to catch them. The wood-framed windows were weather-worn, stiff and hard to open. But I loved it. I loved its tiny size, the woody smell of the old house, the comfort of the encircling woods, the surrounding stillness and the starlit nights. It was there I first saw the Milky Way.

About a year later, Muriel and I dated again for a short while. But she had not changed. She still went to hell, that place to where she retreated when her eyes went black. And I still wanted what I could not have with her: a mutual emotionally wholesome and faithful relationship. One Friday evening, she drove to my house and planned to stay the weekend. I had arrived home from work earlier and was outside, enjoying the pleasant springtime breeze and thinking of what I would say when she arrived. It was half-past 5. "What are you doing?" came her question as she exited her car and walked toward me. "You look lost in thought." As I turned my eyes toward her, my thoughts kept going in the same direction as before she had arrived. The dipping evening sun made her cropped brown hair shine and her eyes squint when she removed her Ray Bans. "I'm leaving this relationship, for good," I said. "And I think it's best we don't stay in touch."

When the lease expired on the cottage, I bought a 900-square-foot house in the cul-de-sac of a working class neighborhood not far from the railroad tracks and airport. I fixed it up nicely. Crammed every stick of imposing furniture I owned into it. Along with the new house I had a new yearning to know why my life was not turning out like I'd hoped it would. I decided to read the Bible in search of something, of what something I was not sure, and to read it all the way through, beginning with the New Testament. Perhaps enlightenment would come upon finishing the holy book. I still went to gay bars. Spent time with gay friends. Dared pray for a marriage partner thinking she would appear. But I also wanted to know more about God. I wanted to understand this thing called faith. I wanted to know about Christ. I wanted to know more than I had learned at the hands of priests, nuns and religious routine. No, I wanted more than merely to know. I wanted to believe. I wanted to spend time in something different and maybe then I would learn something different, and as a result, have and be something different. All I knew was, I wanted to read the Bible.

So, on Sunday afternoons, with Cristi at my feet and Priti at my side, I sat on my couch that faced the sliding glass doors to my backyard and read the Catholic Bible my parents had given me. I read my way through the black letters and through the red letters and through all the thees and thous. I read and read until I had read all the New Testament and was working my way through the Old.

One Sunday, as I sat reading my Bible, Muriel phoned to ask how I was doing. Admittedly, I wondered at the irony of hearing from her while I was searching for answers. But my resolve to stay apart was resolute and I told her so. Was my thirst for Holy Scripture at play in my newfound liberty from the tyranny of pain and frustration? Was I beginning to wake up to the truth: that I deserved respect and happiness, and maybe I was the one to manifest it for myself rather than chase after it in another person? Perhaps my work life that put me in mutually respectful company of colleagues and clients had shown me I was worthy and capable of satisfying relationships in my personal life, too. One thing I knew for sure: I was sick and tired and finished with pretending something was OK when clearly it was not.

I tried not to think too much, to focus on what gave me joy, such as keeping my yard manicured. The previous owner had been the quintessential gardener and I tried to maintain what she had planted. I was outside frequently and friendly with my neighbors and enjoyed walks with Cristi around the neighborhood.

I did not, however, enjoy the culture. I harbor no prejudice but it was readily apparent I was different than my neighbors, including the ones next door. Our tiny houses were true garden homes with the garage wall of each house forming the backyard boundary between adjoining lots. The house facing my backyard was painted bright blue. Old pickups sat in the driveway and street and the chronic waft of gasoline filled the air. On Saturday nights, some of these neighbors converged in one of their front yards to carouse. I did not imbibe with them. On weekend nights, unless I went out, I tucked myself inside, watched TV and went to bed early. I lived a quiet tame life. During the week, I focused on my job, fit in freelance projects as able, and thought of returning to college for a master's degree.

But no matter what I achieved on the work front or how much of the Bible I read, I still was an emotion junkie. How sick was I, for instance, to find myself one evening sitting in a back row at a funeral for a colleague's father, scoping out women in-between sniffles. Just when I thought I had gotten my head and heart right, I did something absurd like scan a funeral home packed with grieving people for that special someone, or at least that one person I might, maybe, perhaps, be interested in after an initial hello. So, I caught myself in the act, and feeling quite disgusted at my thoughts, redirected my attention to the bereaved colleague.

When the service ended, I walked outside to look up at the new moon and single star shining nearly as brightly, and at that fleeting moment, I had a straight shot at God and I took advantage of it. I said, Thanks. Thanks for my life, for bringing me here, for my wanting to think about, care about the feelings of someone other than myself. And then, I climbed into my Tacoma and drove home. When I arrived, I called my mother in a blurting sensational moment of extreme gratitude for having learned from her and Daddy to go to funerals to support people in pain and mourning. My mother wept at hearing my friend had wept grateful tears at seeing me there and that I had wept with her and that it had felt good to do something selfless, better than if I'd closed a profitable deal or caught a fish.

One Saturday night, I drove to a bar I frequented on those infrequent nights when I went out and on this particular night met someone new. Sara was tall and fit with short blonde hair swept back and a wide white smile. We introduced ourselves to each other at the bar when she asked me to join her and her friends at their table. Sara was friendly but my defenses came out in gentle but no less defensive words. Perhaps I was afraid of liking someone too much too soon and getting hurt again. Perhaps I had not yet learned to be discerning or cautious concerning matters of my heart. Perhaps I still knew only how to navigate relationships at full throttle or not at all and that scared me. My past was a clear reminder. A short time later, when I announced I was leaving, she walked me out and we exchanged phone numbers. Admittedly, I was not smitten. I was curious, though, and lonely. It had been a year since my last affair and I had kept to myself. My life had revolved around work, home, pets and Scripture.

One day, Sara asked me to a party. That night, we returned to her home with a few friends in tow and I stayed the night. With someone. I did not know. When nightcaps were had, the tagging friends bade adieu, leaving us alone. I was yet again plunging into the unknown. I let myself fall while all along I knew, then and there, my heart was not altogether involved. I noticed something else early in our dating. I noticed but did not dissect it for far too long. One evening, Sara came to my house for dinner and that night she asked if she could rearrange a few things. A bit startled, I acquiesced, considering the gesture considerate. But what became clear was my decor was not up to her standard. She reshuffled furniture. Relocated artwork on the walls. Rearranged keepsakes on tabletops and the mantle.

In the weeks ahead, we spent most of our spare time together. Typically, I was the one who initiated, but I began to wish it was not so. The more into it I went, the less my heart followed. One Friday night, we were at my home in the living room. It was a clear evening, with a pleasant breeze wafting in through the front screen door. When the doorbell rang, I answered it to find three sloppily drunk female neighbors on my porch. They each held a tall opened can of beer, their features contorted from too much of it. The women in disjointed unison proceeded to inform me I was not welcome there and slurred out soppily with inebriated venom they wanted me gone. They further informed me never to ever speak to their daughters again. Immediately, I slammed the door in their faces and with trembling fingers secured the deadbolt.

In retrospect, I find it grotesquely peculiar these drunk women were concerned about their teenagers being in the company of a gay woman, yet apparently they gave no consideration whatsoever to the emotional and other untold damage their drunken viciousness was inflicting on their daughters. Until this night, these women had been affable. Their daughters had visited with me in my front yard and played with Cristi. But tonight, their obvious intense hatred was even more petrifying than their hate-filled words. I quickly realized when they saw Sara and me together, hate consumed them, as wholly as their drunkenness. And I was afraid. Afraid of what they might do next. This time was ugly talk through a locked screened door. But what would the next time bring? I believed these women capable of anything.

Sara spoke right up. "Why don't you sell this house and move in with me?" Her words reverberated Muriel's not long before. I had lived in this house barely 18 months. To sell it so soon seemed wrong. Irrational. But it was wrong to wait for what the noxious neighbors may do next. The following week, I phoned the realtor who had sold me the house to ask her to list it for sale, and a buyer came quickly. I moved to Sara's and told myself I had done the right thing.

Her home was twice the size of the house I had sold and in a newer more upscale neighborhood. It had an ample dining room to suit my oak dining table and six chairs and a bedroom to myself where my four-poster pine bed and writing desk fit well. She welcomed Cristi and Priti, too. Once again, I had sold my home to move in with a woman I did not know well. And parts of what I did know I did not like. As the months passed, I realized once again the vision I held in my head for what tender and genuine partnership would look like did not manifest with Sara, just as it had not manifested with Muriel or my former spouse. Like others I chose, she was not gentle or tender. She was not emotionally present. And she was domineering. Yet, I did the very thing I purposed not to do anymore: I pretended. I pretended to be in love. I pretended her selfish nature was OK with me. But I knew in my heart I did not trust her and I did not trust what I was doing with her. A condition such as this is bound to fail. But I did not, not then, think of failure.

Thanksgiving arrived and I got excited about the holiday. I decided to prepare a traditional feast for us two, her brother and his partner, and a friend, Shannah. While the men smoked lamb, I roasted a turkey and cooked all the side fare. I baked six pies from scratch. Cooking, baking and hosting Thanksgiving was a welcome revel. And later that day, several of my nieces and nephews dropped by for dessert. I was delighted at the sight of my dining table crowded with guests. The scene brought me as close to a family gathering as I had known in a while.

But throughout the day, I sensed a close rapport budding between Shannah and Sara. The two of them seemed especially warm toward each other. They laughed openly at each other's jokes, complimented each other with silly flattery and looked at each other often while smiling nonstop. The next day, I went to work. Upon returning home in the early evening, I found the pair sitting next to each other, with Shannah seated at Sara's feet and her arms resting on Sara's legs. While not surprised to see me, their discomfort was noticeable as I walked through the door. Their whitewashed faces signaled deception. I felt an urgent sense of dread, a queasy gut feeling that alerted me to the worst imaginable thing. And now the two of them were trying to hide what could not be hidden. I fumbled through the discomfort, mumbling something mindless in response to meaningless prattle they began to voice while standing up and apart from each other.

That night, behind closed doors in the master bedroom, Sara and I argued. I wanted to know, to hear, the truth, about what she had done in secrecy that now knocked me to the ground emotionally. She denied it. Everything in me disbelieved her. Now in tears, my pain spun into incense, shock and deep hurt. I marched from her bedroom to mine where Shannah lay and confronted her, now yelling. "How could you have done this? How could you dare come to my home and do this, to me?" Her face went blank, emotionless, exhuming ignorance and innocence, but she said nothing except she had done nothing wrong. But I knew. And she knew, I knew. I turned from her in sobs and walked numbly back down the hallway to where Sara lay in bed. I sluggishly climbed in on the opposite side with my back to her, in sickening sorry silence.

The next morning, I lay stone still feigning sleep while Sara dressed and left. After I heard her truck engine turn and fade as she drove away, I rose, groggy and depressed, and walked to my room where Shannah had slept. The door stood open. The bed had been stripped of its linen, which had been laundered and neatly folded and placed on one corner of the bare mattress. And Shannah was gone. She had laundered her way out of nasty betrayal but there was nothing she could do to scrub it from my heart. I never spoke to her again. Meanwhile, Sara and I did not speak of it and our rocky relationship worsened from the wear. I knew action on my part was imminent but I did not know what to do. I turned my attention to other things, to my job and walks with Cristi, but I knew my growing anxiety would not subside till I made a plan. So instead of packing, leasing an apartment and moving, the thought of which overwhelmed me even more than staying, I decided to stay put and busy myself with work and a return to school. Obviously, I was not thinking logically and my decision to stay put would carry with it foul consequences, but Sara was in full support of my plans.

It was around this time Cristi fell ill. She had been diagnosed four years earlier with a mast cell tumor on her right rear leg that when biopsied proved malignant. I had chosen not to subject her to the rigors of debilitating treatments, but as the tumors spread, she lost interest in everything. She paced back and forth across the backyard and stopped eating. One day, she looked up at me, and I knew. She was ready to go. Sara helped me hoist Cristi into my pickup truck and I drove her to the vet. He placed her on an examination table, administered something to calm her, and then left me alone with her to say goodbye. I thought about the times we had laid on the floor in front of the fireplace and silently watched the flames dance, the countless miles we had walked, the squirrels she had chased, the camping trips and swims in the river we had shared. She had been my constant companion for 13 years. And now, all that life and sharing was almost over.

When the vet returned and administered the euthanizing agent, Cristi melted in seconds. The vet kindly delivered her remains to the crematorium and I drove home in tears. The next two days were difficult. I missed my dog. And Priti was growing old at 16. And then the chirpy call came from the crematorium, "Cristi's ready to come home!" I was delighted to be handed a black ceramic urn, not the plain wooden box I had expected. I tucked it close beside me and drove us both home. Cristi had had a happy life.

Turning my attention elsewhere, I indebted myself to student loans and thus began a 2-year graduate program with the University of the Incarnate Word to earn a Master of Arts degree in Communication Arts. I planned to complete the 36 credit hours by fall 2005. My second and final year's challenge would be the all-consuming thesis and I was eager to do it. I believed pouring myself into scholastics would calm my anxiety by redirecting energy away from a yet-again nauseating private life. School seemed my sanctuary. But I was anxious, too, about living with someone untrustworthy. I regretted selling my house. And the condo before it.

Graduate school proved intensely stimulating and hard work. A sweet distraction were the kindred friends I made of classmates. Unlike the undergraduate classes I had taken 10 years prior that hinged on theory, my master's field of study focused on real-world application of mass media communication, including thought-provoking research and literature. I hungered for it and dove in headlong. On the work front, as I became increasingly disinterested in what had become mundane daily details of my job, which I had learned quickly and as quickly out-performed, I received another award. I appreciated the accolade but longed for something fresh. I wanted to scratch the itch in me for the pursuit of greater purpose and I needed to fill the emotional emptiness in me left by a dingy home life. So, I emptied my humanity and that of my subjects into my articles for the energy company. I wrote from the perspective of the human experience not the technical, mechanical or managerial point of view and my work was well-received.

Early in 2004, my cat Priti stopped eating, even refusing water. On the final night, I lay her down next to me and fell asleep. As dawn arrived, I heard my cat meow, release a final breath, and with that, she left. And it was a beautiful experience. Priti died naturally and quietly at the break of day. The day after, Sara and I buried her beneath the shade of a tall cedar at my property in Boerne. In less than a year, I now had said goodbye to my two prized pets who I had loved and cared for since both were tiny.

As Father's Day approached, when I was 49 and Daddy was 81, I wrote an article about him that was published Father's Day weekend. It appeared in the Express-News titled "Through Tough Times of Every Sort, Daddy Never Gave Up," as well as Mama and Daddy's hometown paper, the Gonzales Inquirer, which retitled it "Daughter Fondly Recollects Father's Finest Legacy—Himself." The papers later reported they received outpourings of readers' compliments on the story. And my father shed humble tears at its reading. I would reflect later on this article's timing and know it was by no accident. One month later, as Daddy's 5'11" frame waned to 149 pounds, he complained his food tasted bitter, "like quinine." When his doctor reported a "thing" on his chest, I began taking copious notes concerning his health.

In August that year, Mama and Daddy celebrated 60 years of marriage. As we planned a congratulatory gala inviting a host of friends and relatives to St. Benedict for the event, I drafted the happy declaration for newspapers to print and poured over several hundred family photos, selecting 145 that paid apt tribute. After compiling the snapshots chronologically, I ordered them set to music of the Big Band era in a filmed homage to air at the party and as my gift. I arranged to have a mic on hand for well wishes and on that day led the effort. As I spoke into the mic of reverence for my parents, natural emotion cracked my voice when I observed the gentle swell of tears in Mama and Daddy's eyes, as their fingers fumbled for handkerchiefs. My sisters followed with brief quips of wit.

On Sept. 2, at 3:30 in the morning, hard sobs awakened me from a vivid dream. In it, I had accompanied Mama and Daddy to see St. Benedict's pastor Fr. Eddie's newly built 700-square-foot hall. As it turned out, it was a 700,000-square-foot beige and rose stone structure architected in a half-moon contour that towered 12 stories, spanned a city block, and was garlanded in front by three tall lush green trees. The vision quickly transferred us to Roger and Kelly's house but it did not look like the real one on Prairie Sun. The living room stretched endlessly from the front door to the dining room. My niece Heather sauntered in with her and Jason's first born, Soleil, who was 2 and dressed in a brown plaid business suit, like a miniature executive. She jabbered happily as she strode past me, smacking my backside with her briefcase in jest! Heather sat down next to Soleil who sat next to me, and Heather and I watched as Soleil faced another child, which was Heather's inner child, also 2, and the two 2-year-olds sang a song they both knew.

At what was supposed to be Roger and Kelly's house, its dark paneled interior changed to brightly painted white airy rooms, into which Roger strode. My family seemed unsurprised. He was barefoot wearing faded blue jeans and an untucked plaid cotton shirt. His hair touched his shoulders and the ends were wet as if just out of the shower. He looked a bit pale and had a small white chalky spot on his jaw that covered a shaving nick. He sat down smoothly in a chair. I looked at him, amazed; he is alive! I flung myself on him, buried my head in his neck and sobbed, at which he sweetly whispered, "Don't cry… don't cry." But I could not help but weep. At that, I awakened, still sobbing, feeling the ache of 17 years prior. Hugging Roger felt real, and for hours afterward, the emotions and images lingered.

I pondered the dream's meaning. I supposed Soleil's tiny size and business attire reflected my currently stunted career. The 12-story building and three trees spoke to me of biblical references, to 12 apostles and the three persons of God. And Fr. Eddie had officiated Mama and Daddy's 60th wedding anniversary Mass. In truth, I dreaded my parents' deaths more than I wanted to admit. I did not want to suffer the anguish I had endured through Roger's. But in the dream, Roger's soothing words reassured me upon awakening he lives in spirit.

Two days before Christmas 2004, my father was diagnosed with esophageal cancer and a grim outlook. My stomach churned at the news.

By that time, I had resigned my full-time position with the energy company to research and write my master's thesis, but now I also would become a considerable contributor to my father's healthcare oversight and my mother's consequent need. The ensuing 10 months absorbed in Daddy's declining health, aside my unemployment, graduate studies and deteriorating personal relationship with Sara, compounded by rising familial rifts, all would go in directions that were anybody's guess.

Daddy's Sick, Hell is Real

Eleventh Spiritual Death

Daddy's embittered journey during his final months engraved itself on me like a tombstone epitaph, transforming the course of the rest of my life. I did not know until I walked alongside him through hell the cataclysmic and lasting impact his disturbing circumstances and consequential defenselessness would have on me. And with it came the shattering of life as I had lived it and the tearing down of our family as I had known it. Daddy's firsthand experience with elder abuse and my witness to his suffering fed my master's thesis and spilled putrid memories into my soul. Either I would leave it festering inside me or take it into my hands, look at it long, and do something with it. So I tell his story irretrievably laced within mine.

My father's battle with abusive neglect began at Christmastime in 2004 when doctors diagnosed him with esophageal cancer and an equally grim prognosis. My mother, siblings and I fell numb at the news. Soon after celebrating Daddy's 82nd birthday in early January 2005, we bid safe farewell to Jo Ann and my father on their exploratory drive to a cancer clinic in Houston. There, a team of doctors concluded Daddy's cancer "likely could be cured." This cure would begin with an aggressive daily dual regimen of debilitating chemotherapy and radiation, with treatments administered Mondays through Thursdays.

Doctors said daily doses of chemo and radiation or radical surgery could kill him, but he had a small chance of surviving if he withstood the cure. And if he did nothing he'd be dead in nine months. While on the surface the news seemed somewhat hopeful, it frightened me. I feared my father would not survive the rigor of it and implored my parents to let me research at least one other option before he undertook the clinic's regimen. They agreed. I took him to a local oncologist who had graduated from Baylor Medical School and was the daughter of an oncologist at the cancer clinic in Houston. She employed the same regimen but with less aggression to preserve quality of life throughout treatment. But Daddy opted for the Houston clinic, likely at the prompting of another family member. I believed it a grave mistake but treks to Houston would commence in February.

As my preoccupation grew with Daddy's illness, Mama's personal and medical needs, and my graduate coursework, unemployment and dwindling savings, so did my anxiety. It would have been nice to have had a sympathetic arm around my shoulder but there was none and I wondered how much more I could carry.

Daddy's medical regimen required my sisters and I each take turns driving and staying with him in Houston four days and alternately taking care of Mama's needs at home. At the time, Mary and Lynn lived out of state and my other two sisters had jobs. I had no steady income only freelance work, and was in the second and final year of my graduate program with a full course schedule and a thesis to research and write. Kelly worked full-time, was pursuing a bachelor's degree and had pets to care for but she offered to pitch in. Meanwhile, Mama was battling a skin disorder, likely caused by nervousness and ointments that made matters worse.

Then came my turn. Arriving at the cancer clinic was like landing on another planet. I'd never seen so many busy bodies in one sequestered place; there were swarms of them like bees on a hive. They never stopped coming and going. From early morning till after night fell, they still came and went. Many of their heads and limbs were slick as shiny apples. And some wore masks.

Valentine's Day arrived but was not giftwrapped in tenderness. As the chilly winter day extended, so did my heartache. I came to the conclusion on top of everything else I was bearing that I was not able or willing to bear more pain caused by my sick relationship with Sara. I asked her to find a healthy way to manage her pain-inflicting anger aimed at me. I again considered leaving but did not know where I would go or how I would manage it. I was afraid, too, with the worries I held, that I would collapse, go crazy. But I told myself it would be easier to hang on to my sanity than to come back from insanity. I thought of delaying school, but I was indebted to it and my master's would boost chances for lucrative income. In the end, I decided to stay the course on all fronts but felt trapped. Sara's response to my request was predictably apologetic. I knew better but I bought into the facade yet again from pure need to believe it. I busied myself while steering clear of her.

In the beginning, Daddy came home weekends. But soon he could no longer manage the road trips and so he and we spent weekends in a guest house adjoining the cancer clinic. Increasingly and often, Daddy threw up and weakened, unable to eat. One day when I was with him, he told me how deeply concerned he was for Mama, that if he should not survive, she would not be able to manage on her own. Daddy told me my Mama had become a "mental and emotional invalid." I swallowed hard at that. From where I sat, my mother had infinite capacity for kindness, admittedly intermittently sprinkled with harsh judgment, and was strong. But Daddy knew Mama better than anyone. He had lived alongside her 60 years through everything those years delivered. And he lived with her through hers and his advancing aging. Daddy was genuinely, deeply worried about Mama. And I did not know what to do with his worry.

My 50th birthday came and went in early March without notice. By midmonth, my father had landed in the hospital bordering the clinic an invalid and skeletal. He had lost 30 pounds in four weeks, the result of incessant nausea, vomiting, and a charred throat preventing eating or drinking. Daddy became progressively incapacitated. Doctors told us there would be no more treatment and Daddy would be released home. As I had feared at the onset, the hardline regimen was more than his 82-year-old body could stand. Having no experience with a seriously sick older parent, I was ill-prepared for what lie ahead or the sordid end, which I would learn had to do first and foremost with my father's severe medical regimen and secondly discrimination against the old. In the end, Daddy said he would rather have died than lived through the "hell" of debilitation from the chemo that landed him in negligent institutional "care."

The first evidence of neglect came at the hospital adjoining the cancer clinic. Doctors initiated intravenous hydration but neglected to insert a feeding tube, which caused malnutrition and accelerated the chemo's toxic impact on Daddy's major organs and functions. This was the first in a series of tragic missteps that prevented my father's recovery and ultimately led to his untimely death. At the start, Daddy entrusted doctors with the whole of himself, body, mind and soul, and plunged high-spirited and headlong into a supposed cure and rescue from too-soon a death. But neither he nor we could have known what would follow in its wake: a negligent medical and healthcare system that grossly disregards older people. Following his debilitation, our family would find a "healthcare" system, "rehabilitation" centers and "nursing" homes steeped in ageism. Whenever I think the words "elder abuse and neglect," they pop in my brain like bullets. We found ourselves face-to-face with widespread indifference observed in attitudes and actions, or inactions, of medical practitioners, many of whom ignored our growing despair. We found ourselves confronted by the unconscionable and unstoppable.

When the imminent was clear, Mama, my three sisters and I converged in Houston to hear the prognosis together. The doctors determined Daddy was cured but debilitated and needed rehab straightaway, which we would arrange for him in San Antonio. We spent the final night at the guest house five minutes from the hospital. The next day, I planned to drive Mama home while my sisters would follow Daddy home once discharged. That night was terrible and unforgettable.

My sisters and Mama had left the hospital for showers and food while I stayed with Daddy till visiting hours ended at 9. When I asked Jo Ann to pick me up then, she said blankly, "Take the shuttle." When I informed her the shuttle stopped at 8, she replied, "Take a cab." I left at 8 to catch the shuttle to the hotel.

Mama had long suffered with intermittent migraines but with Daddy's wasting condition her head pain recurred without relief. In the one-room suite we occupied that night were two double beds and a foldout couch. Mama lay on one bed, Jo Ann reclined on the other where I had taken a seat, and Debbie and Mary sat a few feet away watching TV. At seeing Mama's struggle with a headache, and realizing the dreadful emotions that must have been swimming around inside her, the doubt, worry and wonder about Daddy and what would become of them both, I asked the TV volume be lowered.

I had presumed Mama would sleep alone in the bed she occupied, Debbie and Mary would share the foldout couch, and I would share the other double bed with Jo Ann. But when I went to lie down, she said, "You can sleep on the floor."

I instead slept with Mama, lying with my back toward the other bed. When I tried to go to sleep in silence, Jo Ann next threw a full unopened bottle of water at me, hitting me hard and square in the center of my lower back, I got angry, and retrieving it from the floor flung it back. I reminded her Mama had a migraine and needed to sleep and Daddy lay debilitated only minutes from us, as if either should require a reminder.

I then witnessed in bewildered sentience my eldest sister's personality change, as she sat up in bed cross-legged, dialed her cell phone, and whimpered complaints to someone on the other end. Mama saw and heard and said nothing. Years later, I supposed Daddy's declining health that seemed to spiral Jo Ann's emotional decline in the midst of our father's fate was more than she could bare, and perhaps she did the best she could. Still, her behavior was hostile and bizarre. It was not the compassionate acts of a daughter or the sister with whom I had once been friends, with whom I had travelled and laughed, with whom I'd held hands and witnessed Roger's head trauma. I wondered to where that sister had gone.

The following morning, Mama and I left Houston with plans for the next day; I would drive her to a standing hair appointment. Meanwhile, my sisters would follow Daddy's ambulance home. But by the next morning, I awoke hot with fever and felt as weak as a newborn. Sara dialed my doctor who presumed the flu and called in a prescription. Before Sara left for the pharmacy, she dialed my mother's phone number for me. I informed Mama I was in bed with the flu and suggested she call her cousin a few blocks away who I knew would be happy to help. We ended the call. Sara returned with the medicine, and I took it and fell asleep. Later when I awoke and dialed the voice mailbox of my phone to check for messages, I shuddered when I recognized the voice on the single message was my younger sister, spewing a series of obscene curses because I had not driven Mama to the beauty shop. Her venomous words hit me like missiles, one after the other.

There later came no expressed regret over the hurtful behavior in Houston or the vicious voicemail. But I would learn to forgive it all and to shield myself from such assaults in the future.

The next two months dichotomously welcomed spring while demanding a chilling assiduous effort overseeing Daddy's transition to so-called healthcare recovery facilities. There was not much time to plan. When Daddy had first left the cancer clinic March 24, he made the three-hour trip by ambulance. Upon arrival, Jo Ann checked him into an acute-care hospital, one we believed safe. But I arrived there early one morning to find abusive neglect rearing its ugly head. Over the first few days, at every turn, my sisters and my eye-witness observations and reporting of things gone very wrong to hospital administrators, charge nurses, case workers, rehab therapists and aides went unheeded.

Our reports included their neglecting to sanitize the peripherally inserted central catheter (PICC) line previously installed in Houston for chemo treatments and their repeatedly drawing blood from the PICC line despite Daddy's doctor, medical chart, and us telling them not to due to threat of infection. This they continued until I asked the cancer clinic to call the facility's administrator with orders to stop it. They placed Daddy in a shared room with a very obese patient in freezing air-conditioning that left Daddy's 113-pound frame, warmed only with thin bed coverings, shivering while recovering from pneumonia; and took him to a common area for baths then left him sitting in a wheelchair ignored, unattended and trembling. X-ray technicians entered his room in utter impersonal silence, placed cold metal plates on unclothed parts of his body, took the images and left without a word. They left no water pitcher or cup by his bed and laid the phone on a side table he could not reach; ignored his tangled and bundled bedsheets, blankets and pajamas leaving him uncomfortable despite knowing he was too weak to straighten them himself; left his food trays sticky and stacked with uneaten smelly food sitting next to his bed; and kept the door to his room wide open, next to the noisy nurses' station, rendering badly needed sleep for him impossible.

One morning soon after his arrival, I found him in bed, disoriented, and the window of his street-level private room wide open. Given Daddy's vulnerable state, I asked the admissions director about the open window. He smiled a superior smile and replied, "Some patients like fresh air." When I asked why Daddy's false teeth, which lay on a bedside table, were disgustingly dirty and smelled, the congenial admissions director kindly blamed the dirty dentures on the ambulance company. Daddy confided in me he felt "pushed," and "no one is listening to me. I feel lost; I may as well be sitting alone in the middle of my front yard." Alarmed, I spoke to the charge nurse, informing her I did not question her staff's expertise, only their lack of courtesy and communication. I asked that everyone speak to Daddy with respect, treat him with dignity, and listen to and respond to his concerns. I asked her to tell everyone to introduce themselves to him so he knows who they are by name and their purpose in his care.

My concerns were met with defensive excuses. Daddy was unsure about what his physical capabilities were and did not, rightly so, trust strangers with his care, particularly when they were seemingly unaware and worse, unconcerned, about all he had been through already and that his recovery depended highly on them. I constantly had to remind the charge nurse and staff he had a short time ago had some 25 rounds of concurrent chemo and radiation in only a few weeks' time, had lost substantial weight, was recovering from double-pneumonia and needed to be kept warm.

These kinds of ongoing red alerts had to be attended to and remedied nearly always immediately and caused me incessant mental and emotional anguish. I was on high alert around the clock, an apiary of angst. But I was willing to go through it because no matter the atrocities I witnessed, it was Daddy who lived them. I could not, not, be vigilant and vocal each and every time something was wrong. In Daddy's situation, something "wrong" was not merely a mistake or oversight. In his case, "wrong" could be lethal. Daddy was right. No one was listening at that place.

It became clear no one had reviewed his medical chart despite our being told in advance Daddy would see a doctor and therapists within 24 hours of admittance. But on Day 3, I was informed the facility's doctor would not review Daddy's condition for yet another day and that scared the hell out of me. How can you care for an acute-care patient day-to-day, much less hour-by-hour, when you don't have a clue about his recent medical history or current condition and need?

I typed a list of our family's instructions and phone numbers, posted it on the wall behind Daddy's bed, and had one placed with his chart at the nurses' station. Even that, we would learn, would go ignored by nurses who apparently considered themselves above reproach.

Finally on Day 4 the doctor and therapists convened to discuss his care plan. It was reassuring they affirmed he was lucid, functional in his judgment and strong in his upper body, but his radiated throat and debilitation from chemo rendered it painful to eat or drink, which left his lower body frail. Ways were found to work around that, and soon he had gained 8 pounds. Our family had to be so detailed as to tell staff what to feed him and when. He occupied space in a place with people in crisp uniforms milling about, but we, Daddy's family, were the ones who took care of him on a daily basis.

We observed other unsettling situations there. Nurses dropped pills on a highly trafficked floor, picked them up and put them back into small plastic cups on the trays they carried, and headed into patients' rooms with them. Instead of addressing older patients by their names, nurses and aides used pet labels in patronizing tones as adults do with babies. They spoke to us about Daddy in third person as if he were not present. And incessantly we asked where the doctor was. By early April, Daddy had taken a grave turn and seemed justifiably depressed. His mouth was sore and swollen from the chemo and radiation, and sores around his lips rendered him barely able to speak and nearly unable to eat or drink. So his stamina was low and he could not oblige physical therapy. I started taking soft food to him, such as yogurt and mashed potatoes, of which he managed only a little. He liked miniature Musketeers so I took some to him and occasionally he ate one.

One day I popped in before class and was told Daddy had been found sitting on the floor in his room earlier that day. He had told the nurse who found him he had tried to walk to the bathroom. When alone with Daddy, I sat down next to him, held his hand in mine, looked into his eyes, and asked what had happened. He said, "I called for help but no one came." Naturally, the charge nurse denied it when confronted. And Jo Ann and Mama were livid when I told them of Daddy's fall because the nurse had not called them when it occurred. I knew Daddy told the truth and the nurse lied. And knowing we were being lied to by employees of this acute-care hospital, knowing my father's well-being was in jeopardy, was almost more than I could stand. I felt smothered by anxiety and powerlessness. So I phoned Daddy in-between visiting in person, which was often.

A couple of days later, Daddy requested a feeding tube be inserted into his stomach so he could get stronger. On April 8 he was provided one after ambulance transport to a hospital for the procedure, for which my elder sister and Mama were present. And later that day, he was transported back to the acute-care facility. My father was willing to suffer through yet another invasive medical procedure to regain himself and come home. Coming home was his perpetual goal. And I aimed to see it through. The tube was near his naval, about the diameter of a small finger, and would require meticulous daily sanitary care. When I visited him the next morning, I saw others had availed themselves of most of the bite-sized Musketeers I had brought him the day before. I put ointment on the sores around his mouth with a Q-tip and gave him a long drink of water. He was spent.

That same day, I felt angry when I heard a nurse call Daddy "papa" instead of Mr. Guckian. Her using a pet name and condescending tone someone might use with a child was disrespectful and unacceptable. I watched nurses continually make suppositions about Daddy's needs based on generalizations not his medical chart. The nurses presumed because he was in his 80s and weak at the moment that "he's a very sick man," and "he's not going to recover, we're here only to make him comfortable." I told one nurse who said the latter never to say that in my father's presence again. They told us "he's no trouble at night, he just sleeps," but I believed they secretly administered tranquilizers to him when the sun went down.

Every time we visited, we had to warm the room for him. Nearly three weeks after my family and I told them repeatedly not to draw blood from Daddy's PICC line, they continued to do so anyway unless we were present and intervened. The chemo had rendered Daddy incontinent and he wore disposable absorbent adult underwear, and often, as we learned when he called us on these occasions, they delayed helping him with a change for 30 minutes or longer. Only God knows what happened to my father when we were not with him. This kind of worry can eat a person alive.

Anyone in Daddy's shoes would be depressed and anyone in mine should be angry. I refused to hide my apt emotions toward insensitive staff, and that included everyone from the doctors and nurses to the simpleton aides and higher-up administrators. My admonitions did not sit well with my family, but I was willing to absorb their wrath to continue making sure everyone at that place knew beyond a shadow of doubt I would call them out on every infringement against Daddy's best interests and his doctor's orders. And neither they nor my family should ever expect otherwise. I was not in this situation to be popular. I was in it to take care of my father who took care of us his entire life. I at once was my father's advocate and an alien in my own family, which clearly showed signs of shattering.

Alarmed, we arranged for Daddy to relocate from the acute-care facility to a remodeled skilled nursing and rehab facility in another part of town. By now it was mid-April. As Daddy was transported, I fielded calls to home healthcare agencies and another rehab center to gather information about

Daddy's next steps along his road to recovery that would lead finally home. On April 15, Daddy transferred by ambulance to a private room at the privately owned nursing and rehab facility we chose based on its remodeling, location, and spotless and seemingly well-run appearance. It was a welcome relief from the torture Daddy had suffered at the acute-care hospital and my taut senses slacked a bit. In the beginning, everyone there was courteous and friendly, and the schedule of Daddy's therapies and activities seemed strategic, productive and safe. Nurses and aides were responsive but Daddy was angry and depressed. He still had hefty challenges to surmount, not the least of which were incontinence, extreme weakness, and sore gums and throat. But he was gaining weight albeit negligibly, talking a bit more, reading the newspaper and watching westerns on TV.

Despite its freshly painted walls, spongy new carpet and spit-shined workers wearing pressed uniforms and smiles, again we found the underlying attitude toward elders impersonal, indifferent, dangerous. On visits, Daddy kept saying he wanted "to get out of here." He told me what he had been through in mere months was "pure hell." Hell is the same and only word he used to describe the bloody European front in WWII.

I learned appearances are deceiving and the old are disgraced. And it sickened and tormented me. On one day, I found the door to Daddy's private room standing wide open to a public hallway. Inside, an aide lifted him, naked, from bed. As she pulled him trembling to his feet, he suddenly lost control, like an infant without a diaper. I will never, ever forget the shame and incomprehensibility of that moment on my father's face and the sorrowful words that escaped his mouth when his eyes met mine. It does me no good to swipe away the unwelcome, recurring memory; it is stuck there, returning, like a filthy, pesky fly. It was as upsetting as immediately clear the aide either did not know or did not care about Daddy's debilitation, incontinence or inability to stand. She seemed not to care that he was unclothed or that the door to his room was wide open. This deeply, deeply disturbed me.

As Daddy's stay reached two weeks, I saw more of what I had seen at the acute-care hospital: abusive neglect. And each time I saw things gone wrong, I brought them to staff's attention as I had done in the prior place and expected them to address them on Daddy's behalf. It was never-ending. Aides used wet or dry soiled towels from Daddy's bathroom, for instance, to clean him after he used the bedside toilet, even while knowing he still was fighting infection and had a feeding tube in his stomach, and left the dirty towels and rags sitting on his nightstand. The aides sometimes accidentally knocked over the bedside urinal spilling its contents onto the floor next to Daddy's bed and mopped it up with towels from the bathroom, missing some of it and leaving the residue unattended while serving Daddy lunch. Nurses began avoiding or having eye contact with me.

My careful oversight was met by Jo Ann's angry phone calls to me, and later to my mother about me, that informed me the facility had complained I was demanding better care of my father. My sister gave me no benefit of the doubt in the face of lies by the facility's staff, and Mama having not witnessed what I saw disbelieved the dozens of daily wrongs happening. In one such case, a nurse advised me to enter a patient's room to request the aide help my father, but that same nurse told my sister I forced myself into the room demanding the aide stop what she was doing to attend to Daddy.

Jo Ann apologized for her unfair words and asked I continue my vigilance. Still, I began to want to run from that responsibility, from the appalling situation my father faced 24 hours a day, in a strange place with people who did not care about his welfare any more than they did a flea on a stray dog. While I wanted to bolt I also feared for my father's life. I was increasingly struck with angst over my belief the longer he stayed in that place or anywhere but home, the more assured his ongoing humiliation, suffering and untimely death. I was torn between caring for Daddy and hiding. But I did not scram. I did not bolt. I knew if I did not keep showing up to keep an eye on Daddy for however long he had to be in that hell-hole, he would suffer even more. And I, with him.

The last straw came on a Sunday in early May when Daddy told Mama and me of the nursing supervisor in charge of the afternoon shift who threatened him at his refusing medicine he knew he did not need and we noticed a bruise on his right cheek. Like clockwork, she brought him a cup of pills, but when he refused them with clenched jaw, he told how she held the cup to his lips, leaned in within an inch of his eyes and said: "Open your mouth and take it or else." Because of his vulnerable state, Daddy was scared to talk about it, afraid of the consequences. When I brought the incident to my family's attention, they initially insisted I "not cause problems," concerned the facility would discharge my dad and then where would he go? But I told Mama she must report it as abuse, which she did by telling the social worker in charge of Daddy's care. I also called an attorney about Daddy's legal rights in light of the negligence and believed physical and psychological abuse taking place. Talking with the attorney fueled my fervor to diligently speak up on Daddy's behalf. A few days went by and Daddy continued to show lethargy and non-responsiveness to family and therapists' promptings, but he knew and told us the drugs he was forced to take were the culprits, not his will to get well.

I found myself blindsided at every twist and turn, which were many and constant. It was sharply clear, elder neglect and abuse was pervasive. It was, is, a ubiquitous cancer. Daddy knew this better than I. Meanwhile, my father wasted away. Over-drugging had followed Daddy place to place, as absent doctors prescribed drugs sight-unseen that held him prisoner in a bedridden body.

Mama finally arranged for him to undergo an exam by his cardiologist, who upon inspection hospitalized Daddy, taking him off nearly all drugs the rehab center had administered around the clock. With healing healthy lungs and heart, the only medicines Daddy needed were an aspirin, antibiotic for bronchitis, a blood thinner for stroke prevention and temporary oxygen treatments using a nebulizer. While in the hospital, Daddy grew more alert and stronger and his mantra persisted, "I just want to go home." I heard him loud and clear. I wondered if anyone else did.

The skilled nursing and rehab center from which he had been transported to the cardiologist's office now refused Daddy's return without explanation. But we knew why. Their overdosing him along with countless other instances of abuse created legal risk for them. While I pushed to bring Daddy home under private-pay home healthcare, Mama and my eldest sister, at the urging of Mama and Daddy's former primary care doctor, pushed for Daddy to be placed in a cheap state-run nursing home in a penurious part of town paid for by Medicare.

Alarmed and adamant to instead bring Daddy home where either he would recover or die, I mailed Mama a letter believing her reading my words would be more convincing than ongoing discourse. In it, I reminded her "unless Daddy has a serious medical condition, he does not belong in another facility," "HE WANTS TO COME HOME," and "I will help you." I reminded her Daddy needed to be in familiar safe surroundings, with her, at home, where he could sleep in his own bed, shave in his own bathroom, look out the windows at his yard, sit on his porch, and eat meals with her, and where friends and neighbors could visit. "Remember when we prayed, when he was in Houston, that if Daddy was going to die, that God at least bring him home to die?" I wrote. I reminded her of the advantages and affordability of home healthcare, which would cost the same as a nursing home. And I vowed to bring him home, warning Mama I could no longer bear watching my father wither away in institutions where he hated being and did not belong.

Despite my letter to Mama and urgings to my siblings to bring Daddy home to recover, my mother—confused, scared, suffering her own medical ailments, and relying on bad advice of the former physician and perhaps other family members—deposited my father into the dilapidated nursing home. There, he was left in a gloomy gray room with no phone or TV. Supposedly, he would receive physical therapy twice a day. I strongly urged my mother and sisters to monitor whatever medications the nursing home tried to administer, including tranquilizers easily disguised and mixed with liquids placed in his feeding tube. I told Mama to begin preparing for Daddy's return, because I was bringing him home. I also told her if she did not bring him home, he would die in that rotten place. It was his right and wish and had been for months to come home. I assured her again she and I would make all preparations, I would follow through when he got home, and she need not worry. Gratefully, my mother edged her way into agreeing with me, as did Lynn.

While I researched a plan to bring my father home, I visited him at the nursing home during the three weeks he was there, often finding him clutching the mobile phone we had given him. He was anxious about not having all our mobile phone numbers handy, so I typed a list, taped it to his phone, and told him to call anytime. He called Mama that day, telling her he was itching to get out of bed and into a wheelchair, and from there get moving, get strong and come home. He phoned me early the next morning with a chirpy hello.

From its place on my nightstand, my phone rang one morning at 2 a.m. I knew who it was before I answered. It came from the ramshackle nursing home and made the scared 6-year-old in me shudder. "Hi, Daddy. Are you OK?" This time, he said he had been lying an hour in cold sheets wet with urine, too weak to do anything about it himself. He had repeatedly pressed the red button clipped to his bed to alert the nurses' station, but no one came to help him use the bedside urinal. Full of zip and lighthearted mischief before the cancer,

Daddy still suffered from incontinence caused by chemotherapy that had ended two months earlier. I swallowed hard pushing down the sad swell in my throat and asked him to hang up so I could call for help. I promised to phone him right back and did. I lingered on the line till someone arrived. In a few minutes, Daddy said, "They're here now. Thank ya, Sugah. G'night." I think back on that night and remember the grace in his voice despite his circumstances. I know what heartbreak is, and I know my heart cannot hurt long enough or grave enough to ever come close to what he must have felt. What hurts the most is he suffered in silence and alone.

These calls would recur, with Daddy phoning me, me phoning the nurses' station, then me phoning Daddy again to ensure he was OK. This would prove to be, which came as no surprise to me, the dreadful neglectful standard operating procedure of the nursing home. They did help him regularly out of bed and into a wheelchair but then left him there for over an hour, which was too long for Daddy who needed to return to bed intermittently. It was at that time he told me he had lost interest in everything, even fishing. All he talked about was coming home.

In an ongoing push to rescue my father, I kept researching options for home healthcare and scoured the internet for reports about the nasty nursing home. After finding much more than I wanted to know, I shared the results with Mama and Daddy. I wanted Mama in particular to see a printed report about the truth of Daddy's lot. The Center for Medicare and Medicaid Services had scored that place extremely badly overall in its most recent survey. I also gave Mama a step-by-step list of what she could do instantly to prepare financially for Daddy's homecoming, such as reducing charitable donations and her housekeeper's time.

I scheduled several two-hour interviews each with registered nurses, case managers and administrators of each of three private-pay home healthcare and medical and service agencies with Mama and me. And I kept Daddy updated on progress to fuel his hope. Mama and I hammered out potential schedules for home healthcare along with cost and a payment plan. We ordered delivery of a prescribed hospital bed and other medical equipment and stocked up on healthy groceries.

In late May, as Mama and I hammered out Daddy's discharge plan from the nursing home and solidified full home healthcare services, I was in the middle of two graduate classes and hustling through the beginnings of thesis research headed for a November course deadline and December graduation, all while looking for full-time employment. I contracted with an executive career counseling and coaching firm to lend a hand. My finances were very thin. I had dipped into my tiny life savings and was worried about my ability to care for myself. My money was nearly depleted as were my emotions. Sara was in the background, offering obligatory support as I asked for it but I asked little of her. Mama historically a perfectionist seemed ever more insistent now. I understood she was afraid and uncertain and her life had changed dramatically as had Daddy's, but I felt no matter what I did it was never enough. It took strength and prayer not to unleash pent-up anger and fear. I felt on the verge of fracturing and breaking into a thousand pieces.

Near the end of May, Daddy's disgruntled phone calls increased along with his gratitude for me and my sisters' remote help with his calls. He understandably expressed impatience, unhappiness and discomfort with his whereabouts. I faced more heart-wrenching splintering and disagreements with family about my doing what Daddy wanted. But he was my priority, I focused on him, and he was getting excited about coming home. Home, the place of safety and comfort he had built for us long ago. The place he had not laid eyes on for four excruciating months. I was ecstatic for him and eager to help with his homecoming.

On a Friday, May 27, I emailed my siblings a detailed letter telling them the nursing home, at Mama's request, had begun Daddy's discharge process. I told them he was coming home within a few days to a well-researched, pre-arranged, complete home healthcare environment and described it. And I implored their full support. I identified the home healthcare and hospice agency Mama and I had picked and explained it would provide Medicare-paid registered nurse, physical therapy, occupational therapy and hospice if needed. I identified the non-medical nurses' aides services agency we chose and services to be provided by feeding tube-trained aides. These included all personal hygiene and help with walking and wheel chairing as Daddy was able, and light housekeeping, cooking and errands for Mama. I named expected related costs and reminded my siblings of two primary facts: Our parents had money saved that now would be put to suitable use, and Daddy must be allowed the dignity to make his own decisions about his care, including medical treatment, the latter of which would occur only with his express knowledge and consent.

I also advised them of the registered nurse's assessment of Daddy, that neither Mama's nor our family's medical power of attorney's goals for him were the primary concern. Daddy's wishes were primary. I passed along the registered nurse's explanation of his physical limits: the chemo and radiation poisoned and destroyed Daddy's esophagus and upper stomach, which were his principal sources of nutritional health and hormones, and which he may never regain, but eating several small nutritional meals a day would help. She told us not to push him to eat, drink or do anything he did not wish to do and that he knows what's best for himself. In light of all my father had endured, his spirit and mind were intact; he was extraordinarily strong and brave.

I visited Daddy May 29 to explain how his transfer would happen and what to expect once home. He was eager to leave what he called "a miserable place." He and I knew, no matter what came after coming home, home is where he needed and longed to be. I told him, "It's your decision what to do with your life and where to live it, not ours, not Mama's, and I stand by whatever you decide, and I never want to see you institutionalized ever again." His reply was short, "Good! I plan to exercise that right." And then he downed the homemade split-pea soup I had made him. It was one of his favorites.

On May 31, Daddy came home by ambulance to his Dysart homestead that was abuzz with fresh caring faces and optimism. Mama and I successfully had orchestrated it all. How propitious, for a WWII veteran, my father, to return home around Memorial Day, at a time we honor and also mourn members of the American military who served and died bravely on behalf of the United States. Daddy now had survived yet another war, but there were battles yet to fight.

At home, the hired nurses' aides fully bonded and insured with successfully completed criminal background checks were supervised by a veteran registered nurse and worked around the clock in three shifts to guard against burnout. They helped Daddy from bed and into the wheelchair every day every two hours for 15 minutes. He took three meals a day at the kitchen table with Mama and consumed protein drinks mixed with whey bran three times a day via his feeding tube. His hands stopped shaking and his cheeks turned pink. He even watched TV in the living room. And he used the bedside urinal himself. He was doing well. On the financial side of homecare, I negotiated down from a standard market rate for the aides and obtained Daddy's protein shakes from the American Cancer Society for free. Daddy was well-attended to and Mama had help.

Once Daddy was home, as the well-oiled home healthcare machine took over 24/7 to care for him and ease Mama's worry—in fact, both agencies complimented our organizing them so well—I took a few days away to focus on schoolwork and classes for which I had fallen behind and feared failing. I prepared myself mentally and spiritually to trust the hired caregivers and the rest of our family to do their parts. No matter what came next, Daddy was home and that settled me. I had done my duty as his daughter and willingly. I had made his wish come true. I had gotten him home.

Enlightened by Daddy's plight, I requested and received approval from my professors to write a persuasive thesis on the subject of elder abuse and neglect, tying it into my major field of study in communication arts. I would show mass media's neglect to expose and explain the disgusting and growing phenomenon. I set about researching and writing the 100-page scholarly paper based on Daddy's experience and my firsthand witness blended with reviews of books, academic and professional journals, studies and interviews. I aimed to expose the complex, pervasive social illness of elder abuse, show the nation's top major newspapers do little to uncover and thus contribute to it, suggest what society should do to prevent it, explain societal conditions that lead to violence against old people, and urge mass media to expose and explain the daily reality and horror of elder abuse.

I contacted the American Cancer Society about a support group; I wanted to learn how others handled similar situations with poise and grace without destroying their own lives in the process, as I felt I was doing. My beloved sister-in-law Kelly reassured me at every turn, reminding me it is better to disappoint by saying no than over-commit. That balancing my needs with commitments, and focusing on graduate work and career would pay off and better equip me to help my parents. Her words helped me keep striving for that bewildering thing called patience particularly with family. I would keep trying. Kelly was as judicious as she was kind. Her amity and moral support were inextinguishable candles in the dark. Whenever I was downhearted, alarmed or upset, she brightened my outlook with wisdom mixed with welcomed humor.

She and I shared many uplifting emails and phone calls. She assuaged the guilt I carried delivered intentionally or not by Mama or my sisters. She bolstered my resolve to finish my degree and get back to work. She advised me to make time, even if little bits, doing what brought me joy, such as camping, gardening or hiking. She calmed my simmering anxiety by reminding me of the twofold design of life: "It's not much worth the effort if you can't enjoy it!"

About two weeks after coming home, Daddy suffered three separate episodes of a shooting pain that "felt like lightening." They began at the corner of his mouth and burst from it, accompanied by feeling faint. A six-hour visit to the ER and a myriad of tests showed no stroke, heart attack, neurological problems or blood clots; a pleasing blood pressure; and an excellent oxygen level of 97. Daddy reported no headaches, nausea, numbness or pain elsewhere. The only issue was his erratic heart rate, which at rest ranged from 115 to 120 and appeared to skip a beat. In the end, the doctor's exhaustive analysis revealed nothing wrong with Daddy's health except the enormous jolt caused his body by chemo and age. He was to keep doing what he was doing: Eat, be mobile, and give his body time to recover.

We also learned should Daddy's health take a terminal turn, hospice care strictly was an at-home comfort-care program that precluded visits to the ER or life-saving actions. Hospice meant conclusively, death at home as comfortably as it can be. Daddy opted out of hospice.

As June crept by, I confided in Kelly a harbored heavy burden. While coping with my parents' shaky ground and crucial needs, family conflicts, unemployment, dwindling finances, pressing master's program with demanding coursework and looming fixed targets for completion—sometimes I wrote papers the very day they were due—and living with Sara who vacillated between considerate and callous, there was nowhere for me to rest my head or heart, nowhere to exhale, nowhere safe or devoid of fear. I was awfully scared but pushed fear aside to press on to the next task in front of me, but the fear inside me swelled. I seemed to be losing everything including my sanity. But I knew it was up to me, and only me, to hold on. I had spoken with my pastor and a priest, joined a support group for families of cancer patients, read the Bible, prayed and exercised. Despite all that, I often either felt I was sinking into a deep, dark hole or on the brink of shattering. I kept telling myself over and over again it would be easier to hold onto my sanity than to come back from losing it. I felt discouraged even while pressing ahead with everything I had to do.

I asked Kelly what she had done to rise up and out of the emotional darkness she surely must have fallen prey to at losing Roger so tragically so soon. Anyone in my shoes, she said, would feel as I did. And no one could make those feelings go away. How well I knew. What worked for her was finding a new direction in life. I didn't correlate that idea to my circumstances, yet. Kelly's virtuous counsel for me to stay calm amid stormy, angry and angering times was extremely vital for me to keep in mind in my managing both contentious and affectionate relationships while making solid judgments. That proved to be a tall order, though. When fright or unbridled emotions boiled they exited my mouth. As much as I disliked it, that was my systematic stress-and-fear-induced reaction.

Kelly kept cuing me to stay calm through each encounter and situation. We two decided to form a support alliance to check in with each other regularly. We shared our goals and progress for personal improvement and career advancement. Prodded each other to attain our aspirations and shared fresh ideas about solving problems. In the process, we helped each other manage stress. Kelly's love and support was a gift from God, an angel sent in my time of need. She had been Roger's angel and now she was mine.

I began penning random thoughts on snips of paper and collecting them in a folder to fuel the writing of a book someday in which I would tell the story of me and my father, and I returned to my habit of journaling. I continued coursework, conducting research for my thesis. By June's end, a month after Daddy's homecoming, the home healthcare and hospice agency discharged him from their care when he hit a positive plateau. We were happy with the four weeks of strengthening he had attained but with each physical therapy try his blood pressure erratically spiked and his heart still raced. Thankfully, the nurses' aides agency stayed on to help Daddy with daily activities and Mama with chores.

On Daddy's behalf, I contacted the case manager and doctor who had coordinated and administered his treatment at the Houston cancer clinic to ask how long it would take for the chemo to leave his body and for him to regain strength and stamina. I asked whether the chemo was the culprit for his spiking blood pressure and racing heart and would that self-correct and by when. There were no clear answers to my questions. I continued painstaking diligence including lengthy instructional emails with the nurses' aides agency, advising them of desired changes to Daddy's daily care and coordinating implementation. For instance, the supervising registered nurse suggested stopping Daddy's vitamin supplementation but we disagreed, knowing his gaining weight and strength hinged on supplementation and use of the feeding tube, given he was unable to eat as much as his body required to recover. I reminded them, again, Daddy wanted natural nutrition not medicinal solutions and all aides must be trained in use and care of his feeding tube, which he and we believed was instrumental in his healing. I was particularly upset after discovering one aide did not know how to use or clean his feeding tube and so advised the agency this was unacceptable.

By Independence Day, Daddy was faring well. He was walking to the restroom with the walker folded and rolling at his side vs. in front of him. He ate hardy meals. And he talked about removing the feeding tube.

That month, I completed two courses with A's but the rigors of research and weekly writing assignments for my developing thesis continued as I also attended career coaching workshops and kept up with daily walks. I was immersed in reviews of literature related to my formulating thesis proposal. And I was ecstatic about the prospect of writing a scholarly document about a topic that not only impacted my father and family but people everywhere. Each step of my effort was coordinated with and reviewed by the Thesis Committee, which gave me glowing approvals at every stride. I set about interviewing my second cousin, a doctor on Daddy's side, and national elder abuse prevention organizations. At long last, in August I began my final semester and continued meeting with the Thesis Committee on progress and approval of my influential paper. The composition would tell Daddy's story of elder abuse and abusive neglect backed by published authoritative documentation. Concurrently, I ramped up my work search.

About this time, the feeding tube was removed and Daddy began outpatient physical therapy three times a week with a rehab facility close to home. Since his former physician had dropped him like a hot potato when we did not abandon my father for good to a nursing home, Daddy was in need of a new primary care doctor and I offered mine. In advance of their appointment, I provided her with Daddy's complete medical history and contact details for the more than two dozen doctors and six institutions he had been shuffled among in the past six months. At home, matters were not going well anymore with the aides responsible for Daddy's care.

Symptoms from an emphysema diagnosis 14 years prior had been negligible. He had taken quality vitamins every day and eaten healthy food. And he had been very active until debilitation from cancer treatment. But now, my father began showing clear signs of wear and tear. He was angry at the ravages the chemo had inflicted on him and depressed and who wouldn't be? And now he had bronchitis, which left him disinterested in food or medicine that would help cure it. I knew he suffered. That he had been stripped of his dignity and independence. I loved my father and kept praying for his recovery.

To help offset the cost of home care, Daddy sold his Ford F150 pickup, which he hated to part with; it had been his motivation to get back to driving and fishing. I had never seen Daddy bitter before then. He had been a fun-loving man with a wholesome attitude and resilient. He had friends and independence. Now, his life and body were wholly stripped of all he had known and been. I felt helpless to help my father. I did not know what to say. I did not know anything anymore.

Through summer, my father spent several brief stays in the hospital for recurring bouts of bronchitis and unexpected maladies. During one of the last times, the doctor-on-duty misdiagnosed him with Parkinson's and prescribed hefty medicine with toxic side effects levying an irreversible toll on Daddy's body, not yet recovered from chemo, and producing among other hazards sudden fainting.

Shortly after Labor Day, I reported to the home healthcare agency's management its quality of service to my parents had declined. One of their aide's recurringly reeked of nicotine and arrived late or not at all, leaving Daddy no ride to scheduled outpatient rehab, which was catastrophic for him. I questioned, since the agency employed 300 people, why they had not honored their word to us that Daddy's helpers would be consistent, experienced, reliable and trustworthy, and why from among 300 they would send someone obviously unfit. I tired of repeated empty apologies and finally told them in no uncertain terms we were firing that one aide and she was prohibited from returning.

It was then Daddy unburdened himself to me and Mama about another aide, one with whom they formed an amicable rapport when she first joined our team. Mama liked she could take explicit instruction about laundry and dishwashing and the lady seemed happy to oblige. But Daddy finally told us when he was alone with her, when she was helping him into and out of the shower, she was pushy, mean and rude, and had said things to him that were disrespectful and hurtful. I advised the agency of this, and that aide, too, was fired from our employ. I hope she was fired from the agency as well, but the sad truth is, we found abusive neglect is pervasive in home healthcare just as it is in facilities everywhere.

As I reflect on what Daddy endured often with empty eyes in silence as he watched his body erode, the family he loved and lived for fall apart, and caregivers abuse him, I wrestle with the unsettling memories and struggle to find meaning in them. The unpopular fact is elder abuse and neglect is real and the ageing explosion is making it worse. For the first time in human history, the oldest among us outnumber the youngest. Daddy's story is a warning that speaks for those who cannot or will not for fear of repercussion. This is not the whispered cry of a single individual suffering in the dark alone; it is a loud collective scream from increasing numbers of our vulnerable old. Every one of us either will die young or grow old.

The recurring hell I came to know as abusive neglect would exact a permanent irreversible toll on my father and on the family we once had been.

Daddy's In the Ground and I Climbed In

By early October 2005, I had completed my classes, dissertation research and 90 percent of my thesis. Graduation loomed in December. Meanwhile, I ramped up my hunt for full-time work. Unless gainfully employed by the end of the year when my savings would expire, I would have to live on credit while repaying student loans. It was then a CAT scan revealed spots on Daddy's liver as he again complained his food tasted bitter.

While we awaited the oncologist's prognosis, Daddy's appetite waned but one Sunday he ate heartily. He devoured one-half of a T-bone steak, protein shake, sliced tomatoes, bread with butter and one-half of an acorn squash, and washed it all down with iced tea. And he played a game of dominoes with Mama and me. I felt encouraged. Only later would I understand Daddy's brief and temporary resurgence was a precursor for what lie ahead; his spirit was giving him a final taste of life as he once had known it before that life was over.

Daddy's diagnosis quickly grew grim. After a fainting spell, he was rushed to the hospital. When I arrived, my sisters were in the ER where Daddy lay, feeble and silent on a metal exam table. The young physician attending to Daddy showed us X-rays of his lungs that indicated severe pneumonia, which came as a complete surprise; the hospital had neglected to detect it two days earlier when it dismissed him from a previous admission. Now, the prognosis was "certain death."

Against my sisters urgings for me to be quiet I asked the doctor, "If Daddy's condition was ominous, why is he lying on a cold hard table in the ER instead of in monitored comfort in the ICU?" No reply. I demanded my father be relocated to the ICU and made comfortable. I pushed for it despite fuming words, hard looks and harsh gestures from family. I pressed the doctor again. I asked if hospital policy held an age limit for ICU admission. Still, no reply, and the doctor walked away. My family was outraged I would badger the physician about hospital policy. They did not know what I knew, that some hospitals refuse an elder person ICU care when a younger patient vies for it or they want to reserve a bed.

Despite my parents' top-of-the-line insurance with a prominent provider, there he lay in the ER waiting to die and us watching him. This was all wrong. At even the most basic level of human kindness, do we not comfort the dying?

A human being is not road kill waiting to be swept up and the mess disinfected. This was my father.

A moment later, a nurse emerged, attended to Daddy in the ER, and a short time later my father rested easily in ICU. We all watched the clock. Relatives arrived and kept vigil in the waiting area a short walk from Daddy's bed. The last time I saw my father, his face was shielded by an oxygen mask, his lean body covered in clean soft blankets. My mother sat next to him. Daddy was too weak to open his eyes but I feel sure he knew we were with him. He did not want to go; he was not ready. But he was dying, after months of suffering abusive negligence. I told him I loved him. What else could be said? I was living this moment while disbelieving it real. I wondered what was going through his and Mama's minds.

The nurse said it would be "any time." How could she know? Mary and I left his bedside so Jo Ann and Debbie could join him and Mama. I walked in a hush looking into air as my feet carried me to the waiting room. I had nothing to say to anyone. Not even to myself. It was no more than two minutes later, at 4 minutes to 8 p.m., Debbie broke from Daddy's bedside announcing alarmingly, "He's gone!" Dread fired through me. I rushed to Daddy, thinking, no! He lay so very still. The oxygen mask had been removed. There was no breath. His eyes, closed. His strong hands that once worked hard, held tenderly, fought bravely, prayed fervently, were still. Mama told how Daddy had taken a couple of breaths and winced, never opening his eyes, and when she whispered, "It's OK, you can go," he did. Just like that. Just that quickly. My 82-year-young father no longer lived "on this side of the grass" as he once put it. He was somewhere else, gone fishing with Roger, I supposed, on the banks of a cosmic river in some well-stocked pretty shady cove.

Onlookers described his passing as peaceful, without suffering. Not I. His death certificate stated his demise was due to "respiratory and cardiac failure with sequential contributing factors of aspiration pneumonia, Parkinson's and esophageal cancer." But those were lies. Daddy suffered negligence starting with the too-aggressive combined chemo and radiation regimen that wholly poisoned him, and the overtly unethical diagnoses and forced overdoses of detrimental unwarranted drugs administered to him in hospitals, rehab centers and nursing homes. Yes, he did suffer. Badly and recurringly. I would remain forever grateful to have had the fortitude to fight my way through what I had to do so he could in fact pass in peace and comfort in the ICU. Thankfully, his final minutes were not of misery but tranquil. My father had suffered dreadfully, often in silence, and now, he suffered no more. That much I knew.

After leaving the hospital, after leaving Daddy there, all alone, among strangers, I went to Mama's. She did not ask but told me to stay and help her write Daddy's obituary so we could pass it to the newspapers the next morning. But I did not want to stay. I did not want to write about my father's passing. To sum up his life in a few short paragraphs. It all was very wrong and I could not reconcile it within myself. I wanted to scream. To go home. Even in Sara's callous house, at least there was a room where I could be alone with my grief.

Mama and I argued. After all, she said, who else but me to write the words. I would look back on that moment later, see it through different eyes, and make amends to Mama. But in the thick of it, I wanted to grieve my loss my way. I did not want any more responsibility. I did not think at that moment that writing Daddy's obituary was the honor and privilege it was. I was torn between taking care of myself and taking care of Mama yet again and did not see how I could do both at once. I wanted to be a caring daughter. But I also wanted to flee. I had nothing left to give. I, too, was in mourning.

Begrudgingly, I stayed. And together Mama and I wrote down all the words we hoped would pay apt homage to an extraordinary and great man's life and tell newspaper readers the deeply sad news of his passing. Together we wrote my father's epitaph, into the wee hours we wrote, until we penned it precisely right. It began in a standard manner, "Eugene Patrick Guckian passed into eternal life at the age of 82 on Oct. 13, 2005, in San Antonio, Texas. He was born in Lockhart, Texas, on Jan. 12, 1923…" and ended with a common plea, "In lieu of flowers, the family requests contributions may be made…." Despite the floral concession, lovely fragrant blossoms soon would abound. Daddy's epitaphic decree cited the visitation Saturday at the funeral home, rosary Sunday at St. Benedict, and funeral Mass and burial Monday. A meal would follow at the Knights of Columbus Hall, where Daddy and Mama and us kids had frequented, where family weddings had been celebrated, where now we would remember my Daddy without his presence among us for the first time in that place.

The awful morning arrived and, at Mama's urging, I drove us to the funeral home to arrange Daddy's services. My mother moved through her dutybound decision-making with a stoic disposition I did not share. I hated every minute of tending to my father's burial plans. You cannot make burial plans for someone who is alive. I scarcely could bear it, could barely sit through all the conversing and head nodding, talking about burying this man, my father. My protector. My Number One. My archetype. At one time, my business partner. The man whose spirit loved all things natural and outdoors. And barbecue and rivers and fishing and laughing and old country music and Mama and us kids and Woolie Boolie and Marlboros and his mother's seven-layer lemon cake with pecan frosting. He called her, affectionately, Mother. He was his mother's firstborn son.

While I sat uncomfortably with Mama in comfortable leather chairs across from an expansive mahogany desk where sat the funeral director, as they passed papers back and forth agreeing to moneys spent and that which would be paid, in walked a woman my parents knew well. She was a pint-size lady, warm and friendly, my parents' hairdresser at the salon they had frequented for years. She had come to style Daddy's hair for the open-casket service. Mama instantly invited her to sit with us, telling her she was "like family," as we discussed and planned the most intimate of details of my father's interment with the funeral director.

How could my mother invite an outsider to sit with her and me to pour over the painful intricacies of Daddy's last recognitions? That she could do it hurt. I felt swept to the curb. But the woman saw, and likely felt, my scorn for the absurdity in Mama's offer and politely excused herself to tend to Daddy's hair. I later would recall my feelings of then and forgive my mother's unintentional slight and myself for what I felt and thought at that moment. Mama, after all, was grieving the loss of her husband, with whom she had spent pleasant times together in laughter and light conversation with this woman with whom my parents were well-joined. I imagine my mother seized the opportunity to share a part of "Pat" with the hairdresser, and in some way, that likely comforted Mama while she dealt with the reality of what she was in the middle of doing.

Ahead of the funeral Mass four days after my father's final breath, my three sisters and I met with Fr. Eddie who would officiate Daddy's eulogy. He was a tall, handsome, kind-hearted man and a dedicated priest who knew our family. Daddy liked him. As he listened to each sister tell of our father, he scribbled snippets onto a waiting yellow ruled tablet sitting on the small table around which we sat. I waited until my sisters had offered their parts and left. And then I wept and confided to Fr. Eddie about trials we had gone through over the past months as a family. He was sweetly consoling and told me Daddy had been my advocate and I had been his. His words were warm and welcome. I had not thought of it that way before.

He asked me to describe Daddy. I said many things but one stood out as Father wrote it down: "He was a lion with the tender heart of a lamb." Daddy was strong with a tender sensitivity rarely seen in men. Roger and Lynn had inherited that endearing trait. And so, at Mass, Fr. Eddie repeated our descriptions of Daddy and when he spoke mine his eyes met me from where he stood near Daddy's casket.

We buried my father and into the ground went the rest of us. Buried went the family we had been. Buried went my advocate. Buried went the anchor of our lives. Buried went hope and trust. Buried went understanding and faith and everything that once made sense. All of that fit oh so neatly in the hole in the ground with my father. And it left plenty of room for me. And in my heart, I climbed in.

I was 50 when they lowered Daddy into the earth. He was 82 but until the fateful December of 2004 seemed younger than his years. My mind had kept him young, too, kept me from facing he was aging and one day would up and die and leave me alone. Leaving me without his eyes and voice and hands and temperament and answers to every question I could possibly imagine to ask him, and without his patient answers that came even when he was tired of all my questioning. It went too fast. But it went. And when it went, a sizeable part of me went down in that hole at the cemetery with Daddy. And the rest of me wrangled with what was left.

When Daddy's light went out of him, I captured and carried it inside, a patrimonial model of my father, I thought. But I knew the world wasn't the same world anymore without him in it, and nothing would ever be the same, not even close. Not the way I looked at myself or others. Not the way I felt. Not the way I talked or thought. Not the way I prayed. Not the way I saw what was beyond the window of my pickup truck days later as I drove away from that covered hole in the ground where my father lay. That vile, disgusting, hideous hole covered in dirt. And a few feet from it, where Roger lay, as silent as Daddy, he in his very own undercroft. I wondered whether father and son conversed from inside their respective earthen pits, from within their comely caskets that shut them off from the rest of us.

Instantly, the world was bigger and scarier and left me adrift. I felt wholly lost. As lost as my father had felt in those godforsaken rehab facilities and nursing homes. I had lost my anchor in a sea that now was my new residence marked by unmarked horizons in every faraway direction. He had been my stronghold when I ran to him in fear, and when Daddy died, my fears were magnified. Daddy was the one, the only one, I trusted. Now he was gone, but I still needed his steady presence. Maybe now Daddy and God would be for me one in the same.

The End to Abuse: A New Beginning

Twelfth Spiritual Death

Daddy had never judged me even when I deserved it. That was Mama's long-held yet well-intended role she assumed particularly and wholly upon Daddy's death. And she was good at it. Even though he disagreed with us kids at times, and rightly so, Daddy gave each of us the time and dignity to pull out of our mistakes ourselves and helped us through them if he could. Maybe once do I recall him shaking a finger at me with "I told you so." But he was gone, and life as I had known it was over, and where did that leave me at 50?

I cannot recall with certainty but believe every living relative and friend known to Daddy and our family attended his funeral, the burial and the meal at the Knights of Columbus Hall. It was abuzz with sympathizers who came to be with us and share Daddy's memory. But the place concealed the ghost of Daddy's footsteps and laughter. They were around every corner and in the kitchen, and now Mama, and we, were there without him but surrounded by people who remembered. After filling a plate for myself, I took a seat where there, as it happened, sat Brenda. Up until the age of 8, we lived across the street from each other on Charcliff. She was kind to me that day. We ate our food and chatted, reminisced about people and places now gone, and exchanged phone numbers. I was grateful for the safe haven of her friendship, and kind eyes and words that day. In coming days, and soon, in fact, Brenda's re-emergence would prove providential.

Throughout the afternoon, my sisters and I were politely cordial but withheld. I watched my familial relationships, as if from afar, disintegrating in real time. There were pictures taken of us together, side-by-side, with compulsory smiles on their faces and stoic forbearance on mine. My sadness was apparent and I could not hide it. Surely they must have been sad, but if they were sad, it did not show. We each went our separate ways that day talking with and being consoled by others who came to pay their respects to my father and us. Sara was there, too, offering dutiful moral support. There was a chilly air of detachment between myself and her and myself and my sisters; there were no shows of affection between them and me.

But on the other hand was Aunt Marie, Daddy's youngest sister. She had come from Louisianna with her girls, my cousins Jeannie and Sharon, who all three met me with familiar comfort. Uncle James had preceded Daddy in 2002 and here now was Aunt Marie who thankfully still was able to travel. My aunt and uncle had been wonderful to us kids and Daddy when Mama was sick when we were little. Aunt Marie was a tough, robust lady I admired but now she struggled with emphysema and lugged an oxygen tank everywhere she went.

I will never forget what she said to me as the three of them piled into Jeannie's pickup truck at the end of that day to head home. My aunt was like Daddy; she didn't need a lot of words about situations to recognize and understand them. She had eyes and a heart and used them readily. She obviously had seen or heard unloving undertones. In parting, she said, "Betty Lou, I want you to know, you are welcome at my house anytime. I love you." I wept at her words as I knew she meant them. Indeed, she had my father's heart. That was the last time I would see Aunt Marie on this side of life. I always will remember her, as I will my father's unconditional love. It is a rarity even and especially in families.

With Daddy departed, no one needed to tell me because I inherently knew my life was fixing to change in major ways. I was not sure how but I felt it. I knew as sure as I knew from cool sweet-smelling air and sudden wind to expect a rain shower. That night, I sat in Sara's backyard beneath a clear sky filled with stars and a full moon. I later went to bed feeling a blank exhaustion and awoke before dawn from the first sound sleep I'd had in ages. I noticed the closed blinded window was aglow in calming light and peeked through the slats to find my face awash in the same soothing moonlight emanating from the nearly full moon of the prior night. Its unhindered luminescence streaming down on me from the eastern sky delivered Daddy's presence, reassuring me he was watching over me. This waning moon for the next two nights and mornings shown bright. It shown from the east, from where Scripture predicts Christ will come again, from where divine life appears.

Later that day, grief came on me hard. I wept deep and long and fever overtook me along with nausea and fatigue. I slept most of my way through the afternoon and night. The following sunrise, I called Mama. In hopes to comfort her, I told her about the moon, that Daddy was in its brilliance and looking out for us. Sara, however, was no source of comfort. She was aggravated I asked for chipped ice and a spoon and snapped back, "I have things to do!" Her coarse conduct was painful. She may as well have stricken a blow to my body. Hatred for her filled my heart as rage spilled from my mouth, spewing all the dreadful feelings about my father's suffering and death now heaped onto and worsened by her insensitive cruelty. Not only had she mistreated me in a downtrodden state but she in so doing disrespected and disregarded my father's memory. Despite Daddy's feelings about women sharing a life, he had treated Sara kindly. I apologized later for my words but I was not sorry. I could not regret reacting to her cold-blooded meanness. Forgiveness was neither in my heart nor in my belief it ever could be.

I spoke to Mama again that afternoon and told her of Sara's disdain. Mama said something she'd never said before. She told me, "Betty Lou, you are a very sensitive and compassionate person, aware of other people's feelings, and many people are not that way." I had no idea my mother knew me at all. But she did after all. She suggested I try to forgive Sara, as Christ does us. Our conversation turned to talk of Daddy. She had gone into the backyard to find the birdbath empty. She filled it with water and then threw stale pieces of bread at its base for the birds. We remembered and laughed about the time Daddy pitched stale biscuits on the lawn for the birds, and when I asked if he was going to break them apart, he replied, "Hell no. Make 'em work for it."

Welcomed messages of genuine sympathy penned in pretty cards and emails began streaming in with soothing words I sorely needed. Words that expressed sorrow over my father's passing, prayers for me and my family, and kind overtures of help should I need it. A former colleague told me of my good fortune in having a moral father and mother and added my personality was missed around the office. A schoolmate noted, "He was so lucky to have a daughter like you; I admire you for all you have done." One of my professor's wrote, "I know how much you loved him as I witnessed your devotion to his care from the day I met you. May he rest in peace and you find solace in those around you and in the worthy work I know you will do." People with whom I had worked in the past who had read Daddy's obituary mailed condolences. Even Muriel posted a lovely card, in which she wrote it had been her good fortune meeting Daddy who was kind to her and she would never forget him.

The two weeks after Daddy's funeral were strained, both with Sara and my mother. I distanced myself from my sisters and the discomfort I felt when with them. My full-time focus shifted from caregiver to student, to finishing my thesis, attaining review and approval from my professors and attending my commencement. I had to put everything else aside, my grief, my anxiety, my fear, my guilt, my depression, to concentrate on nothing but schoolwork. Either I would focus or I would fail. I had sent numerous emails requesting insights to fuel my paper, the abstract for which I provided along with examples of what Daddy and our family had endured. One reply was unexpectedly encouraging. It came from an old friend of our family. She had known Daddy, attended his funeral, and was aware of my current personal and familial struggles, too. She wrote concerning my thesis so far, "All you wrote about your dad is true. Don't shortchange yourself. You are interested in people and are a loving, giving person."

One Friday night, 11 days after we buried my father, I left my bedroom where I had been working on my thesis to the living room and asked Sara if she would like to watch TV with me. She answered, OK. So, we sat together on the couch as I tuned the TV to a live jazz performance. As I chatted excitedly about how talented were the performers, wanting so badly to connect with her, with anyone, she turned a cold eye toward me and said flatly, "Well, if you keep talking, I can't hear the music." Her words fell on me with a dull thud. Why, oh, why did I live this way? I simply had hoped for a modicum of human compassion. I knew I was in mourning. I knew not to expect comfort or caring from the callous individual she was. Yet, I needed comfort. Where in these instances does one draw a line between need and availability? I did not know. I did not see a line.

I asked how she could be so cold toward me when I had just buried my father. A rational person would not have bothered asking such a question. A rational person would not have expected a compassionate response from an uncompassionate individual. But I was not rational then. I wanted her to know she had hurt me and done so at the worst possible time and it was not OK. Predictably, she stood and swung. Before I knew it, she was sitting on top of me, yelling, spitting hate. She had been rude to me often before, yet I recurringly rationalized her abusive onslaughts. She then hit my right arm and next delivered a punch to my chest. I was horrified. Even she seemed surprised at what she had done. This experience was not unlike others I had suffered with other people yet I was shocked as if it had never happened before. I was that battered woman I'd heard about. A statistic. A victim. I was disgusted, ashamed and scared.

Instead of being withdrawn at her rage, I became hysterical and fought back with words. At one point I grabbed my cell phone to dial 911 but a slap of her hand sent the phone sailing across the room. She hurried away down the hallway to her bedroom and slammed the door shut and locked it. I found myself following and begging her to open it all the while disgusted by my pursuit. She did, came after me, grabbed my shirt, shoved me down the hallway and into my bedroom, and pushed me to the floor before slamming the door.

I sat there, stayed put, trembling like a beaten animal, unable to cry anymore or move, realizing quickly my head could have been gashed open by the sharp corner of the writing desk as she thrust me to the floor, or my face could have been bloodied by her fist, or one of my arms could have been broken. My body and brain were numb with cold disbelieving belief. After a while, I pulled myself up from the carpet and drug myself into bed. I never called 911. I remained withdrawn in my room, in the dark, covered up with my blanket, trembling uncontrollably, knowing I had to get out of there and quick. I regretted not having done it sooner. The past year had wiped me out emotionally. Regret amid tragic circumstances is exactly that: tragic. Tragic that I had put myself in this ugly vulnerable position… again.

The next thing I knew, it was morning. I lay very, very still, breathing as quietly as I possibly could, so as not to be heard, until I knew she had driven away. It was Saturday and she had left for the weekend. On that morning of Oct. 29, I took a long deep breath, exhaled, and then dialed the first of seven phone numbers.

I first called Kelly, endearingly more a sister than in-law, who said to pack, that she would prepare her guest room and come for me after work the next Tuesday, and I could stay with her until I graduated and obtained work. I called Mama, who sympathized but balkingly wanted to know what I had done to cause Sara's wrongdoing. I called the Battered Women's Shelter and arranged for free counseling. I called my doctor to tell her I was crumbling; she knew already I was grieving my father's death. I told her of abuse at home, and the need to pull myself together to complete my master's and looming graduation. I told her I must relocate immediately. And I told her I felt dejected, confused, despondent, scared and deeply hurt. She prescribed the temporary help of antidepressant and anti-anxiety medications, both of which I began that day.

I called my nephew and a friend to help me move. I called a storage company, rented space and collected boxes that very day. Finally, I called the old family friend and neighbor who appeared at Daddy's funeral and offered her phone number. When I told her what had happened, she said, "You need to get to an open Alcoholics Anonymous (AA) meeting or Al-Anon meeting or both," and offered to mail me a copy of "One Day at a Time in Al-Anon" or ODAT and a meeting schedule. When I asked why AA since I was not alcoholic, she said only that I would find the answers there.

Suddenly, after a few calls, support poured in. I was taking positive productive action and breathing sighs of relief. I believed God was watching out for me after all, or Daddy or Roger was with me from across the other side, or maybe God, Daddy and Roger were all mixed up in it together.

It's curious, the treasures and memories I keep of those passed. Their handwritings, for instance, like my father's the summer of 1997 in which he detailed standard rigging to keep in my tackle box, and the Christmas card he gave Mama, in which he underlined the typewritten words, "I need you and love you with all my heart," and added, "… and I mean it. Your sweetie, Me."

I had a long way to go to get to OK. But I believed if I did what I needed to do, then the OK would come. I recently had bought a book entitled "Each Day a New Beginning, Daily Meditations for Women" by Karen Casey and read it religiously every day for strength and insight. The day following my seven phone calls, its reading for Sunday Oct. 30 reassured me that one way or another, by one means or another, prayers always are answered.

This book, my story, is by no means by chance. Its events and timelines like my life unfolding were pre-ordained to unfold precisely as they have, with God redirecting my course constantly, even and especially when I was unaware. It is God saying to me in a wordless whisper, "Your life, your book, are providential, keep at it." It is God who decided long before He created me I would be a writer. God who put me into or helped me navigate through progressive circumstances that molded and shaped me as a writer and a person with a specific story to tell. God who made the work I have toiled over and published so far that which He intended for me, and only me. God who gave me an appointed time in life to do what I have done and am here to do. As I reflect on the events of my life and notice how each has stacked on top of the next, I realize it has been God's doing all along. His book. His timeline. His unfolding… in the happenings of me.

On Hallows Eve, a Monday, the day before I was to move to Kelly's, I attended a women's support group at the Battered Women's Shelter and returned to Sara's house feeling empowered. She asked about the meeting and I told her all I had learned. That never is there a reason or provocation for someone to physically attack another. That she had been controlling either with passive avoidance or forceful physical violence. That it was healthy for me to expect her to discuss problems rather than shut me out or physically afront me. And after sharing all this with her, Sara shunned the information, wholly discounting its validity.

The following day, Tuesday, the first of November, I packed and kept at my thesis. That night, as promised, Kelly came for me. She told me when a decision is right, everything falls into place. It most certainly had. Wednesday, I awoke in Kelly's guestroom unwell from scant sleep but that afternoon drove to Family Counseling Services and cried to Bill, my assigned counselor, before setting a follow-up date. Thursday, Brenda and her husband helped me move more things to Kelly's, and that day and the next I finished packing. Saturday, movers stowed my furniture in a nearby storage unit. And Sunday, my nephew and a neighbor loaded my lawn furniture and the BBQ pit that once was Daddy's into the bed of my truck and I stored them at Mama's. Everything I owned now was warehoused in three separate places but my belongings were stowed and I was free. I left Sara's house and Sara forever and settled into Kelly's guest room.

My new beginning had begun.

Daddy during WWII, Naples, Italy, 1943

Mama and Daddy, 1944

Me on my trike, 1957

Me and Daddy, my First Communion, 1962

Mama and (L to R) me, Roger, Debbie, Victoria, Texas, 1963

Daddy placing a "lucky penny" in my shoe on my wedding day, 1973

Kelly and Roger, 1983

The "R" Word

I sometimes wish I held the memory of my first beginning. I don't remember the day of my first cry on Earth. The one that came nine months after my parents conceived me, when God surely said, I'm sending her to them, made in My image and entrusted in theirs.

Most first beginnings are embraced, even reverenced, for their tender and telling timing and predestination, into which I emerged on this side of my mother's womb: in the middle of the morning, in the middle of the week on a Wednesday, in early spring. Amid the middles came I, to join a growing brood of kids who from the start and by the finish would find me… in the middle, fourth of six. My birth day sang of springtime and sunlight, announcing the unwrapping of new life assured of budding goodness, as sweet as dew, as promising and pretty as dewy rosebuds.

But as I reached a half-century, this newborn's promise had steadily faded into a woman's unfulfilled yearnings that wistfully yet whispered: Someday I will be married to a moral man who loves me and treats me well. Someday I will have a happy and wholesome home life where I feel safe and wanted. Someday I will have a family around me that cares about me. And Someday I will defeat financial famine. I cannot count the innumerable looks backward at the risky minefield that deafened my Somedays and defined my life's lot when I asked the unceasing empty question: Why did God save me from myself time after time after repugnant time?

Typically, when people enter their 50s, they are near retirement and enjoying grown children and grandchildren. Their mortgage is paid. They take vacations. They have money in the bank. Not me. I was single and childless with no job, money or home of my own, and had little to look forward to. I had shown up to suffer verbal, emotional, mental and physical abuse. The proverbial poster-child for victim, I had grown angry and offensive. I had allowed myself to be used and deluded myself into believing I was the rightful user. And I talked myself into believing that being a user was OK.

In all fairness, I had achieved a few remarkable feats by mid-life, including professional recognition of published work, a stellar academic record and a successful business venture. But my personal affairs were nowhere near as notable. How awful to come face-to-face with the terrible truth midway through a lifespan that what I wanted most was missing. And what I wanted most was love and all the Somedays that came with it. But I did not know how to get what I longed for. I did not know how to have or hold onto something as vital, human and esoteric as love. The idea of it eluded me except in the reveries of my imagination, mingled with remembering the dirty road I'd traveled to find what I thought it was. After everything, despite it all and because of it all, I still wanted my Somedays and something inside me said to hold on to them.

Sometimes I wondered how this could be happening to someone like me. I had not grown up in squalor. I was not raised by alcoholics or drug-addicted parents. I came from a religious background. I was not sexually abused at home. My parents were not shady or lazy characters. So from where did my abuse-seeking nature and seeming predisposition for trouble originate? I wondered, What's wrong with me? I was in a bad spot but was I a bad person because of it? I was not a liar, thief or cheat. If I was not bad but good, I asked myself, then why was my personal life in shambles and why was I angry and sad?

When I received the promised ODAT and meeting schedule from Brenda, I selected a location near Kelly's house. Two days later on a Tuesday evening on Nov. 8, 2005, at 7 o'clock I attended my first recovery meeting. It was called the Coker Family Group and was open to both alcoholics in AA (AAs for short) and those who love alcoholics, called Al-Anons. I had no idea what to expect but went to the meeting held at a church in a tiny outbuilding. I parked, walked pensively up the ramp, and wandered sheepishly through the open door into a room filled with unfamiliar faces that met mine with a familiar warmth I had been missing. The place was organized with folding chairs arranged in a circle. A long table stood next to one wall and atop it was a freshly brewed pot of coffee and Styrofoam cups.

Small square boxes of tissues dotted the floor near the chairs. Someone smiled at me as I entered and spoke for everyone, saying how happy they all were I had come. The kind greeting touched me so profoundly and immediately that tears welled in my heart and leaked from my eyes. Across the room near the encircled chairs sprawled an imposing couch stretching the length of one wall. The obviously time-worn fabric of dark hues of maroons, blues and browns swallowed me when I sat down upon it, or more so, when I furrowed into it, its seat cushions so cavernous my feet dangled like a toddler. I quickly claimed one cushy corner and sat awaiting the meeting's start.

Quietly I continued surveying the place. On the plain beige walls hung large scripted illustrations of consoling words in great big letters that spelled out something similar to Scripture. Instead of the Ten Commandments were 12 Steps and 12 Promises of recovery that conveyed, in other words, biblical principles.

As I sat still and emptied my eyes into the room, my thoughts of Sara and my family ricocheted across the confines of my mind. I had fought against their denial of hurtful offenses and didn't want to keep living that way. Did refusing to live like that while watching my own behavior sink amid it make me wrong, or did it make me rightfully unwilling to endure abuse? I was fighting for my right to dignity while fighting with my guilt over battling my family, the ones supposed to love me, the ones whose blood and history I shared. I found it impossible to calm the conflicting echoes.

As the people filed in with smiling hellos and hugs, I kept watching in hushed anticipation as they poured steaming cups of coffee and took their seats. I did not know or care whether I was an AA or Al-Anon or both or neither. I simply was a willing observer come to watch and wait for the miraculous answers Brenda promised. The meeting convened promptly at 7 as a leader took the helm. A notebook was passed for people who wished to jot their first names and phone numbers in it for others to copy and take home for future use. The practice struck me as very caring. A few traditional words were read and said and it was explained, "Who you see here, what you hear here, stays here." I liked that immensely. It rang happily in my heart that still contained stockpiles of pain caused by relationships poisoned by betrayal. Here was a fresh breath of trust, and, oh, how I needed it. Those words were the first words I would take with me and remember and learn to live by. Those words told me, Yes, this is how we are supposed to live with each other. Respecting one another. Affording each other the anonymity and confidentiality healthy relations require and expect. Already, I was an agreeable fit.

I watched as individuals took turns speaking, sharing only their first names and declaring whether they were an AA or Al-Anon, and then saying at the end of their brief treatises, "Thank you for letting me share." I found their humble declarations and genuine appreciations relaxing and refreshing. But I remember not the details of what anyone said, only kind eyes. When I stated I watched, that is precisely what I did. I did not hear most of the words. My mind full of its own misery had plugged my ears. When a brief pause in-between others' sharing happened, I seized it. I spoke my name and then set about telling everyone through unceasing sobs of my despair, Daddy's death, abuse at home, an estranged family, unemployment and fear about that and looming graduation, and the pain I carried.

I do not know for how long I rambled, but I do recall the loving and compassionate faces of those who sat in the circle. Their eyes met mine with tolerance. No one told me to shut up. No one told me my time was up. No one rolled their eyes at me or whispered to his or her neighbor. No one rose and walked away. No one laughed at my tears or made light of my plight. No one told me what to do with my pain. They all simply sat and listened and let me cry and talk. Someone handed me a box of tissues while the whole room full of strangers handed me a long overdue dose of delicate validation.

I did remember one thing someone said during that first meeting: "Come to six meetings, and if you're not sure whether these meetings are for you, then come back to six more, and if you're still not sure, then come back to six more." The humor in that sentiment was obvious but so was the wisdom. When the meeting adjourned precisely one hour after it had begun, I stood from my sunken spot on the sofa, and as I did, a few made their way to me. They thanked me for coming and hugged me. Two of them were David and Mary Frances who had been married most of their lives and in recovery about three years. David placed a reassuring arm around my shoulder and said tenderly, "Keep coming back, Lou. We hope to see you next week." I sensed he meant it.

I left that friendly space and faces on a clear fall night feeling as if my scary new world was a bit less daunting. I did not know those people, all strangers then. But they talked and treated me differently than my own family and those I'd chosen as partners. These people were tender and accepting, like Kelly and her parents, Gil and Joyce. Like Brenda. Like Aunt Marie. Like Lynn and Judy. Like Mama could be. Like Daddy and Roger had been. I could not, not, keep coming back. I was hooked on their humanity and the hope of feeling as happy again as they seemed to be. I simply knew I belonged there. I did not know what was to come of my attending those meetings. I did not understand yet what recovery truly meant. All I knew was, I felt soothed and safe there and would keep coming back.

The following afternoon, I kept my follow-up counseling session with Bill. I told him of the countless times I stood crying in front of Sara, asking her please to get past her anger and meet me halfway, but she didn't. He explained the more she avoided me emotionally, the more abandoned I felt. And the more abandoned I felt, the more fearful I became. He explained it was normal for me increasingly to feel anxious, hurt and scared, and despite my emotional outbursts in those instances, my reactions were a natural result of her increasing indifference.

He also explained no amount of love or support on my part could have made the difference because she was unwilling or not ready to make her recovery from growing up in an alcoholic home a priority. Bill reminded me I, on the other hand, was reading books, seeking counseling, attending recovery meetings, and constantly looking for healthy ways to solve my relationship problems. Bill gave me three instructions: Make a list of what I will not tolerate from anyone and walk away should those things occur; go slow in a new relationship, that is, "don't speed through the parking lot at 80 miles per hour;" and don't divulge everything upfront. I also learned from him my need for emotional intimacy was innate, something I should expect. And finally I realized physical intimacy without emotional warmth is hollow and sex is not love.

From the Coker group, I heard of other meetings, including an open Al-Anon meeting held Saturdays at Club 12, San Antonio's hub for recovery meetings, and frequented those as well. Upon my first visit to Club 12, I saw a bland timeworn one-story building that needed paint and scouring and seedy characters milling about, which left me feeling a twinge of embarrassment. I thought, What if someone I know sees me here? After all, I was on the hunt for professional employment. My image was at stake. Nearly immediately, I checked my haughty attitude and humbled myself to where I belonged, in a state of gratitude. After all, I had been a seedy character in the past myself, and no building's ugly outsides would ever be as ugly as my insides or behavior had been. Besides, I thought, people are here not for brick-and-mortar aesthetics but to get well. And from that day forward, I was proud to arrive at Club 12 and park my vehicle out front.

I found Al-Anon to be a place of deep insight particularly about the emotional side of recovery. Whereas AA focused primarily on abstinence, Al-Anon was fixed on abstinence from destructive emotional and psychological addictions, such as obsession and control. The Coker group showed me both sides of the addiction problem and the Al-Anon group at Club 12 surrounded me with kindred others who understood more about recovering emotions. I now recognized the Al-Anon is addicted not to a substance but to a person. I learned the deeper meanings of two words that beforehand had been foreign to me: codependence and boundaries. I did not understand, yet, why I had warped my life so defectively as a codependent personality. I was impatient to feel better, but I kept hearing to take recovery 24 hours at a time, sometimes one hour or even one minute at a time, no matter how anxious I was to get past the pain, anger, fear and confusion.

Learning to trust and adopt this new way of thinking, versus what I had always done before, which was to control circumstances and predict outcomes so I could feel safe, was hard. In recovery, I heard, "one day at a time," but I wanted to get fixed quick and know what was coming. Recovery does not work like that. A recovered way of living takes time, time to unlearn self-destructive mindsets and habits, time to grasp why I had behaved as I had for decades, time to live out and manifest everything beneficial and wholesome I was learning. People in recovery reminded me it took 50 years to get to where I was and it was going to take time for me to recover. That made sense and helped me persevere. In meetings, I heard a host of useful phrases I easily recalled when in a rough spot: "easy does it; keep it simple; to thine own self be true; when in doubt, don't; I didn't cause it, can't control it, can't cure it; do be humble; do pray; don't be a doormat; do the next right thing; progress not perfection."

Thanks to Bill and my recovery fellowship and literature, I began to learn about adult children of alcoholics (ACOAs) and the defective impact of parents' alcoholism, most notably, distrust and emotional absence, on their children. I began to realize people with whom I had had intimate relations were ACOAs. And I began to see my own codependent predisposition, or addiction to the ACOA or addict/alcoholic, was at play in all these affairs. And that my mistake had not been in loving the ACOA but in trying to change or control the object of my love. At the same time and on the upside, I also began to define and appreciate my own character traits that formed my personality and interactions. A few of these were passion, resourcefulness, a pensive and complex nature, and emotional depth, among others. I was learning who I was as a person, an individual, not someone attached to or living in the shadow of someone else.

I had journaled in the past but now heard regularly in meetings about the cathartic and transcendent effect of journaling. So I committed to chronicling my thoughts and feelings to heal from injurious pain and the resulting sorrow that had cast its shadow over me. Journaling became a fitting addition to my counseling, recovery meetings, reading and prayer. I discovered when I put pen to paper, my spirit within took over and the words flowed onto page after page after illuminating page. Sometimes I looked forward to it and sometimes I did not. And so it went, each time I picked up the pen. I allowed my notions, moods, memories and sensitivities to spill onto paper. I allowed my pen to usher in the raw truth and with it, ultimately, enlightenment. I allowed my mind to reserve judgment on what came from the pen as my hand guided it, or more aptly, as the spirit within me guided the pen in my hand, to what manifested. And what manifested was not always pleasant. Sometimes I whimpered and sometimes I wailed because the truth is not always pretty. Life is not always pretty and the truth about my life often was ugly. And I learned something else. Not only was I capable of looking at the ugly in me, I was willing to learn from my repulsive past.

I sensed a building renascence that told me with God's grace I'd heal. I'd finish my thesis and graduate on time. I'd find lucrative employment, and a safe, comfortable, affordable home for myself. And I would be fine. I began repeating a mantra in my mind and out loud: "Good things are happening to me today!"

Along with "Each Day a New Beginning" and my ODAT, I read the Bible and purchased and regularly read more recovery literature, including "How Al-Anon Works for Families and Friends of Alcoholics;" "Paths to Recovery, Al-Anon's Steps, Traditions, and Concepts;" and "Twelve Steps and Twelve Traditions." I jotted down wise and uplifting messages from recovery meetings and books onto index cards, used them as bookmarks and carried them in my purse. I told myself I would get through this hard time day by day, step by step. I told myself if other people could overcome their maladies, then so could I.

About that time, it was suggested I choose a "home group" in recovery that would be my mainstay and I chose the Tuesday night Coker group. My home group was where I got to know the people and they got to know me and we bonded. Some of them opened their homes to our fellowship for meals and holiday celebrations. And always, we encouraged each other through struggles from a recovering and spiritual point of view. I would form beloved lifelong friendships with some of these folks. I didn't know it then but they were becoming my new family. I found Sundays, which growing up had been family days, particularly hard. But I made it through by fellowshipping with God and people in Al-Anon and AA who willingly and mutually drew close and encouraged me. And I took long walks in the fresh uncluttered air.

I redirected recurring negative thoughts to positive ones and had to exercise this new skill regularly to keep my mind hopeful. Coincidentally, I began receiving uplifting notes and cards in the mail from Mama, signed endearingly with her love. In one, she wrote, "Everything will work out for you, God has a plan. Ask to be guided in His direction. Always remember, let go and let God. Nothing is too small or too large for Him to solve. I love you, Mama." And in another, "Everyone has troubling days, you are no different. You work hard and you are intelligent! Be patient." My mother's words often repeated what I was hearing in recovery meetings and reading in Scripture and recovery literature. There had been plenty of times I had felt unjustly judged by Mama, misunderstood or unloved. But in truth, my mother always had loved me and would.

Recovery was not a straight smooth road without troubling curves or bumps. Even as I made the earliest of strides, I mercilessly still blamed myself for my shortcomings and mistakes and obsessed over the past. But I reminded myself again and again to refocus on my recovery with persistence and practice.

The more counseling I got, the more recovery meetings I attended, the more I listened, the more I read, the more I heard what I needed most was to take care of myself. And setting healthy boundaries would have to play a key role in self-care. Even so, the idea of it was obscure. I did not know wholly how to do it. I knew how to eat well and exercise. To study. To work. To cook and clean and care for my property. To pray. But I did not know how to care for that part of me living on the inside: my mind, my feelings.

The unseen in me, my insides, was my problem, the part I needed and wanted to figure out and fix. I wanted to feel calm and assured on the inside and not merely look like it on the outside. I wanted to resolve the guilt, shame, blame and anger, and fear of an uncertain future. I wanted to be whole and happy. Healthy boundaries I was told would help get me there.

In all honesty, I continued obsessing over my aimless relationship failures for many months, even after admitting I was at fault first and foremost because I stayed where I did not belong. I had tolerated the intolerable, even from myself. There were two of me on opposing sides—the codependent one and the recovering one—warring against each other. This is what addiction looks like.

I yearned to understand how I could be so wrong in believing people loved me, when all along, they did not or could not, and why I stayed in relationships with them, even to the point, albeit benignly, of trying to force them to be who they were not or feel what they did not. In short, I needed to rid myself of codependence. Often, I heard in Al-Anon meetings, "You can't get bread from a hardware store." This simple phrase taught me that I couldn't get love from someone who didn't have it to give. And expecting otherwise was futile and would only cause more pain.

Epiphany

I was well enough to entertain the idea I was lovable and that anyone else's inability or reluctance to love me did not make me unworthy of love. I also recognized not everyone will love me or like me, but it was important I love and like myself.

Upon these realizations, I began another new practice. I began to pray for Sara and all those who had hurt me. And I liked myself for doing it. Every time I developed a resentment toward someone, I opened my Big Book of AA to page 552 and repeating its words prayed that everything I wanted for myself be given to those who harmed me. The book further suggested I pray this way every day for 2 weeks and if I did I would be free of any and all resentment. Sometimes, I had to pray longer than 2 weeks. But my discovery: it worked.

As I grew in recovery, I came to realizations repeatedly and had one prominent epiphany in particular: I had not been in love with the emotionally unavailable people I picked. I had been in love with the person I believed they could be.

Soon, it was raining epiphanic insights, like pennies from heaven. One day, while reading the Al-Anon magazine, The Forum, I came across a story about a woman who realized her tendency toward control and perfectionism stemmed from fear of abandonment as a child, which manifested as anger, and how fear and anger had a rollover effect in her marriage. The story made me think about my childhood, that I had developed a fear of abandonment. I presumed it was due to Mama's mental illness and resulting emotional and sometimes physical absence. This fear showed up in my adult relationships as controlling behavior that usually appeared after someone I cared about shut me out. And being shut out not only scared but anguished me.

I had not seen myself as a controlling personality before. Driven and determined, yes. But now, I began to recognize duplicitous behavior by someone close to me triggered fear, and fear produced emotional pain. The more hypocritical or outright mean the behavior toward me, the more pronounced was my fear and pain and kneejerk attempts to regulate the situation.

Up to this point, I had been unconscious of my tendency toward domination, or the fear that drove it, or that my anger was a byproduct of fear.

This insight splintered my illusion of control but left me a bit apprehensive about what life would be like without it; then again and of course, I remembered, control is an illusion. The only person I can control, after all, is me. The only behavior I am responsible for is mine. Accepting this would take time. A long time, for me, in fact. I heard in meetings, accept what is; things are what they are, not what I want them to be; and to be happy, I must accept what is. I understood the principle of acceptance. But I did not accept that acceptance was appropriate all the time.

I had to learn acceptance is not approval but a virtue all its own. Like a vast wide open prairie, acceptance reaches across the depths of one's interminable soul. It permeates every thought, feeling, word and decision. The ideals I wanted for my life often did not match others' morals, so the principle of acceptance was teaching me rather than convince people to change I instead must accept people and things as they are. And once accepted, it was up to me to take appropriate and thoughtful action for my own sake. I was learning I had no authority over anyone but myself. This precept of Al-Anon and AA recovery recurred repeatedly so I could not escape it and I hoped one day to master it.

I shed a river of tears in the earliest days of recovery. But through them I began noticing a rising power and confidence in me that told me it is a much healthier, sturdier person who seeks the truth than one who lives in denial and blame. I was pleased with the effort I was making to understand myself and to change—to adjust, shift, transform. I began to recognize confident people are happy people capable of congratulating others' successes, but those who lack self-worth are consumed instead by bitter envy. Another phrase I heard in recovery reiterated this idea: "Hurt people, hurt people." I was beginning to understand. But understanding did not by default excuse or forgive.

As people in recovery and literature reaffirmed my worth, so did I reaffirm my capacity to love and be loved. I made a first-ditch effort alone at the 12 Steps of recovery, despite realizing I needed a guiding sponsor. I accepted my powerlessness over other people, places and things, inasmuch as I understood how to accept. I believed in God and His ability to restore my sanity but still struggled with God's decision-making; after all, God had let my brother suffer and die at the hands of a drunk driver and my father likewise at the hands of abusive neglect, and if God let those I loved suffer, then what plans did God have for me?

Turning my will over to God was a scary prospect. I wanted, half-heartedly at first, to turn my will and life over to God, because it seemed the better plan, but I did not know how to do it. I had learned simply saying so or praying so did not necessarily make it so. I made a fearless and searching inventory of myself, taking stock of my numerous faults as well as my favorable qualities, the latter of which I was pleased to discover outnumbered the former by double. I began feeling grateful for the demise of my relationship with Sara, because, had I stayed, I may not have been able to complete my thesis or graduate on time or discover recovery.

With Thanksgiving approaching, everyone it seemed had plans but me. I was not on any family member's invitation list. But I was beginning to recognize and define insulting behaviors and learning to protect myself from harm. I was learning to prefer my own company or the company of people in recovery because they treated me with respect and kindness. I was learning when I became uncomfortable with a person or situation to remove myself from it until I was well and strong enough to handle it with self-respect and dignity. And that required, once again, I become skilled at setting healthy boundaries. Like the alcoholic, the Al-Anon learns she must change her playmates and play places if she is to recover. And she must check her mouth to avoid regret. Instead of expressing every thought I had, I was learning that some things deserve quiet contemplation. Sometimes that meant resolving a thought or feeling within myself without revealing it to anyone else, especially to a provoking or insensitive person.

My earliest experiences with hard clear boundary-setting occurred between me and my sisters and a bit more delicately between me and Mama. I was not adept yet at setting boundaries without anger or harshness, but in time I was sure I would soften with practice. Mama had hoped I would spend Thanksgiving with the family. But when I explained I may not be able to do that, she told me, pleasantly and surprisingly, to do what was best for me, that she would be there for me when I was ready, and she loved me. But Mama was not consistently accepting of boundaries. On another holiday a few months later, I declined spending Easter with the family, explaining that steering clear of conflict by choosing to be absent was in everyone's best interest. At that, she replied: "You're one tough cookie!"

But I did not want to be alone, either, throughout the long Thanksgiving holiday weekend, left to wallow in my own thoughts. So I volunteered to help serve the Raul Jimenez Thanksgiving Day Dinner at the Henry B. Gonzalez Convention Center and later attended the Thursday night Al-Anon meeting at Coker. At the same time I was doing what felt like all the right things, I worried I would not find work or a home of my own soon and that would strain my stay with Kelly and wear out my welcome. Her dog, Button, continued to bark at me and frequently I felt underfoot.

Friday after Thanksgiving I went to an open AA speaker meeting and potluck supper where someone said "God is in control" and "things are as they should be." Those words reminded me if I did my part, then God would do His. At times, my part was to wait. David was there that night and suggested I get an Al-Anon sponsor to work the 12 Steps. I knew David and others were messengers, that God spoke to me through them, as He did through recovery meetings, literature and Scripture. These messages and meetings all began to represent a different breed of church. I was drawn into it and trusted it.

Some days I still had a long cry and some days I forced myself to count my blessings. I heard in meetings how crucial it was on the road to recovery to find something to be grateful for every day, particularly when I felt defeated. One morning, I recorded 22 blessings and felt better after seeing them written out. I prayed over them, first thanking God for them all, and then asking He help me be strong and brave and wait with trust on Him.

And then an empowering thought returned to me and caught me by surprise. I said to myself I was the one responsible for where my life was. Not God or Sara or Muriel or Scott or my sisters or anyone else. Me. I saw the stark difference between making a choice and making excuses, blaming others for my lot. And what I saw from all my journaling and all my pondering was God had been there all the time, as if sitting next to me, answering every prayer I whispered or screamed, and in one way or another, giving me what I needed when I needed it most.

On the home front, I chipped away at my thesis; worked with a realtor to canvas neighborhoods for a suitable house, condo or townhome believing I would land employment soon in the new year; and basked in the light of Kelly's ever-loving moral support and elevating words. One evening in early December, as we lifted a glass in a holiday toast, she exclaimed, "To your

Independence Day, Lou!" Kelly had declared it and I grabbed it with both hands. I felt a wave of revolutionary change coming as the Christmas holidays drew near, with Kelly's bright star the quintessential silver lining behind what had been a gloomy gathering storm.

Within my first month in recovery, I had a few short-term sponsors. It was not uncommon to have more than one or even a string of sponsors over time. Sometimes people's schedules, personalities and priorities did not align, and that was acceptable cause to switch. Both sponsors and sponsees understood this tenet. I had not realized how uncomfortable it would be to ask someone to sponsor me. Asking for help seemed a weak thing to do even though I had done it for other reasons in the past and recently. I still felt it a weakness, to admit I needed even more help. But when I understood that a sponsor derives as much benefit as does the one sponsored, that understanding relaxed my pride and insecurity.

My first temporary sponsor asked me to phone her daily for 30 days, which was intended to help me learn to ask for help. I liked the practice and indeed it did help. She also suggested I purchase a daily devotional, "Courage to Change," which I bought that very day, excited about reading and discussing each day's entry with her. Our relationship ended two weeks later, but I continued attending meetings, reading recovery literature daily and staying in touch with others in the fellowship, all the while praying for a full-time sponsor. My next two sponsors attended Al-Anon meetings and took my calls but were lackadaisical about working the Steps with any fervor. That was not enough for me. Recovering myself was a matter of life or death.

I did not want to pussyfoot around with my mental and emotional health, dragging out my promised awakening. I already had spent 50 years doing life the wrong way and I was eager to start living it the right way. I wanted to get straight to the crux of the matter and to do so required I be sponsored by someone who had cut her teeth on all 12 Steps with a sponsor who had done likewise and come through it transformed. Transformation is what I wanted and I was not willing to settle for less. I was on the scout for the ideal sponsor.

Five days before graduation, I went before the Thesis Committee to defend my composition, receiving unanimous accolades and a grade of A. My work, "Elder Abuse: More Is Expected Unless Society and Newspapers [Mass Media] Intervene," soon thereafter would be recognized by the National

Institute on Aging's Journal of Elder Abuse and Neglect as unique in the field of research and inducted by the University of the Incarnate Word's scholarly online library, The Athenaeum, for perpetuity. My beloved professors and I sipped champagne to commemorate completion of an arduous assignment, and thus, my master's degree. My coveted credential was in hand. I was proud of the hard work now culminated in a bound book supplied by the university and I hurried to submit a copy to the U.S. Library of Congress Copyright Office. I did not know then this work would shape a nationally published article I someday would write.

The day before commencement, I visited Mama, where I was presented opportunities to put into action what I had learned so far in Al-Anon. Jo Ann phoned while I was there and asked to speak with me. Her call was not congratulatory. She phoned only to ask I leave a check for her with Mama, for my part of the cost of Daddy's funeral flowers. But when I told her I would reimburse her once employed, she became angry. Rather than lose my temper, I simply repeated what I was able to do and while unsettled by her anger I did not allow it to ruin my excitement about attaining my master's. My other two sisters visited Mama while I was there. Neither one so much as mentioned my graduation or asked how I was doing since moving to Kelly's. I was disappointed but not devastated. This, was progress.

Later that day after I returned home, God sent me affirming angels. Lynn and Judy had phoned Mama asking how I was faring and afterward phoned me. They congratulated me on graduating and asked me to send them a copy of my thesis. Lynn and Judy's genuine concern enveloped me in light. When I called to invite Brenda to my commencement, she heartily accepted and congratulated me on my degree and the impressive efforts I had made in recovery. That afternoon, a woman I had met at a networking event emailed me requesting my resume to share with her managers. Barely a month prior, I had been panicked and petrified. But now, here I was, graduating, healing through counseling and recovery, and being considered for employment, all while learning, albeit awkwardly, to walk steadily with God. And then it hit me. I had begun to have regular dialogs with my Creator.

In the past, I had read the Bible and prayed, often out of desperation or want, but had not talked to God like a trusted friend. I had pleaded but had not waited, listened or watched for His response. But now, I was paying attention to God. I realized when I did "the next right thing," doors swung open and God was the doorman. He opened the door to my heart, to others' love, to good things coming out of the bad. And all I had to do was the next right thing. It seemed and sounded so… simple. I had not been used to simple. I had been accustomed to chaos, and so, hoped neither my past nor my own often-misguided will would interfere with the goodness God surely had in store for me.

In early December, the university held to its annual tradition of decorating its campus peppered with trees with jolly Christmas lights. And on the much-awaited momentous day, commencement found us graduating students on a proud promenade in a march toward the auditorium, flanked all the way by cheering professors, family and friends. I had done it. Through the unforeseen rigors of the unexpected when first I'd decided to aim for it, I had attained my Master of Arts degree and attained it with distinction, illustrated by the bright gold cords I wore atop my black commencement robe. I beamed. Mama was there, along with Kelly and Brenda. I was and would be the only of us six kids to attain not only one but two post-secondary degrees. It had been a mere two short months since Daddy's passing and the photos Mama and I took together that night showed unmistakably the grim sadness she carried. But her presence showed pride and love.

A week before Christmas a Santa in a Cessna appeared bearing holiday tidings and transporting gifts. It was Kelly's dad, Gil, who had flown his private plane from Georgia and landed it at a tiny airfield mere blocks from her home. Next to Daddy, Gil was a charmer, and one of the kindest and most remarkable men I have known. He seemed to wake up with a cheery face and wore it all day. Since I occupied Kelly's guestroom, Gil slept on the foldout couch in the living room in homey company with her cat, Felix, and dog, Button. The next morning, Gil gave me two gifts. I excitedly unwrapped the first, a cushy Rudolph the Red-Nosed Reindeer stuffed animal. The second was a 40-Day diary called "The Purpose-Driven Life Journal" holding scriptural verses and ruled writing space. I would begin it Jan. 1.

Kelly gave me a God Box. It was my first. I didn't know whether the box had been hers or Roger's or something she found at an antique shop or estate sale, but it was crafted from textured metal stained in brown and beige and trimmed in brass with a clasp in front. On its slightly rounded lid was a noble coat of arms of gold and blue. It looked like a tiny treasure chest and obviously had changed hands a number of times, evidenced by its dents and tarnishes. Inside I found a fountain pen and small notepad. Kelly explained: I was to write down each of my prayers on the small snips of paper, fold them, pray over them, and then drop them in the God Box. After all my prayers had been noted, prayed over and placed in the box, I was to close it and put it away, leaving my treasured prayers to God.

The idea was to give my heart's desires to God and let God work them out for me. A simple notion and coincidentally a tenet of Scripture and recovery: "Let go and let God." I followed Kelly's advice poste-haste, as I was eager to let God set to work on each prayer. That diminutive God Box proved a little miracle. As I write this long after the fact, I still use it. Every year, at Christmas, I open it, unfold and read the paper prayers, and to my cheery surprise find many have come true or are no longer wishes.

One day, Gil invited me for a ride in his two-seat airplane. After completing pre-flight inspections, he welcomed me aboard and we took off. We flew 110 miles per hour but from the cockpit it felt as if we were floating. Flying over the Texas Hill Country with the Guadalupe flowing below us in clear view, he turned and told me, matter-of-factly, "Lou, you're going to fly the plane." At first, I thought he was kidding. I was terrified of flying the tiny craft 2,000 feet above the ground but willing. Gil took his hands off his yoke instructing me to take hold of mine. He told me to tip or lift the steering wheel and nose to climb and speed up or to descend and slow down, watching the nose of the plane and staying at a steady speed. I followed his instructions exactly with trembling hands and a wildly beating heart. After circling Boerne to head back home, I eagerly returned control to Gil. But I will remember that plane ride always. Thanks to him, I can say, I flew a plane! And in commandeering that Cessna, my confidence soared, which was Gil's idea from the start. He was a sensitive and intuitive man.

That night, the elation I felt while flying went aground when I attended another women's support group at the Battered Women's Shelter and heard myself sharing feelings of self-pity and anger at having lost so much so recently: my father, my residence, my relationship, myself. The women reminded me I was going through normal stages of grief but I had the love of others. And I was loving myself back to health. I needed to hear those reassuring words over and over again. I thought, too, if I could get back to work, I would feel better about everything.

I spent Christmas weekend and the New Year's holiday with Mama. She later told me how much she enjoyed it, despite Daddy's absence. And when the holidays and graduate school were behind me, with a recovery program and fellowship around me, I ramped up my work search, believing something good was bound to come of the building momentum.

The end of the year found me as it does every year, in reflection. The past 12 months had dealt brutal blows and hard knocks leaving me in varying stages of shock, sorrow, regret and strained familial ties. I was afraid and defensive. I could not understand why the people I loved were cruel and insensitive, but upon arriving in Al-Anon and through all the loss and heartache I found the beginnings of understanding. For decades I had blamed my failed relationships and life circumstances on others' betrayal and inability or unwillingness to love me; on my colleagues and bosses for unethical, discounting behavior; and on my unfulfilling relationship with God. But my heart now leapt with hope for the future, as Scripture told me: "I would have lost heart, unless I had believed that I would see the goodness of the Lord in the land of the living. Wait on the Lord, be of good courage, and He shall strengthen your heart" (Psalm 27:13-14 NKJV).

I found hope in Scripture and the optimism of the recovery program, fellowship and Big Book, the latter of which paved a way to problem-solving. It told me in the chapter entitled "Acceptance is the Answer" to focus on the answer, not the problem.

The tenets of recovery were clear-cut and simple to grab hold of, especially in troubling times. I woke up one day to find the pain was not gone but tapered. I was sad. I was grieving. But the incessant torture that had taken up residence in my gut was gone. I decided to make a pact with myself. I would not court another affair until I had finished working the 12 Steps and recovered my emotional health.

Through the healing rooms of recovery, did everything suddenly change? No. Did I experience clear undeniable corner-turners nearly immediately? Yes. Were the promised answers to my questions beginning to reveal themselves, as Brenda vowed? Most assuredly. But mostly it was and would be an ongoing unfolding. I was then and would be journeying toward something all the time.

I was like a river, ever flowing. I could not possibly have known then what lie ahead for me in the rooms of recovery or outside them, but I was ready and willing to find out. I was ready to treat and heal from the bleeding raw emotions that lay open like gaping sores on my heart. At long last, I had chosen the novel uncertainty of the path of recovery over the certainty of my former self-destruction. And I saw on the horizon a fresh frontier, full of potential and promise. But ahead of the coming promise came my mother.

My Mother, My Judge, My Friend

In-between my painful past and emerging emotional health was my mother.

As a new year began, I faced two giant hurdles: landing lucrative employment, and mourning my father's passing and with it the demise of my family as once I had known it. At the same time, Mama was coping with the death of her husband of 62 years along with the fear and anxiety of living alone, and the uncertainties ahead fed by her advancing age and weakening health. Was it any wonder my mother and I would come to recurring conflict. I aimed to steer clear of clashes and that meant staying laser-focused on recovery. After a few weeks' exposure to Al-Anon, open AA meetings, recovery literature, dedicated prayer and counseling, I fully understood if I let lapse any part of it, I would fail at all of it. As if God wanted to encourage me, on a taciturn morning in mid-January, I shred 36 scribbled requests from my God Box, which gave me hope. The discarded paper prayers had come true or no longer posed problems.

At this time, dealings with my mother and sisters fluctuated like the wide swing of a pendulum, never settling in a calm middle for long. It was a strain and draining as I grieved through the emotional sways. Al-Anon was teaching me to trust my Higher Power, God, yet I wept habitually. And the longer I lived without income, the more fear and tears were mine. I'd heard people in meetings say when they struggled with a haunting problem, they ramped up service to others, even in small ways, such as smiling at people or saying hello. They said it eased their burden a while and sooner than later something sweet always came from those small gestures. I decided to give it a try. When people confessed in meetings or group counseling they were troubled, I promised to pray for them, told them I would, and listed their names in a prayer notebook I referred to each morning. Praying for others by name fueled my faith, while Al-Anon and daily devotionals taught me to be less scared and more attentive to the struggles of others. I felt a growing strength.

Then one night, Mama screamed at me on the phone after I called to check on her. We had gotten into a conversation about her completing and mailing papers concerning Daddy's passing and I asked if she had kept copies, to which she said, "Yes, but not everything." I then replied, "Oh, Mama, why not?" She explained she wanted to be rid of those papers. And then I committed an egregious error; I repeated my remark about her not keeping copies and that's when she screamed. In her defense, she sounded exhausted. I asked her please to not scream, to which she asked, "Was I screaming?" I quickly remembered I, too, had screamed at people in the past when I was afraid or spent.

It also reminded me to keep my advice to myself unless asked. Since I had not known what was best for me most of my life, how could I possibly know what was best for Mama. And thanks to Al-Anon I was learning pressing someone more than once about anything more often than not was not an act of concern but control. In that brief moment, I also had not taken time to consider those papers made Mama re-live the reality of Daddy's death. I made amends to her on the spot.

I was learning invaluable lessons in Al-Alon that served me in my relationship with Mama. "Principles before personalities" was teaching me to practice tolerance and compassion, refuse the cancerous spread of gossip, consider feelings fluctuate, and grant the other person might be right. On the flip side, there were times Mama labeled something I had said or done in my clumsy effort to practice the principles of recovery as pure stubbornness rather than healthy resolve.

I am a slow learner sometimes and impatient with my own snail's pace. Even after all I was doing and learning, I still backslid to "God, what else do You want from me!" As if God was withholding my ability to handle every situation, especially with my mother, with ease. And here I had another epiphany. No. It was not God withholding anything. I was working on changing and change takes time. In dealings with Mama, I had to get ahold of and remove negative thinking! It did not require I do more or be more. Only that I treat myself more gently, more lovingly. And if I could do that for me, then I could do it for Mama.

Ultimately, I conceded to coping with mine and Mama's grief by completely trusting God and putting God first. I decided to start asking God for help with every little thing, even the threading of a needle. I doubled-down on worrisome thoughts whenever they bubbled up by replacing them with a reassuring mantra: "I think only harmonious thoughts." I began to realize God must occupy my first thought instead of my last-ditched cry for rescue. I understood what He wants of me is to ask for His help, and then, expect it, in God's idyllic time, not mine. Waiting on God's timing, now that was something else altogether. I still felt a sense of urgency to act. To speak. But Al-Anon had an answer for this, too. If I acted or spoke because I felt anxious, then it was not God but the "ism" and old behavior prompting it.

I began feeling deeply grateful for my mother. For our relationship and time together. Through Al-Anon, God was giving me insight into my character defects and a program through which I could change and become healthier for myself and my rapport with Mama. I realized God allowed me to suffer as long as I chose to but was there when I called for help.

I also was eager to grow my faith as a Christian and live it. Doing so was sure to bolster my patience with Mama and myself. During one Sunday service I heard a strong resounding theme: Patience is the most important attribute a Christian develops. I wondered, was God talking to everyone or just me? One winter night near January's end, my remade resolve to patience was tested. During a phone call, Mama raised her voice again, accusing me of not listening and expecting me to understand her without question. I had spent the entire day with her and had taken her to church that evening. I explained I could not understand what she had tried to tell me and naturally asked questions to clarify, and I could not accept her yelling or screaming at me anymore. That led us into upsetting back-and-forth finger-pointing. I apologized for my part quickly and Mama apologized, too. I knew she missed Daddy terribly. I, too, missed my father.

After that happened, I phoned Lynn. A saving grace on numerous occasions, he explained Mama may be closer to me than my sisters and was in her third stage of grief: anger. This boiled down to me being a safe harbor for her simmering pent-up feelings and fear. Immediately afterward I phoned Mama and told her I understood she was afraid and missed Daddy. She apologized again, but I suggested we forget it and we swapped I love you's.

During the months I lived with Kelly, Mama had peppered the mailbox with caring cards and thoughtful handwritten notes addressed to me. If a week or two went by without my receiving one, it was unusual. I read, saved and savored each and every one. My mother was someone I turned to and looked up to, but I was concerned she would worry each time I spoke of hard times I was muddling through, so I did not tell her everything.

I had promised Kelly in November if I was not working and able to move within two or three months, then I would ask Mama if I could stay with her till on my feet. I discussed it with Mama who happily agreed. We talked of my helping her around the house, running errands, taking her to appointments and offering familiar company in an otherwise empty home. When I told Kelly I'd be moving to Mama's by early March, she said my being with her had been helpful and bonding and wrote me a note one day that read: "You're a good friend, Lou, and it's a blessing for me to have you as a sister." In light of my then estrangement from my three biological sisters, her note filled my heart with warmth and hope. I thanked Kelly profusely and repeatedly for all she had done for me, letting me stay for months with her, Felix and Button, all the while underfoot. But she did not want more thank you's. All she asked is I "pay it forward."

In early February, I vacated Kelly's guestroom leaving her to her solitary status quo and headed to Mama's, where I occupied Daddy's room. Mama seemed pleased to have me, along with Cristi in her urn, which I sat on the dresser next to my beta fish, Miracle, in its miniature bowl. It felt good to be there.

Despite progress in recovery, failed attempts to find work left me with recurring feelings of failure day after day, and I kicked myself mercilessly and fearfully for failing. I slipped in and out of all I had learned in recovery and even questioned the existence of God. I cursed the devil and I cursed God. I hated everyone and everything. I cried a river. And when I was spent yet again, I realized how ridiculous I was to be angry at God in whose existence I refused yet to whom I turned for help and chuckled at my own absurdity. And once again I was humbled by my roller-coaster emotions and frailty. I was scared; after all, anyone in my shoes would be. And increasingly, I was eager to work the 12 Steps with a sponsor.

Returning to my childhood home was not as placid as I'd hoped. I wanted to strangle my beloved mother after experiencing a side of her that left me bruised and bewildered. Growing up, she had been a tough taskmaster. Demure, she was, but a force to be reckoned with, like a reticent sleuth. An often demanding wife and mother, Mama had issued high alerts to Daddy and us to do her biddings, executed to stringent standards. On the flip side, my mother was a most considerate and faith-filled woman. It struck me one day Daddy surely had endured decades of her perfectionism-turned-obsessive compulsive disorder and now, I unfortunately had inherited the incessant transfer of expectancies.

Please understand, there were plenty of glimmers of bright light in my stay under Mama's roof. We ate meals and watched TV together and baked Grandma Floy's kolaches. I was glad at first to be there. But with each passing week, her harsh tone stemming from repudiation of my gay lifestyle, despite that I was not dating, was unendurable and her expectations of me were draining. I had no time to myself.

At sunrise one early April day, I drove to the park on Lord Road a few blocks from St. Benedict and there walked the paved trail a while listening to Christian music. I then sat down atop a picnic table painted the color of a red barn, the same color Daddy had painted our house one year, and phoned and talked a long while with a friend in recovery. When we ended our call, I thought back to 1977 when I had sat atop a table at this very park, maybe this very table, and bawled my eyes out to God in excruciating agony. Now, nearly 30 years later, here I sat, same place, different me. Broken, but on the way to putting myself back together. Instead of tears, desperation and isolation as it had been before, my eyes were clear, a phone was in my hand, and I had someone caring to talk to.

Instead of unbearable anguish, I often felt happy for hours at a time. I was meeting new people, attending recovery meetings and church, and choosing to steer clear of confrontations with my sisters, and with Mama, as much as possible. And I had a growing knowing my future would be unlike my past. The difference had nothing to do with expectations of a trial-free future. It had to do with the healing of my mental, emotional and spiritual selves, which strung altogether day after day would create a healthier and, I believed, happier me.

I tried doubly hard to grow a thick skin off which to ricochet Mama's unkind words that held propensity to level me low at the most inopportune times, usually when I had gotten a bit of good news. I tried to work my Al-Anon program, to keep my hurt feelings to myself and share them only with the Al-Anon fellowship, to remember Mama was grieving loss of Daddy, to zip my lip. But unfortunately and progressively, I was unable to follow through. My own grief was fresh, and in dealing with my needs on top of Mama's expectations, my limitations became regularly and obviously apparent. I repeatedly was met by my sisters' scorn as well; anything negative that happened between me and Mama was by default my fault. When Mama spoke mean words and I told her the words stung, sometimes she said she meant them and then nearly immediately restated, "I guess that was mean," or "I guess that was smart," in a roundabout apology. It seemed a hopeless situation. I didn't know what to do but keep up with my recovery and work search.

As I had done since the start of the new year, I made a full-time job of looking for a job, regularly attended recovery meetings Tuesday and Thursday nights, and devoted Wednesday evenings to previewing houses and apartments for rent. These simple acts took me out of the house and gave me something to look forward to, a potential light at the end of a dismal tunnel. One night, I called Aunt Frances to check on her and Uncle George Edward and asked what she'd do if one of her daughters moved home. She said in not so many words they'd likely kill each other. While her response made us both laugh, the sentiment was true.

I began reading about detaching with love from people, places and things. At first, I did not understand what it was or how to do it. How do you "detach"? I learned it means emotional detachment and not necessarily physical removal, but it can be both. I wanted to stand for myself in a tense situation while being as respectful of others, of Mama, as possible. Given my newness at practicing loving detachment, my first attempts were awkward.

I also knew I had to set boundaries if ever I was going to find a job and my own place and keep my sanity. But every time I took time for myself, my mother tried to lure me back into doing something for her or said something unkind to guilt-trip me if I declined. I simply could not do it all. So when I said no to something Mama wanted, to say yes to myself to something time-urgent and important, the fiery cannonballs that were my mother's wrathful words came hurling at me. The more awkwardly I tried detaching with love and setting boundaries, sometimes at first with an inadvertent fit of temper, details of which my mother reported to my sisters, the more my sisters consorted against me, with one calling Al-Anon a cult. They did not grasp the principles of detachment or boundaries so they could not appreciate my clumsy practice.

One day, the three of them took Mama to lunch and pumped her with "Betty Lou is abusing you," misconstruing my efforts at boundaries and condemning my random lapses into a lost temper. They asked my mother,

"You want us to come remove her?" as if I were a fugitive. When my mother told me later of my sisters' words, I was hurt upon hearing but should not have expected otherwise. Mama and I, on the other hand, had our conflicts but thanks to Al-Anon and my counseling we were talking them through, making our apologies and forgiving each other. My sisters however seemed hell-bent on seeing me thrown out. That evening, tired and puffy-eyed from crying, I attended a Mozart concert and afterward paid Kelly a visit. When I told her what had happened at home, she urged me to stay the night. I did and slept nine hours. In the morning, she served me coffee and a filling breakfast of more of her steady moral support.

Finally the day I strived for arrived. I landed a full-time job as an advertising executive with a news-talk radio station starting in May and found a third-floor one-bedroom apartment for which I leased with plans to occupy by month's end. It was only a few miles from Club 12 and access to meetings. That very day, when I was hired and pre-let the apartment, I received in the mail my first student loan bill. The job had come in the nick of time.

And oh, how I missed Daddy. Sometimes I'd sense his presence, in a grand blue jay squawking or a bright red cardinal chirping loudly from a nearby tree limb. While he was alive, my father had kept everyone harmonized and held back the ugly wave of strife. He told me once, "Betty Lou, you cannot trust anyone, not even family." I had not grasped his meaning then but now was facing the brunt of its truth. Mama and my sisters seemed to have formed a consortium that seemed swayed against me. No matter how hard I worked, for Mama or my recovery, it didn't seem to matter to my family. Mama's attitude toward me was intermittently and perplexingly hostile and unrealistically expectant insofar as my caring for her every need. One morning, for instance, I drove her to a hair salon, left to do her grocery shopping, and then circled back to pick her up. But when I arrived at the salon, there was no thank you, only her complaint I was late.

Once home again, we found Mary waiting. Mama greeted her kindly while at once ceased speaking to me throughout my sister's entire visit, except for one comment. My mother handed me a snip from the newspaper and said, as an order, "Check this website to see if I've won something," returning her full attention to my sister. I apologized I couldn't comply, explaining I had spent most of the day on her errands and I had paperwork to complete for my new job. Mama refused to accept what she asked of me would take more time than she realized. I reminded her she rarely thanked me for anything but expected more. Her response was flat: "When I have time to get down on my knees, I'll do that." And so it went with me and Mama. I began to feel loathsome of my own mother and of myself for harboring such sorry feelings toward her. I did not like who she was then. And I did not like myself when with her. She was cold to me but to my sisters and everyone outside home she was warm. I kept reminding myself Mama was grieving and so was I. She was angry and scared and so was I. I loved her. But I did not like her much right then. How I hoped and prayed this would change. In recovery, I heard, "Let it begin with me." I was willing to keep trying.

As planned, I started my new job and eagerly awaited my first paycheck, which would bring with the money my again newfound independence. Over Memorial Day weekend, two months after having moved in, I moved out of Mama's house and into my apartment thanks to friends from church and Al-Anon who lent a hand hauling my belongings up three lofty flights. Once resettled, I emailed my pastor a plea for support in overcoming the guilt and shame I carried about being gay. I explained every time I was around my mother since Daddy died, all I heard was how sinful my life was and how I was the cause of every family problem. My pastor's response was predictably kind: "Precious Lou, I'm so sorry you're dealing with being guilt-tripped! Yes, there's a series coming up on this subject. Please, please join us."

As I resettled in my apartment and fitness routine, I worked full-time at my new job that albeit unknown to me at the time would lead to fresh professional horizons. I continued my recovery, counseling and weekly support group at the Battered Women's Shelter. I journaled copiously. Daily entries in the 40-day journal Gil and Joyce had given me for Christmas became my recluse, a place to reflect and unburden, another indispensable source of insight.

In all my looks at myself squarely in the mirror, I saw I was weakest in patience and acceptance and that these impeded my progress. I committed the Serenity Prayer to memory: "God grant me the serenity to accept the things I cannot change [others], courage to change the things I can [myself], and wisdom to know the difference." And I struggled to know my purpose. Perhaps growing through weakness and trouble would lead me to it, I thought. In recovery, I heard "pain has purpose." That laying down guilt means picking up acceptance. And acceptance starts with giving God the wheel. I chewed on all that a long while. Al-Anon was teaching me to detach rather than resist. Yet, as simple these concepts, changing my own behavior was much harder to carry out than contemplate. Despite stormy ends to my most intimate relationships and heartbreaking tensions with family, I began to believe I had gleaned a morsel of something good from those awful experiences. "But as for you, you meant evil against me, but God meant it for good..." (Genesis 50:20 NKJV).

I strove to take life in stride but often remained impatient with people, including my mother, the pace of my progress, and lagging answers to my questions: Would I ever break free of self-criticism and futile guilt? Would I ever learn to love myself despite others' scorn? Would I ever see myself in a loving light considering my mother's condemning angle? Would I ever truly forgive those who had hurt me? When would I stop feeling this low boil of anger? I kept hearing "To thine own self be true" as a key stepping stone to recovering myself, but I did not know yet how to do that; it sounded selfish and self-centered, traits I hoped to relinquish.

As I dove into work and recovery, my relationship with Mama softened. She was not able to navigate three flights but wanted to see from the ground the outside and balcony of my apartment. I imagined she missed having someone with her in the house and our times together now were less strained. I visited often and took her out to eat occasionally but spent the bulk of time rebuilding my life. One day, I realized my faith in a Power greater than myself, which I had found in recovery, had found its way into my relationship with Mama. Whenever I recognized her anxiety, I encouraged her. I had been reading Psalm 23 and memorizing it by accident through daily repetition recited it to her sometimes. She sat quietly listening and then complimented me on having committed it to memory. Hearing it recited soothed her. She commented how spiritual I had become.

Even though I experienced recurring rounds of sadness, loneliness or lapses in faith, Al-Anon helped me return to trusting God. The closer I felt to God, the closer I felt to Mama. For the first time, I understood worshipping God was not something I did to gain a grade in a spiritual point system. It was as Mama and Daddy had tried to instill in me through their example: that prayer and worship are what we give back to God for all the good God has given us.

Checking my tongue, being patient, showing compassion, respecting myself and others, all these are forms of worshipping God. Al-Anon is what brought me to this understanding. And suffering had brought me to Al-Anon. So my suffering God used for my good. It finally clicked: God had never given up on me. And I knew He never would. Could I live placidly in this knowing? I seemed to be doing precisely that.

What the future held was anyone's guess but unfortunately Mama and I would conflict again and again and sometimes the conflict would feel irreparable. There would be times when she would profess and confess aversion to my gay life and even nausea at hearing the word gay, despite her priest's attempts to console her, telling her God loves us all. My mother's concern went far beyond discomfort; it seeped from her lips reeking contempt. But Mama, after all, was doing the best she could with what she believed and what she believed was that I would burn in hell for eternity if I stayed gay. Maybe she was right. I believed not. Through it all, despite her methods, I knew Mama loved me and did not wish me harm. But I would become increasingly unable to recover myself while exposing my heart to what felt like hatred, for whatever reason and despite any underpinning of sincere concern. I would ultimately make the heart-wrenching choice to keep distance from my mother, and sisters, for gapes of time.

I knew from Roger and Daddy's passings each human life has a beginning and an end and the end date is a mystery. I hoped, passionately, Mama and I again would be friends, for good, someday.

Feelings of angst continued haunting me at times but the anxious days alternated with those of peace. Not because everything was going my way but because I was willing to grow. To grow in faith by practicing what-if. What if, I just believe Almighty God is real and His promises are true. I still struggled with turning over my will completely to God but I was willing to keep trying. I returned to practicing what I'd learned as a child but had left by the wayside. I began again to kneel before God every morning and thank God for my life. For my father and brothers. For enduring childhood memories of my sisters and me. And for my mother, my judge, my friend.

An Inside Job

Recovery is not a religious practice but a spiritual process that allowed me to define my own understanding of God. But make no mistake, recovery requires belief in and turnover of self-will to a Higher Power, a Spirit.

My Higher Power revealed itself rising out of a sea of salty tears. I wept my way through countless boxes of tissues my first three years in the rooms of recovery. Beyond a roller coaster ride, those years were cliffhangers complete with continuums of high elations and cavernous lows. The recovery program was straightforward and simple, but unraveling the tangled mess of my life and heart was going to take time and hard, diligent work. I had a long way to go but I kept hearing to take it one day at a time all the while striving for balance, which I'd find if I worked this simple plan.

Despite the brutally honest effort required of me, I was head-over-heels with Al-Anon. I didn't understand it all; of course I didn't. By January 2006, I was only a few weeks into it. But already its principles were operating in and through me, almost by default, as I put my butt in a chair at meetings and opened my ears, read the literature every day, and stayed in touch with my fellows. The program and its people fortified me. Aside from a rare few supportive individuals in other areas of my life, the rooms of recovery were nearly my only oasis of encouragement. And I needed it. Desperately. I needed to see some promise of potential for feeling better. For climbing out of the dark pit I had tripped into and still dipped in and out of in-between brief encounters with something resembling happy and lucid. Gratefully, it seemed the lows and highs were evenly split, which was far better than the nadirs consuming me, as they had unrelentingly before Al-Anon.

I did not know at the onset, and I'm glad I didn't know, it would take my first three years of spiritual reclamation to relinquish and remove the accumulated garbage living in my insides. It would take those years to turn my will and details and outcomes of daily life over to the care of a Higher Power. That it took three years of steady effort through the first three Steps in particular, which deal with admitting powerlessness and relinquishing control to God, roared thunderously about my record tendency to take charge.

I'm jumping ahead here but it's appropriate to mention I lost all desire for alcohol. In fact, I didn't drink anything alcoholic for those initial 36 months.

This was not deliberate. And because the desire for alcohol left me, I wondered whether I was an alcoholic. One Tuesday night, soon after New Year's Eve and two months past my three-year mark, I shared this wonder with the Coker group. I explained I had bought a bottle of champagne to drink a midnight toast, poured a single glass of the chilled bubbly, put the rest in the fridge, sipped the champagne, and went to bed soon thereafter. The following morning, I emptied the remaining wine down the drain. A friend in AA shed light on my question. "That you had one glass and discarded the rest shows you are not an alcoholic, Lou. An alcoholic would have drunk the entire bottle after opening it and went looking for more. A bottle of alcohol never sits undrunk in an alcoholic's home."

I accepted his words. They made sense. I was not an alcoholic. But I knew and shared in meetings I had drank alcoholically, that is, habitually and heavily, from my mid-20s to my mid-30s and possessed the propensity to be alcoholic. I was gratified to know I had chosen to recover from the effects of past chronic alcoholic behavior on my mental, spiritual and emotional selves. Even without actively drinking those first years in recovery, alcoholic isms were my constant unwelcome companions. Al-Anons and AAs alike spoke of similar isms, such as obsession, emotional outbursts or overbearing behavior. Some alcoholics reported they were unrecovered Al-Anons before admitting to being alcoholic and some Al-Anons said they discovered they were alcoholic during the process of recovery. Many had been ACOAs, raised in alcoholic homes regularly exposed to an alcoholic parent, grandparent, aunt or uncle.

In my case, I had not grown up in an alcoholic home. But as I read and heard about the generational family disease and long-term effects of alcoholism and listened to stories told by recovering AAs and ACOAs, I learned emotional abandonment is a common malady passed along to children who grow up in alcoholic homes. It often haunts them as adults until, if and when they realize and treat it. In adults, abandonment sparks insecurity and fear, which can fuel anger and controlling behavior. This resonated strongly with me. Through this awareness, I began to understand Mama's mental illness had created a similar dynamic in our family. In me. Her emotional unavailability due to mental illness and its therapies and Daddy's stern structured parenting as a result of Mama's illness often resulted in their inability to be warm or attentive, which left me feeling abandoned. On the flipside, when I did get attention, it seemed aimed at blame. As an adult, I had carried all that like dragging rocks. Although unintentional, the fallout of feeling abandoned and blamed scarred me with something resembling the ACOA. I thus was marked by alcoholic isms.

Later than sooner, I recognized the disease of alcoholism seemed common across family, friends and coworkers, and that the isms were no discriminators of age, finances, education, intelligence or any other context.

Thanks to recovery, I had numerous spiritually founded insights. I was starting to see "church" less as a building and more as a body of believing people. A group of people in recovery who believe in the 12 Steps and practice those principles in everyday life is a church. The natural world is an expansive tabernacle. And churches are bodies of people who collectively worship God. Over time I had tried different churches, including Catholic, Baptist, Lutheran, Methodist, Presbyterian, United Unitarian and nondenominational. The only ones I had not tried were mosques and synagogues. I was uncertain as to where all this church-going had led me. But I did know this: I belonged in recovery because from the start I felt better, stronger, healthier. And I belonged in nature where I felt nearest to God's straightforward might and majesty. Ever more, I also saw God cleverly disguised as people, in Brenda who pointed to recovery, in Kelly who gave me safe haven, in Bill who counseled me into rational thinking, and in the kind faces of my fellows in the rooms of recovery.

I worked resolutely to change my wrong thinking, feeling and behaving but still unwittingly held on tight to unwholesome behaviors, people and situations. In retrospect, it was a disgusting habit. Some of this clarified itself in short order through the process of recovery. Some of it would take years to uncover and purge. I was learning I could not improve anything about myself until I understood my character defects, one of which was perfectionism. People throughout my life had told me I am too hard on myself. I supposed that had been true, perhaps the byproduct of my mother's high standards and Catholic acumen. But I wanted to figure out how to cut myself slack while striving for excellence. I did not want to remain perfectionistic or to accept mediocrity but to learn balance, an aspiration I heard about often in recovery.

To live in balance, I had to get free of unjustifiable injurious anger. I was learning of two types of anger. Virtuous, or moral, anger is healthy. But uncontrolled angry outburst, the result of giving in to impatient impulses, is destructive and to be overcome not excused or fed. One day, I attended two recovery meetings back-to-back where others' insights on anger strengthened my determination to be free of it by steering clear of provocation. I looked forward to a full-time Al-Anon sponsor.

I kept up with my 40-day journal. It reminded me God "shapes" each of us for a particular way of life, call it "service or vocation," using our "spiritual gifts, heart, abilities, personality and experience." I believed what it said about pain, too: "… your greatest ministry will most likely come out of your greatest hurt." I had been hurt by self-destruction, other people and uninvited tragedies. I had witnessed people I loved deeply, my younger brother and father, suffer horrifically. I thought about this a while, and journaled about it a while longer, and had yet another epiphany: I would write stories that benefitted others. Perhaps that was my purpose. I did not want to write solely for money. I wanted my work to mean something, to be of worthwhile use. I felt affirmed in my pursuit of my purpose in the written word each time I articulated and shared a circumstance in recovery meetings and afterward was told by others my words had touched them, or whenever I published an article and a reader commented my words had resonated with them. I aimed to turn the hurts in life into help for myself and others through writing.

I also realized I no longer shrank from talking about my newfound connection with God. The topic was easier to raise than it had been prior to Al-Anon. And I noticed I was not as afraid about my future. If I kept doing the next right thing and trusted God with the rest, I would be fine. I would at least try. I found it curious when I professed and practiced my faith in God around the corner was another trial, but equally so was resolution. It was reassuring to know to expect trouble but also to expect to move through it.

My new resolve to live morally modified my social life, which largely consisted of my recovery fellowship. Instead of frequenting bars, I sought other forms of fun. One night, I attended a book reading. It gave me insight into how newly published authors handle themselves in public, how and what they read, and what goes on at such events. I imagined myself at the podium, orating words from a published book I would pen. On another evening, I had dinner with a school chum from St. Benedict whose father had been in the Knights of Columbus with Daddy and who had passed away on my friend's birthday two months ahead of my father. Smoking Marlboros till we emptied a pack, we talked a long time, reminisced, and shared our stories of relationship struggles.

As the weeks in recovery passed, I became keenly aware God's universe was vibrantly alive and so was I, a part of it, and if I kept God first, praised and honored and thanked Him first, if I constantly tried to fill my mind with hopeful trust, then there would be no limit to who I could be or what I could achieve. It seemed an optimistic outlook was a straight line to an unlimited universe of possibilities. The previous year had been a titanic trial. Before Al-Anon, I struggled and pushed my way through everything. Now I was learning to pray my way through, and to watch and listen for God's promptings instead of rushing headlong into potential disaster. Still, I was new at this novel conduct.

I learned to begin each day with gratitude. If I was busy thanking God, then I'd have less time to fret over bothers. If I succeeded, then my thoughts, words and actions would reflect appreciation, which would dissolve in me fledgling bitterness. And this in turn could only benefit everyone around me. It did not take long for me to see it is not God who causes suffering. I had chosen it by showing up willingly to be in the company of those who held capacity to harm me and often through provocation had behaved in a manner far beneath who I in truth am, the woman God created me to be.

And now comes the hard part of all I was learning: Putting the principles consistently into practice. It was harder than I expected. And I would need spiritual mentors and a proving ground to practice what I learned. About this time, my allotted counseling with Bill ended.

Since the start, recovery meetings with some exception had consisted mainly of my Coker home group on Tuesday nights and Saturday morning Al-Anon meetings at Club 12. There, I met an unassuming man named Edwin who was a military veteran and chaired the Alateen meetings. He was a tireless advocate of Al-Anon. After observing him a while, I approached Edwin one morning, telling him I was in need of a sponsor and asking he be mine. At my meek inquiry, he advised it was usual for obvious reasons a man sponsor men and a woman sponsor women, but since I'd shared I was gay, he agreed, but only for a time and for how long he was unsure. Once I related the rundown of my life, he told me three things: Allow myself to grieve my losses. Get settled in my new nest, Edwin's name for my apartment. And, "Write your story, Lou. Get it out there to help other people." I had hoped for a sponsor but had not anticipated one who would reaffirm my plan to write with purpose.

One sunny Monday after Independence Day, I phoned Edwin to tell him I was mad as hell and had been all weekend. I had spent it regurgitating my past. His advice was wise and straight. He told me to put aside my anger, get to work, and that night write down the reasons for my fury. Later, looking at my list of 40, I was appalled at my incessant habitual unregulated obsession; I was unsurprised yet again that often I was the one who allowed the inexcusable; and finally, I was grateful to return full-circle to the wholesome choice I had made to enter recovery and get well. After sharing these insights with Edwin, he suggested I read the chapter in the Big Book titled "The Doctor's Opinion." Those words pointed the way and simple means by which a new life is formed: grounded in God. But nearly as soon as I resolved again to trust God, my resolve flew away like a bird fleeing a whooshing broom. And I would have to recapture my faith in God again and again.

Outside the rooms of recovery, where I was challenged to practice what I was learning inside the rooms, I labored to learn the radio advertising business, get along with colleagues, and meet expectations of the sales manager to whom I reported. As the months passed, however, the more I experienced the intermittent wrath of my boss, the more I wanted to quit. Whenever my sales fell short, he belittled and yelled at me in open meetings. The more he verbally beat me, the more I kicked myself after each "you don't measure up" beating and wanted to flee from his abhorrent harassing tactics. I held my tongue while holding on to the principles of recovery that helped me navigate abusive and worrisome waters at work.

In early August, my employer treated everyone to a party at the lake on a pontoon boat from which folks were free to swim, ski or Sea-Doo the day away. As the day wore on, cliques formed and stuck to themselves. People got drunk and loud. And while I forced myself to socialize, few reciprocated. The day was very long and very boring and I was very glad when it ended. That night, I reflected on the day and people and came to some conclusions. I never cared for cliques. I am not a swimming, skiing or Sea-Dooing person. I am a fishing and camping person. And I did not like, trust or respect most of the people with whom I worked.

Sometimes, I found my imagination on brief excursions from cares I carried. After church the Sunday after the lake party, for instance, I stood in the breezeway in-between the chapel and fellowship hall aimlessly immersed in people-watching. I watched a woman with whom I had spoken several times as she mingled with other churchgoers. She wore a sleeveless blouse that exposed a large prominent scar on her right shoulder I had not noticed before, and I wondered why, where, what in the world happened to her? I quickly realized my thoughts were lighthearted, and it dawned on me, I was not occupied with pessimistic worry. This, was progress.

I began taking notice people were taking notice of me. I was asked on casual dates with women and in accepting exposed myself to a variety of personalities, some unwholesome. When, for example, a new acquaintance without word broke an appointment, leaving me in the lurch and then excusing herself after the fact, I let her know I expected people to be courteous. Naturally, I declined a second date. Being a person of the desired moral character I aspired to and expected in others with whom I associated felt far better and healthier than playing along with conduct that did not serve me well. Edwin congratulated me on the breakthrough in beginning to break my codependent pattern. And, I was lonely. But doing the right thing does not always feel good. As Lynn once told me reiterating a famous quote dating back to the 12th century, "No good deed goes unpunished." I supposed my practice at moral behavior was punished by loneliness.

I was getting better at practicing the principles of recovery, often detaching emotionally and sometimes physically, and often without angry outbursts, guilt or taking others' behavior personally. It felt good to do it. I remembered what Mama and Daddy tried to tell me before I married Scott: I am no better than anyone else but I am different. Despite my failings, I was returning to who I was born and raised to be, a woman with an inherent sense of moral courage, spiritual sensitivity and integrity. Edwin told me never to lose my integrity trying to please others. From what I knew of him, he had survived extreme abuse. He helped me realize I had developed a rotten habit of being with people who made me feel anxious and insecure and that had become normal for me. I already had figured out I migrated toward the emotionally unavailable, which I traced to childhood, and now, Edwin's insight reinforced for me that emotional distance was the direct cause of anxiety and insecurity. He said I could break that stinking habit by surrounding myself with people who fed into me. And above all, accept and believe God loves me.

I knew it was sound advice. I wanted to stop chasing after love and acceptance from people and instead find it in God and myself. I wanted to live as if every part of my life depended on God, He Who created me. But I didn't know how to follow through. I was learning and trying to live by what I learned. But no matter my positive progress, my mind was a mesh of conflicting thoughts still riddled with self-reproach. I was tired of teeter-tottering emotions and the consequent slush they made of my brain. Or was it the other way around? Did my thoughts drive my feelings? I couldn't figure it out. Neither could I comprehend why, after all I heard and learned in recovery, was I not yet able to apply it consistently. I felt like a flibbertigibbet making a limp effort.

One day, my journaling shone silver light on the black-and-white fluctuations. Likely since the age of 4, I had tried to fill the bottomless hole in my heart. I now realized it was I who had perpetuated that emptiness and it was I who had the power to fill it. The reason the emptiness remained was because I still allowed unloving people into my heart. This had to stop. True loving detachment is exactly that: detachment. My own recurring hypocrisy was precisely what held me back. It kept God's wholesome all-encompassing love from saturating my heart. And without my letting His love reside in me, I would not let God have all of me. I had to do as I had purposed from the start… stop whining over feelings of being unloved or lonely. Focus every day, all day, on my relationship with God.

I was beginning to grasp my repetitive back-and-forth thinking and feeling was my struggle with myself to let go and let God. I never had imagined it would be a tangible fight. But there it was. The hurt in me was fighting against the recovery in me and sooner or later one or the other would win the contest.

I would never have the loving relationships I craved with myself or anyone else until I let God fill the void in my heart, and the void in my heart was caused by the void in my spirit. And the only way to love was through God, who is Spirit. Living in and through the spirit changes everything, how I think, feel, speak, behave and discern. Only then would I feel His unending love and love myself. Not only would I read, hear and talk about it, I would live it. As sure as I clutched this new clarity, I would fail to follow it. A major and apparent shift in behavior still had to happen. So I asked God every day to guide me in everything and take care of Mama.

Shortly after Labor Day, Edwin gifted me with a paperback, "Serenity, A Companion for Twelve Step Recovery, Complete with New Testament, Psalms, and Proverbs." Inside the cover he inscribed, "Lou, I pray this book will help you find true serenity. Love in Al-Anon, Edwin, Sept. 2, 2006."

As he guided me through Step 4 to list my shortcomings in earnest, beyond the meek effort I had made months prior, the first task he asked of me was to inventory my virtues ahead of defects. The exercise proved uplifting and preparatory. My virtues, those traits like dependable, truthful, intuitive, imaginative, open-hearted, clean and ethical, far outweighed my defects, but the deficiencies that damaged my life had to be dealt with. A few of the glaring failings I identified were anger, control, ego, fear, impatience (a fault for which my mother had chastised me and one I upheld as a virtue when an abusive situation justifiably called for intolerance), insecurity, talking instead of listening, aggressiveness versus gentleness, candor over compassion, and disagreeableness versus considerateness (excluding defensible brusqueness toward cruelty). My discovery: I liked me.

I liked that when I bought pictures to hang on my walls I selected those reflecting who I am: an untitled portrait of a young woman in anguish from misplaced love; a brightly hued watercolor of sleek wispy female figures, like fairies with wings, titled "One day fed up with hell she simply up and left" (Falk January 1994); an untitled pastel watercolor of a woman wearing a wide-brimmed rose-colored western hat standing alongside her horse; and a framed print of a girl with her hair swept into a ponytail, standing alone and pensive next to a barn, with yellow wildflowers in her hand and a faraway longing in her eyes that were turned toward a beckoning dirt road. I liked that many of my belongings held deep sentimental value and family history. Daddy's Stetson. Grandma Floy's maroon coin purse and pink bud vase. Dish towels Mama gave me. Flannel pajamas and matching robe with coffee cups on them from my parents one Christmas. The quilt Grandma Guckian lovingly handstitched and inscribed January 1954 as a gift to my father, now folded over Great-Grandpa Mercer's rocker Daddy gave me.

Step 4 was a rigorous exercise demanding a serious and scrupulous self-analysis. I deduced at this Step's depth many may not venture near it; ourselves are very difficult to face. I was grateful I was willing to do it. A profound revelation of the exercise summed up the whole of my work in recovery must be focused on… myself. Not on those who had hurt me, unintentionally or maliciously, the ones I sobbed over early on at Coker. Not on circumstances. On me. And only me. And for the first time, I truly understood recovery is "an inside job."

As I worked on myself, strained relations with my sisters persisted. At times I still reacted angrily but other times I responded with poise. I still toyed with the idea of disconnecting from them and Mama altogether until I was healthy enough to handle hurtful behavior without regret. I did not know yet whether I should act on the idea or would be successful. I was, however, sure I did not want to hurt anymore and I did not want to hurt anyone else with pent-up anger from being hurt.

As I worked to recover my emotional self, still guarded and tangled, I boldly marched my professional self toward a green adventure and gravid hope. When winter turned frigid so did my feelings for the job I held with the radio station. It was increasingly evident the sales manager and I had come to a standoff. I was fed up with his unprincipled hostility, as fed up as he was with my decreasing sales. The more I felt like a misfit there, the more I considered resigning. I had dallied in part-time freelancing as Writer for Hire for nine years and now dared to envision myself in a full-time sole-proprietorship as a communication pro, striking contracts with companies large and small. Being my own boss appealed to me so I devised a grand plan to pursue it.

After Christmas, Edwin told me he had melanoma, chose hospice over treatment, and put his affairs in order. He withdrew from meetings and Step work. I was sad and panicked but kept up with meetings and Step work on my own through journaling and using the book he had given me.

As 2006 drew near its end, so did my radio advertising job. I knew self-employment was doubly hard work with its own set of risk and challenge, but after all I had survived I felt sure I could handle whatever came. My emotional self still perplexed me, but I believed in my professional self. I was an educated experienced writer with marketing know-how. I decided to remake my former freelance project into a bona fide communication consulting enterprise where my clientele would reflect my ethics. I christened my new venture FishHook.

Every January, I take stock of my life and set fresh goals. In the prior year, I had entered recovery, left what I swore would be my last abusive relationship, attained my master's degree, and lived on credit. In the present year, I had begun my second year in recovery, joined a church I liked, leased an apartment, held a job until resigning from it to launch my business, and was paying down debt. The inside job I'd begun with Edwin was fresh but progressing. I still hungered for recovery and was convinced I would propel mine by working all 12 Steps with a new sponsor.

Edwin was my friend and teacher and he died in March two days after my birthday. And when he died, he left me gleaning a generous harvest from his seeds of time and wisdom. Edwin loved me unconditionally as a brother when members of my own family did not. He reinforced that I kneel before God every day to ask for knowledge of His will for me and stand through pain.

When I attended his burial, there were only myself, the minister, and scarce others but his adult offspring. It struck me odd, how this humblest of men who had come alongside me and given me the incalculable gift of time when he had so little left, would leave this world with so few bidding farewell. He was buried in a simple wooden coffin following a military ceremony complete with a three-volley gun salute, the playing of "Taps" by a trumpeting soldier, and the reverent American flag-folding with crisp pointed edges finishing the triangular shaped glory handed gently to his children.

I saw few tears in the eyes of mourners but observed through my own when filing past Edwin's family extending sympathy. A kindly lady I did not know approached me thereafter, smiled, looked into my eyes and said, "You will be blessed," and walked away. I never saw her again. But her words told me God and Edwin wanted me to know reinforcements were on the way. Later that day, I found an unexpected check in my mailbox for several hundred dollars' backpay from my former employer. The money came at a time when money was in short supply.

Some members of my family didn't get me. But Edwin did. As had Roger and Daddy. As did Kelly, Lynn and Judy. Those six saw my soul. And they cared. Edwin was a spiritual mentor, my first Al-Anon sponsor, and I would remember him. I was healthier for having known Edwin, who helped me build the foundational framework of my recovery and restored rapport with God.

Thanks to recovery, when I turned 52 that March, it was a perfectly serene day. It began with a phone call and "Happy Birthday" song from Mama, followed by a massage, aimless browsing through a department store, reading, taking calls from friends, and journaling. I made a list by name of the people who had hurt me, including myself, and proclaimed I released them all from my thoughts and heart. Then I took a long soak in a bubble bath and thereafter relaxed watching "The Cowboys" starring John Wayne in fond remembrance of Daddy's and my love of the outdoors and westerns. It occurred to me, because of my father's unwavering sacrifice and dedication, I knew what love was. And as much as he loved me, I knew God loved me infinitesimally more.

Like sound science, on the shoulders of Edwin came Judith. She had been in Al-Anon for years and had a sponsor. As with Edwin, I shared with her the synopsis of my life, family and relationships. Afterward, the first thing she asked of me as her sponsee was every night before bed to list three things for which I was grateful. The task proved encouraging. Instead of three, I often uncovered more. Gratitude lists became my bastion. Like my God Box and answered prayer, they reminded me of underlying goodness and lessened my perception of lack.

As winter bowed to spring, Judith and I sat together on a bench at the Lourdes Grotto at the Oblate Missions, a popular serene meeting spot, and there I cried my way through yet another litany of troubles involving family. Troubles sometimes left me feeling like a little girl instead of a grown woman, unable to measure up, deal, or let go of hurtful people or situations. I still held to a pattern of making strong resolve and then backsliding regularly. I could not stay grounded in what I was hearing in meetings and learning through Step work. She listened a while and then pointed to a small leafless tree limb where a bright red cardinal perched confidently, and said, "Did you know that whenever you see a cardinal, it's there to tell you everything is going to be OK?" I thought of Daddy. And then she told me if I did not attend at least three meetings a week, every week, she could not sponsor me. Meetings, she explained, are the core of recovery and would catapult mine. Sitting in tears was getting me nowhere.

I exceeded Judith's challenge by attending four or five meetings a week. I also began chairing Al-Anon meetings and sharing my story. Being of service cultivated humility and empathy in me. I left every gathering feeling more tranquil than when I had arrived. Judith had told the truth. My crying lessened as my confidence rose. Yet still I struggled with the heartbreak stemming from the pain of strained relations with my sisters. I did not understand it and wondered what I had done so awful, so deserving, of hatred. Was it my gay life?

If not, then what? Each of us had made our fair share of mistakes but were mine worse? The reason escaped me. Perhaps there was none. But Al-Anon had answers for me even when whispered subtly through the sheer act of heeding my sponsor's prompts. As Judith guided me through the Steps at the heart of them was journaling. I penned page after enlightening page of scribbled answers to questions posed in recovery guides.

On the work front, I was equally eager to learn all I could about growing my fledgling writing business and so spoke with a life coach named Mike referred to me by a friend. After I told Mike of my plans for FishHook and a bit of my background concerning negative experience with corporate America, he said in a gentle voice, "You need to heal from the corporate hurt."

Corporate hurt? Mike elaborated. When I spoke about FishHook, he said my tone filled with enthusiasm and passion. But when I talked of companies I had worked for, my tone and words soured. He reminded me corporate clients would be the most lucrative and long-lasting for FishHook, but before I could court them or talk with anyone else about my business, he suggested ever so softly but frankly, I'd have to lose the attitude.

Mike's words stopped me cold. I chewed on them for an entire week and decided he was right. I did harbor corporate hurt. I did feel scornful and negative and it was coming across in my attitude and speech. Pain had been a common denominator in both my professional and personal relationships. I looked forward to improving my attitude and letting go of pain. But meanwhile, I'd breathe and sleep and start all over again every new morning.

Aside from launching FishHook, reading recovery literature, attending and chairing recovery meetings, working the Steps, and attending to my prayer and exercise regimens, I read books by Christian authors and listened to evangelists on TV. I flashed back to Mama and Daddy sitting in their recliners in the living room watching Billy Graham. Here was I, a younger them. It made me smile. The authors I read and evangelists I watched each at varying times and ways told me the same thing: by turning to God I would rid myself of the fear and low self-worth I'd accrued. Their godly philosophies were akin to and echoed the spiritual program and principles I knew in recovery.

As spring announced Easter, I missed Mama. To forestall more pain from spilling into my bruised heart, I had seen and phoned her less often, preferring missing her to feeling sour about myself. I understood my vulnerability; I was shaky over getting hurt, again, believing the slightest thing could crush me. I could not afford to be crushed; I was launching a business and needed all the emotional reserves I could muster. I became progressively careful about who I shared what with, intending to keep myself from harm's way. A friend in recovery assured me once I finished the Steps I would be a changed person, able to handle situations and individuals with ease, and that fluctuations in feelings and resolve were normal and expected.

Memories of Daddy and of Mama and Daddy together kept me going in the face of my indistinguishable family. Sometimes the raw pain of some family members' indifference was excruciating. I felt if I did not release the building internal anguish I would explode like a bomb. I was a walking hemorrhaging heart harboring a pyramid of pain that had reached its pinnacle and I had no capacity for more. Sometimes, the pain was so fierce my stomach ached. Sometimes I wanted to scream. Sometimes I did scream, at the top of my lungs until I could scream no more. It was terrible and terrifying. It was, insane. The love I wanted to share with my family could not endure the cruelty with which I was met. I was learning love and cruelty cannot coexist yet I tried to force it. This dichotomous conflict was killing me.

A wonderful thing happened after Easter. I secured a lucrative contract for FishHook with a federal government contractor located at the air force base where Daddy once worked. On the first day on the job, as I neared Building 2000 at the top of Security Hill where on its second floor Daddy had spent workdays, I pulled off onto the road's shoulder and parked. I sat staring through the chain link fence topped with barbed wire and remembered my father. There he had occupied a small office furnished only with a desk and chair dwarfed by tall locked metal cabinets lining every wall and filled with documents Daddy either had written or reviewed. Everyone liked Gene. He was a lean, young, muscular man then, with thick dark wavy hair he kept slicked back with hair cream and a white nylon comb in a leather sheath Lynn made for him in Cub Scouts. Daddy always carried it in his pocket.

That afternoon, I struck up a conversation with a man named Billy as we walked to the parking lot. I happily blurted out all about Daddy, how he had passed away but used to work there, how it felt strange and good to be where Daddy had been; I could have been tracing the very footsteps he had taken hundreds of times to and from the office, chatting along the way with coworkers and Generals. Billy was attentive and kind in reply, "This is good closure for you." And then I shared how much Daddy loved fishing, when Billy exclaimed, "Now, that's the magic word!" Billy was friendly like Daddy. My father touched me through him, a stranger who spoke to me in a tone and words Daddy would have used. As it also happened, the initials of the company with which I was engaged were E.G., the same as my father's initials.

And herein I had another epiphany. When I live in God's world, I recognize His grace. Merely being in the world is not living in God's world. God's world is spiritual and affects the physical. Had I not been receptive to God's delicate messages, I would have missed His soothing touch.

Mentors of the Spiritual Kind

In the spiritual work of recovery, each sponsor typically asks a novice sponsee to work the Steps anew and Judith was no different. At Step 1 again, admitting to powerlessness still felt frightening and nervy. If I admitted to having no power, then where would that leave me? But once I admitted powerlessness over what I had no power to control—the weather, Mama's aging, my sisters, others' opinions or attitudes, outcomes, the past, the future—it made sense.

Judith also suggested I do more service work, promising me the more service I did, "God would bless me double." I decided to try. Again, she was right. The more I chaired and shared at meetings, the more I volunteered with my church, the more clients and income flowed into FishHook and confidence into me.

By Mother's Day, I felt emotionally well enough to visit Mama. That Saturday, I purged her storage shed in the backyard and Sunday drove us to Mass and then to a restaurant for lunch with my sisters. I observed as if from the sidelines my Al-Anon program working that afternoon, allowing myself to feel uncomfortable without reacting. I evoked what I'd heard in recovery: "Don't take the bait."

Sometimes I felt overwhelmingly alone and lonesome for family as it used to be, long before Daddy fell ill. I recalled how we rallied and helped each other through Roger's tragic death and all the Easter Sunday barbecues and Christmas Eves we had shared. But I could not resurrect the past or live in make-believe. Later at home alone with Mama, I dared talk with her about my observations of my sisters and found her receptive. She was aging but not blind or stupid. She was painfully aware and asked me several times to visit her again. That evening, feeling weary, I spent the night with her, fully intending to rise early and return home to prospect for FishHook. But in the morning after Mama and I had breakfast, she began talking about her memories of Daddy and her. And then she took me by surprise.

She gave me her original engagement and wedding rings, which over time became threadlike so Daddy had given her a new set. When she told me she knew I'd appreciate having them, that I would take loving care of them, I realized she did know me, after all. Daddy had called her his angel. Mama talked of their wedding day and when she talked I saw the 17-year-old bride with stars in her eyes. I told myself, the day will come when I won't be able to sit and listen to Mama's memories or see her face, so I suspended work that day to spend time with her. And thanks to Al-Anon, cherished friends, and my church and sponsor, I was learning never would I want to trade places with anyone who subsists in bitterness, who misses out on memory-making opportunities as I was involved in at that very moment with my mother.

Undertaking Step 2 meant professing belief my Higher Power could restore my sanity. It sounded harsh to hear people in meetings say they were sick, or in other words, insane, much less say it of myself. But after looking up the word insane in the dictionary and finding synonyms for insane include foolish, stupid, impractical and unreasonable, then by definition, I was, in fact, insane. I was insane if I believed I could control or change another person. If I kept chasing after people, places and things that hurt me. To think my decisions and actions had no consequences. To think I could be both halves of any relationship. To think the past 40 years of my life did not have a profound and destructive impact on the way I think, feel, act and speak. To share my innermost thoughts and feelings with anyone who lacked compassion or ability to emote. To believe I was in love with anyone I barely knew. To obsess over people and circumstances, as if fixating would change anyone or anything. To pretend to be something or someone I was not to please others. To think people were other than who they showed themselves to be. To not ask for what I needed expecting others to intuitively meet my needs. To see the axiomatic red flags of dysfunctional behavior and rush toward them anyway.

Yes, I was insane, foolish. But, I observed God restoring me to sanity, albeit intermittently, through recovery, counseling, prayer and practice. I also began to see when I placed faith in God's abiding presence, some form or another of blessing appeared nearly immediately afterward, like a reward. It may be a phone call or note in the mail from someone kind at a time when I needed a boost or money when I could not make ends meet. I began believing that is all God asks of me, to trust Him, through everything. And if I did, then one way or another, the rewards would come.

Undoubtedly, Step 3 was the most demanding thus far. It required I relinquish my will and life to the God of my understanding. Somehow I knew through Step work and faith in God I would be OK. Still, I did not know how to turn my will over to God. It was a pleasing idea, to let go of the wheel and let God drive. But I found repeatedly I could not do it with any consistency. Not yet, anyway. As much as I wished otherwise, Roger's tragic death remained a gristly hindrance to giving my will to God. I wanted to but was afraid to let go entirely. Even saying, "Your will be done not mine" stuck in my throat. I supposed when I could accept God had allowed my brother to die in his 20s, knowing all the while He, the omnipotent, omnipresent and omniscient God, could have rescued Roger but chose not to, then perhaps I could surrender my will to God. But I also supposed my surrender was unlikely until that epitomical acceptance came.

So acceptance I presumed would lead to surrender, which would lead me unquestionably to relinquishing my will and life to God. Turning over my will, my life and everyone in it seemed a serene endeavor, especially where my aging Mama was concerned. And Mama was saddened by disintegrating relations between me and my sisters. I mentioned this to Jo Ann one day, telling her I prayed we all could reconcile someday, but for the moment we should focus on Mama's well-being and she agreed.

Around Memorial Day, I visited Fr. Eddie at St. Benedict. He was widely known in the archdiocese as a Catholic priest who neither condoned homosexuality nor condemned the homosexual. He taught only God's love. I asked him to pay a visit with me to Mama to soothe her worry over whether God loved me. Mama listened and seemed to hear and accept his consoling words. Two weeks following Fr. Eddie's visit, I thought it OK for me to start spending the second and fourth weekends of each month with Mama. Our relationship had smoothed and she did not throw fiery balls of damnation at me for being gay. One morning, I planted two bright yellow Esperanza's, Grandma Floy's favorite, in her backyard, along with yellow lantana and pink vincas. Our time together was enjoyable. That night, we watched "True Grit," both of us missing Daddy and his western-watching.

With my business slowly growing and my relationship with Mama fairly steady, I felt fortuitously euphoric, even danced alone around my living room listening to lively music. I had secured income making top dollar. I was spending weekends with my mother twice each month. But doom loomed.

Fr. Eddie again met with Mama and me to talk about God's love for all people including gays and again Mama seemed sympathetic. But later, after a visit from my eldest sister, Mama broached the subject with me when alone.

She told me even to say the word gay made her sick. My mood swung swiftly from cheerful to sad. In the face of my mother's aversion, I tried not to let her words hurt. But her tone left me feeling as I did when in proximity to my sisters. And those feelings left me scared. And scarred. I was scared because I knew I was getting to the point where I would have no other choice but to walk away from family, from all of them. I felt scarred because I believed the damage done was indelible.

Torn between self-care and losing my family, I did not know how to keep both me and them and be healthy. It was by no accident my friend Phin phoned me the next day to invite me to lunch. We broke bread as he fed my heart, reminding me I deserved to be loved, wanted and treated with dignity.

Insanity, or foolishness, as I described it earlier runs in my family and takes many forms. But no one admits to it. My insanity was that I kept expecting sanity. When away from caustic people and situations, everything around me seemed serene, but inside I was not. This was the dichotomy, to be surrounded by pleasantries, like birds and flowers, but feel disturbed within. I knew two women who cut their own skin to relieve emotional pain. My release was less severe. On this particular morning, I smoked a Marlboro, felt the intake of smoke imbue my lungs, and tasted and smelled the sharp tobacco on my lips and fingertips. I knew it was no good for me, but I smoked it. It was the same with my family's conditional love; it was no good for me either, but I kept embracing it. With every exhale I blew the pain into the air. And after the Marlboro, a Musketeer chocolate bar was had for breakfast. And for lunch, another pain reliever; a leftover piece of chocolate cake with thick, fluffy chocolate icing went down hard and fast with an ice-cold glass of milk. Tomorrow, I'd choose a healthier way. I sincerely wanted the cycle of insanity to end.

Gripping hope, expecting torment, I kept my bimonthly weekend commitment with my mother. Again, she confronted me with, "Daddy did not accept your being gay," while conveniently neglecting to remember my father never convicted or preached at me about my lifestyle or anything else. He mentioned it once and that was that. Again, I questioned whether I was strong enough to keep coming back no matter how much I wanted to help Mama or how much I loved her. She was hard on me and condemned me no matter what I did or didn't do and constantly brought up the past as if I could change it.

And she neglected to mention the role she or my sisters had played in our problems.

I was not able yet to walk away from these confrontations without feeling I had to defend myself, which was futile anyway. In speaking with Judith, she confirmed I was indeed not ready to deal with my mother's attitude. She suggested it was because I did not love myself yet but I was getting there. And she explained that when I'm comfortable in my own skin, I will be able to walk away from harm without words or guilt. I imagined how wonderfully empowering that might be.

As I entered Step 4 with Judith, I again took inventory of myself, as I'd done with Edwin. It comforted me to learn beneath every defect hides an asset. For instance, the defect of fear could have an underlying asset of decisiveness. My list of character flaws was long, which surely meant a long list of plusses was hiding behind them! My first pass at naming my flaws when I worked this Step with Edwin had revealed the obvious, but this time I was more stringent, identifying envious (of what I did not have), judgmental, resentful, self-critical, self-doubting, self-justifying, self-pitying and untrusting.

A year and seven months after my first Al-Anon meeting, I was not yet a glowing illustration of an emotionally fit woman. I was in recovery from the isms of codependency. I was in counseling for mental health. I was in church to deepen my faith in God. And now I was in a gay support group. But so far, none of it had produced in me, not yet, profound change. I was not yet fit enough to handle my family's attitudes. And as Mike the life coach had predicted, my professional life suffered, too. The distrust and negativity emanating from familial dysfunction combined with corporate hurt was spilling over into my dealings with clients.

I sometimes obsessed, for example, over delayed payments. When only a few days past the agreed-upon date, I feared I was jilted. That feeling set off a roaring train of fears over my financial well-being and I acted on those fears, probing clients' intents and projecting my anxiety onto them unaware. My thinking still stunk. Thankfully, I learned in time to recognize it for what it was and harnessed my thoughts more quickly than not. I allowed my business dealings to take their course and no one cut me short.

I wanted, needed, to change how I thought and felt! I was impatient with what I perceived as slow progress in recovery. When would all I read, heard and practiced take hold once and for all? I petulantly craved peace. I often smiled by force but wanted to walk around with an authentic beam. I kept falling short. And that made me edgy. I still wanted a quick fix because I wanted the hurting and confusion to stop. But change would not come quickly. I was going to have to muddle through the transmuting muck of transformation. I kept hearing in meetings, "this too shall pass," and "progress not perfection," and, oh, how I clung to those words, but at the same time, I detested them.

Predictably, I had another clash with Mama that finally broke through my thinking I'd have to stop putting myself in the line of fire. I'd been spending every other weekend with her. On the first morning of my second stay, she dug up the past, again, regurgitating a situation I admittedly mishandled with one of my sisters several months prior and for which I had long since apologized—and for which Mama neglected to admit my sister's equal mishandling. As when a child blamed, all fingers pointed to me. I stayed that day but told her before I left she was breaking my heart and being around her left me like a picked scab: I could not heal from the wounds of pain because of constant picking.

After this episode, Judith suggested I seek outside advice, as in a therapist. Later that week, while having lunch with Phin, I told him I wanted to see a counselor but could not afford it. Luckily, he knew of a qualified therapist and provided his name and number. I quickly followed up with his referral to Don, who at our first session the second week of July said, "Lou, I'm seeing you pro-bono because my old friend Phin referred you, but you have to do the work or we stop."

Don had materialized at a most pertinent moment. Yes, I'd do the work. In our first session, after I explained my dilemma with my mother and sisters, he issued his first counsel: "Cut it off." He had said it matter-of-factly. Grimly. Eye to eye, with his looking straight at mine from atop his eyeglasses as he leaned in from his chair. The man was dead-serious. He explained I was accepting what they gave me and it was up to me to stop accepting it. His goal was to help me live free of the pain I carried. His shocking short advice hit me square, like a mallet. But he was right. I was accepting abuse. I had set boundaries but when they were breached I went back for more. Again and again. This is what insanity looks like. I wanted to be sane. I wanted finally once and for all to say No to anymore abuse, from anyone. And that is precisely what Don was telling me to do.

In the midst of ever-changing changes, I read a book about dream interpretation and along with it began practicing Don's advice to keep a dream log. The prospect of annotating and analyzing my dreams excited me, like a buried treasure awaiting discovery. Don said to place a notebook and pen at my bedside and whenever I awoke from a stirring dream, switch on the light, jot it down in detail, and then go back to sleep and in the morning review it. Or, if I had a question, write it down and then go to sleep, because answers can come in dreams. My dreams were not revealing always but more often than not contained messages for me. Some affirmed, some reflected, some predicted.

Prior to waking one morning soon after starting my dream log, I dreamt I saw many exceptionally bright tiny lights shining from behind a shower curtain, as if suspended in air. When I pulled aside the curtain, I saw a sudden burst of dazzling white light, as if all the tiny lights had combined into one large one that resembled a star beaming in all directions. I awoke sensing it true. I could not predict then that this same brilliant light would revisit me again much later in an even larger and astonishing form and would not occur in a dream but in reality. Perhaps the vision of lights signified my recuperating spirit.

A few nights later, I had another, stranger dream. I was in a place that at first seemed an office but suddenly turned into a zoo with alligators crawling around loose. Let me segue briefly from the dream to state I often had heard and used in business dealings the phrase "I'm up to my eyeballs in alligators," suggesting a busy, challenging schedule. Returning to the dream, my mother was present at first then gone. I saw two men I thought I knew but did not know their names and sensed romantic interest in one of them. Suddenly, my nephew rode his motorcycle past me and then disappeared. Everything—walls, floors, furniture—was brown. Here was a dark dream unlike the dream of light a few nights prior. And I would dream again later about motorcycles, a recurring beguiling theme of my adolescence and predictor of my future.

The following night I dreamt again. This time I was in a small space with my former husband. It was nighttime and late. Two women stood in our living room, one of whom Scott kissed. Feeling hurt, I began to cry, and the women laughed before yelling and cursing at Scott, calling him a liar. At one point, he and I sat on the floor, and with his head in my hands, I banged it against the hard floor, calling him a terrible name for having hurt me.

Some dreams leave me wanting to stay in them, inside that pleasurable floating sensation of part sleep-part awake. But some dreams I wish I never would have dreamt. The latter was the case when I dreamed the next night. I saw maggots. Then Merlin the magician. Then, I stood in the middle of a massive busy intersection where a cop directed traffic, and I approached and poked him in the chest. Standing at the margins was Mama, smiling. Three nights later, yet another dream came in which I was in cohesive company of my sisters, when the eldest phoned crying, saying Mama was in the hospital.

What to make of these dreams? Recent ones revealed a spectacular light, dug up the ugly past, put images on feelings circulating through my healing heart, and, as I would learn, predicted the future.

During a session with Don, he said something that broadened my thinking about my sisters and mother's attitudes. He believed Daddy, unbeknown to me, had run interference among my family members on my behalf, especially since my gay declaration and despite his own disagreement with it. And when he died, my father was no longer there to protect me. His insight echoed Fr. Eddie's, who had told me the same thing when we had talked before Daddy's funeral. When Daddy became frail, my sisters' disdain for me magnified and when Daddy died my mother's did as well. I had never questioned Daddy's love or loyalty. Not ever. Not once. Don's insight left me warmly assured my father believed I deserved respect and had ensured my safety in the family while he was alive. Realizing that fortified me despite Daddy's death.

Don also enlightened me as to why I had chosen intimate partners devoid of emotional capacity, a habit I held that caused me pain. He said I had become my father and married my mother. Like my father, I was hardworking, accountable, brave and strong. I married my mother in that I went looking for intimacy with people who were emotionally unavailable. Mama's emotional capacity nosedived after her nervous breakdown, which left me yearning for my mother's touch. Gender had nothing to do with Don's analogy. My marriage and affairs all were with emotionally empty people. This is precisely what Edwin had told me as well.

I did not choose to cut if off, as Don had suggested, from my mother. My time with Mama was guarded but informed thanks to Don's insight and my recovery. I continued to help Mama inasmuch as I could without allowing myself to be hurt in the bargain. And I was worried about her. She had begun making poor judgments at home when alone that jeopardized her safety. After dark, she put out the trash. Our neighborhood had changed beyond recognition from the safe haven we grew up in to a crime-ridden, neglected area with aging, vulnerable residents. I suggested she sell the house and move into a reputable senior-living community. She admitted to having considered it, knew widows who had done it, but she was concerned if she did, she would be unable to leave us kids much inheritance. I told her to forget the money, as we all had jobs. I reminded her she and Daddy's legacy was in memory not money, and she could live a safer, healthier life in a senior community with kindred friends. She agreed to consider it.

What I was learning in recovery helped me when Judith and I arrived at an impasse and I had an opportunity to practice detaching with love with her. While surprised at my decision to work with someone else, she conceded and wished me well. She had left me in a better place than when we had first met and taught me a lasting lesson: God is my source. Instantly I prayed for a new sponsor to appear.

After the positive outcome of practicing loving detachment with Judith, I flexed this principle's muscle by detaching from two acquaintances I had struck in recent weeks that turned out to be much less than good for me. And TV evangelists I watched were preaching the same sermon. They taught, if my associations do not foster growth, then I should detach from them and surround myself instead with people who exemplify who I want to be. It was as Edwin had said: surround myself with people who feed me. The more I detached with love, the easier it became and the more confidence I carried. Instead of asking everybody else what to do, I was learning to listen to and trust myself. And I was making lucid decisions I could live with. Through this came another epiphany: As my feelings healed, so did my trust of my feelings. I found power in this exercise and result. My life, however much I would be given, was much too precious to live it placating people who were a fatiguingly poor fit.

By the second anniversary of Daddy's passing, Mama continued endangering her safety, venturing outside after dark. It was undeniably clear; my mother would soon have more, and more frequent, needs and likewise expectations of me and my sisters. I quickly volunteered to switch my 11 a.m. Saturday morning Al-Anon meeting with another one so I could make her monthly 10 a.m. hair appointment, buy her groceries that same day, and tidy her yard and porch. After Mama and I agreed to this, I conveyed our plans to my sisters. At the time, I was $70,000 in burgeoned debt from school and business loans, a land loan, and credit debt that swelled when I resigned my job to finish graduate school and help care for Daddy and Mama. I told my sisters I was unwilling to absorb more debt as a result of not working my fledgling sole proprietorship or wreck my physical health again by spreading myself too thin to be on-call. I held to this, especially in light of knowing Mama's finances were sufficient for her to have in-home help or move into a senior community. Inevitably, the alpha sister imposed it was I, not Mama, who'd have to rearrange my schedule to suit the situation.

How grateful was I to have learned to set boundaries and care for myself. In a final communique with my sisters, I told them that each of us was responsible for her individual emotional, physical and financial well-being, that each daughter would have to figure out her ability to help Mama, choosing to jeopardize health or livelihood in the process or not, and their attitude toward me was none of my business. In conversations with Mama, she and I discussed her aging and increasing needs at length on several occasions and amicably resolved between us my part of the total family contribution to her care.

Afterward and by necessity, I evenly turned my attention away from family toward earning my living. Still hankering to help older people somehow through my profession, I threw my hook into the river of opportunity bated with an idea I had hatched. I would write an article about elder abuse, based on my master's thesis and personalized to Daddy's experience, and I proposed the coming article to editors of several nationally recognized senior-oriented magazines. But I learned quickly after a string of gracious but obvious snubs that publishers were more intent on retaining lucrative advertising dollars paid by organizations purporting to cater to seniors than telling the truth about elder abuse. While let down, I was not swayed. I was adamant to find a way to tell Daddy's story but put my article on simmer.

Over a weekend in late October, I attended a spiritual retreat with 60 other ladies. During a workshop we were asked to pick an "angel card" from a basket full. Each card had one word on it and this word would be the area to focus on. My word was "synthesis." I looked it up in the dictionary. And then I felt pretty darn powerful. Synthesis is synonymous with fusion, production, creation.

I welcomed autumn as temperatures cooled and chilly winds chased fallen leaves across lawns and streets. But I was not invited to the family meal Thanksgiving Day. It was not so much to be left out that was hurtful. I was getting used to sharing holidays with friends. It was my family's painful indifference, as if I did not exist. But acknowledging pain, admitting to my feelings whatever they are, is a strong tenet of Al-Anon recovery. I had covered up my feelings for decades. Learning first to admit to them and then to release them to God was not easy or quick. I had to learn to live with the discomfort of growing through pain and sorrow while making hard decisions and learning how to be free of misery.

I decided, yet again, to remove expectations I held of my family and to break free of the pain I felt by completely detaching, at least for a while, from most of them. I had known I needed to take this leap for a long time, Don had affirmed it, but I had not been able to sidestep the guilt I knew I'd feel if I followed through. But now, I knew, it was time. I had to detach until mentally and emotionally strong enough to withstand the winds of disdain without allowing squalls to break my heart or pollute my mouth. My mother understood and admitted my sisters' wrongdoing in leaving me out but she sided with the three. She explained that, at her age, she could not risk losing their help with appointments, errands and chores. Here I found myself, again, drowning in tears over the same thing I'd cried over countless times before. I prayed intensely to forgive them all. And I knew whatever detachment I mustered may not last. Don had suggested two months earlier I take this healthy step, to separate myself from them all, yet I had waited. As I always had, waited, waited for the abusive behavior to change, to stop, for someone to say she was sorry.

On the morning of Thanksgiving Day, I again admitted powerlessness. I admitted defeat and the death of any expectation of my mother or sisters' attitudes or behavior toward me changing. I knew what had to be done. That, in and of itself, was progress. I asked God please to help me raise myself up and take care of myself, to treat myself with the love I deserved. I rose from bed and begrudgingly wrote a meticulous list of every person, place and thing in my life for which I was grateful. And by the time I was through, I felt relieved. And then I dressed and attended the Thanksgiving Day dinner at Club 12 where I shared hugs, food and laughter with friends, who reminded me to pray for those who hurt me and enjoy my day anyway.

The Friday after Thanksgiving Day, I felt angry at the world. I lashed out at a clerk at a department store, making a public scene and then apologizing for it. Here I went again. I did not like my behavior or how I felt. I recognized it was leftover hurt I could not seem to shed. And grief-induced anger at the perception of deep loss. I had to continually remind myself, minute by minute at times, this too shall pass. I went home and listened to a John Denver album. I cried, sang along, napped. Sometimes, the best thing to do when I didn't know what else to do was to listen to John Denver and sleep.

Two weeks after Thanksgiving, Mama phoned. Apparently, as most mothers do, she wanted to smooth things over. She had talked with my sisters and wanted me to know Debbie told her I "can be really nice sometimes," and Jo Ann had suggested "why don't we all let bygones be bygones." I appreciated the call and words but remained skeptical at the seesawing swing of behaviors, one day hateful, the next day complimentary. No wonder I, too, was fickle.

I informed Mama I was glad for the news and would be open and cordial but I also would observe how it goes. I told her I had forgiven my sisters for what was done and said in the past, but without their expressing remorse over the loathing they had shown me, I did not believe I would be able to reconcile. I would have to pray about it. I also told Mama I no longer was willing to be around anyone who treated me hatefully or disrespectfully. I was unwilling to deny I was not gay or suppress myself from sharing normal life events with my family. At that, my mother told me my eldest sister had said her behavior toward me had nothing to do with my being gay. But if that were true, I said, then not pretending to be straight should not be a problem.

The following Saturday I spoke at the 11 a.m. Al-Anon meeting at Club 12, where I shared details of my phone call with Mama and my experiences with my sisters. It was clear even to me I was taking small steps at setting healthy boundaries. Afterward, a beaming Judith gave me a bear hug and others approached to say they gained from hearing my story about the challenges I was overcoming. I left Club 12 and drove to my property in Boerne, where, feeling quite like a pioneer, cut down a 5-foot tall cedar tree, took it home and trimmed it for Christmas.

Shortly before Christmas, I thought about my mother missing Daddy and was moved to phone her. I asked if she'd like me to visit late Christmas Eve after the rest of the family had left, spend the night with her, and make breakfast and dinner for just us two on Christmas Day. She sounded happy at that, told me Debbie planned to take her to church Christmas morning, and asked if that would be OK. I said that would be fine. It was progress, that Mama had asked for an OK at all.

One night soon afterward, I had a bizarre dream in which was the hostile radio station sales manager. In the dream, I had a small motorcycle and it had been stolen. I wore no shoes, was skimpily dressed, and carried no purse, money or phone. I ambled aimlessly among strangers, whimpering. Reflecting upon awakening, I supposed the dream was prompted by my fear of failing at my business that would lead to homelessness and my skimpy dress indicated vulnerability. I decided to write a list of all I had accomplished that year, and when I had finished, I saw numerous successes. At the top of the list were new friends-turned-family, progress in recovery, and lucrative strides I'd made with FishHook.

After 24 months in recovery accompanied by counseling and Scripture, I knew it was God who walked with me through every circumstance, softly, lovingly, abidingly. He had tapped gently and repeatedly on the door to my heart, till one day, I paused, listened and heard the strumming that was His gracious voice. And I answered Him. Invited Him in. Listened. And tried to follow His counsel. I knew I never would revert to who I was before. Now that I knew, how could I not share it. And in the sharing was God's plan, perfectly timed and executed, with outcomes far bigger and brighter than I ever would have been able to imagine. Perhaps sharing my pain and deliverance from it was part of my purpose all along.

Thanks to Bill, Edwin and Judith, I had been introduced to the power of lists, and lists had taken their rightful places as invaluable instruments I used to unclutter my mind, create goals and make decisions. I discovered at seeing things written out, my ideas became tangible and thus attainable, or at times, dismissible. So, as was my custom, one morning I wrote across the top of a sheet of ruled white paper the titles of three columns: What I Want/Need In A Relationship, What Is Negotiable, What I Will Not Tolerate. And then I commenced to listing entries in each column. I was thorough, jotting down 25 in the Want/Need column, 7 in the Negotiable column and 21 in the Will Not Tolerate column. I had my map; now what? I decided I would share it with my next sponsor and find out.

Scarcely did I know, the toughest and most transforming season of my recovery was looming, closer than I knew, and it would come through the kindness of one man whose name was Jim. And little did Jim or I know I was about to step onto the teetering brink of coming astonishing transformation.

In Step

Jim was an angel arrived on the heels of Judith.

A retired U.S. Army colonel of stout stature and crusty character, Jim was married to a woman in AA, taller and more talkative than he, and they helped start the Coker group. I had listened to Jim share in meetings and thought, here's a man strong enough to handle my equally strong personality and emotional swings. Jim was someone who seemed to have a steadfast grasp on recovery and the 12 Steps and he sponsored men in AA. When I asked him to sponsor me, he unhesitatingly agreed as Edwin and Judith had, but told me, as Don had, I would have to commit to doing the work. He further informed me he was supplanting his standing Saturday golf game of 14 years to instead meet with me for an entire year and he needed to know I was serious. Without flinching, I committed.

The first thing Jim asked of me was to read the first 164 pages of the Big Book. He asked I read them a second time highlighting anything I related to. When I finished, we would begin Step work. The things I highlighted were alcoholic isms—in me. Every Saturday after the 11 a.m. Al-Anon meeting at Club 12, Jim and I met. I told him even though I had worked Steps 1 through 4 with Edwin and Judith, I still struggled with recurring flareups with family and turning my will over to God. He regularly assigned me homework on the Steps we studied, each in turn, and encouraged me to keep at it, keep journaling, and call him as needed.

As I stated earlier, I cried my way through my first three years in Al-Anon. Step work was not the cause of my tears. Working the Steps was satisfying and productive. On the contrary, I called Jim often in sodden sobs because something hard and hurtful had happened, mostly between me and a sister, or because of yet another toxic relationship I'd slid into partway despite my promise to myself I would steer clear of dating till after I'd completed all 12 Steps. But Jim was not available 24/7. Luckily, I had collected phone numbers from trusted others in recovery, and when Jim was busy I phoned them to vent my burden, get out of my head, and get through and past the hurt and confusion. But I did not reclaim composure fully until I heard the soothing sanity of Jim's sound counsel.

Jim was strict but gentle with me as a situation necessitated. Like Don, he knew I was headstrong and so took whatever approach was called for at a given time. He was known broadly as shrewd and belligerent in his business dealings and in openly disconcerting disagreements with others, but with me, Jim was sensitive, a reassuring and able anchor. He had an uncanny knack of reeling me in when my mouth and tears took me too far into a frantic sea of emotional turbulence. It was the same in sessions with Don. I cried a lot, recounting every slight, till Don said to me with straight candor, "Lou, you talk too much. We're going to try hypnoanalysis." Hypnoanalysis, he explained, would employ the trance state, or hypnosis, to reduce the time it would take, as compared to talk therapy, to get to the core of my recurring emotional pain problem.

My therapy with Don was bolstered by Step work with Jim, which was the heartbeat of my recovery. I share here the Steps I moved through with Jim and the associated awarenesses I came to from working through each one, one by one, in order. I want to show you who read this account that during the process and at the conclusion of working the 12 Steps, an undeniable, recognizable transformation within me occurred, irrefutably obvious to those around me. It would produce in me the visibly apparent and permanent behavioral change I'd craved.

Working Steps 1 through 12 in order had strategic purpose: to unfold and produce in me qualities I could embrace, practice and be proud of. Each quality was built upon the shoulders of the previous quality attained in the previous Step. And each Step presented not only the principle aimed for but relevant readings, discussions and journaling, which consumed necessary blocks of my time. All 12 Steps and the venerable qualities they engendered—honesty, hope, faith, courage, integrity, willingness, humility, love, discipline, patience, awareness and service—would successively and altogether bring about my utter transformation.

I worked Step 1 from late November through December 2007 (Honesty): "I admitted I was powerless over other people, places and things, that my life had become unmanageable [by trying to control other people, places, things]." Through the grueling process of finally admitting to addictive codependency and that it had made and kept me emotionally sick, I admitted to powerlessness over addiction to an unhealthy person and to any illusion of ability to control the object of my addiction. This was hard because to give up power was frightening. Because of codependency, the strength within myself to persevere had mutated into an illusionary need to control what caused me pain, strain, fear or other perceivable threats. Admitting defeat over my attempts or ability to control anyone or anything was a crucial first step.

While entering the rigors of Step work, I built FishHook, around which I regularly admitted to having no control over its outcome.

Step 2 consumed the month of January 2008 (Hope): "Came to believe a Power greater than myself could restore me to sanity." This believing oftentimes vacillated but increasingly steadied. I had admitted powerlessness over other people, places and things, and now I relinquished any illusion of control. God would be my strength and sanity. It felt comfortable to believe in this Power, in God, to restore level-headedness to what I thought, spoke and did. But this palpable belief was hard-fought before won; it did not come quickly or easily.

While working Step 2, I launched the FishHook website and in reviewing my business's progress, happily found in its first year of operation I had earned enough to meet six months' expenses. There seemed a correlation between belief in God and in myself and efforts.

January also was a tumultuous time in my family, particularly in the ongoing interactions between me and Mama and me and my sisters concerning our mother's health, aging and well-being. As the elder sister attempted to ramrod the situation giving orders, I repeatedly restated my inability to contribute more than one entire weekend a month. I offered to give more if and when I could and reminded my siblings home healthcare was a viable option Mama considered and could afford. Despite my mother agreeing and understanding my limitations, I received berating emails from two of my sisters. They accused me of "refusing to help" and labeled me "selfish" all while deeming their commitments to volunteering at the San Antonio Stock Show and Rodeo held higher priority over my earning a living.

At the time, I was launching FishHook working six days a week on my sole means of income and had no health insurance. Meanwhile, my three sisters all had regular income streams. Al-Anon and Step work were instrumental in my repeatedly resetting boundaries with my family and staying a healthy course for myself. I refused to entertain homelessness or bankruptcy to satisfy my siblings' opinions. By January's end, I closed the discussion with my siblings while spending the final weekend of the month with Mama. We baked Grandma Floy's peach kolaches and visited Mary who was home recovering from a minor surgery. Discovering her computer had crashed, I donated my old printer and dispatched a willing friend, the president of a technology company, to resurrect her hard drive pro bono. Lynn generously financed home healthcare for Mama for February, which indirectly blessed me with ability to latch on to FishHook's building momentum.

I worked through Step 3 in February, March and April (Faith): "Made a decision to turn my will and life over to the care of God as I understood Him."

By far, this was the most laborious step, spiritually speaking. I had to find God in my own time and way. And it took some time because I worried over everything. It took a lot of back-and-forth faith flipflopped with will and worry. I gave people, places and things to God. I took them back. Repeat. Before I could be free to let go and let God, I had to remove every smear, every stain, every tiny drop of unbelief, self-will and fret. I had to walk across coals of painful mistakes again and again and again and again until I was sick and tired of being sick and tired of dwelling in anguish. Psalm 37:5 NKJV told me "Commit your way to the Lord, trust also in Him, and He shall bring it to pass." But it took persistent decisive aim and a long time to trust.

To help me through, Jim suggested I keep a worry journal every day for 30 days. I was allowed 15 minutes a day to worry and document the worries in my journal. But I was not allowed to worry any other time. He instructed me to read the "Acceptance Prayer" on page 417 and "Third Step Prayer" on page 63 in the Big Book daily, and every week, review my gratitude list and the Promises of recovery. And then Jim did a most unexpected thing. He gave me a small blue rubber duck with a yellow beak smile, the kind a child plays with in the bathtub. It had a tiny hole in its bottom so when squeezed it squeaked. Jim told me, "The duck is 'everything' you worry about, Lou. Give it all to the duck. And when you can tell this duck what to do, and it does it, that's when you can take back your worry."

Worry and control go hand-in-hand. Having lived for decades in self-will, I was trying to let go of controlling behavior; that's what growing up is. Healthy mature adults do not attempt to control other adults. I had to remind myself with help from my recovery fellowship it had taken half a century to mold me into who I'd become and it was going to take a bit of dedicated effort and time to remake "Lou."

By the start of March, I added a second weekend each month with Mama but given the fluctuating volatility of our relationship, my intent would not stick for long. Every weekday and two Saturdays a month were full work days for me. I completed projects for existing clients, wrote articles for the San Antonio Business Journal (SABJ), continued cold-calling, met with prospective new clients, and introduced my business to chambers of commerce members. Cashflow and prospecting were critical at that stage of business growth, as critical for me in growing my faith as edified in Step 3. I believed with due diligence I would square my debt. And I dared believe in myself as a book author someday.

Despite my worry journal, I awoke often with a head full of random worries, mostly to do with my business, income and Mama. She now was accidentally overmedicating herself, so I created charts in a binder for medicine entries but she did not use them. She still ventured outside after dark, unlocked her door for deliveries and other strangers, and chatted with random callers who asked personal questions. I was deeply troubled by these things and concerned for her well-being. Daddy had been accurate. Mama was at times a mental invalid, well-intentioned but at times devoid of reason. So one unrelated thought followed another. I did not like my mind's preoccupation with ricocheting worry. I wanted a calmer, slower mentality. I wanted the blue duck to take all my frets and keep them. I wanted to awaken rested and at peace. I wanted my mother to be safe.

The unforeseen but welcome happened just before my 53rd birthday. Barely a year after launching FishHook, I was nominated and won two SBA Home-Based Business Champion of the Year awards. Congratulations from friends, colleagues and Lynn rolled in. In an email from one of my sisters, there was no mention of the awards, only a sharp accusation: "You put Mama in a state of depression, so why don't you stay home and Mary and I will take care of her this weekend." Apparently, my sister was unaware Mama had asked me to stay the weekend with her but I had declined. I was reminded of Don's wise advice to cut it off and by the end of March, I had done precisely that. Due diligence in recovery was paying real dividends. And I was increasingly grateful for Lynn who gave me sound guidance when I asked it. He told me, respect is a two-way street, and if you don't get it in return, then drop that person off your list till he or she can treat you with the same courtesy you offer. His words echoed Don's and a tenet of the recovery program.

Throughout April and May, work poured into FishHook and revenue although modest exceeded the prior year. It was, I supposed, like housebreaking a puppy. One day you find your due diligence and hard work have paid off. Another unexpected yet welcomed surprise happened in May. The Express-News interviewed me for an article about FishHook's two SBA award wins and published the piece in its Business section. I began believing the higher road I was traveling was being blessed by my Higher Power.

Also in May, I completed Step 4 (Courage): "Made a searching and fearless moral inventory of myself." A dually self-degrading and gratifying Step, I had, and wanted, to admit to my deficiencies and fears. But I had to temper my brutally honest look with an equally celebratory survey of my favorable qualities. Because I tended to whip myself for being far less than perfect, I named more faults than admirable attributes. And this, in and of itself, was telling. I had to learn, and did, to let go of perceived defects of character, because in fact, they were not; they were spinoffs or results of glaring deficiencies and those were the ones I nailed. Only in working this Step did I realize I had fewer defects than I thought and I decided to focus on the original relentless six: anger, control, ego, fear, impatience and insecurity. It was correspondingly gratifying to appreciate my noble qualities, which I aimed to nurture. I continued noticing some attributes were defects in disguise. For example, when my innate desire to be generous exceeded my physical, emotional or financial capacity, then generosity was a defect that robbed me of the ability to be sensible and I suffered. I gave away too much of myself at times, holding no reserves, and that caused me harm. I had to temper my want to give with my need to live.

I completed Step 5 in June (Integrity): "Admitted to God, to myself, and to another human being the exact nature of my wrongs." This Step involved my sponsor primarily but also trusted others in the recovery program when I wanted to confess a Step 4 backslide coupled with a Step 5 awareness. It often was important to me I take this Step in real time, delaying neither identifying and admitting to the defect in action nor the relieving satisfaction that came from confessing it. I did not want to wait for a more convenient time in the future, which made my circle of trusted others in the recovery fellowship invaluable to my progress. Practicing this Step cleared my mind and heart, which allowed me to let things go. The resulting transparency and integrity was soothing and confirming. In short, I learned to hold myself accountable.

Throughout Step work, I logged my dreams. In early June, I dreamt I was a superhero or double-agent, flying high above people's heads with a large balloon in one hand, and flying after me was a man in a uniform with a gun. I outflew him, descended, and hit the ground running. I ran into a large office building where there stood Daddy, whose hand I grabbed. He looked worried about me but smiled. I didn't like leaving him but had to keep running. When I wrote of this dream, I figured flying and escaping may have pointed to my learning in real life to rise above or steer clear of damaging behaviors of others. And maybe Daddy represented God, an extension of the Divine, always watching over me.

I continued familial distance and had not spoken by phone with or visited my mother since late March. But we did mail each other warm notes. When Father's Day arrived, I honored Daddy's memory by going fishing. Lynn told me one time he often thought of Daddy when he went fishing and the way Daddy felt about "hooking a keeper." I first fished the Cibolo Creek in Boerne where I snagged only reeds. I then tried my luck in the Guadalupe River where I caught a small catfish after wading into the cool water with my pole, a pocket full of bait, and endless memories of Daddy's smile. It was the most fun I'd had in recent times.

Also in June, I began writing my article on elder abuse, envisioning Daddy's story a revealing expose spanning some 5,000 words. I wanted it to be perfect and perfectly persuading. And my break into national publication.

I moved through Step 6 in July (Willingness): "Were entirely ready to have God remove all these defects of character." Oh, what a relieving Step! To be ready to let go of the illusion or practice of presumed control over other people, places, things; of anger, control, ego, fear, impatience and insecurity, all of which had held me back and down. Yes, I wanted them gone from my mouth, mind, heart, soul, actions. I wanted freedom from all that hindered the tranquil life I craved and one for which I could be proud.

Willingness surfaced everywhere. I was willing to guide my first sponsee through the Steps. I was willing to ask for help, to admit I didn't know sometimes, to admit I was scared sometimes or even much of the time, and to admit to glaring behaviors I would be much better off discarding. At the time I worked Step 6 and apropos to Independence Day observances, our church hosted the campaign manager of the U.S. Department of Peace and Nonviolence to speak about proactive peace initiatives underway across the country. Upon learning of Phin's involvement, I willingly answered the call to volunteer for administrative chores.

Coincidentally, phone calls with Mama resumed and became more frequent and in one such call she spoke more about home healthcare and a senior-living residence. I missed her and dropped by one day with a dual purpose for the visit. I had collected data about a senior-living campus called Morningside Ministries and a few home healthcare agencies' brochures I had screened for her to peruse.

Hesitant at first, I completed Step 7 in August (Humility): "Humbly asked Him to remove our shortcomings." It must sound strange, and it was strange, to realize that despite the trouble my shortcomings had yielded, I hesitated to ask God to remove them. I only can surmise it was the soul sickness that wanted to hold on to each and every one. This Step, too, involved powerlessness. Stinking thinking that held me captive was vying for control over me and I had to fight yet another internal battle to gain traction on the field of war for my soul. I would not relinquish my faults and failings to God until I knew there was something else with which I could replace them. This internal battle waged between a heart filled with anguish and the feared emptying of that anguish to only emptiness. But I fully knew if I did not give God my shortcomings, I would keep them. This was yet again another leap of faith. Like a lamb, I sheepishly leapt toward faith.

The first time I worked this Step, I was not wholly free of every glaring defect and I would have to revisit this Step when force of habit kept me holding on to faults. But eventually, with repetition, my requests to God to remove shortcomings became more sincere and I became more committed. And once banished completely or with only slight occasional resurgence, defects of character gave way to assets through which I strove to practice and live. Giving anything to God must be done with purpose and follow-through or the effort is in vain.

While I completed Step work, I also finished broad research and screening of senior-living communities in San Antonio beyond what I had shared with Mama earlier and shared the results with her and my siblings. I suggested they likewise do their own research and make suggestions. I urged them to consider that for-profit places were concerned with shareholders' earnings not residents' welfare and most had a caregiver-to-resident ratio of 1 to 8-12 versus faith-based facilities at 1 to 4. Ultimately, I advised Mama to deem Morningside Ministries her only option.

My mother already knew all too well after Daddy's horrific experience and reading my thesis the reality of elder abuse and was rightfully wary, as was I. Decades in service to elders, Morningside was the only local privately owned, faith-based, church-funded organization and residential campus for elders, complete with independent living quarters, assisted living units and a skilled nursing section. Its campus was designed uniformly to accommodate progressively aging residents. It was the only one with a reasonable staff member-to-resident ratio, making for a safer, more responsive environment for the elders who lived there.

August 2008 also delivered with its sweltering heat the start of an economic downturn but FishHook was thriving. And I started thinking about an extended road trip, making it an annual affair, to see beautiful places and stay at posh lodges across the country. Meanwhile, I was content to tent camp occasionally on weekends at Texas state parks.

After Labor Day, Mama and I toured Morningside Ministries where we talked with the administrator who treated us to lunch in the dining room. While eating dessert, we were surprised by a tall spry redhead wearing a bright red pant suit and with feet outfitted in sparkling white tennis shoes, one of which she flung up and plopped down on the seat of an empty chair at our table, exclaiming, "I'm 95 and still can do that and walk 2 miles every day!" The lady in the flashy outfit had been a federal marshal in her youth and now lived at Morningside. Mama liked the place and people. While there was nominal discussion among my siblings about other options, Mama chose Morningside.

A thorough Step 8 consumed September and October (Love): "Made a list of all persons I had harmed [including myself], and became willing to make amends to them all." My list was exhaustive! I aimed to apologize to everyone for everything I had ever done in my entire lifetime and do it all, once and for all, and then, release it all. I typed a 3-page amends list, organized by columns entitled Age, Grade, Year, Event, and Person Harmed. I set about recounting every single thing I could recall where I had hurt myself or someone else, even by accident. When Jim saw the list, he asked me to separate the names of persons harmed into three groups: Those to whom I would make amends, consider making amends, and never make amends. I did not realize then Jim's wisdom, but nearly everyone would have their amends in the end. This Step prepared me mentally, emotionally and spiritually to make the actual apologies.

One afternoon immediately after having had an upsetting phone call with my eldest sister, I phoned Jim and told him, amid cusswords and in no uncertain words, "I will never make amends to her!" As usual, Jim listened patiently and then stated the obvious. "You do not have to make the amends until you are ready. Place her on the 'never' list and let it go, for now." How simple it was, yet so far away from my ability, at the time, to conceive letting anything go until later. It had to be decided right then. But no, it did not have to be decided right away. And herein, another epiphany: Because all habitual behavior is deeply engrained, letting go of it seems a never-ending endeavor.

Step 8 was all about love. Love for myself. Love for others. The act of love for self and others in letting go. While working this Step, I heard from Aunt Frances who told me she had spoken with Mama who seemed very excited about moving to Morningside. I was most grateful to hear the happy news. Even more happy news was on the way.

From Strayed to Straight

First Spiritual Awakening

I welcomed and finished most of Step 9 in November, quickly followed by Steps 10, 11 and 12, which easily hurried past on the heels of the miracle of Step 9 (Discipline): "Made direct amends to such people wherever possible, except when to do so would injure them or others."

At first I shivered at the thought of apologizing to people who had harmed me. But Jim informed me as did the Big Book, I make amends for myself. He said I must have no expectation of their forgiveness, much less their asking my forgiveness for harm they had caused me. The focus of Step 9 is, once again, on myself. Jim taught me the invigorating influence of humility through which amends flow. Distinctly different than humiliation, humility embodies the fortitude to be tender and poised and as needed, firm. And he told me to make my amends and then end the meeting and not linger.

Some people to whom I would apologize I phoned first to set a date and place to meet for no more than 30 minutes. Some people I phoned to request a block of time of 15 minutes to make amends by voice only. And to others I mailed letters of amends. It did not matter how I made the apologies. What mattered was I made them. Step 9 aimed to free me of any and all wrongdoing I had levied. This included amends to those who had harmed me, because I had chosen to be in their company and the hurt they dealt me provoked in me unsavory behavior that now necessitated my apology.

For those apologies made in person, I penned the amends on paper, referring to it as I spoke so I did not forget anything. I began each one the same: "I regret having caused you hurt in your life and for that I am deeply sorry." And I meant it. Then, I stated those things I had done or said for which I was making amends. I went so far with Debbie to apologize for accidentally slamming her thumb in the front screen door when we were kids. At the end of each apology, I asked if I had forgotten anything. The addons proved rare. Once the amends were made, as recommended by Jim, I explained I would never speak of the things for which I apologized again to them or anyone and considered the matter closed forever. To my surprise, nearly everyone welcomed and listened to my amends and one or two also expressed regret and apologized as well. The most important amends was to myself and came last. But my first was to my mother.

I did indeed owe my mother apology. As a teenager and young woman, various "me's" had done her harm at one time or another in one way or another. On the appointed day, I arrived at her home with my amends letter in hand. We had talked by phone earlier when I explained how it would go. As we sat at the breakfast table in her dining room, I referred to my letter as I made my apologies. When I finished, she said, "I forgive you, Betty Lou. I forgive you everything." And as we stood to hug, for the first time in memory my mother reached out to me, held me tight, and we cried at once. Then, still embracing, she eased back a bit still with arms around me, looked me in the eye, spoke of pride in me and thanked me.

Mama next asked if it was hard for me to do it, to which I replied, "No, not hard; right." When I asked how she felt, she replied, "Wonderful! You have made my prayer come true." I closed the amends by explaining I would never speak of it again, that in recovery I am becoming a new person and the past will be left in the past. My mother accepted and agreed. When I left, I went with exceeding joy. Instead of mailing letters to my sisters, I instead met with them one at a time in person on neutral ground. Mary first, at a coffee shop where we sat at a small table in the corner of a covered patio. She listened and when I was done told me she had forgiven me long before. We reminisced and laughed and after a long warm embrace went our separate ways. Mary and I would strike a renewed friendship as sisters and remain so.

Amends to Debbie happened at another coffee shop, outside on its patio in a secluded spot. She listened attentively and had one comment: "Why are you apologizing for slamming my thumb in the door when we were kids? You don't need to do that." I told her I aimed to be thorough, to apologize for everything I remembered. As we walked together to our vehicles, we hugged, and as a rare tear escaped her eye, Debbie said through a trembling voice, "I don't want to be angry anymore." I told her she did not have to be. We hugged again and separated.

I made amends to Jo Ann at Mama's on a frenzied afternoon. The family had been in the throes of packing Mama's belongings, preparing for her move to Morningside. My sister and I were alone for a block of time. We sat at the small breakfast table in the dining room. As I moved through it, my sister occasionally interrupted with her varying recollections of the events and circumstances I noted. At the conclusion of my apology, I asked if there was anything else that had harmed her for which I could apologize, because I would not bring up ever again anything we discussed that day. She cited one of my amends made, wanting to rehash it at length. But I explained, again, her acceptance was her choice, but my part, to make the apology, was done. She then accepted the amends and offered a general apology, without citing anything in particular. I concluded my amends and left.

After the initial four, I called Lynn, then extended family members, and finally Muriel and Sara. Lynn was graciously accepting. Muriel and Sara expressed appreciation.

Daddy and Roger were puzzling cases. Both had passed away before I entered recovery and I did not know how to make my amends to them. But Jim assured me amends could be carried out at their gravesites. He suggested I do so and when finished, while there, ask each one to confirm he had heard me and patiently await a sign. I was happy to have a way.

At my father's grave one sunrise, I spread a blanket on the ground and sat upon it with my amends letter in hand. I spoke toward the tombstone to Daddy. I cried all the way through it and then I hushed and waited, as the sun climbed in the east and a slight breeze swept the air. Presently, a pair of mourning doves flew overhead, then one of them perched in a nearby tree. The other one flew farther to land on top of the 20-foot marble crucifix of Christ that stands watch over the cemetery at its entrance some 20 yards from where I sat. The dove perched atop the cross a long while, seemingly staring squarely in my direction. And I knew.

I next made amends to Roger. I stood near his tombstone recounting my amends, the most glaring of which I recollected happened a few days shortly before the Christmas Day he suffered fatally in the car wreck. I apologized for not letting him drive my car the day he asked to take it for a spin around the block. And I apologized for the night he drove his crazy selfish sister 100 miles for a final fling with her soon-to-be ex-husband and waited in the car in the cold two hours. I knew without needing a sign Roger had forgiven me.

I found amends-making stimulating and humbling. The act of sincerest apology raised in me a surprisingly salubrious self-esteem. I was legitimately happy to admit I had been wrong. I was happy to unburden my heart and soul of wrongdoing and genuinely sorry I had hurt anyone. Through it all, I held my head high, respecting myself and the other person, and in the process observed in me two transforming vicissitudes: I humbled myself with those who had harmed me who never apologized, and, the practice of humility produced in me a spiritual vitality I had never known.

Amends to myself was deeply purifying. As a maturing adult, I made amends to the child in me, to the teenager in me, and to the young woman in me, for having put my former selves repeatedly in harm's way. I apologized to myself for the harm I had done myself in every familial row, intimate affiliation, workplace conflict, and instance of physical injury due to overexertion, and for the financial pickle I had gotten myself into. I promised myself from that day forward to be kinder, gentler, wiser and more caring with me in every area of life.

I was most rigorous with the account of my past transgressions against myself, listing and describing nearly 50, all of which I shared with Jim and all of which affirmed how disparagingly I had treated myself. My sage sponsor helped me hone down the list to a focused few. And he suggested I put the short list someplace where I could see it daily and read it when I felt low. He told me to practice two concepts of recovery always, and if I did, then assuredly I could live truly in a state of "happy, joyous and free," and doing so would improve all my relationships in all areas of my life. The two concepts consisted of accepting people the way they are, and not taking others' inventory, which is thinking, wondering about or judging what anyone else is saying, doing or thinking.

And now, wholly for the benefit of you who read this, I share my amends to myself, the ones Jim honed to a few encapsulating all the rest. This to say, you do not have to live with your past transgressions, no matter how dark or dire they may have been. I was absolved through the process of amends and self-forgiveness, and you, too, can know liberty if you choose it. My amends to myself:

"Dear Lou, I am sorry for every thought, word or action that hurt you. I am sorry for scaring you, abusing you, treating you as if you were of no value, scaring the little girl in you who has for most of your life needed to be loved, acknowledged, affirmed, nurtured and protected. I failed you in many ways, many times, for many years, and I am truly sorry for having hurt you so much for so long.

"For the times I felt ashamed. For the times I reacted to others' unloving hurtful behavior with hysterics that only served to make me sick and sicker. For allowing myself to be cussed at, hit, pushed, shoved and otherwise mistreated. And all the while, blaming myself.

"For allowing myself to feel and think as if I'm not good enough or skilled enough despite my accomplishments and positive qualities, not attractive enough, not talented enough, not witty enough, not smart enough, like I don't belong, like I don't deserve to be loved, respected, nurtured, treated with kindness and respect, for not acknowledging my self-worth.

"For carrying the sickness of guilt, taking on everyone else's problems and attitudes as if they were mine and my fault. For allowing intolerant others to judge me and then owning their judgment as if true, all the while lashing out in hurt and anger. For resentments I held onto about other people, which kept me imprisoned by anger and bitterness.

"For mistaking sex for love and beating myself up over not getting the love I needed. For every sordid act and instance of promiscuity and immorality. For drunkenness and its ugly accessory behaviors. For giving too much too soon. For not allowing myself the dignity and time to get to know someone before having a physical relationship that never ended well and drove me deeper into self-hatred.

"For forgetting I am the daughter of God, no less than a princess; my Father is the One Almighty God and Creator of the universe, Who made all things and Who loves me and wants me to be happy, joyous and free! I am powerful in God, my Father, Who created me perfectly, in His image, and I can do all things through Him!

"For the worry, stress, hysterics, weeping, spiritual neglect and decline, emotional and physical neglect and decline, and mental neglect and decline I caused myself, in trying to control everything and everyone so I did not have to be scared, hurt, left, rejected, abandoned. None of that stuff ever worked for me. It only made my life miserable. For trying for so long to force solutions, which only kept me in pain, discontent and disharmony. For trying to control the outcomes instead of feeding my spirit; for playing God, which only fed my ego and kept me living on the lowest level and in misery.

"I'm sorry I have hurt myself for these and other things I don't recall; for loading my life and spirit, heart and soul with ugly anger, impatience and anxiety; for lying to myself and others directly or indirectly, intentionally, arrogantly or ignorantly; for trying to control the pain I carried by turning it outward in frustrating anger; for breeding insecurity and self-contempt within myself through immoral decisions for years.

"For all of these things I have done to hurt me, I am truly sorry and ask myself to forgive me. I ask the child in me to forgive me. I ask the teenager in me to forgive me. I ask the adult in me to forgive me. I ask God once and for all, please forgive me for these and all the hurts I have done to myself. Please take away all my guilt, shame and regret, all resentment toward myself; take away the anger, control, ego, fear, impatience and insecurity I have hurt myself with for so long. I give it all up. I give it to You, God."

Step 9 taught me to forgive myself and others because I came to believe we had done the best we could with what we knew and who we were at the time. But reconciliation does not always follow forgiveness. Sometimes, the most loving thing I can do for myself is walk away from a relationship when someone's behavior is unchanging and noxious and therefore a threat to my well-being.

Step 10 (Patience): "Continued to take personal inventory and when I was wrong promptly admitted it." My sponsor told me after completing Step 9 I would complete Steps 10, 11 and 12 in one day. I would do so come March 2009. The amazing grace afforded by Step 9 was unmistakable at the time I made all amends, and Step 10 required and constituted a vivid behavioral change fulfilled at Step 9. Step 10 required every day forward that I apologize on the spot when wrong. And this would become a lifelong habit. The goal was to live in my changed behavior. If I strove to not regress, then I would have little to apologize for.

Step 11 (Awareness): "Sought through prayer and meditation to improve my conscious contact with God as I understand Him." I love this Step. Al-Anon brought me closer to God, God brought me closer to Himself, and through intimacy with God, I am becoming the woman God created me to be. I already had begun and practiced a daily morning ritual of praying for myself and others and reading recovery literature. I continued to read the Bible as well and came across other books that widened my spiritual lens. Some of these deepened my Christianity while others inspired the professional in me. But all of them kept stepping me along a path of continued enlightenment.

Aside from reading, I also began practicing deep breathing most mornings. I had read about the healing effects of deep concentrated breathing, how it reduces stress, for instance, but now was discovering firsthand the true tranquil effect of performing it. In me, it produced a fully awake trance-like state from which I departed feeling as if I had awakened from a sound and peaceful sleep. Science and religion tell us meditational practices, including deep breathing, heal the body, mind and soul. I am convinced this in practice is true.

Over Thanksgiving, I planned to spend a final night at the family homestead with Mama and my sisters for old times' sake. But I changed my mind. Instead, I had dinner with friends on the eve of the holiday and then dined with other friends Thanksgiving Day. I was letting go of pain and embracing love. I had learned "family" is not united only by blood; family are those people with whom I share love, trust and respect. I loved my biological family and fond memories of us, but I could not trust some of them with my heart. Being blood relatives does not by default mean we relate.

About this time, Lynn told me: "Trust is a strange thing. Once earned, it can quickly disintegrate, and once lost, it takes a long time and proof to earn it back." I could not have agreed more. The shedding of tears over losing the family I once knew or hoped of ever knowing again slowed, and as the future would tell, stopped altogether.

From when I had first met Edwin two years prior to now nearing the finish of systematically and meticulously working the 12 Steps with Jim, I remained as thirsty as ever for recovery and its promise of spiritual awakening. Already, it was happening, evidenced in changes in my behavior and decisions, which happened from the inside out. And I did not know it then, but in the very near future, I would uncover another layer of self-reclamation. I would step into a special place of God's presence, which without having experienced I never would have believed possible.

Step 12 (Service): "Having had a spiritual awakening as the result of these Steps, I tried to carry this message to others, and to practice these principles in all my affairs." I talked about my recovery everywhere I went. But more than talking about it, I lived it, and it lived in and through me.

Tom was a professor at a prestigious private university, my friend and kind. We met at the Saturday morning Al-Anon meeting at Club 12. Soon after I completed the 12 Steps, he wrote me a note. His gentle sincere words affirmed the spiritual distance I'd traveled and the truth in the 12 Promises of recovery: "Betty Lou, as I've quietly observed your growth, as you've progressed in your recovery, it seems to me you've become more centered, much less angry and needing to be in control, and clearly more caring. You seem much more at peace. That's the spiritual. Further, you are a physically attractive woman. But as you've grown spiritually, your inner growth shows on the outside as well. You radiate your recovery. You've moved from being pretty, which is to say, pleasing to the eyes, to being beautiful."

Caye was a temporary sponsor and dear friend in Al-Anon with whom I formed a deep and honest friendship. I doubt I'd ever known a more faithful, caring, genuine, compassionate, patient and giving human being, except for my parents and Kelly. She was a mighty collection in a tiny package. I first met Caye at the Saturday 11 o'clock Al-Anon meetings at Club 12. She always dressed in bright happy colors, typically toted a tall glass of water and wore the brightest smile in the room. She could cast a colossal net of meaning with few words. We talked often. Whenever she grew frustrated with my emotional binges, she'd moan, "Oh, Louuuuuu," stretching out my name in a long syllable string and that snapped me right out of it. And no matter her circumstances, when I asked how she was, Caye's answer often was, "Fabulous!"

As I completed the 12 Steps, Caye told me not to be timid in wielding my newborn power: "You're a flower opening up but spreading an umbrella to prevent raindrops (God's blessings)." She sensed coming abundance and suggested I let it come without reservation, to accept strong spiritual connections without having to analyze them or know future outcomes, and to complete Daddy's story about elder abuse without further delay. Caye was one of a few individuals who powerfully and enduringly impacted my life in wonderful lasting ways.

After completing three dedicated years in recovery, the third of those with Don in weekly therapy sessions that coincided with Jim's sponsorship and weekly Step work, my heart had lightened, my mind had eased, my attitude had softened, and my spirit had been freed. FishHook was growing, and I was engaged in the business of living, no longer subsisting submerged in chronic emotional and mental anguish, no longer tee-tottering continually between sane and insane. The sometimes soft whisper and sometimes heavy whip of recovery had reshaped me into the deliberate, decisive woman gone hushed on the inside far too long.

Back in December 2005 after one month in recovery, I had promised myself I would not court another intimate relationship until I had finished all 12 Steps and recovered my emotional health. About the time I completed the Steps in November 2008, except for the final three maintenance Steps, Don taught me that a lasting lifetime relationship, marriage included, manifests only through a series of successive building blocks: acquaintance, companionship, friendship, loving. He said if I jump from acquaintance to loving without developing companionship and friendship, then the risk of never attaining emotional intimacy and the corresponding risk of being hurt if one withdraws is high, even imminent. Mindlessly jumping was how I had lived prior to recovery, a way of life I wanted no more.

I have heard few to none share an experience with the vivid spiritual reawakening as I experienced later that November. I'm sure each individual has a distinct encounter, and mine was my own and that is how I tell it. Angels' trumpets did not blow, the sky did not burst into a sensational blanket of endless blue, I was not floating above the earth—although this came close. It happened at a crowded speaker meeting at Club 12. These Sunday meetings were jam-packed with hundreds of people filling every available seat and standing space that spilled into the hall toward the entry. I had taken a seat near the podium in front. After both speakers finished and the meeting adjourned, all the people milled about noisily.

Suddenly, like the Red Sea in Scripture, the crowd parted and my eyes were drawn directly and only to one man, and this man was enveloped in a halo. His cropped silver hair was thick and behind his ears. He wore a long-sleeved blue cotton shirt dotted with tiny red and yellow flowers and a wide white-toothed smile he opened readily. I was taken aback by the halo's radiance but felt attracted to what I saw. It seemed to me for an instant he was the only person in the room aside from myself. For what was presumably only an instant, I saw and heard no one else. I later discovered our paths likely had crossed at Club 12 for more than a year, but I had never noticed him prior to that day. When later I shared this with Don, he suggested my higher essence that was awakening saw this man's higher essence, and thus, the halo. Don had experienced something similar when first he met his wife.

This was the first time in 17 years I had taken notice of a man. I drove home that day in reflection. Was there indeed a halo around this stranger? Had God put it there to draw my eye? I barely dared think it, much less speak it, but believed it my spiritual awakening arriving on the heels of completing the 12 Steps; I knew instantly I had turned from women back to men, back to the woman God had created me to be. Was this haloed stranger God's medium for my awakened turn? Was he more? I would find out soon enough.

Interestingly, I soon heard from the female sheriff with whom I had ridden in her squad car that frightful Friday night. She apologized for angry words she had said to me long ago. I accepted her amends and informed her I no longer lived a gay life and had been in Al-Anon. She then told me she had learned she was Indian, had taken up riding a Harley-Davidson motorcycle, had a horse named Montana and followed the Red Road, which she described as a dignified life. How interesting I would discover the silver-haired haloed man at Club 12 also was Indian, rode a Harley, rode to Montana, and followed AA and the Red Road of wellbriety. A stunning coincidence.

What I knew for certain was all interest in women and the gay life left me. Spiritual reawakening had come like a bright light flicked on in a pitch black room. God took over my insides and that altered my outsides. It was exactly as the Big Book promised: "We will suddenly realize God is doing for us what we could not do for ourselves." My Step work had yielded immeasurably. It taught me to trust my true instincts, the spirit within. I knew, despite mistakes in the future, and there would be those, I would never revert to who I had been. There would be struggles, but the struggles would be fewer, less severe and shorter-lived.

I had learned to pray earnestly for my sisters, asking God bless them with healing from wounds they held. I had learned not to allow fear to drive my decisions and to steer clear of compromising situations. I had learned to ask questions before jumping to conclusions. I had learned from Don when I needed advice to ask Daddy. Daddy had been my loyal advocate while he was alive and still was, around or behind or through the invisible hedge we call death. And as soon as I asked, the answer would come and I would know what to do.

In early December 2008, Mama sold our family homestead to move to Morningside Ministries. She selected in its independent living section a one-bedroom flat on the second floor where she could cook in her kitchen or take meals in the dining room. And when age and time came calling, she could transfer to a single room in the assisted living section and from there if needed to skilled nursing.

The house had sold quickly. My sisters and I busied ourselves emptying closets and cabinets, and carrying out furniture and other items of our parents' former belongings. Mama was set but plausibly a bit reticent facing yet another loss and sorrow. On one of the last remaining days there, she was dressed impeccably as usual with makeup applied, hair coiffured and jewelry laid on but looked thin and absent at the goings on. It must have looked to her like a flock of vultures descending on a waiting carcass on a busy roadside. The eldest and youngest sisters seemed aloof or tired. Jo Ann commented the place I had selected that Mama had preferred, Morningside, clearly was the best choice. A few of the eldest of Mama's granddaughters and grandsons converged like human squirrels to carry away treasure while the littles darted here and there hugging and kissing everyone in sight.

But Mama, oh, Mama, my beloved my dearest my mother; I was so proud and reverently awed by the fortitudinous disposition with which, in the midst of history leaving, she left the dwelling where she and Daddy had settled inseparably as one. Where she and he had raised six children and the four daughters had dressed for their weddings. Where friends and relatives had been in steady supply. Where people and special occasions had graced its welcoming halls and laughter had lightened the heaviness of sorrow. Where countless meals had been cooked and countless ills had been endured and countless condolences had been extended when her youngest son and husband had died. Where now a million memories would live but she would not. If her heart emptied tears, no one saw them.

That night, I dreamed I sat in my apartment in the wee hours in the dark on a tall stool gazing out the sliding glass door that led to the balcony. Beyond it, a thicket of live oak trees, and beyond the trees a herd of restless black cattle running in all directions chased frantically by frantic cowboys afoot and on horseback. The stockmen scrambled to contain the cattle and wrangle them back into a fenced area through an open gate. I was glad I was not on the ground with the chaos and the cowboys and the cattle but only watching it unfold from on high. Suddenly, it began to rain and the cowboys' intensified efforts seemed even more futile. I awoke feeling calm. I believed the dream meant I no longer courted rowdy drama or wrangled with anyone over anything. I had a program for life.

Bill, Edwin, Judith, Jim, Caye and Don each followed the other in divine orchestration, each one in successive turn. Each one teaching me something I could learn only after having learned the preceding mentor's lesson. When I made the choice to say Yes to healing, God stepped in and set everything and everyone in motion. Like a river, my recovery flowed, sometimes a trickle, sometimes a roar, but it kept, keeps, flowing to an often unknown somewhere, someday, every day.

The lessons I had learned and would continue to learn would be infinite. The most poignant of these were faith in God, loving detachment, proper boundaries and self-love. I had learned the sheer acts of wanting and craving triggers pain but acceptance produces peace. I had learned life cannot be lived backward or forward but right now. Minute by minute. Hour by hour. Day by day. Step by step.

In light of the character and timespans of my personal relationships thus far, I indeed was progressing on a positive track. When the next conundrum came along, I would be better prepared, I told myself. Perhaps I would recognize and steer clear of imminent danger early on before getting too deeply involved or perhaps I would steer clear altogether. Sooner or later, these waters would be tested.

I had arrived at the stark awareness I would rather feel the occasional passing pinch of sadness or loneliness brought about by healthy choices than the indelible stain of pain. I no longer was willing to tolerate dysfunction emanating from elephants in the room any more than I was willing to suffer a blow to my head or being set afire. I fully realized this new way of being and relating would be anomalous and unacceptable to some people I knew or would meet. And often, I would walk alone as a result. But I was comfortable with aloneness because in truth I never am alone. I finally knew I belonged first to God and second to myself, and never would I put myself under the crushing foot of anyone or anything again.

The Step work I completed, including and most importantly the amends I made to myself, freed me of soul sickness. No longer was I an indistinguishable extension of someone else. I stood firmly on my own two feet, affirmed by the rhythm and fluidity of a pure pulse of peace in my spirit from where and through which I would live, from then on. And even though predictably I would oscillate intermittently in the winds of life's storms, I still would stand after the squall passed. I would be shaken but would not be shaken loose. I would be frightened but fear would not immobilize me, at least not for long. Because I had said Yes to spiritual mentors and their wisdom, Yes to the 12 Steps of recovery and done the work of it, I had established my roots deeply in the ground of God. And from where I had strayed, I had been made straight.

FishHook

It's one thing to dream of doing a thing but quite another to do it. I tell of FishHook to inspire people to aim high in life and to prove that dreams do come true with hard work, faith in God, and faith in oneself.

My career is peppered with risk-taking explorations that ultimately fed my entrepreneurial niche. I did not need to specialize in a single offering with my new business. I could capture more because I knew more and I knew more because I was unafraid to learn. And I had inherited grit, that measure of the entrepreneurial spirit exhibited by the men and women of our clan who made lives for themselves by the sweat of their brows and faith in God.

Throughout 2006 while employed with the radio station, I discreetly applied for more satisfying jobs in my career field. But after months of canvassing the job market for full-time work at a fair salary and reaping only deficient offers or rejections, I told myself I did not measure up. But that was a lie. The truth was employers were unwilling to fairly compensate my profession or expertise as a writer. They did not understand the dons of a bona fide writer and often handed communication projects to others who were not writers themselves and produced acceptable but mediocre results. I recognized this fact and considered self-employment to fill that void; the barbecue sauce business and my early freelance writing venture had taught me well. A new business venture called me by name. I named it FishHook.

FishHook would constitute the commercial side of my writing life and account for my daily bread. But I would make time for creative expression through bylined articles published in business journals, major dailies and magazines, all with the aim of telling stories of moral merit on the national stage.

By the time I had sold myself on sole-proprietorship, I had been distinguished as an award-winning writer. Because I had worked for the federal government, in mass media and multiple commercial industries, I was well-positioned as a well-rounded researcher and writer. I was equipped to provide my skillsets to the marketplace, casting a wide net while pinpointing nearly 40 types of services of a seasoned writer. I defined potential clients as organizations and individuals with a need to strategically conceptualize, contextualize and produce ideas, projects, policies, programs, or varying sorts of documents or plans aimed at improving operations or increasing efficiencies and revenue.

Working with a clear profit in mind was Priority No. 1. I had heard that a new enterprise either must offer a niche product or service or provide what already exists but better than the competition. I indeed already had defined my niche; I also had been described as "an artful storyteller" whose work was "compelling" and "error-free," someone with "gifted talent," which I would leverage with a unique marketing strategy fulfilled by meeting my promises. I decided to promote my business through aggressive cold-calling, targeted networking and timely delivery of uncompromising superior quality. And I was confident positive word-of-mouth would spread and my clientele would grow. Doing business with FishHook would be methodical and easy, starting with a fact-finding meeting with decision-makers. If their needs matched my abilities, then we'd strike a written agreement, including conditions for the work, timeline to accomplish it, fees and payment terms.

I designed a logo and wrote a slogan reflecting the technical and creative services I planned to provide. My motto said it all: "Words turn heads. Close deals. Open minds. Don't leave yours to chance." In creating the emblem, I set the image of a fishhook into the center of the words Fish and Hook, choosing green and brown colors reflecting my love of nature. By its memorable logo and in-demand product line, FishHook would distinguish itself from the competition, remind me of Daddy's passion for fishing, and "hook" clients with a catchy name.

I also connected with the local SBA SCORE: Counselors to America's Small Business office. It provided free workshops and mentors who taught small business owners how to structure a business, manage finance and records, create a business plan and locate sources of capital. Through it, I learned of the South Texas Business Fund, which offered more free guidance on starting and growing a business. This led me to yet another cost-free resource provided by the UTSA Small Business Development Center. I seized every existing reserve to learn beyond what I knew already how to launch FishHook in short order.

While taking full advantage of this resource treasury, luck found me in fellowship with a successful freelance writer who taught me how to set and negotiate rates and walk away when the money or pact was a poor fit. She said,

"With talent and determination, you can get where you want to be." I seized her words as mine!

When freelancing part-time as Writer for Hire, I had set a single hourly fee for any type project or duration. This rate became FishHook's base rate for long-term, 40-hour-per-week contracts. At the onset, my rates were purposefully lower than market. I started with a zero budget and scarce capital and had to earn money right away. But after a few months, I introduced more competitive rates based on regional pricing localized to San Antonio that varied depending on type of client, industry, project and timeframe. I separated these groupings by corporate, agency, individual, academic and nonprofit, assigning each group a distinct rate. I planned to partner with credentialed graphics and website designers and photographers to support my clients' more complex projects, with FishHook providing oversight. And I would assess a premium fee should a client require immediate turnaround.

I also created an annual service agreement featuring a discounted rate with services billed monthly for repeat clients with recurring needs. The annual contract would make doing business with me cost-effective for clients and establish recurring revenues for FishHook. By late January 2007, I was hunting and chasing after every potential lead.

To build momentum fast, I followed a strict regimen starting at 6 a.m. and ending at 5 p.m. If I had an existing client, most of my workday was devoted to it. But when without work or with small projects that required small outlays of time, I cold-called 15 prospects, replied to email and made follow-up calls. Prospects included those named in the SABJ's "Book of Lists," which identified the 25 top companies for multiple industries; the "Reference USA" database offered free by the San Antonio Public Library; and local chambers of commerce. I aimed to cold-call every company on every list, introducing my way to top decision-makers, amicably advancing through gatekeeper personnel with witty chinwag.

Each workday I devoted an hour or two to penning my story on elder abuse and researching national magazine publishers in hopes of securing one. I knew I had to hold myself to firm parameters as a home-based business owner and operator or fail. I found it excruciatingly hard mentally, emotionally and physically starting a home-based business from scratch, particularly during the first year. Some said it would take three to five years to establish but I boldly hoped to do it in two.

I registered "B. Lou Guckian DBA FishHook" and through the South Central Texas Regional Certification Agency in conjunction with the Texas Unified Certification Program certified FishHook to boost premier of my brand and garner invitations to bid for government and corporate contracts. I attained accreditations of Small Business Entity, Woman-owned Business Entity, Disadvantaged Business Entity, and Historically Underutilized Business Entity. Next came creating my business card. On the front I printed, "B. Lou Guckian DBA FishHook, Professional Writing Services," etching certifications and contact data. On the flipside I wrote: "Any size organization, Any industry, Anywhere," intentionally not limiting myself to geography or specialty, and notated core services. But I was wide open to all things scripted.

At the time, I lived in a 535-square-foot apartment that became my home office. In the tiny combined dining/living room, my dining table served as a desk, outfitted with a computer, printer and mounds of prospecting files. In practicing my cold-call prolog, I became adept at getting through to business owners and other senior managers who ran communication, public relations, marketing or human resources departments and often received my calls with interest. Several told me no freelance writer had contacted them much less offered services. This confirmed my niche in the marketplace. Cold-calling and follow-ups were vital to my early business strategy. In fact, these simple but crucial calls led to my landing lucrative contracts with some of the biggest businesses in town, including one of the country's largest banks and a national industrial commercial construction company.

I logged every call and email in a spreadsheet for reference and follow-up. Whenever I was met with a No, I politely ended the call and moved on to the next prospect. It all was extremely exciting despite having to brace myself against many Nos. Admittedly, I had to grow a rhino's skin to bear the Nos and muster every modicum of determined tenacity to ask for the business when I neared a Yes. But each call became easier especially after snagging a few meetings with new clients. Within mere months, I had secured three repeat clients and was earning more per month than I had with the radio station. I was hearing from people with whom I networked "good writers are hard to find." This early success and affirmation convinced me FishHook would become a long-lasting, profitable venture providing a lucrative living doing work I loved. I began envisioning a website featuring a services portfolio, published work and client testimonials.

I was self-employed writing and editing technical documents, articles for employee newsletters, slogans, promotional ads and website content. I delighted in the diversity of the work and the industries and organizations in which I found it. Since starting FishHook with a zero budget and Herculean faith, within seven months I had generated nearly $13,000 in revenue plus triple that in projected sales for the next 12 months. To be profitable in the coming year, I needed to borrow for working capital and debt consolidation. At summer's onset, I applied for a small business loan collateralizing my property in Boerne. The SBA approved it at a low interest rate and 5-year term. With it, I consolidated debt, upgraded my computing system, joined the North San Antonio Chamber of Commerce and American Marketing Association (AMA), developed my website and kept the rest in an operating fund.

At a most unexpected yet welcome time, a nice surprise surfaced. I struck a lucrative service agreement with my first nonprofit client, Personal Energy Transportation, or PET, to provide grant donor research and grant writing. This was yet again a new frontier in which I was eager to learn. PET made and provided free hand-cranked mobile devices to people in poor and war-torn countries who were immobile due to lack of legs or feet. This being my first grant, I came alongside a grant-writing veteran through SCORE who mentored me through the basics. She was surprised and complimentary that not only would I write the grant, I also would create the nonprofit's media kit, conduct grant donor research and recommend top picks, and pitch the nonprofit to media outlets via press release. I learned grant writers usually did none of that. Another niche for FishHook.

Rounding out PET's media kit, I wrote a compelling press release and personally delivered it to multiple radio, TV and print outlets via email and followed up by phone. Within 48 hours, a longstanding San Antonio news anchor for KENS-5 TV phoned me stating she wanted to interview PET. Within two days, she visited the PET workshop and videotaped the interview including her riding one of the PET carts and aired the segment that night during the evening news. The news anchor told me she had never read a better press release. My client was over-the-top ecstatic as was I.

By Thanksgiving, I had begun writing bylined articles for the SABJ, NSIDE Business Journal and NSIDE Medical Business Journal. While modestly compensated, these published works broadened my exposure. Clients were referring me to others and offering testimonials and my business was growing with an official website soon to launch.

Nearing completion of my first year constructing, unveiling and operating FishHook, with all its excitement, stress, expense and hard endless labor, my emotions dragged during the holidays from recurring pain I still carried concerning my family. I sometimes felt knocked off balance. But I had worked relentlessly on my recovery and my business and refused to let those scars steal my newfound joy or energy that drove it. I rededicated myself to what I knew to do. I prayed for those who hurt me and for prosperity. I ate healthy meals. I exercised. I worked diligently at my craft. I attended recovery meetings especially my home group and devoted each morning before dawn to reading recovery literature and Scripture. I remembered the sound counsel of my Al-Anon sponsors, and Don and Mike. And most importantly, for my heart's sake, from where my fortitude came, I acknowledged the pain and connected with trusted others who offered healing perspective.

By Christmas, I had run my first biweekly ad promoting FishHook in the SABJ and launched guckianwriter.com. I emailed the announcement and internet link to more than 400 individuals who were current and prospective clients, former colleagues, friends, family and relatives. In launching my website, in no small measure were the efforts of two gifted colleagues and friends. One's in-depth knowledge of the high-tech digital domain was an immeasurable asset to the FishHook site. She worked tirelessly and patiently with me as I sketched its layout and wrote and rewrote content. And Robert, an exceptionally gifted photographer and trusted confidante, who not only spent the better part of an entire day photographing me at the lovely Japanese Tea Gardens for my website but also spent countless hours talking with me through very trying personal matters.

By the end of my first year in business full-time, I had earned enough to cover six months' expenses thanks to a growing clientele and published articles. I had secured a small business loan and my DBA, certified my business, debuted my website, joined two professional organizations, completed 300 sales calls and advertised in the SABJ. I had become a vendor with the State of

Texas, City of San Antonio, Bexar County, and 17 corporations and agencies, submitted bids for proposals, and made new friends along the way. FishHook was a bona fide business. I was giddy, beyond thrilled. My birthday was just around the corner and I was in the mood for a treat. So, on a chilly afternoon in February, I sat through a two-hour tattooing of a large tiger on my left shoulder and a small butterfly above my right ankle. The imposing cat roared over all I had overcome and the butterfly reminded me to love myself as tenderly as did God.

In March 2008, the South West Texas Women's Business Center, an SBA and City of San Antonio Economic Development Department-supported organization catering to women-owned businesses, phoned me. They had nominated FishHook from among top small business entrepreneurs across the nation for two awards and I had won both the SBA 2008 Home-Based Business Champion of the Year for District and five-state Region VI. The district award considered nominees from 79 counties in South Texas, while the regional contest spanned five states: Texas, Arkansas, New Mexico, Oklahoma and Louisiana. Only one winner was selected for each honor. Stunned, I asked, Why me? The answer came, short and sweet: Tenacity and a solid business and marketing plan. The SBA presented the awards in mid-May at a luncheon covered by local press. The Express-News, which a decade earlier had published my first article "For a Song," interviewed and photographed me, reporting my award wins prominently in its Business section.

My initial year had been lean but exciting. By the end of my second year, I had contracted with 32 clients nearly doubling my revenue. I was getting calls from prospective customers referred by current clients and had published six bylined articles. As I had foreseen when first conceiving FishHook, I had served clients large and small, in a wide array of industries, doing a diverse range of writing and editing. FishHook was off and running.

On Jan. 1, 2009, I journaled strong optimism: "Today is an exciting day! It is a new year, a new beginning of a year-long treasure hunt! I set my sights on goals with faith I will, I can, I am succeeding!"

But the new year soon delivered a global financial crisis marking the start of what would become known as the Great Recession. Described by some as "the worst worldwide economic disaster since the Great Depression," it would wage economic war throughout 2009 and ripple its devastating effects for another three years after that. I barely held FishHook steady that third year. From a rolling boil to a slow simmer, revenue shrank as clients dripped contracting dollars to a bare trickle or shut them off completely, dwindling my client base from dozens to four. I barely was able to meet expenses and still carried enormous debt. Despite feeling overwhelmed, I kept believing in myself and God's provision. Unsure as to what the future held for FishHook, I took three part-time jobs and continued writing articles for three periodicals while planning for a somewhat cheerless homecoming to a salaried job. My brother, the realist, would be proud, I thought, of my decision to reconsider full-time employment in light of the downturn and shaky outlook.

My self-confidence and faith vacillated, though. I was a dual personality fraught with panic on the one hand while on the other filled with expectant confidence I would see fruit from the seeds I'd sown the previous two years. Meanwhile, I reinvented FishHook's services portfolio emphasizing technical work and adjusted fees accordingly. I had noticed a rising trend in technology use across public and private sectors and with its increase surely would come an amplified demand for technical documentation. I raised my standard rate in line with what the market bore for technical expertise while extending a deep discount for contracts guaranteeing a set number of billable hours over a long period.

And, I worried over what seemed a mountain of monthly expenses and outstanding debt and felt an urgent need to run down commercial work or a salaried job fast. But I felt equally urgent about finishing my article on elder abuse. Again I did what I'd learned to do when in need of help: I prayed for guidance. Shortly after my prayer, the phone rang. It was Mama, offering me a portion of my inheritance early. She wanted to help alleviate worry over expenses so I could focus on completing the elder abuse story. She said, "Betty Lou, your Daddy would want you to finish this article and get it published for the good of so many others who suffer." God had given me clear guidance, delivered through my mother.

I accepted her gift and labored to finish the article. And I looked for work. I found little but was grateful for what I found. I applied for jobs overseas. I connected with local companies and potential clients and was diligent with cold-calls. Recruiters and the Texas Workforce Commission had me on their radar. And I prayed boldly in expectation that no matter what the economy said, God said differently where my business and I were concerned. I asked God to flow prosperity into my life like a river. To bless me with peace. To take away all fear and reservation. I asked to be led.

In mid-September, SCORE nominated FishHook for its SBA 2009 Success Story award. And I won. I was beleaguered, barely making it, yet I won. God, determination and dogged pursuit had won the day again. I also completed the article on elder abuse, my father's story, and submitted it to national publishers and groups dedicated to the advocacy of our most vulnerable old. One month after receiving the SCORE award, as the economic downturn continued swallowing up my former business clientele and income, the National Consumer Voice for Quality Long-Term Care in Washington D.C. published my article, titled "Daddy Suffered in Silence—Are You Next." I was not paid but its publishing was a sure sign my writing career was on a purposed trajectory, despite the loss in self-employment income or current hard times. I was deeply pleased at the article's publication on the global internet by a reputable source. Mama was pleased I had achieved the great goal. And I sensed Daddy smiling, nodding avowal from his ethereal stay, as if to express, "Well done, daughter, well done."

By fall, I had earned enough to scarcely meet expenses for the year but was unable to satisfy longstanding creditors as well. I had paid off my auto loan by then, deferred my student loans, and obtained refinancing or reduced monthly payments for credit, property and business loan debts. But that was not enough. I fully understood robbing Peter to pay Paul; I was living it. Other writers I knew who freelanced had a husband or wife at home bringing in steady income, which eliminated their concerns about lulls in their businesses. But I was operating solo. I looked for work in and outside my field, including full-time, part-time, seasonal and contract, mostly to no avail. I learned when employers who offered lessor jobs saw my resume, they hesitated hiring me believing I would leave at the first chance of something better. I must confess, they were, of course, accurate.

2010 was nearly a repeat of 2009 but worse. My income continued to plunge particularly the second two quarters while I occupied myself with four clients and two part-time jobs.

That summer, the lease on my apartment in San Antonio expired. I had tired of the property management's neglectful and unsafe maintenance practices, so I leased a modest townhome 20 miles north in the small town of Boerne and made the move to Diamond Drive. The back porch of my new leased home was my favorite spot and a comfort; Daddy's barbecue pit sat there. Looking out the window from my second-story home office one day, I saw eight cows grazing in the field next door. One calf was nursing. The scene comforted me somehow.

When my existing contracts concluded in the fall, so did all existing income. And with no news from the numerous federal and other jobs for which I'd applied, I joined the ranks of the unemployed.

Sometimes, on morning walks, I meandered through the cemetery one-half mile from home. I have for a long time been intrigued by graveyards. To think of all those people who once walked the earth but now occupy space in a plot in an obscure cemetery, all but long-forgotten by the living. But I have not forgotten. I know tombstones mean something. They don't merely mark a gravesite. They tell a story about a person who once lived, and breathed, and laughed, and loved, and cried, and accomplished things, and traveled to places, and endured hardships the rest of us will never hear about. So tombstones, some more than 100 years old, intrigue me. One day, my time above the grass, too, will be marked by a stone.

As much as I did not want to do it, I asked local churches for help with utilities and rent and "shopped" for free groceries at food pantries. At the end of my financial rope, I asked my family for help, and surprisingly and gratefully was met with gifts of several hundred dollars each from Lynn, Jo Ann and Debbie. Mama offered $2,500, which I accepted only as a loan. It was a most humbling and oppressive time but I refused to believe it was the final word on FishHook or my success as a professional writer. In a last-ditch effort, when all resources had been had, I placed a desperate call to the Texas Department of Health and Human Services and applied for food stamps. From my perspective, I should expect a hand up from my state. I had paid into the tax system for decades and now I needed a brief assist. Nothing became of my plea.

I did my best to find work but exhaustive efforts yielded little. In the midst of my search, Don, former chairman of the board of the American Academy of Clinical Hypnoanalysts and a certified medical hypnoanalyst, asked me to research and write an article on behalf of the Academy. The article would cover a unique form of hypnosis involving psychotherapy administered in an altered state, which I had undergone formerly as Don's client. The topic fascinated me. I deemed the article a challenge and form of service benefiting countless others when published.

Don's patient would be the key subject of the article and had agreed to volunteer as the case study observed during a hypnosis conference held at the Concept Therapy Institute in San Antonio. He was a military veteran who had experienced war, separation from his family, alcoholism and drug addiction, and loss of everything. He had survived multiple car crashes and a drunk-driving arrest and lived with the trauma caused by sexual abuse as a child. He had seen Don for several months, joined AA, and attended group therapy for post-traumatic stress disorder (PTSD) through the Veterans Administration. Don asked me to attend the conference, and observe and interview this man, along with attending psychologists, medical doctors and authors, and licensed professional counselors. He asked I try to get the article published but not to worry if I could not.

When the conference convened, attendees described Don's patient as "morose and downtrodden." But by the end of the 3-day workshop and nine hypnoanalysis sessions, he laughed and noticeably walked taller. Attendees expressed astonishment at witnessing the shift.

In August 2010, the American Counseling Association published my 3,000-word expose in its Counseling Today magazine, entitled "Fast-tracking recovery." This was my second nationally published article I considered of merit to humanity. Don and I could not have been more delighted. The article's publication demonstrated yet again that even though my finances suffered my creativity and generosity did not. And that God surely had orchestrated the effort as He had done with my thesis and article on elder abuse. I was keenly aware it was not I alone who had arrived at and written these worthy works. God orchestrated the connections, guided the pen, and inspired the editors who published them.

That year otherwise was a gut-twisting period. Through it I learned no matter what my academics or business acumen, no matter the awards attained or drive possessed, an unforeseen economic crash cares nothing about anyone's well-being. I learned I was stronger than I thought, of the goodness in people's hearts and the benevolent resources available to folks who fall on hard times. Most importantly, I discovered a confident humility within myself in struggling through and overcoming shame over circumstances affecting me I did not invite and could not control. I survived 2010. But earnings continued to nosedive and by the final quarter had dried up completely. When they did, I was fortunate to qualify for unemployment compensation, of which I gave 10 percent to charity. I indeed believed whatever service I did would be doubled back to me by God. And as needy and scared as I was to let go of a single dollar, I gave it anyway.

In 2011, I made a weighty decision as aid trickled and then ended and despite gaining 10 small clients for FishHook. I sold my beloved 3 acres in Boerne to transfer the proceeds to debt. Before closing the deal I visited my property one last time. Kneeling on the ground, I thanked it for giving me enormous pleasure over the past 12 years, with its wide open cedar, prickly pear, and persimmon-dotted landscape and flowing Guadalupe River, where on its banks I had sat, pondered and fished, breathed immaculate air, and felt the sweet sweeping of wind on my sun-kissed skin. I paid off most of my debt, including $2,500 owed Mama. Only later would I realize the letting go of my land was preparatory for what else was coming.

And so, the future unfolded, as it always had. In 2012, I returned to federal government civil service as a technical writer/editor, from which I retired five years later to re-enter the more-lucrative private sector.

FishHook was, and is, alive. My wild ride with full-time self-employment had been daring, sometimes frightening, and often deeply satisfying and affirming. It taught me more about life, business and myself than academics or the safe haven of salaried employment ever could. I had developed and operated my own enterprise, had done it as a single woman, and in so doing, discovered a power and prowess in me that otherwise may have gone untapped. Yes, I was helped along the way in hard times, but most of the time, I triumphed through the ebb and flow of uncertainty and elation of success, if not in financial gain then in artistic and spiritual profit. Since first publishing a story in a major daily newspaper, I had published more than 175 articles in corporate magazines; multiple features or guest columns in major dailies, magazines, business and medical journals; and via the internet through the Texas Associated Press and national affiliates. And I became affiliated with and grew professionally through relationships with dozens of clients and organizations. These institutions and people are forever an integral part of my life story.

The pinnacle of a 25-year career would find me in 2022 realizing yet another dream. I would begin writing my first book, the one you now read.

How far I had come from the broken woman I was at 24, divorced with only a high school diploma and scarcely else to my name but a king-size brass bed and broken heart. Despite danger and desolation, the spirit within me had survived. And from it flowed all that would be. Again and again, I had seen and would see a recurring common thread in my life story of God making a way when there seemed none, of God turning what seemed hopelessness into goodness, for me and through me. Like a surging river, my spirit re-emerged, by God's grace.

And here, as someone who has worked in the communication arts for decades, I leave you with something to consider concerning evolving technology. Since the advent of the interactive internet in 1995, technology has sped forward at lightning pace. And with it, the convergence of mass media has corralled a technology-consuming world into one global database, nearly obliterating human individuality and privacy, and with it, human dignity. Personal and moral boundaries have all but disappeared. Instead of using technology for the benefit of humankind, humankind has sacrificed its soul on the altar of ease and speed, at a high cost. Adolescents and teens are abandoned to a digital universe by absent parents and a civilization at-large opening wide the doors to programmed shaping of them, and worse, societal scum to prey upon them.

Arguably, there are viable uses for technology. But through its excessive use and misuse, human beings are digressing from their God-given humanness, and with this digression comes vile indifference and irreverence for God's highest gifts of instinctive human intellect, ingenuity, compassion and language. This mockery of the Creator's finest design destroys human sensibilities that inform human language and interaction in the sharing of ideas, hearts and minds—transmuting God's design for human communication from its once most pure and effectual best to empty gibberish. And with that, the degradation of the human heart.

Indigenous People, Native Spirit

Second Spiritual Awakening

Life is a circle. The journey I'd begun at the conclusion of the 12 Steps had no end but would continue revealing itself, taking me with it through an escalating awareness I only can and must call sacred. Native Americans have played a vital role in the increasing spiritual unveiling and evolving of my inner self, my spirit.

Initial connection with Natives came in the person of the silver-haired man I'd met at Club 12 in 2008 whose name was Paul. He was a mixed-blood Chickasaw raised on the reservation or "rez" in Oklahoma and interchangeably called himself Nashoba (Choctaw for wolf or coyote) or Coyote. A Vietnam veteran and survivor of pervasive generational alcoholism and sexual abuse as a child, Paul had led a sordid bibulous life until AA in mid-life. Once sober, he became a "spirit rider" traveling to Indian reservations on his Harley spreading the good news of Native sobriety. He had discarded material things keeping only what fit on his motorcycle and in so doing set himself materially free.

One day, he spoke at length about carrying the AA message to Indian Country. We struck a friendship agreeing he'd fill me in on my curiosities about Indian culture and prayer ways. I wondered, too, about the leather jacket he wore, its fringe-trimmed buckskin overlays, Native beadwork and a back patch that read "Sober Indian Riders."

On Valentine's Day in 2009 I attended at his prompting my first intertribal United San Antonio Pow Wow. There, I watched as indigenous people gathered from different tribes and places near and far to celebrate and venerate their ancestry, sharing their heritage with the interested public. I was enamored by the feathers and attire, by the poise and posture of the Indians who drummed, sang and danced, all unlike anything I had come across. The spirit of that experience would linger long, long after I'd left the event.

As I stood on the outer parameter of the arena, the Master of Ceremonies instructed spectators to respect their sacred ceremonies and not step inside the circle unless invited. Pow wows are sober and smoke-free events, which I liked immensely. Dancers were not to be photographed, and regalia, some of which embodied family heirlooms and sacred memories, was not to be touched without permission. The dancers wore ceremonial regalia, often handmade, donning feathers, deerskin or other buckskin leggings, vests or dresses, beautifully crafted cloth skirts and shawls, head dressings including war bonnets and animal skins, and moccasins and belts adorned with skillfully sewn beadwork.

The Grand Entry that marked the start of the pow wow was moving and spectacular. In the center of the arena and central to the ceremonies sat the heartbeat of the pow wow, the large sacred host drum, and around it sat its drummers and singers. During the "Flag Song," spectators were asked to rise, hold hat in hand and refrain from picture-taking. Accompanying presentations of the American flag were pennants representing participating tribes, as a procession of veterans and dignitaries filed in ahead of the dancers who then filed into the arena in clusters representing their particular style of dance. Touched by the drum's beat, I stood awestruck at the magnificence of what I beheld and felt. I watched with delight, impressed by the preciseness and agility of the men's Traditional, Straight and Fancy dances, and the women's Jingle and Shawl dances. By and by, the crowd was invited inside the circle to dance along, as the drums played and the singers sang. And I watched the sacred Gourd Dance, into which no one except participating Indians were permitted.

As the weeks passed, my parleys with Paul increased and focused on Native American culture. He recommended I read a book that explained the historical and contemporary truth of Native America. I read the book, entitled "Custer Died for Your Sins: An Indian Manifesto" by Vine Deloria Jr., a Sioux of the Standing Rock Reservation and Christian. And indeed I was enlightened in its reading. I realized, for instance, that I, and likely most non-Indians, did not know much about American Indian history. It is not taught in American schools. We had not learned the deeply and widespread disturbing truth of the atrocities done to the Indian race dating back to the beginning of western civilization. As I learned about Indian sovereignty, I understood American Indians did not invite assimilation but were forced murderously into it.

I would continue reading books, some penned by Natives and some not. Indian friends suggested numerous films and I would watch more than two dozen about the first Americans, including "Bury My Heart at Wounded Knee." Reading about and watching actual accounts concerning the unfolding American West and Native Americans' experience with it over several hundred years of near-annihilation disturbed me. Just as it had to witness and write about elder abuse done to Daddy, and the irreversible ravages of a driver's alcohol abuse done to Roger. I asked myself, can there be a clear line drawn between one atrocity and another, marking one more horrific than the other? All brutality is catastrophic and unless acknowledged and remedied repeats itself.

Through Native friends, books and films, I learned of the deeply spiritual and religious nature of indigenous people. I heard of God by other names: Great Spirit, Creator, Grandfather. I heard of Mother Earth. I learned to see anew the all-encompassing nobility of God's natural world and human beings' relationship to it and to appreciate ever more God's creation. I heard of the "circle of life," that people "walk on" not die, as in eternal life. I learned about civilized (assimilated) tribes and traditional tribes. That some Indians are Christians and some are not. That some live on tribal lands and others in urban cities. That some pursue institutional academics, others learn traditional disciplines of their ancestors, and still others strike balance with both. That some speak and preserve their Native tongues, some speak English, and some practice both.

I learned about the burning of sage or tobacco as an accompaniment to prayer and began enjoying the sweet aroma in the mornings when I prayed as well; I found the scent of sage, like lavender or pine, soothing. I learned Natives are men and women of valor and tenacity who have served in America's military when advances of foreign adversaries threatened the United States and in peacetime. I learned each tribe was unique in language, look and lifeway; some were warriors, some were peacemakers. I learned some tribes fought each other. And some tribes coalesced. And in all my learning, I realized Native Americans pray to the one God.

Through the pow wow, I met a Lipan Apache Christian pastor and became involved with his drum circle. Those monthly gatherings were held at participants' homes, where there were drumming, singing, dancing and Bible-based teachings contextualized to Native culture. I was invited to wear a shawl and dance with the women in a circle around the drum as the men drummed and sang and was moved by it. At the conclusion of each of these services, the pastor burned sage as we all lined up to receive a blessing of the sweet-smelling smoke, which he administered with gentle swoops of an eagle feather. I embraced the practice wholly and appreciated the blessing, peace and sentiment it left with me.

My cherished circle of Indian friendships grew. The more time I spent with them, the more I learned and experienced, the more aware I became of a subtle rising echo on the inside, similar to what I felt when alongside the river.

It was then I offered to chair my Coker group every Tuesday night in November, marking my Al-Anon anniversary. There, I told my recovery story. On the first sharing, a woman with 25 years' recovery told me she'd watched me transform, witnessing the courage I exhibited of being in my own skin, of being my own taskmaster in identifying my character defects and emotions and staying vigilantly aware of them. She complimented my doing the work, doing something prayerful and positive with my flaws and feelings, and inspiring her by speaking openly about it. The emotional sobriety I had been able to achieve in a few short years, she said, was something she only in recent years had been able to do. My spiritual nature was revealing itself more and more.

Around my fourth Al-Anon birthday, a man in recovery heard of my interest in Native American culture and introduced me to Laura. Well-respected in the local Indian community, she led a traditional sweat lodge ceremony for women. Initially, she was unreceptive to my participating in the sweat and tried to dissuade me, stressing its sacredness and Indian legacy. But when I told her of my recovery, our mutual friend's referral, and my developing spirituality, she acquiesced and forewarned it may not be something I would like or want to repeat. I was eager to go. I had read sweats are thousands of years old within Native culture and wanted to experience it. Laura advised me to wear clothes I didn't mind getting dirty and no jewelry. She explained, if I was claustrophobic, I may not be able to handle the darkness or small enclosed space shared by other people, but afterward, there would be showers, fellowship and food. The nearly all-day affair would last from sunrise to late afternoon. She asked only that I contribute something to the meal. This was no commercial trick. No money or favors were involved.

On the property, the six of us gathered with Laura. All the Indian women were warm and welcoming. The lodge had been erected permanently on an area of land cleared of trees and brush a short walk from the house. It was a small, dome-shaped framework of willow limbs, which we all surrounded and covered with tarps and blankets, arranging, overlapping and securing them to utterly darken the inside. On the inside, in the center on the ground, was a circle of stones. At the onset of the ceremony, several ladies built and minded a bonfire a few feet from the lodge. As the intense flames roasted the stones, we all stood encircling the fire pit in silence. Once the fire burned low, we were instructed to enter the lodge one by one. I watched and followed those ahead of me, each of us dropping slowly to our knees at the entrance and crawling inside till we all had entered, sat, and formed a circle around the center of stones. One woman remained outside. She shoveled in hot rocks and placed them into the circle of stones, and then she, too, crawled inside letting fall the flap.

Intermittently, Laura sprinkled water, and sometimes cedar splinters, onto the hot rocks creating sizzling steam and pleasing aroma. On the third round of prayers and singing, we passed and smoked a tobacco offering, each taking four puffs from the hand-rolled cigarette. On one pass, I said a healing prayer while blowing puffs of smoke onto my right ankle, which had been painful after I had twisted it recently during a hike. I was wholly consumed by the powerful spirit present in that place and came to tears. I welcomed the steamy heat, darkness, collective petitions, aroma of cedar smoldering on red-hot rocks, and the cool earth beneath me, which along with my focus on prayer helped me withstand the intense ceremony all the way through. I lost all track of time. But after a time, I was delighted and astonished to see slight flickers of light dancing in midair, much like the tiny lights suspended in air I had seen two years earlier in a dream, in which they had shone from behind a shower curtain. In the lodge, I saw one flicker here, another there, and a few together. Some appeared near the walls and others danced in air near the steaming rocks.

Near the end of the ceremony, Laura invited us to speak, one at a time, to say whatever was on our hearts. Through gentle tears of joy, I said I felt connected to God in that place. The other women met my sharing with comforting affirmation. And finally, precisely as we had entered, the flap was flung open and each woman exited the lodge in turn, on her knees. Some sat outside here and there and some walked slowly about but all of us in a quiet reflection that shown on our faces. We all watched the sky slowly turn orange as the sun made its way toward the horizon. It was refreshing to be in cool air again. To let what had happened settle in me without words. No one spoke for what seemed a very long while. I noticed I was awash in perspiration and my right ankle no longer hurt.

I went from that place, journaled of it, and then slept well and long. The sacred sweat had cleansed my body and soul. Perhaps much like focused meditation, I am told a sweat can redirect a person's purpose, putting her on a path she had not realized was hers to chart. Some people say they receive visions while sweating. I believed the lights I had seen in the sweat lodge to be spirits of foretelling signs of something significant. And within what I had seen and sensed I supposed was a message specifically for me, even though I did not know yet its full meaning. I trusted the meaning would unfold in its own time. I would wait and watch for it. I would remember what I had seen and sensed that day and return in coming months to participate again with this welcoming band, arriving early to help prepare the area and fire. In a subsequent sweat, I became extremely overheated; I was told to lie down on my side with my face touching the cool ground. Once revived, I sat up again and finished the ritual. Sometimes, I attended a sweat in the morning and the Lipan Apache circle in the evening.

I continued going to pow wows, too. At the Sacred Springs Pow Wow held outdoors at Aquarena Springs in San Marcos I recognized Indian dancers I had met before. They shared hugs and hellos and gave me tickets for a meal and drinks. At the invitation of an elder who sat at the Northern Drum, I was invited to touch it for prayer and blessing and offered a chair to sit with them. That afternoon brought nothing short of joy.

One Saturday, I attended the Annual American Indian Heritage Pow Wow in Austin. By then, I had been to several pow wows in San Antonio, San Marcos, and Bandera, but this was the largest and most remarkable, reportedly the largest 1-day pow wow in America. Competitive dancers from 25 tribes numbering 300 came from across America, Canada and Mexico to dance; scores of vendors peddled handcrafted jewelry, Pendleton blankets, Indian frybread and more; and 30,000 spectators like me poured into the stadium and grounds. It was a magnificent experience after which I drove home feeling utterly content.

In spring, I attended the Fiesta Pow Wow in San Antonio. There I purchased a sterling silver bracelet set with blue turquoise and a matching ring made by Effie, a Zuni Indian elder from the Four Corners where a sacred Sun Dance ceremony happens. I also bought a Native American five-hole cedar flute, determined to learn to play it, and made new friends, including Virgie who agreed to give me lessons. My heart beamed.

My first flute lesson was an enlightening surprise. I was so moved by Virgie's flute I wept. I wanted to match it but of course I could not. She told me my spirit was very sensitive and beautiful. I had shared that recently a snake with a stripe down its back crawled up the glass door to my porch and another one crossed my path on the sidewalk. Seeing a snake is about transformation, she said, shedding the former year's skin. Coincidentally, at that time, my relationship with Paul was nearing its end. I also told her of the hummingbirds that come around. She said the little birds are special and to feed them, and whenever a four-legged, such as a deer, crosses my path it is a spiritual sign.

At Virgie's suggestion, I researched animal totems for my birth date and found mine the wolf. That finding intrigued me, since for years I had displayed a framed print of wolves in my home, had dreamed about a wolf soon after meeting Paul, and a year afterward had been attracted to and purchased a painting of a wolf. I read that the wolf is a deeply emotional and passionate animal. And while self-reliant, headstrong and often preoccupied, the wolf in a nurturing environment is gentle and generous. I liked the parallels between the wolf's character and mine. And I did not consider the musings of recognizing the wolf's character as representative of my own at all contradictory to my Christianity. My heart and mind were open wide to experiencing all that Native people wanted to teach me.

My connection with Native people was not by chance. As sponsors in recovery had been stepping stones on the pathway back to myself, so were my Native friends. They brought me full circle to the marrow of my spirit. Life indeed is a circle. I was born of God but went astray, which led me to recovery. Recovery led to spiritual awakening, which led to indigenous people, and they led me closer to my Creator, which led me ultimately back to Jesus Christ upon Whom my life and faith are hinged. Discovering and experiencing Native customs and prayer ways in no way diminished or compromised my Christian faith; on the contrary, it all strengthened my relationship with God. One day, I will close my eyes to this life and open them in the next, when my life circle will be complete. I will find myself in the presence of Almighty God and all those in faith who went ahead of me.

Through the sweat lodge experiences, I met a woman who had served as an American diplomat to Mexico and lived in Hunt, Texas on a wooded hillside bordering the Guadalupe River. There, she had built a yoga camp and spiritual retreat. In late June 2011, she invited me to the Yoga Center in Fredericksburg where I met a shaman of the Huichol people of the Sierra Madre Occidental mountain range in Mexico. The shaman had just attended a Sun Dance ceremony and had come at my friend's invitation to offer purification ceremonies to those interested, me among them. At the time, I was broken-hearted and unemployed.

The shaman spoke an ancient language mixed with Spanish and his interpreter translated. I had worn capris that day, so I was wrapped in a blanket as a skirt, seated in a chair with my feet resting on an ottoman and my eyes closed, and I was told to relax, breathe and listen. My friend played a Native American flute softly while the interpreter, who was tall with thick wooly salt-and-pepper shoulder-length hair and dressed in a colorful striped short-sleeved shirt and white linen pants with finished creases, spoke words over me. I felt as if in a hypnotic sleep, breathing steady and deep yet aware of what was going on around me. I was touched by feathers; I heard soft voices and footsteps.

I then was ushered to an adjoining room to where the shaman had preceded me. My friend informed him in Spanish I had a broken heart and was unemployed and stressed. I was instructed to lie face-up on the table where she covered me with a soft lightweight blanket, comforted my head with pillows and left the room. The shaman rose from his seat and walked to where I lay. He closed my eyes gently with his fingertips and began speaking words I could not understand.

He gently touched my forehead, ears, cheeks, fingers, arms, legs, feet, toes and stomach. At various times, I felt his cupped fingertips or perhaps his mouth against my skin in a pulling or sucking motion but it was featherlight; one here, another there; and then I heard him step through a nearby doorway that opened to the outside where there he spat and then returned to me. He did this several times. At one point, he put something silky and light, what I guessed was water, on both my eyes and then softly swept it away with a feather. The entire encounter was soothing and pleasant.

As the shaman exited, the interpreter entered and told me the shaman said, "Eat!" He told me I had not been eating wholesomely and to drink more water. He told me I think too much and was clouding my mind and blocking the spirit. He said, "Let go … of the former companion." And he warned, "If you do not, it will block your heart's desire from materializing."

I offered a modest $25, all I had on me, in trade for the ceremony and a colorful beaded bracelet with images of deer, peyote cactus and mountains; it represented natural elements meaningful to the Huichol and used in rituals. I then watched a small crowd, most of whom were artists and yoga instructors, file in and out of their time with the shaman looking as peaceful and happy as I felt. When all had been seen, we were served a meal of bison roasted in gravy, cucumber and tomato salad, and asparagus, all fresh and delicious.

I left that place knowing some things. I knew the best and most powerful thing to do was pray. I knew by any other name there was one God. And I knew God had been in the midst of that place and those people.

I had a second cleansing days later at my friend's yoga camp in Hunt. When I arrived that morning, the shaman already was there with his interpreter. I was led to a small cottage near the main house where inside I lay comfortably on top of a quilted bed, which the shaman and a few others encircled while speaking words before he performed a ceremony similar to the one in Fredericksburg. Again, there was a splendid meal afterward. And following the meal, we all gathered in a large airy room with high ceilings and wide open windows to play instruments and share thoughts. Albeit it awkwardly, I played my flute.

My friend suggested I journal my experiences with cleansings and expect to see changes in coming days and weeks. She also mentioned to write out my questions and hold them to my heart, asking for guidance and direction. I was given other instructions. To remove voicemails from Paul and delete his phone number from my phone. To not refer to him by name but as "the one who left." And she asked if he had lived at my home. As I answered yes, she suggested it be cleansed as well and the shaman would do it.

The shaman further instructed me to fill a lidded jar with fresh water, keep it at my front door, and splash the water on my face and hands before entering to protect against remaining negative spirits in my home. I considered the water sprinkling similar to use of "holy water" from my Catholic upbringing and gladly obliged. He also said to place a candle next to the water jar, and to light and let it burn all day while I was home. Again, I did not consider indigenous rituals, ceremonies or people pagan. Native people recognize all God's creation is sacred; their rituals and materials are not believed gods but symbolic of dedication to prayer and faith. I viewed and received them all as prayer ways to the one and only Creator.

That day at the yoga camp, the shaman had noticed my silver Tacoma and thinking me wealthy told me through his translator his tribe packs supplies on mules up the mountains and having such a truck would be of rich benefit to them. I was sure he was right. But I kept my truck. Driving home that evening, I felt a surge of energy… and determination to eat well. I stopped at the grocery store and once home cooked a pot of chicken stew, ate a generous portion, and enjoyed fresh strawberries for dessert. The food tasted especially delicious.

Within a few days, in early July, I purged my home. I deleted the phone number, email address, voicemails and emails from Paul. I kept photos of Montana that gave me joy, relocating them from frames to an album I stored. I gave away items he had given me. I went through my drawers and closets and discarded anything that resurrected upsetting memories. While I was at it, I threw away photos from other relationships that had caused me pain and sorrow. It was emotional and tiring but a helpful exercise.

I cried a good cry and afterward wrote my short list of questions for God: "Where do I go from here? How do I detach with love and blessing? What did I learn?" I journaled my thoughts around these questions. Then watched for God's reply.

I would keep warm memories inside my heart from where I could retrieve and look at them whenever I wanted. I would keep some of the words, too, in my heart, the ones that had been spoken to me that I believed sincere. And as with warm memories, I knew abiding love does not perish but changes form. From this place to where I had come I would travel still farther to reclaim and raise my spirit. And I would be ushered there by God, the spiritual gifts and wisdom of indigenous people and Native spirit, and my willingness to discover, develop and change.

Of Bliss and Sorrow

When we met in late 2008, Paul was in what he termed a devoted relationship and I introduced myself as having been gay. But I did not go into detail. I knew I no longer held interest in women. If our friendship deepened then I would find the right time to tell him about my awakened change.

By spring 2009, I learned his alleged committed affair was more unsteady than devoted and hinged at times on what he called "emotional strangulation." He spoke of returning to the rez to "sleep with all the pretty girls." I noticed early on Paul's sentiments spilled from a man much younger than his age. He was 70, educated, intelligent and articulate, but behaved at times as if half his age. He regularly left for yet another spirit ride and then reappeared for a time before leaving again. Each time we met, the more I learned about Indians, the more interested I became in Indian culture, and in Paul. I wanted to know more about his personal history growing up on a reservation and current ambitions.

Since adolescence, I had been enchanted by motorcycles and their riders and likewise was intrigued that Paul rode a Harley and was part of a sober riding group he had fallen in with in Montana called Sober Indian Riders or SIR. Its leader, Francis, otherwise known as SIR Redroad, was a Kootenai Indian of the Confederated Salish, Kootenai and Pend d'Oreille tribes of the Flathead Reservation who had fathered the Chief Cliff AA Group in Elmo, Montana. There he lived with his wife Deanna of the Spokane Tribe and to Montana is where Paul would ride.

I was enamored with Paul and charmed by his multiple names. He was ruggedly handsome, witty and obviously well-read judging by his eloquent vocabulary. And often he wore an inviting smile. It was not long before I realized my interest was past platonic. That I was interested at all was novel. The more we met the more my heart came along and sooner or later, all of me would follow. Still, I was hesitant and with good reason. He was not to be trusted, what with his ongoing back-and-forth abdications with a love affair, simultaneous flirtations with me, and plans to leave town. He had no roots to speak of. And by his own self-declaration he was dishonest. Paradoxically, I found our differences alluring. Despite all that and in light of my leaving gay life behind, mixed with the introduction by halo the previous autumn, I wanted to see to where it all led. One thing was certain. I did not want to get in the middle of his ongoing affair. My thinking was self-contradicting, though, since I kept communicating with him, caught by intrigue and morally confused by it.

One Saturday in late March we spoke by phone. That night, I dreamt I was alone inside my Tacoma with windows locked when an imposing dark-hued wolf appeared at one window. I perceived it male by its size and it scared me though it did not snarl. As he pawed at the window it came down a smidgeon but I managed quickly to push back his paws and reclose it. Suddenly, the wolf disappeared as instantly as it had materialized, and a second wolf, perhaps a coyote, emerged outside the opposite window. It was smaller. I tried to keep it out as well, but the windows slid smoothly down on their own, and the coyote jumped inside, encircled me, and then jumped out again and was gone. I awakened, unafraid. Neither wolf nor coyote had touched or harmed me and I wondered the dream's meaning. I had never before dreamt of a wolf or coyote. I later would learn from an Indian friend the wolf may be my totem, or spiritual guide, that wild, natural, free spirit given to me by the Creator before I was born.

In early April I talked with Paul after a meeting at Club 12; he was leaving in May. After a warm hug, I confided I did not want to bid goodbye. Before parting, I asked to kiss him but before I could he leaned close and kissed me once and then again. I kissed him because I wanted to know. I wanted to know for sure whether I had switched. I wanted to know after 20 years of not kissing a man what it felt like to kiss this particular man. I was not looking for this when we met. But here it was. I wanted to respect his ongoing albeit troubled relationship and his dual reason for leaving town, and the kiss was morally wrong and I knew it. Yet, I had done it.

With Easter came admission to myself of feelings of love for Paul and this love was not the kind I felt for everyone. I told him of it as he readied to leave Texas and that I no longer was two-spirited, his word for gay. I was not entirely sure whether what I felt was fascination and endearment for all things Indian, or for him, or both. Still, my brain warned, You barely know this man, but my heart said, What I feel for him I have not felt for anyone in a very long time. What I sensed went deeper than skin. No matter the source or reasoning, I wanted to explore my feelings and believed myself emotionally strong enough to take whatever came with the exploring. Saying No to protect myself from possible, even imminent, disappointment or heartbreak paled compared to the allure of what-if.

Before he left town, I invited Paul to brunch at my apartment. I had written a poem called "When You Go" as a parting gift. We sat on the couch nibbling fruit and apple-cinnamon tarts, I read the poem, and he hugged me warmly. He talked of coming travels to Colorado, Oregon, Montana and finally to the Pine Ridge Reservation in South Dakota and agreed to keep in touch. Given my feelings for a man again, I wondered what a wholesome relationship might look like; I had never had one, and wondered whether it thinkable with a wanderer like Paul.

After an hour's stay, he stood to go and then made obvious attempts to seduce me. I shrank from it. It seemed in conflict with the tender easy embrace we had shared on the couch, and his deep kiss felt forceful and was unwelcome. Only God knew what was occurring between him and his girlfriend, whether they were one or apart or in-between. And I was wavering and he was leaving. So I gave him the poem. He gave me a book. I then gifted him with a brown leather key ring shaped like Texas with a red G and star engraved on it. It had been a Father's Day gift from me to Daddy. When I told Paul it had belonged to my father, he winced and asked if I was sure I wanted him to have it, but I reassured him, because it carried love. I opened the door, ushered him through it, and trailed behind down three flights with my fingertips on his back.

Several weeks passed with no word. On Father's Day at sunrise I went to the river and sat on the rocks that sloped facing east above the water. I had my fishing line in the water, Daddy's Bulova on my left wrist and my journal in my hands. I was alone, except for the overcast sky, the plop and gurgle of the river coursing within its stoney bed and the birds chirping from cypress-thickened banks across the streaming water. Just being there, was a prayer. I wondered how I could lend my writing skills to Native people in recovery and hoped to do worthy work for the benefit of others.

In August, Paul answered a letter describing himself as a "restless spirit." Here again, a declarative caution. He also informed me he and his girlfriend yet again had rejoined their "committed" relationship and "hoped I would want our relationship to remain in good standing," and "You have added to my life in good ways and I care for you very much." He spoke of his admiration of my "grand" heart and love for people. I agreed to friendship and wished them both well. How ecstatic was I to have stood on moral albeit shaky ground at his prior sexual overture at my apartment three months prior. I wondered, Is this how men are? Do they carry one woman in their hearts and sleep with others who are handy? Daddy had been honorable but I doubted many, even most, men were. My therapist believed Paul's words to and about me were true. Don also educated me about a man in his 70s; he thinks of two things: completing his purpose and contemplating death.

I did miss Paul. I missed our discussions about Indian Country, Native ways and Indian sobriety. I heard from him periodically and one day in an email he told me the mended affair with his girlfriend had failed, again. I wondered whether his spirit rides were more accurately getaways from obligation and whether he would linger in old ties forever. My sponsor, therapist and trusted friends in and outside recovery supported my inkling toward a romance with him but warned me to go cautiously. I was like a teenager in love. I admitted it. And I knew to watch out, but would I? Given my history, I considered Paul a proving ground, as well as an opportunity to learn about Indians and Indian prayer ways. Most assuredly, interactions with him tested my emotional maturity or lack thereof. It was hard to know where I stood sometimes. Not with Paul necessarily but yes, that, too. Mostly though, within myself. I wrestled with wanting and warning. I began to pray God remove all sense of expectation where Paul was concerned.

In the wee hours one night in October, I was startled awake as if someone had clapped loudly in my face. As both eyes opened quick and wild, I remembered the dream. In penetrating shadows, I was inside a group of nameless faces on a towering flat rooftop encircled by lower rooftops and treetops as far as I could see. Suddenly, I toppled over the edge and thought I would die. But as quickly as I had fallen I landed easily on my feet with a stunned smile on my face. I knelt quickly, uttering, "Thank you, God," and as I did, was aware I felt unashamed of praying in public. As I stood in the dream, I awoke at the clap.

Don supposed the dream meant I was rebounding, leaving a dark place, landing on my feet. That was true enough. But I did not feel particularly resilient. I felt off-balance. All that day, I thought of my losses, of Roger and Daddy, and of Kathy, an Indian jingle dancer from the Apache circle I had joined who was dying, and now of Paul's exit after what had seemed a telling halo intro. I felt afraid of liking the man too much only to lose, but lose what? I barely knew him and we were not involved, not really, not yet. My mother reminded me, "Life is loss but God knows our grief." She surely knew, after the passing of her youngest son, husband and parents. I was tired of grief, though, of loss and its pain. Right then, I committed to 30 recovery meetings in 30 days to refresh my perspective.

The river was a soothing poultice for me, too. That weekend, I went fishing along the banks of the Guadalupe where the air carried the near-distant rumble of a Harley. I thought of Paul and dreamed about him that night. I dreamt he was leaving on a spirit ride and asked me to go, saying with bright enthusiasm, "You camp!" When I declined, he asked, "Who will you date?" At that, I awoke, smiling. Perhaps I declined the ride because I wanted to date a man who offered potential for permanence while acknowledging Paul's fleeting disposition. But the dream also left me wondering if not him, then who? And when? By Christmas, we had traded dozens of emails in which I had begun to sign, "Love, Lou." I am certain I emailed him far too frequently, which likely annoyed him, though he seemed not to mind and never said. We posted several letters and in one he wrote he was riding to Texas to formally end his failed relationship; their wavering commitment seemed more a swinging door.

In January 2010, I saw Paul briefly at a mutual friend's home after not having seen him for eight months. That day, he stole a kiss in the kitchen, and then was gone again. Over the next few weeks I shared my backstory with him and we flirted across the phone lines and email. Sometimes I mailed letters enclosing colorful photos of pow wows I had attended and of me with friends with whom I had spent holidays or other gatherings. He wrote of despondency on the rez due to alcoholism and drug addiction and the loss of life that came with it.

The next few months found me uneasy; I had not heard from him after regular contact. What I knew from recovery was that a perception of abandonment was resurfacing and I aimed to curb it. At my home group, I requested a desire chip. When asked, Why, since typically they are offered to alcoholics who need a reminder of an inward desire to be outwardly sober 24 hours at a time, I explained. I was in an uncertain place that threatened my emotional sobriety and wanted a chip to remind myself to stay emotionally sober. I was given the chip, after everyone laid prayers on it. I carried it with me everywhere in my purse or pocket and slept with it on my nightstand. It helped. I told myself the geographic separation between me and Paul was God's will and held purpose.

A dear friend and temporary sponsor helped me to see that my emotional capacity was uniquely vast, and many people, especially those in AA, may not possess the same capacious depth. And in relating with recovering alcoholics, I would fare well to remember. She also taught me to sit with discomfort before acting. Caye was another wise influence, reminding me to journal about whether I saw God manifesting in the people I spent time with and activities I pursued.

Paul resumed contact, inviting me to Montana. He had rented a duplex near the Flathead Lake and spoke of the area's breathtaking beauty and Big Sky Country. He told of depressing prolific occurrences of teenage suicide, alcoholism, prejudice and the long winter and seemed eager for my visit. He planned to take me motorcycle riding, only us two at first and then with SIR on a grand excursion.

I was excited but wary. The trip might hold more for me than majestic scenery and thrilling bike rides. It might also present an emotional quandary. I was up for the adventure but did not know whether I was prepared to spend a week alone with Paul. I cared for him and our flirting had been fun but I was figuring my way out of a long history absent of men, his past was peppered with infidelity and lying, and he suffered from untreated manic-depression. It did not seem either of us was ready for a healthy relationship with each other.

I began noticing his vacillating moods and random resurfacing mentions of his former girlfriend, and that worried me. Based on what I'd learned in Al-Anon, I was worried about becoming an unhealthy emotional outlet for Paul's choleric shifts. But there was more. I was bothered by his emotional immaturity and wondered whether I could care about him and for myself at the same time. I knew I was no longer capable of physical intimacy without mutual emotional closeness and trust. To share my intimate being, something I finally had learned to respect, with another person I hardly knew posed the greatest risk of all.

Paul was a strong personality not used to anyone setting hard boundaries with him, but I did so then and knew I would have to do likewise if I visited him. After weighing everything, I opted to go and we considered late-August. On the whole, the trip seemed a thrilling prospect. But while on a call with him one day, he told me a story about his uncle, Gray Hawk. As he spoke, I spotted a red-tailed hawk soaring in the distant sky above the treetops and a moment later it flew directly in front of my window. I wondered, what had the hawk come to tell me?

The next few weeks found me doubtful as his communication with me waned again. When it resumed, I found myself emphasizing a platonic friendship over physical attraction. Soon after, I received his letter. It told me of the hard country there, a young Indian boy who took his own life, the astronomical suicide rate, and hopelessness everywhere among teens who see only a future of poverty, abuse and abandonment. And he wrote, "I cannot divide myself. This is where I belong. You want and deserve to develop a loving relationship with a partner who reciprocates in gentleness, passion and commitment. I am not him. You deserve so much more than 'half measures'." He underlined the words, "I thought I could do both and it might be with you... I cannot."

I wondered whether my platonic posture had sparked the letter but swallowed the news and afterward kept our talks affable. I still hoped someday to visit Montana to see what he saw. Thereafter, he shared in emails and occasional calls his experiences bringing sobriety to Indians including taking AA meetings to them in jail and told of extreme prejudice against Indians. I shared news of work, weather, my move to Boerne, and refurbishing the barrel barbecue pit that had been Daddy's, occasionally signing my emails, "Love, me." I was used to telling people I cared about I loved them. I still cared for Paul; to omit it seemed strangely false.

Paul phoned in mid-June and spoke again of my visiting Montana. As the trip drew closer, I suggested we have blood tests. I did not plan on an affair. But we were two people with feelings and desires, and if intimacy happened, I wanted to be safe. Recently, I had completed my annual exam with my doctor and knew I was fine. At my suggestion, he became incensed and told me to cancel the trip. Sucker punch. To my stomach. I steadied my voice and explained that blood tests were a loving gift to each other, especially considering our ages and relationship histories. But he had none of it.

After that call, I spoke with Don, my sponsor and close female friends in recovery who all affirmed my feelings and one implied God was protecting me. I had heard, "rejection is God's protection," and maybe that was true in this case. I even spoke with Mama who said Paul's reaction was only ego. I was amazed I was having this conversation with my mother who thankfully was sensitive and understanding. She said he likely would rethink it and have a change of heart, but if not, then he did not care for me, and it was not God's will for me to be with him. Mama said, "You deserve to be loved, Betty Lou, truly loved, by a man." Mama was wise and Daddy had loved her well. I hoped to be more like her and find a love like theirs. I prepared to cancel the trip and rethink feelings for Paul.

It was increasingly clear, drawing closer to this man was a dangerous proposition. My past was peppered with dangerous risk-taking. But since recovery, I was more discerning though not yet wholly wise. I was caught in the middle of conflicting thoughts: God pointed Paul out to me, and, Once God pointed him out to me I realized I was no longer gay, and, Am I supposed to be with him? I decided albeit with caution to inch forward. The risk-taker in me, although tempered by softshell prudence, wanted to know what I would find. Then one day, he called. He claimed a case of ego but much more that prompted his negative reaction to blood tests. He pointed to insecurities, old behaviors, aging, long-time single life, and my raising a sensitive subject no one had broached with him before that forced him to be honest with himself. He wondered what I saw in him. I had been doing my utmost to show and tell him what I saw was his higher essence, that part of him that mine called to, that person in him long ago all but buried, the person I saw that day of the halo. I had caught its glimmer and it was beautiful.

He asked me again to make the trip and I agreed. We now talked openly about the prospect of intimacy. I had not been with a man for two decades, had not dated or been in a relationship for five years, and had never experienced intimate tenderness with a man. The closer the flight date, the more I contemplated the inevitable outcome. I knew what I wanted was not attainable with Paul. But I wrestled with wondering why God had put us together.

When I arrived at the airport in Missoula, I found it cradled by five mountain ranges. From that moment on, I would look in every direction to see astonishing splendor that amplified with each unfolding day. After stowing my gear and climbing aboard White Thunder, we rode 70 miles to his home. I was on my great adventure! That night, he introduced me to Francis at the Chief Cliff AA meeting at the Elmo Community Health and Wellness Center. When we walked through the door, Francis met us with warm hugs of welcome. The meeting was sparsely attended and set up in a circle with sage burning in its center. I enjoyed it but was extremely tired by then, now dusk. I barely could keep my eyes open.

My week's stay began happily but quickly became riddled with confusion. And tears. I had planned to sleep on the couch while Paul took to his bed. But that was a difficult proposition, given the mounting anticipation we both had fed. I would have welcomed a night alone to sleep but against my better judgment I joined him. What I had known with certainty long before arriving in Montana is what I still knew, that being physically intimate would attach me to Paul—of course it would—and usher in all sorts of emotions on top of those I carried already. The first time should have been unhurried when I was not fatigued. My yielding was a grave mistake. I did feel desire for him but my tiredness left me neutral and I felt more handled than valued. He became frustrated, impatient, rose in silence and left for the living room. And when he left, I felt what I had felt in the past: abandoned.

I went to him and told him of my feelings and reminded him I was exhausted. He asked why I had come to Montana. I told the truth; I wanted to see him and beautiful country. I waited in silence for him to tell me to leave. But he put his arm around me. After that first night, his aggravation turned to gentleness and I relaxed. And then we found out age and time had played tricks on us both. We talked through the unexpected surprises. He was thereafter at times tender and at other times impatient and openly frustrated with the pace and expression of our intimacy and his anger began to fuel in me a growing distrust. His dual personality was confusing and hurtful and I wondered how much and for how long I would endure it. Still, I had chosen to be there. Even so, I had wanted our time together to unfold not by force but naturally.

My misgivings that first night and following week would set a precedent I would not overcome. Over time, my wariness would prove valid again and again. Without mutual respect and trust for one another, in the most intimate setting, at least for me, lovemaking would never be satisfying or complete. I could not abandon myself to utter vulnerability with Paul without trusting him. And I did not trust him with my heart since I knew his anger was always hovering. Yet, we wrapped up in each other every night and enjoyed a most picturesque place by day.

The day before I departed, we rode to Missoula to stay the night at a hotel before my early flight the next morning. That afternoon, he caught me by surprise, tackling me onto the bed, and we laughed like teenagers. Times like these endeared me to him and made it almost easy to forget his wounding words. After an historic week of sightseeing the wilds and wonders of Montana with SIR from the comfy back seat of White Thunder, when we parted we casually claimed commitment across the miles. Montana was not simply a place I had visited. Montana was a place in time that became a part of me, a pulse of my heart, and I became a part of Montana. It always would be that way.

When I returned to Texas, he readied to leave for Dallas to be with his son and family. They were in trouble and Paul wanted to help, apparently in a last-ditch effort to make up for his alcoholic failings during his son's upbringing. Once I was home, every day for the next two weeks he phoned or emailed saying he missed me, loved me, was in love with me. He described our time together in Montana as "bliss." He told me he had known before Montana I was a giving person but when he knew me better fell in love with me and wanted never for me to be hurt again.

On frequent morning calls, we shared a prayer and meditation from recovery literature. And at day's end we bid good night. In mid-September at Paul's invitation I flew to Las Vegas to join SIR members at the Native AA Conference. While there, Francis gave me a necklace he had made, adorned with a Salish and Kootenai Nation recovery medallion. Our final evening there, Francis, Deanna, Paul and I meandered along Old Freemont Street taking in the lights, vendors, music and costumed performers. We were dazzled by an artist who created art using cans of spray paint. We watched him paint a lush colorful valley scene with a lake in its center, and behind it, snow-capped mountains in the distance, and in the light of a full yellow moon, a statuesque wolf atop a high ridge with its head held back in a howl. I bought the painting to take home.

After we four bid good night, we headed to our rooms, all bound for home in the morning. But I wanted to hug our friends a final time and so started toward them. Paul stopped me short, scolding me openly and harshly that my saying goodbye was "not the Indian way." I was shocked by his fuming display and wondered why he could not have given me this news in a kinder manner and in private. We both fell silent and kept walking, but I wanted to run from him. Once alone, he held me close when I told him his words and tone had been extremely harsh. I reminded him of my past, riddled with abuse, and I could no longer accept it. He listened, speechless. On that trip, I discovered when we were alone he was different than when in the company of others. One minute he was warm. The next, his blue eyes turned black and he became an offensive rogue in atomic rage. I watched in panic as his personality swung like a pendulum. Its impact on me was extremely damaging, leaving me afraid and nauseous. When I told him his incensed fury numbed my heart toward him, he dismissed my words. But I knew love and abuse could not coexist.

The following morning, I flew home to Boerne as he rode his Harley to Dallas. From the road he phoned to apologize for his cruel behavior. "You're the last person I wanted to hurt and now I had," he lamented. His amends seemed sincere and I accepted them. He said he wanted to "start over." But the pain was deeply lodged like a stake in my heart. My emotions and thoughts wove throughout me a haunting tangled web. I had hoped, naively, my reentry to loving men would be tender and affirming but it was not. For days, our calls were strained. In one, I told him I did not want to be with anyone from whom I had to protect myself.

I soon spoke with Don about what had taken place. We agreed, it had been disquieting at best, against the grain of my values and frightening. But I knew I would try again. I still was caught between the woman I had once been and the woman I was becoming and there was Paul in the middle of this evolving. I also believed irreversible damage had been done to my heart by thorny stabs of his rage. Throughout September into early October, as Paul discovered the harsh realities of his son's home life, he phoned and emailed me with constant expression of love. I offered a respite, a visit with me in Boerne. In October, he stayed 12 days and we never had a cross word. One day, we attended a tribal council gathering where I met fellows of his tribe. On another day, I introduced him to my mother. He told me repeatedly he was astonished at my witnessing his imperfections and aging yet saw him as beautiful. I doubted he ever had seen himself in a positive light.

We prepared and ate meals. Biked to my property and sat together on the grassy banks of the river in serene silence. Rode White Thunder to Sisterdale, Luckenbach and Fredericksburg, where we ate ice cream and meandered through shops. We slept. Were intimate. Brushed and braided each other's hair.

Watched movies. Took walks. Listened to albums while lying on the couch in each other's arms. We danced. He spoke of leasing an apartment in Dallas for the remainder of his stay there and said he "hated to leave" me. Then he left for Dallas and my life alone returned to me.

That is when I learned, at Paul's admission, he and the former girlfriend still stayed in touch, which fueled distrust and injury, particularly after recent days together. I talked it over with Don who labeled Paul's tete-a-tetes "emotional adultery." Paul later declared he was not good enough for me but loved me and was unsure what was best to do. I did not want to live with the befuddling ghosts of his past. I detested he hurt me. And, I believed I loved him. A part of me muddled through learning how to be in a relationship with a man again. Part of me believed this was not the man. Yet, I was not ready to walk away. But the time was nearing.

Back in Dallas, Paul rented a tiny upstairs apartment and welcomed my visit over the Halloween weekend. We shopped an entire afternoon for furniture, rugs, and odds and ends, and transformed his modest space into a place of appealing color and comfort. That weekend his son hosted a party and we went. I met his granddaughter with whom I became fast friends, so much so, Paul commented she was closer to me than him sometimes. There I also sensed a certain tension in his family and one particular neighbor. She was a yoga instructor with whom Paul now shared smiles, and as I observed, mutual flirtation. When she arrived, she walked quickly toward Paul but he rebuffed her advance by announcing nervously, "This is Betty Lou." At this, the woman stopped short, turned her eyes from him onto me, said hello, and did not speak to me again. For the rest of the evening, Paul did not sit close or touch me. My instincts told me something was afoul. God was talking to me but I listened half-heartedly. I did not want to believe the worst, that being betrayal. When I brought what I'd seen and sensed to his attention later, Paul dismissed it, denying shenanigans.

The night before the morning I was to return home, while alone in his apartment, he again turned into the ogre he had been in Las Vegas. At my quiet silence, Paul erupted into malevolent rage, yelling, "Go ahead, leave!" And he kept yelling and demanding I go. The part of him who was kind disappeared, replaced by someone, something, vicious. Here I was again caught off-guard by what looked like a complete takeover of his being. I was afraid. Of him. Afraid he might physically harm me. The fear was nauseating. My insides shifted into high idle in a split-second and stayed steady until I left the next morning. I wanted to leave right then but I was tired. So I stayed, he calmed down, I rested and left the next morning.

I did not understand his recurring meanness and sudden shifts when he knew how damaging they were, and why after realizing the pain his manic-depressive episodes caused he refused treatment. He was not in counseling for PTSD. He continued to rebuff Al-Anon. His ongoing response was he was "working on it." I was glad to leave that place and his presence. I welcomed the lonely road home. But I did not end the relationship.

As his family in Dallas struggled through its own turmoil and Paul wrestled with his past and present, he found himself poorly equipped to handle the emotional upheaval and became increasingly irritable during visits with me in Boerne. He was heartbroken by his son's suffering and the pain he had caused me. I told him God was giving him a second chance on both fronts. I wanted to be at his side but I would not if it meant getting hit repeatedly by his angry emotive buildup. Rage directed at me felt like jabbing stabbing pain. I had been observing his pattern of anger for months and it petrified me. The abuse hurt me more than missing him would hurt should we separate. His unbridled furies usually erupted the night before we were to leave each other's company.

Meanwhile, Paul's "I love you's" continued through mid-November. He spoke of the comfort in kissing and holding me and "brushing your lovely hair." He also admitted to his bouts of cursing and irritability and their negative impacts on me. And I admitted to him I loved him, would not want him to go, but would not stop him if he did. I discovered despite my asking him to stop he still stayed in touch with the former girlfriend claiming friendship. I reset boundaries, told him not to bring up his former lover or her life conditions to me, and not to deposit his anger onto me, that neither was tolerable. But it was of no use. Disloyalty and explosiveness recurred. Paul's impassioned outbursts often were followed by amends and tenderness before the next maddened eruption. No one else saw what I saw or experienced in private. I told no one except my sponsor, therapist, and a trusted friend in Al-Anon. Repeatedly, his behavior smacked of every past dysfunctional liaison I had suffered through before recovery, and I had sworn I would never allow that into my life again. But now I had, and that was a hard spot in which to find myself.

He visited me again, this time for six days, before Thanksgiving. I told him in advance I had nothing to offer but he wanted to visit anyway. His recurring amends for the damage he'd done had not expunged the emotional scars burned into my heart. He had used me as an emotional whipping post and we both knew it. Paul said one day, "I admire you. You're doing your best to live the spiritual principles." But I had reached the end of my tolerance. The night before he returned again to Dallas, as we drove home from my home group meeting, we argued. I told him I was no longer able or willing to suffer damage from his wrath and it must stop. I could not tolerate anymore his disloyalty, flipflopping conduct, and empty amends.

Once home, I sat outside on the back porch in the dark a long time and then walked inside where he was packing and without speaking ascended the stairs. Sleep came slow. At dawn, I awoke to the aroma of coffee brewing followed by the rumble of White Thunder but I stayed put under the covers until certain he had gone. I felt afraid, again. Afraid of letting go of something I had thought I had wanted but scared more of keeping it. He was a good man with a bad problem and neither I nor my love for him could help him. I did not cause his problem, I could not control it, and I could not cure it.

When I finally descended the stairs, I noticed the framed photo of us together on an idyllic ridge in the majestic mountains of Glacier National Park taken during the memorable Montana ride with SIR, a photo he had tagged "bliss," had been moved. I supposed he had held and looked at it before leaving. He had left the key ring I had given him and the handwritten pages of his life story, which I had encouraged him to begin. I did not chase after him that morning. A trusted friend told me later I was very strong. But I didn't feel strong. I felt sick at my stomach. Sometimes, doing the right thing hurts, too.

I decided should he contact me, or I him, I would stand firm on two things: I would not take abuse in any form. And if he chose to do the work of getting well, then I would grow our relationship. If he did not, I would not. I worked the 12 Steps with my sponsor around my hurt feelings and Paul's anger aimed at me. I journaled endlessly. Caye reminded me, "If we're pursuing God, we cannot miss God's will." I talked at length and in detail with my friend Robert. I reminded myself of my core values: Integrity, self-support, self-respect, courage, balance, spirituality, forgiveness. I asked Francis for prayers. I burned sage and released it all to God.

In mid-December I mailed Paul a brief letter, returning the key ring and his fledgling memoir. No matter current circumstances, I wrote I would hold him in a special place in my heart and memory. We shared a few phone calls that month, during one of which he told me, "You are a special person in this world and you're doing everything right." Despite the distance, we continued to communicate in support of each other's challenges—his bouts with nasty flus; my financial and spine health hurdles—still professing love. But the love we admitted to was changing into a treasured pearl we put away but knew its whereabouts.

From my intimate experience with this man who had 25 years' sobriety in AA, I learned being in AA for decades does not by default make a recovering alcoholic emotionally healthy. I had listened to alcoholics share in open Al-Anon meetings they had found spiritual reconditioning in Al-Anon in developing and maintaining wholesome intimate relationships. I knew what Al-Anon was doing for me. And I realized I had been trying to rescue Paul. But rescue was not a healthy solution. I believed Al-Anon would help him but he refused it. He also told me he does "not share everything with his sponsor." Those concerning words spoke volumes. My sponsor-sponsee experience was a trusting environment in which I held nothing back. Not sharing everything with my sponsor, to me, was the same as lying, which is morally deadly to spiritual growth.

Finally, I said No to being Paul's depository for pent-up anguish. I recognized abuse commits murder of the spirit, that my spirit had been reborn, and my duty was to protect it. I would not regress or sacrifice my well-being, for anyone, ever again. I forgave his hurtful remarks and deeds but the emotional welts would take time to heal. He visited two days before Christmas and returned to Dallas Christmas morning. Once back in Dallas, he called that day professing love and longing. He spoke of feeling "harmony," describing the "peace" he felt when with me, again citing that as unusual for him. He again phoned mornings to share the Third Step prayer and at bedtime to say good night. Sometimes his calls were sad professions of failing memory or physical sickness. Sometimes we reminisced about Montana. Sometimes we closed with I love you's.

I felt compassion for his circumstances and mailed letters of encouragement. I believed he was tiring of Dallas and his calls were a lifeline that carried him through a depressing season in a hard place. He expressed gratitude for me in his life and said he loved me. Throughout this time, I stayed close to my sponsor, working through my feelings with her. I had heard some people are in our lives for a reason, a season or a lifetime and wondered in which Paul belonged.

Paul began talking of mental illness; that he may say one thing today and something different tomorrow. He warned me I accept risk being close with him at all. Yes, I knew that already. It seemed urgent he said those words to me. And then he told me he wanted to see me.

Soon after we talked, I dreamt I had forgotten about an aquarium on my porch. Fearing the two neglected fish dead, I looked and saw they were alive, huge and extremely colorful with bright circles and squares on their bodies that were puffed out and pulsating with energy. In my dream, I thought, these are my "prosperity cows" and believed God had saved the fish to reveal He soon would work a miracle of prosperity in my life. I awakened refreshed. And then the phone rang. It was Paul calling to say he would be heading my way the very next day.

In mid-January 2011 on a below-freezing Friday, he rode from Dallas to Boerne in bitter cold. When he arrived, chilled to the bone, I warmly welcomed him but was met by his open hand waving me away as he stepped inside. I was offended by his icy gesture, after which he frowned, lowered and shook his head, and apologized. Paul spent the next day telling me things. That he had experienced frustrating and frightening "memory loss" and did not want, because of pride, to ask for help for fear of appearing "old or weak." And he told of his sons, who had grown up amid his disease when he was a "horrible father and unfaithful husband," and he wept at that.

That night, he brushed my hair a long time and we held each other for what would be our last embrace. Before he left on Sunday, he said he still loved me, still "wants," "present tense" he stressed, to be "a better man" because of me. After he left, I took a walk, finding myself in the middle of the street looking down at the yellow dividing line where White Thunder had rolled with me on it. And when I looked up again, I saw a street sign that read: Someday. I broke into a smile.

I was left not knowing for sure what was real or false, truth or lie. I prayed for clarity. I felt sad, relieved, angry. I reached out to friends in recovery. While

I grappled with Paul's sudden comeback trailed as suddenly by withdrawal, and wondered whether the supposed loss of memory was an idle excuse, I decided no matter the reason or how I felt or what I thought at the moment or would feel or think in coming days, this was the way it was destined to be and the best outcome for me. I decided to trust it. A week after he left, the beta fish I named Coyote two years prior died. I buried Coyote in the backyard and burned sage and recognized the telling omen. It told me to release Paul to God. And I did. I put away photos of us. In a sense, I buried him and then I prayed God guide me to my next step.

Knowing the best in myself, and having seen traces of the best in Paul, and loving him for those remnants, I understood I had been an unfamiliar but sincere experience in his life. This man who wished to be seen as honest but was not, to be admired as a spiritual giant but was not. I doubted he could face the sour certainty of damage caused to himself and me by his deceptions and rage. For him to be honest was to look backward and inward at the darkest recesses of his life but neither did he seem able nor willing to do that. And because he denied the truth, he was unable or unwilling to be wholly truthful with himself or me.

I confided in Mama. She pointed out Paul could have chosen to be the type of man to linger, take advantage and live off me, let me work hard and wait on him. But he did not. Many men would have, she said, but he was not that type of man. Her remark pointed to an infrequent display of integrity that at times surfaced through Paul's otherwise dubious facade, and that softened my sense of loss. Whatever our relationship had been or not, whatever words had been spoken in truth or not, whatever sorrows had been suffered in the midst of what was or was not, one thing was for sure. We had given each other a genuine memorable pearl: An ephemeral foretaste of bliss.

A small part of me wanted to hold him, to hold on to him. The larger and healthier part knew better. I realized Paul lived with a dark reality he did not show the world, but I had seen it, numerous times. And he had told me stories, wincing as he spoke, of his childhood. When that insidious shadow overtook the best of him, perhaps triggered by his sensing abandonment, razor-sharp leftovers cut him up on the inside, which he relieved by exacting verbal lashings onto the innocent and unsuspecting. Was it the junk of manic-depression? PTSD? Childhood abuse unresolved? I did not know. What I did know was he knew about the ogre who lived inside him. The cruel one who came out uninvited and unwelcome. The one with pitch-black eyes the color of midnight. And I came to believe the torment that gripped him was mightier than he. Or, more truthfully, he allowed it to be.

One day on my walk I spotted a coyote on a porch. It had rusted with time and weather yet howled with passion and pride. I thought of Coyote. A flock of geese waddled across my path, a four-legged barked hello from a bypassing truck, and nearly home again, a crimson cardinal caught my eye. Honeysuckle, cedar and thundering pipes afar made for sweet air. In this perfect place and point in time, I was wholly present and part of it all.

By late May, our contact trickled. Paul had wanted to keep in touch and I did for a bit. But I knew with too much "in touch" I would be at best an emotional standby, there would be no true letting go, and that was not in my best interest. I remembered my dream of 2009 in which a wolf and coyote each came to me inside my truck. Maybe the truck's locked windows had foretold warning of coming heartbreak and necessary defense from it. Maybe the large wolf had warned of Paul's arrival. Maybe the coyote had foretold of his fleeting appearances. Maybe neither wolf nor coyote harming me meant I would be fine. During a phone call in July, I told Paul I would remember the good, release what was not, and him, and wished him well. And finally, definitively, I followed through, a human woman wrestling with her own soul. Caye told me, enthusiastically, "I am proud of you, Lou. You took back your power." Indeed. Power. An immense and mightiest of words, a superior spiritual construct. Too often we forget to possess it.

In late winter, my instincts told me something was astir but what exactly they did not say. Then I heard from mutual friends Paul had taken up transient residence in Luckenbach 20 miles from Boerne at the Armadillo Farm campground. The tiny settlement consisted of a saloon, small outdoor concert venue, few shops, and scarcely else except the imposing fearless red roosters that wandered loose and patrolled the place. I felt uneasy at the news.

About a week later on a Saturday evening, I felt lonely as I sat on my porch at sunset and watched the sky turn colors as it dimmed in the west toward dusk. The field across the fence was a glorious emerald oasis. It was quiet outside, on the outskirts of this tiny town of 12,000 residents, and I could hear only the occasional thunder of cycles in the distance. I often can sit still and look at the night sky for hours, losing myself in its infinitesimal simplicity and wonder. I can do the same thing watching a fire burn at a campout or in a fireplace. The natural energy is soothing. And it's everywhere, if we but take notice. I wonder at the rare siting of a plummeting meteor we lovingly dub a shooting star. They are lucky sudden sightings for sure. I wonder whether one star carries as many messages as there are beholders. As twilight descended, I went inside and didn't feel lonely anymore. The night sky teaches me patience. So does a pretzel stick, when I let it melt in my mouth instead of quickly crunching it with my teeth into a mushy pulp. There is gallantry in placidity whether colossal or small.

As his lease expired in Luckenbach in early September I heard from others Paul was headed again for Montana. I was happy for him to go. That was the end of my connection as it ever had been or would be with Paul, but it was not the end of me. I had given him something only I could give because of who I was and would be. In the short span of the erratically spent time I'd known him, I had been able to filter through what I had labored with for many years longer in previous affairs. I also understood the codependent pattern I'd held to before recovery still lingered in my existing behavior and that was something I aimed to change.

I aimed to better evaluate with whom and how I spent time. To be more discerning when meeting someone and sensing attraction, to pay keener attention to any recognizable ism that may rear its head and steer clear of it, no matter the commonalities or momentary magnetism. No longer was I willing to sacrifice myself on the altar of dysfunction. No longer willing to suffer through connections that caused more pain than joy. No longer willing to trust the untrustworthy.

I understood life contains pain and loss, disappointment and confusion, but I believed it could be more enjoyable than not. The idealist in me still held that peace should be more pronounced than pain. Scripture tells me in Jesus's words how to do it: "Do not give what is holy to the dogs; nor cast your pearls before swine, lest they trample them under their feet, and turn and tear you in pieces" (Matthew 7:6 NKJV). In my long ago and recent past, I had given the best of me to individuals who had trampled what I gave. I would do so no more. It was entirely up to me. It had been all along.

The end of my season with Paul was not the end of my interest and involvement with Indians and Native prayer ways. Or men. God had given us to each other when our higher essence, our souls, connected that foretelling day at Club 12. Knowing him reopened my heart to men but not to a life with him. There was certain sanctification admitting that to myself. He had introduced and educated me about Native America and for that I would remain grateful. The finish of our former connection signaled progress on my road to emotional recovery and rising spirit, and with it, a higher morality. Parts of my association with Paul were savory. Parts were sharp setbacks, those situations that caused me injury. But the setbacks, I thankfully learned, were momentary, like the debris piled up on the banks of a river after a storm. Once cleared of rubble, a pleasing view reemerges.

By the end of 2012, I sensed a sweet shifting. On a late afternoon on a beautiful blue-sky Thursday, I strolled into Boerne. As I reached the town square, I heard music before spotting its source. A teenager sat on a bench strumming his aquamarine steel guitar with his whole heart. I drew closer and he smiled at me. I asked his name. "Tristan," he said. "Hi, I'm Lou," I said as I extended my hand and he took it and I sat down next to him. "I had a brother," I told him. "He played guitar, too; he'd play for hours and for me," I said. "His name was Roger." He asked, "Dalton?" We smiled. Then he said, "You know, most people don't say hello; they say, 'I'm not giving you money.' So, I'm glad you came over."

As sunset advanced, I still wore sunshades. In them after dark I felt mysterious, in disguise. I stood to square myself in front of Tristan, eased my sunshades down along the bridge of my nose, and met his eyes with mine.

I began, "Tristan, some people are intimidated by life…" and then pausing, spread my arms wide and continued, "…when they see someone living it. Don't let others' opinions concern you one iota. Keep playing." I extended my hand once more and he took it once more and in parting, I said, "God bless you. Merry Christmas." He replied, smiling, "Merry Christmas." I walked away with footsteps a bit nimbler. And I prayed, Thank you, God, for giving me someone to encourage today; please send more. I would never see Tristan again. That I know of, anyway. But connecting with this stranger connected me to God, to my beloved brother, to my grand-nephew also named Tristan, to the expansive, eternal, mysterious universe.

At December's end I found in my mailbox a small bubble-wrapped manilla envelope from "Coyote" in Bozeman, Montana. Inside I found the brown leather Texas-shaped key ring I'd given Paul in 2009. It now had made its fourth and final pass between us, like a symbol of who we had been, back and forth, until finally, returned to ourselves. With it was a small corner torn from ruled yellow paper and on it a scribbled note: "Hi, thought it would be quite fitting for you to attach your motorcycle key to this. Kinda nice for your Dad's spirit to ride with you. Blue Skies, Nashoba." I was surprised he, someone who holds on to little, had held on to the key ring and my address with it. The return carried calm closure to what had been but no longer was.

Unlike I, who grew weary of the pain of spiritual death from which I chose to recover, Paul chose to live in eternal twilight of spiritual death and the lies it told him since young: that people are objects to be used not human beings of value deserving of dignity and love. He elected to exist in and through suffering and darkness, unable to accept honesty and love in their purest forms, which is what I offered. And that is what blocked our bond. Night and day cannot coexist. Darkness is sorrow. Daylight is bliss. Scripture amplifies this in Jesus's words: "I have come as a light into the world, that whoever believes in Me should not abide in darkness" (John 12:46 NKJV).

The radiant light for which I'd been waiting appeared one day, ever so subtly at first, like dawn, from the seeds that had been sewn inside my soul. And then it dazzled as brightly as a pristine daybreak when the blinding sun tops the eastern horizon. On that spectacular day, I found myself yet again dancing around my living room, as an enigmatic smile widened across my face. I danced alone but was not. I had me, a woman I was getting to know more attentively with every experience. I had the spirit within. And I had lasting remembrances.

Sometimes I felt beautiful and strong, sometimes as frail as a newborn, sometimes in-between. I had vacillated for years along a continuum of powerless and powerful and thought it peculiar how power reveals itself in my most powerless state. Ours, Paul's and mine, had been a brief and tragic love story, laced with bliss and broken by sorrow. But time cannot extinguish what is true, decent, good. I would not regret loving him. I had not failed at loving. Despite a relationship's end, as my friend Robert reminded me, one person leaving by choice, chance or death does not make the encounter before it unreal.

Near the end of mine with Paul, I had penned for him a parting poem, a 92-line ode to an elusive love. I called it, "What is this Yearning?" Its pensive, poetic librettos summoned reminiscent tears, he later told. And soon thereafter we were no more.

On a Sunday in February 2024, 12 years after our parting, Paul made casual amends for the sorrow he recalled having caused me. I accepted.

A few golden gains from my loving Paul were camouflaged as hard life lessons. I learned to suffer through a painful outcome that showed itself only through loving a man who could not love in kind. To fail and try again. To be vulnerable for love's sake. To be raw and real risking rejection and impermanence. To be ever more adventuresome in all areas of life. And that for some—not I—to trust sensations of true peace and harmony is too painful to feel for long or at all.

Sober Indian Riders: The Ride of My Life

To say the 14-hour motorcycle ride through Glacier National Park in Montana the summer of 2010 Paul and I made with Sober Indian Riders was the ride of my life would be an understatement. It was indeed that. And, it was so much more. How to put words to the pulse of coursing blood? To the pulsating life in the wind that swept my skin as we rode unencumbered through Indian Country? To the sensations and unseen spirits that surrounded and reached clean through me? To the moon aglow from its nocturnal station in the blackest of blues where it, colossal and unconquerable, occupied a sphere enough for 10 sumptuous moons?

Since I was not used to riding a motorcycle, Paul took me riding every day ahead of the Glacier run with SIR. One day we rode north from Polson past Elmo to Kalispell and another day farther north to charming White Fish where I enjoyed my first-ever huckleberry ice cream. Another day, we toured around the vast, magnificent Flathead Lake that stretches 30 miles from Polson to Bigfork. I felt safe on the Harley with him even though we wore no helmets. At times, he reached back to gently press my left calf with a reassuring hand.

Then that most memorable day began with banded and braided motorcycle riders, us among them, who gathered in Elmo on a chilly sunny August daybreak. Temperatures promised by afternoon to climb into the 90s. The ride concluded at 10 that night when the great moon was replete and dominated the darkness, and the moonlit air turned bracing. In-between were the switchbacks of The Loop along the Road to the Sun with its eye-popping terrain-dropping narrow rims that wound us past jagged forest-covered mountains and snow-kissed crests of the Rockies that stood watch over spacious glens. Rival only to the majesty of the landscape was the equally exceptional camaraderie and warmth of those with whom I was most privileged to ride: Gary, Dan, Emery and his daughter Connie, Frank and Glenda. Absent was Francis, whose cycle was in repair and kept him home.

From Elmo we first rode north toward the Canadian border through the Flathead National Forest, inhaling sweet pristine pine air all the way. The Flathead is a vast, flourishing home to grizzlies and gray wolves, lush with lofty western red cedar, Engelmann spruce, lodgepole and ponderosa pine, subalpine fir, and grizzly favorites, huckleberry shrubs. After entering the park from the southwest at Apgar Village, we took the Road to the Sun all the way to its summit, stopping intermittently for a stretch and to feast on remarkable panoramas. We parked above the banks of the sparkling clear Avalanche Creek, in which we sprayed our faces. We rode next to the cliff wall that wept thawing snow and spring waters that descended in elegant splashes across the thoroughfare. And on a final rest, wild huckleberries got picked and eaten on the spot before we rode southeast through the park then home again—but not before an extraordinary encounter.

Tens of thousands of years past, Blackfeet and Flathead Indians inhabited what is known as the 1-million-acre Glacier National Park. The Blackfeet Indian Reservation occupies the park's eastern periphery while forks of the Flathead River form western and southern bounds. On the final leg of our ride that remarkable day, we rode east in the park along a curvy stretch across a sprawling rise through untold acres of charred forestry. And as we rode I suddenly sensed we were riding not thundering motorcycles but ponies, as if transported backward in time to centuries long gone. I rode with ghosts and felt welcome. I cannot explain it except to describe it as otherworldly. It was one of those occurrences when once through it you shake your head and ask yourself, What just happened? As we rode on and exited Glacier at St. Mary Village, southeast through the Blackfeet Reservation, the present returned to me. But the ghostlike encounter riding horses with Indians through open country was indelibly marked on my heart, where it would remain as vivid an image as the palm of my own hand.

By the time we reached the final 16 miles that stretched from Elmo to Polson, temperatures had fallen into the 40s when I snuggled myself into Paul's back, my head resting on his shoulder as a shield from the wind the rest of the way home. The oversized outperforming moon lit our way, even when veiled by gathering clouds. A few saw us home safely and then bid good night.

This day had been a day like no other before it, and forever and thereafter never would there be another like it. My encounter with SIR and Montana, the marvel and majesty of Indian Country and geniality of its Native people, was now and always would be part of me. It was a distinguishable blink in time and treasured impression that never would come again but would be remembered forever.

This White Light

Third Spiritual Awakening

On the afternoon of July 12, 2011, I was alone at home in Boerne and ascended the stairs to my bedroom to lie down. I wanted to get quiet and meditate in preparation for the next day's ceremony. The Huichol shaman was coming to conduct his final cleansing of my being and my house.

Lying still a while with eyes closed, my breath smoothly taking in air and letting it out in a soft rhythm, I felt composed and tranquil. Suddenly, from the center of my stomach, I sensed and saw a brilliant buoyant white light, in the shape of a spectacular star, burst from me. The light was dazzling and exceedingly white, and nearly as quickly as it appeared, it disappeared. Startled and speechless, I opened my eyes quick and wide and then softly wept with inexplicable joy. A single thought immediately followed: I had seen my reawakened spirit.

Closing my eyes again, I lay extremely still, yearning for its return. The unfathomable elation I'd felt at its electrifying appearance was unlike any pleasure I had ever known. I waited in silence. I did not move. I did not speak. But willfully summoning its return was futile. It had happened, on its own, without prompting from me, and if it returned, I supposed it would do so in its own time. After a time, I rose from my bed, went rummaging for my pad of canvas paper and pastel chalks and rapidly drew a picture of what I had seen. I then placed it on my refrigerator where I would see it often. I wanted to look at it every day, because every time I looked at it, I would remember what I saw, and felt, and experienced. I longed to feel again the unparalleled pleasure it had given me.

After this extraordinary encounter, I recalled my dream of 2007 when I'd seen tiny glimmers dancing in air from behind a shower curtain that when pulled aside revealed a sudden single combined burst of dazzling white light resembling a blazing star. The curtain in my dream had new significance. I deemed it now symbolic of a curtain rising on my eyes of faith. And I remembered two years after that, in November 2009, the small flickers of white light that appeared in the air in the sweat lodge. Another symbol of seeing and believing. And here now was I, another two-year span of time later, seeing the very same light but on a much larger scale while fully awake and which came not from a dream or trance but from inside me. Its arrival produced ecstasy. Who would believe me? Few, I supposed. But I knew. I most assuredly knew. Please understand. At the time of seeing my reawakened spirit and to this day, I did not then and do not now indulge in legal or illicit drug use, intoxication, or smoking or ingesting mind-altering substances.

In the early morning of the following day, which was two weeks after my second cleansing at the yoga camp that had followed the first at the Yoga Center in Fredericksburg, the shaman visited my home in Boerne. Accompanying him were his interpreter and a Native woman from the First Nations of Canada. They arrived within 48 hours of taking part in a sacred 4-day Sun Dance ceremony of dancing, fasting and praying. As I opened the door to welcome them, they all smiled at seeing the water jar on the porch with a candle burning next to it, as they had instructed me before. I hugged the shaman and his interpreter, who wrapped his arm around my shoulder and gently placed me next to the woman, when tears spilled suddenly from eyes. I told them I had cried countless tears and thought countless thoughts since the yoga camp. At this time, Paul and I were past-tense. The interpreter quickly suggested I give away anything remaining that Paul had given me because it kept me in the past and sorrowful. I later followed through.

They first walked through every room of my home, chanting and telling bad spirits to leave and inviting good guardian spirits to stay. Then came the cleansing of my person. It was the same as the yoga camp, with me lying down and the shaman conducting the ritual. And finally, as I sat in my living room in a comfy armchair covered with a soft pastel throw, with my eyes closed and feet raised on an ottoman, the woman sat next to me and blew a soft wisp of air toward my heart. She began to speak, telling me she sees events through the jaguar, which had come from Mexico where the shaman and his interpreter live.

She had run north, to the Midwest, to find five different pieces of my spirit. She put them all on her back, took them back to the desert, and then jumped into the fire to remove all the past hurts on my spirit and release them. The first hurt, she said, was when I was a child of 4 or 5 when I sat and cried and cried. The second was when I was a bit older and hid in a closet or under a bed, someplace dark, crying. The third was when I was a teenager, running and hiding. The fourth was when I was older, hiding my true self, crying. And the fifth was when the jaguar followed me into a deep dark cave and found me, a small girl, afraid and in tears.

Her vision was telling and true. I had cried and run and hid my true feelings much of my life. I told her, when I was 4, Mama had a nervous breakdown. When a little older, I sometimes hid under my bed, thinking myself invisible. When I was nearly 16, I ran away from home. When older, I often hid my way of life and cried then, too. The girl the jaguar found in the cave was the child inside me, I supposed, the one scared and abandoned who cried from and carried emotional pain. She said, "You've had many, many hurts in your life, Lou, but now the jaguar has put you on her back, taken you to the desert, jumped with you into the fire, and released you from all of these hurts and past pieces of you. You are set free. You are doing the work, Lou. You do not have to hide your true self any longer."

When I told her about the dazzling white light, she told me assuredly, "You are blessed, Lou. Yes. That is exactly what you saw. Your own spirit. Your life is going to change now."

The woman with the spirit of the jaguar reminded me, I am strong. That my home and being had been rid of negative spirits through the ceremonies but it was up to me to talk to my guardian spirits who now resided in every room and not to let weak or negative thinking return. She assured me everything wholesome would start opening up to me. Before they left my home, she held and curiously flipped through the pages of a coffee table book in my living room I had purchased years prior, titled "Big Cats: Their Power and Beauty" by Deborah Alexander. In it is a section devoted to the jaguar. In ancient Mayan religion, Alexander writes, the jaguar was revered. Its spirit was believed to protect shamans during healing rituals.

The translator left me instructions for prayer vigils. He told me to burn the candle outside by the door each night, place a glass of water next to it, and then in the morning, fan-spray some of the water from the glass across the door to keep the spirits that had been cast away from re-entering. When the water was gone, refill it with water from the mason jar I had been blessing myself with, repeat the fanning, and when all that water was gone, it would be finished. He told me also to place a glass of water in the center of my table and before I left the house and upon my return, take a drink, and say a prayer to "Creator, Father, the Great Mystery, and to Father Sun and Mother Earth, and to the

Four Winds," thanking them for blessing me and my home. He reminded me, "No more thinking. Invite only positive spirits into your mind. Do not allow negative thinking to return."

I offered them a modest $20 and a package of food, filled with strawberry and whipped cream sandwiches, plums, peaches, a quart of fresh strawberries, two lemons cut into slices, and chocolates. I would never forget the woman from the First Nations or the Huichol shaman and his translator. I would savor and remember their spirit-filled gifts and the unique spiritual prominence and rarity of seeing my own spirit. Their prayers and presence put me back on my spiritual path in a strong and tangible way. I would not forget I am blessed, yes, special. And I would treat myself this way. I would better care for and respect the whole of me.

Three days after the cleansing, I stepped through the front door onto the porch to extinguish the red candle left burning all night and was surprised to see the water in the glass next to the candle had turned red. Was this the materialization of a supernatural transference? Or the mischief of a neighbor? I would never know either way. But it didn't matter. What mattered was what had happened inside me.

My friend in Hunt invited me and I happily accepted to return to the yoga camp in mid-August to join her and other kindred spirits to bathe in the sacred waters, play music and eat. Interestingly, that same weekend, "the one who left" was scheduled as AA speaker at Club 12's anniversary festivity, from which I would be absent but where I often went. There indeed are no mistakes in God's world.

At home, I held to my practice of meditation. When I closed my eyes and freed my mind, I continued to see soft white lights appearing in tiny delicate orbs, bursting softly and increasing and then fading before reappearing again. And I reminded myself, "Eat well and enough. Drink more water. Don't think too much."

On the heels of the cleansings, I made decisions right away. I would not allow my past back into my life wherever it was a source of pain but would retain the beautiful and breathtaking. I would discontinue AA meetings because I am not an alcoholic. I would pray for God's clarity and direction in every detail of my life. And each day I would ask God to direct my steps and then listen for God's soft voice. When memories popped into my head, I wondered whether others who appeared in those recollections sensed the same popups at the same time as mine.

One morning, I looked through the sliding glass doors of my dining room at the pasture next door to see a herd of some two dozen deer grazing. In Huichol culture, the deer is the central symbol representing the herald of God. I took the siting as a supernatural sign of my growing closeness to God and of coming fortune. I also recalled Virgie saying that a four-legged such as a deer crossing my path is a spiritual signal. And here were 24 of them.

In the surreal shade of twilight, slightly before dawn, I walked one morning to the gym at the complex where I lived to exercise on the elliptical while watching an evangelist named Paula on TV. As I listened, she spoke of tithing and referred to it in Scripture: "You have caused men to ride over our heads; we went through fire and through water; but You brought us out to rich fulfillment" (Psalm 66:12 NKJV). And quickly thereafter, she encouraged her viewing audience to plant a $66.12 seed to her ministry and then watch and see what God would do with it.

Historically, I had scoffed at tithing, despite my parents' dedication to it. But right after Paula spoke, she looked straight through the TV at me as if she could reach through it and touch me with her hand and spoke my name, saying, "Betty Lou, are you ready to sew a seed in faith?" My heart skipped a beat, my eyes widened, my jaw dropped, I stopped pedaling the elliptical, I laughed in a strange way out loud, I shook my head in bewildered disbelief, and I asked myself, out loud, Did she just say my name? Woah. What just happened? It took me time to unwind.

I decided to believe, as I could not believe otherwise, that God had caused me to see and hear that woman call me by name. And I wondered, did God do the same with countless other viewers? I asked God if He was asking me to sew a seed, to give, when I had so little. The answer came back nearly before the words left my mind and mouth. Yes. It was not about money. It was about faith. That day, I mailed a check for $66.12 to the evangelist's ministry, pledging to sew that seed every month from my unemployment benefit. I went a step further.

Whenever I attained freelance income, aside from reporting it to the unemployment compensation office, which reduced my benefits in light of the dollars earned, I gave away 10 percent disbursing it among local food banks,

Al-Anon, and other altruistic sources. I believed I had nothing to lose in doing so but everything to gain because it is God who brings me money, indeed life itself. Scripture assured me, which Phin and Caye had repeated, " 'Bring all the tithes into the storehouse, that there may be food in My house, and try Me now in this,' says the Lord of hosts, 'if I will not open for you the windows of heaven and pour out for you such blessing that there will not be room enough to receive it' " (Malachi 3:10 NKJV).

On a chilly October Sunday in 2011, I underwent a full-submersion baptism at a Christian church in Boerne. I had been baptized Catholic as an infant but yearned to declare my rebirth and publicly dedicate my life to Christ. In the company of witnessing churchgoers and two chums, Caye and Mary Frances, I stepped into an outdoor baptismal font filled with warm water and therein was dunked and baptized by the preacher.

A dream came to me soon after baptism. This one was disquieting and woke me up scrambling to grab pen and paper. In the dream were people and things long since gone. In journaling of it later, it occurred to me the dream was telling me to let go of a corroded past, of Roger's tragic passing, of those who had betrayed me, of who I was before. One day, I watched my pen scribble GOD: G for Good. O for Omnipresent, Omniscient, Omnipotent. D for Divine. The letters and words delivered a spontaneous smile that stretched sweetly across my face.

In November, I was offered a job with the federal government and by February 2012 was employed in that role as senior technical editor. After the $66.12 seed had assuredly come the harvest.

One day, I met a clerk at a health food store, a Middle-Eastern Indian man named Leo. We talked of God and I shared briefly the struggle I had come through. He said, "Do not chase the world. Let the world chase you." I liked that and would remember it. It was about this time that people began telling me I "glowed."

Most always, I have been open to what's next and new while holding on to the best parts of my past, of me, and those I love. I'm grateful for an open heart even though it's been broken many times and may be again. The saving grace in all this is acceptance. Accepting that loss will happen, that I will rebound from loss and a broken heart, that I will keep loving, first God, then myself, and then others.

By my mid-50s, I finally began to manifest my Somedays, one by one. It was as if my dreams simply had been delayed, resting in the shadows, always there, patiently waiting for me to make the right choices. My dreams never left me. They were no longer quiet whispers or only wishes but manifestations of new and welcome wholesome realities, attainable and real. And there were more to come.

While attending the church in Boerne, the preacher who had baptized me spoke from the pulpit one Sunday asking us to share transformation encounters. I visited him the next week and told him of my awakening, the changes I had experienced from strayed to straight, the Indian encounters, the white light. He looked at me in disbelief with a grin barely there. "Has this ever happened to you?" I asked, speaking of seeing his own spirit. "No, never." I left and never returned.

I take no interest in arguing anymore or convincing anyone of anything. I only want to show up in life and be who I am. And hopefully who I am will influence others in a good way. Each soul must do its own seeking after God and I thank God I do. Every step I have taken toward God has been a step in reopening my heart to Him, when He has revealed His Spirit in me. I had paid attention to the white light. I believed in it. And I knew it came from God. And that it, He, dwells in me.

"In the beginning was the Word, and the Word was with God, and the Word was God. He was in the beginning with God. All things were made through Him, and without Him, nothing was made that was made. In Him was life, and the life was the light of men" (John 1:1-4 NKJV).

Red Spirit and Me

I rode my first bike when I was 2. It was a tiny metal tricycle with single-stem foot pedals that protruded from each side of the front wheel. I gleefully rode that tiny trike around our sparsely sodded backyard when we lived on Charcliff.

I knew little of motorcycles except for their hypnotic pull and my experience with Paul on his Road King. Nothing before or after Montana compared to riding down a road feeling the bracing wind and I missed it. When I shared this missing with friends John and Robert, both riders, they implied I buy a bike and learn to ride. At first, I dismissed the idea. But it seeped into my thoughts repeatedly and finally one day I agreed. In January 2012, the year I turned 57, I bought a motorcycle. Incidentally, considering the mystery in numbers, this was 55 years after my tricycle ride at 2, and two years following the Montana ride with SIR, when I was 55. More on numbers later.

I spent months researching the best bikes for beginners and settled on a new scarlet red Honda Rebel 250, a 234-cc cruiser, for which I paid $5,200. John told me a bigger bike would afford more stability and comfort, and I trusted his judgment, but I wanted to start small with an equally small investment. I thought it wise to find out whether riding my own bike was for me before spending more on a bigger one. I named my Rebel Red Spirit.

On my first day of training and practice, Robert and I installed a trickle charger on the bike and then I learned proper straddling and leaning. He taught me how to use body posture and strength to pull the bike up after a lean. My efforts were met with his "Very good!" Robert was a patient coach and a trusted, comfortable friend. I practiced rolling forward in first gear, increasing the throttle then letting out the clutch and feeling the bike move itself forward. I learned how to ride the bike up and down the porch step.

At first, I was afraid of dropping it but wanted to learn well so I could ride the pretty tranquil roads of the Hill Country with confidence. I wanted to feel as easy as the young calves yelping in the pasture next door. As with any fear, I learned to move through it by thinking positive thoughts. So I decided to think positively about my riding. But I hadn't learned yet to pair thought with practice where the bike was concerned. On my first day of practice, as I entered a left-veering curve in the parking lot, I was traveling too fast and took the curve too wide. Instead of following the front of the bike with my eyes as I'd learned, my sight drifted to the curb and iron fence beyond it. Sure enough, I jumped the curb but stopped short before plowing into the fence, putting both boots on the ground. That was a close call. But I didn't drop the bike or slam into the fence.

After a week under Robert's wing, he assigned me homework. I was to ride 30 to 50 laps around the complex parking lot practicing all I'd learned. The next day, I rode five hours taking intermittent breaks. I practiced gearshifts, U-turns, wide turns, and quick starts and stops. I learned to scan, swerve and slalom. I looked forward to the safety riding course in May, getting my license, and taking my first ride with friends John and Clarence. Fear still crept into my thinking occasionally, telling me I was going to crash, drop Red Spirit. But I told those lies No!

On May 20, after a weekend of classroom and field training on a Buell Blast 500 492-cc motorcycle with Javelina Harley, I passed the safety course, scoring 100 on the written exam and 87 on range. On the following day, I obtained my motorcycle license through the Texas Department of Public Safety. That Saturday on a bright sundrenched morning John and his wife Deb, Clarence and his wife Audra and her brother, Anthony, and I rolled from Boerne toward Bandera. John and Deb rode point on his Honda Gold Wing, followed single-file by Audra on her Kawasaki Ninja 500, Anthony on his Honda Shadow 700, me on Red Spirit, and Clarence trailing on his Harley Road King. We rode along Highway 46 West before turning onto Highway 16 that took us into Bandera.

After parking in front of the Old Spanish Trail cafe, we ate burgers and then took in the Memorial Day "Redneck" parade before riding back to Boerne. On the way, I dared pass a large truck directly ahead of us and led our band around it, taking point. As everyone followed one after the other, with John and Deb passing me first, they gestured a thumbs-up and retook the lead. We ended the afternoon with ice cream at Dairy Queen and talked about the ride. It had been a fantastic fun first time! Each time we had topped a hill followed by a wide curved downward slope, I felt I was flying. The wind brushed my body and bugs splattered the face shield of my helmet. I had capped my speed at 60, lacking confidence to ride faster my first time out. But I would remember it and the guiding friends who watched out for this novice every mile.

The following Saturday I rode alone to Sisterdale and back, a mere 26-mile round-trip but fun practice. There I met two couples on Harley Ultra Classics stopping like me for a soda. I rode beneath clear blue skies past yellow wildflowers and green grassy fields, over hilltops, and through valleys with strong crosswinds that pushed hard. At a slow roll at one point, I smiled at a bug crawling across the road. And once, I passed a flock of vultures feeding on a carcass on the roadside. Back in Boerne, I parked in front of the Bear Moon cafe, practicing backing my bike toward the curb after turning around during a break in Main Street traffic.

On Independence Day, I rode with a friend to Luckenbach to visit the red rooster patrol and listen to live music. There, we ran into a childhood neighbor of mine who was drunk as a skunk but apologetic all the same. I remembered a very, very long time before when I'd have done the same thing. I was grateful that part of my past was in the past, for good.

Often I rode alone striking out early on quiet Sunday mornings headed east or north through the countryside. Twice I rode with a group I'd met at church. It felt strange being on the smallest bike in the group, but I was out there, I was riding, I was learning, with their support. One day, on a group ride to Luckenbach, after topping a hill, pausing, and then pulling out to go left onto a busy roadway, I steered too wide and wound up on the shoulder in gravel and then into the grass. But quickly I recovered onto the pavement. I saw at once the focused faces of the others that turned and displayed "Oh no!" But I shouted, "I'm fine!" and kept rolling.

On the second of September on another sunny day, John and Clarence rode again with me to Bandera. This time, I topped my speed at 65 taking curves at posted limits. After breakfast, we rode the back streets so I could practice frequently using my turn signals, and stopping and starting at red lights and stop signs. Back in Boerne, we three refueled at a station where a truck nearly backed into me, at which Clarence declared, "You need a bigger bike." John agreed; aside from being easier to spot, a bigger bike would give me more confidence, power and comfort. I considered it.

My favorite ride that fall was the road from Boerne through Sisterdale to Kendalia, an 80-mile round trip. It was scenic and tranquil with the smell of wood burning in the chilly air. As I passed Sisterdale, I descended a hill doing 65 and thought, I feel like I'm riding my lawn mower, and thought again of upgrading my bike. In spring, I rode to the Willow City Loop near Fredericksburg where wildflowers draw crowds and to Boerne Lake several times. Along that stretch to the lake, horses hurried to fences to say hello and a 6-foot-long snake stretched across the road mere inches from my front tire.

By the start of the next new year, I had logged 1,000 miles on Red Spirt and considered trading it for a Harley Springer Softail or 883 Superlow Sportster.

Three days before my 58th birthday, I sold my bike to a man named Larry who bought it for his daughter so she and he could ride together. But another motorcycle was not in my future. Mama's health was failing, and with that my priorities shifted. But I would remember Red Spirit and me and the inimitable thrill of conquering the ride.

Kelly's Gone to Golden Pond

Life is laden with hard knocks. And nobody gets by in life without some. The best we can hope for is to survive them, and keep living despite and in light of them. Psalm 90:12 NKJV gives guarded counsel: "So teach us to number our days, that we may gain a heart of wisdom."

Kelly and Mama were cut from the same cloth. Maybe that's what attracted Roger to Kelly. And she possessed something else. A feisty daring even daredevil trait that made her self-reliant and as nonconforming as a gypsy. But when Roger died, Kelly withered. She cocooned herself and who could blame her. No one knows what happens inside a woman's heart when one-half of her DNA is snuffed out unless that woman has lived through it herself. After years in reclusion, she finally reemerged with a verve that carried her and found her as daring as before.

A first, Kelly worked independently as a craftsman with intricate needlework but found she could not live on her impassioned craft alone. So, she took a miniscule part-time job with the Express-News sorting and organizing photographs and newspaper clips in its library. The library was located in an isolated caged section of a dingy, dusty, musty warehouse. It was a forgotten place planned for demolition. She worked in full humility in that dismal environment, often while seated on a dirty concrete floor. But Kelly stuck with it, no matter how demeaning it was, no matter how modest and lowly the task or compensation. Unknown to her, her managers were watching. What they saw was the emerging woman, survivor, and excellent worker she was despite her circumstances, and ultimately rescued her from it and rewarded her for it. And thus began her newspaper career.

Within a year, Kelly turned permanent and was promoted to assistant librarian working nigh the newsroom. She enrolled with the University of Incarnate Word to earn a business administration degree and did so in 2006. Her big thinking didn't stop there. Kelly planned to win a Pulitzer one day and spoke of it. Eleven years after her part-time start, Kelly turned down a lucrative job offer from the New York Times to accept a premier role created for her by the Express-News: computer-assisted reporting editor and news researcher. Often, Kelly's name appeared with reporters' credits on published stories. She was credited with contributing monumentally to the paper's evolutionary history. And when the economy nose-dived, ensuing layoffs left Kelly's job safely unscathed.

As her professional success soared and finances with it, Kelly sold the little house on Prairie Sun to buy a spacious home in central San Antonio. It was here I stayed a few months with her not long after Daddy's passing. There she and her beloved dog and defender Button and feline Felix often sanctuaried in her backyard within a private palisade of mature enveloping trees charmed and occupied by flirting birds and tricky squirrels. Kelly had taken up birdwatching and planned to buy a small RV and do more of it. Her parents lived in Georgia and to Georgia she drove sometimes to visit them. My time with her there was very pleasant. She was one of the most comfortable human beings I'd ever shared space with.

As Kelly's mother and father reached their 80s, Kelly uprooted from Texas and moved to Georgia to be near them. In January 2012, she took a job at the Atlanta Journal-Constitution and relocated to the city of the same name, where there nearby she purchased a home near a lake. She described the house and location from Roger's point of view: "The house suits me, and Roger would love the location. It's as close as I could get to 'On Golden Pond,' the movie setting I saw the two of us (Rog and I) getting to in our latter years. I just wish he could be here to share it with me. He is here in spirit." She invited me to visit and we planned to sip mint juleps on her veranda. We spoke often about balancing work and play. She once told me, "You only have one life, Lou. So make it work for you. Happiness is a choice. So choose it and embrace it and you'll be fulfilled." I would remember her words always and try to live by them.

In February 2013, Kelly was diagnosed with stage four pancreatic cancer and soon thereafter commenced chemotherapy. But it was no cure and at the age of 54 on June 27, 2013, 26 years after Roger's passing, Kelly joined him. She had never remarried, had never stopped loving him, and now they were together "On Golden Pond." Those closest to her at the end of her life said in retrospect she wished she had remained in San Antonio, to be buried next to Roger. The night before I left for Georgia to attend Kelly's funeral, I watched the sun set over the hay field next door to my townhome in Boerne. Spooled hay dotted the smooth ground. And as the sun slowly dropped behind the field, I saw Kelly all over.

I drove to Georgia to be with Gil and Joyce and Kelly's brothers and their families and attend her funeral. It was terribly sad. But Kelly's spirit rode with me those 2,100 miles to and from where she was laid. I dedicated my drive to her. It was my first-ever lengthy road trip and bittersweet. But much like Kelly, I learned I, too, loved the discovery of places I'd never seen before. In the midst of the mourning I found a new happiness on the road. I was like a child opening presents Christmas morning with each town I passed. Along the road, I stopped at the Stuckey's in Anahuac somewhere between Baytown and Beaumont, Texas, and bought a coffee mug inscribed with: TEXAS. It would remind me of my trip to see Kelly laid to rest. I drove over the mighty Mississippi River in Baton Rouge and across the state of Louisianna on to Biloxi, Mississippi before spending the night in Alabama. The next day, I crossed the bridge that crossed over the Mobile River, taking in the evergreen Alabaman landscape. And I thanked God for clean restrooms at Loves. Arriving in Canton, Georgia, I supped at Cracker Barrel a short walk from my hotel that was nestled next to a lush forested hillside.

Kelly was interred at Macedonia Memorial Park in Marietta. Well, Kel, you're now in a brand new Independence Day! I thought. Free from the binds of this mortal world as with Roger and Daddy. I will see you all again one day. How swiftly life flows from beginning to end to what lies beyond. Kelly was gone from sight but lived on in my heart.

On the way home the following morning, I stopped in Montgomery at the Hank Williams Museum and played a 45 RPM record of Hank's on a Wurlitzer. I felt safe travelling alone and pleasantly surprised at the number and quality of rest stops and visitor centers. Once home, I lie in bed that night reflecting on my solo sojourn to Georgia. On my grief over yet another loss in this life. Kelly was my beloved sister in the truest sense. I loved her deeply and knew she loved me. She always was ready to lend an ear and a hug. I told her my most intimate secrets and she kept them. She taught me compassion and courage, strength and honor, love and acceptance. And to never ever give up on what I want most in life. Forever she would remain my Independence Day cheerleader.

Kelly had taken her leave from my natural world but her spirit stayed with me, along with Roger and Daddy's. I didn't know then but Mama soon would follow.

Mama Died and Grief Stayed Long

Three years after Daddy's passing when Mama moved to Morningside Ministries, she and I started sharing precious time. She was happy for me in all I pursued, personally and professionally, and I was happy to be with her. I visited often. I treated us to meals out and took her to Mass, on drives in the country, and shopping. We played Bingo and watched TV. We made memories hand over fist.

One of my favorite times was in early June 2011. I collected her one Friday afternoon to spend the weekend with me at my home in Boerne. I had made wonderful plans. She could not ascend the stairs to the bedroom so I made for her a comfy bed on my soft leather couch and the first night I slept on a pallet on the living room floor near her. After coffee and breakfast the next morning, we took a drive around Boerne Lake and then returned home for homemade chocolate meringue pie. Later, we prepared dinner together. She sat at the kitchen sink peeling and cutting potatoes for potato salad and then relaxed on the back porch on Grandma Floy's yellow glider I inherited while I barbecued beef ribs and chicken. Afterward, we watched "Lonesome Dove" and ate popcorn and before bed we kissed good night.

Early Sunday morning, we drank our coffee on the porch watching the krowy (Polish for cows, a word Mama taught me) in the field across the fence, followed by breakfast of cottage cheese and strawberries before heading to Mass at St. Peter the Apostle Catholic Church in Boerne. Mama shed tears at receiving Communion; when I asked why, she said, "I was praying to God in thanksgiving for the Mass and Communion; it has been so long." As she told me this, she shed more tears, and then said, "Thank you for being so good to me. I love you."

I had been waiting an eternity to hear those words. My heart burst with joy, too, because me and Mama were together again. I hoped the happiness I gave her made up for all the heartache I had caused her the first half of my life. That afternoon, I took us on a drive through the Hill Country then home again for leftover barbecue and pie. Before returning her to Morningside, I burned sage and smudged her with the smoke, praying for her healing and health. She liked it. When we bade farewell, she hugged me several times, each time telling me how much she enjoyed time with me, my home, all the cooking, baking, and driving I did for her. I told her, it had been my pure pleasure.

On another day, I drove us to Luling for barbecue at City Market where she and Daddy used to go and then for a spin through Palmetto Park. On the way home, we stopped by St. Jerome's Cemetery to pray at Daddy and Roger's graves and then to Dairy Queen for ice cream. Before I left her, she hugged me and said in a cracking voice, "You just don't know how much I appreciate you." I was moved by my Mama's sincerity.

Friends continued noticing the "glow" in my face. And I began noticing Mama's forgetfulness and confusion. It was not long before fainting spells and falls followed and Mama was hospitalized. Doctors diagnosed her with dying brain tissue near the area of the lobotomy she had undergone in 1967 and the onset of dementia with its symptomatic brain shrinkage.

I decorated her hospital room with pictures of Daddy, Roger and Grandma Floy, and brought her a green blanket she liked. Mama knew she was changing and it scared her. She sometimes forgot our names. It saddened me. And it was harder each time to leave her. Once she was home again, sometimes I stayed overnight with her in her tiny assisted-living apartment sleeping on the couch. I did not mind it. I knew my time with Mama was limited. And I wanted as much of her as I could garner. We watched movies, laughed, and ate chocolate, strawberries, popcorn and hamburgers.

One evening before heading home from Morningside, as I walked with her to supper in the dining room, her voice shook and her eyes filled with tears. Mama told me she did not want me to leave until she knew that I knew that she loved me. Throughout my life, rarely had I seen my mother cry. We hugged and I confirmed I knew. When I phoned later to tell her good night, she said she had been thinking about how she could show me she loves me, but I told her, I already knew and she needn't do anything. It seemed urgent to her, that I knew it. I told her often how much I enjoyed her company, how much I loved her, that she was my best friend.

In early 2012, Mama suffered the first of more seizures to come. Her appetite waned. She yearned for visits from family and meanwhile I continued mine. I wished I had a home suitable for her to live with me. We still went for drives and to Mass sometimes. On her and Daddy's wedding anniversary that year, I treated us to ice cream and a drive. At times Mama was perky and other times blue. She began giving things away and her memory continued to fade.

By the end of 2012, I considered moving back to San Antonio to be closer to Mama. I had a full-time job in the city and relocating also would cut my commute. But primarily, I wanted to be nearer my mother who by then was 86 and increasingly frail. In early December, my sisters and I hosted her 86th birthday party where four generations gathered to pay tribute. But the golden treasure of that day came that evening after everyone had gone home. We two, me and my Mama, sat side-by-side on her couch in her tiny apartment as I painted her fingernails a soft rose color. We both fell silent during the nail polishing as if it were a sacred ceremony. Polishing Mama's nails painted a most beautiful memory of me and my mother together on the canvas of my heart and there it would live evermore.

By April 2013, Mama had suffered increasing instances of mental disorientation and physical weakness. Often she spoke of the past, her childhood, her and Daddy when they were young, us kids when we were little. She told me little adages popular when she was young and sang ditties to me that she used to sing to us as children. One of them went like this: "I love you with my whole heart and half my liver. If I had you in my mouth, I'd spit you in the river." We laughed at that one. Sometimes when I visited I brought her favorite candy, a large Hershey chocolate bar with almonds. She ate the whole thing in one sitting. And sometimes when I arrived, she'd say, smiling, "It made me so happy to see you walk through that door." Every next minute with her was more precious than the last.

I had long since noticed, since my 30s in fact, that my Mama had a distinguishing twist to her gait. It was natural. And I had inherited it. The older I got, the more I looked like her, too. I was proud then, as now, to bear her reflection. And her trademark twist. One day in May I wandered through the cemetery in Boerne and phoned Mama to say hello. She was having a hard day. She said, "I'm so tired. Come see me." I promised to and we ended our call. I came upon Mr. Smith standing at the grave of his wife who had dementia and passed away. I saw another man engraving an end-date on a tombstone. I looked up to heaven and asked, "God, are you getting ready to call Mama home? Is she ready? Am I?"

For a Mother's Day treat, I took Mama to lunch at Cracker Barrel. We didn't know it would be our last meal out together. Later that afternoon, I sat on the couch in her apartment while she dozed in her recliner and began to mumble. I sat quietly until she opened her eyes and realized she had been speaking. I asked what she had been saying and to whom. Her reply stunned me but only for a minute. She told me she had been talking to Daddy. And when I asked, Where is he? She said matter-of-factly, "Well, he's sitting right next to you, on that couch." And then she shook her head and said, "That was silly." But I told her, "No, it was not silly. You saw Daddy. You spoke with him. That was real." She then told me she dreamt she saw and talked to her parents. I began thinking Mama's inevitable end was near. And Daddy, Roger, Kelly and Mama's parents were extending an ethereal welcome.

By late July, I had signed a lease on a townhome in San Antonio and scheduled movers for Aug. 17. Everything was set. Every spare minute, I packed. A relocation is riddled with details, physical exertion, and stress, but even more so when doing it alone, and I was, and working full-time and commuting two hours.

In early August, I visited Mama to find her fresh out of the shower and sitting in her recliner pulling on her pajama bottoms. I had not seen my mother in her underwear for who knows how long, but that day her stomach seemed alarmingly swollen. She said it had been that way for a while, that she was getting fat. I did not consider it beyond that. Looking back, I should have. I helped her finish dressing and before I left, she asked, as she often did, when I would come back and how far away I would be once I moved back to town. We planned to have a fried-chicken picnic once I resettled.

On Aug. 10, Morningside staff found Mama incoherent and she was taken by ambulance to the emergency room. I was at home in Boerne when I got the news and drove straight to the hospital where I found Mary, Debbie and several nieces and nephews already there. Jo Ann, at the helm of Mama's medical care, was out of town but headed home and Lynn was on his way from Florida.

Mama's eyes and lips were closed. To me, it seemed family gathered there were very loud, talking and laughing within close proximity to Mama, who was fragile, and it was obvious her condition was dire. But I was quiet, believing this reverent time should be silent time, spent in complete attention and presence of what was taking place—my mother, their mother, their Nonnie was terribly ill. Her abdomen, legs and back were awfully swollen. She screamed in pain when a nurse thoughtlessly and uncompassionately forced insertion of a catheter. I was horrified. Another nurse poked Mama's skin three times attempting to insert an IV as Mama moaned in pain. He showed no sympathy. We all saw and heard but no one said a word about it. Even me. The damage was done and I could not undo it. But it smacked of the abuse my father suffered at the hands of uncaring "healthcare" staff.

After hours of waiting, my mother was moved to a private room. Once she received oxygen, Mama seemed herself, alert and chatty. When my nephew Jason, Roger's son, entered her room, Mama said she had heard his voice earlier and was so happy to see him. He decided to stay the night with his Nonnie. I was glad for them both.

After a CAT scan, doctors diagnosed Mama with presumed metastatic cancer; there were tumors on her rib cage, back and lymph nodes; her kidneys were failing; and her lungs held fluid. But due to numerous complications, we were told, which prevented draining her lungs or performing a biopsy, they could not confirm cancer. I wondered why my mother's condition had not been noticed or treated sooner, how her health could have declined so suddenly. I thought back to when I had noticed her swollen stomach. I wondered whether all the other now-reported problems had been coming for some time but were ignored. But it was too late. Now, doctors advised acute hospice.

I stood by Mama's bedside and held her hand. She then told me she had been in a hearse. I said, "No, that was an ambulance." She then uttered "I am going to heaven" with calm certainty.

When Jo Ann and Lynn arrived, they and Mary and I left the hospital for a nearby restaurant to discuss next steps. Debbie arrived late, grumbling. She and Jo Ann poked over a subject about Mama that turned tense, and when I tried to calm Debbie, thinking I was reassuring her by saying what one person says may not be what the other person hears, she looked at me squarely and said flatly, "I hate you!" At that, I stood, informed the others I was leaving, asked them to call with any news, and walked out. Lynn followed, admitting to my sister's callous remark. My three sisters followed next, with Debbie saying in passing, "I don't hate you."

We returned to the hospital to find Mama lying calmly with the curtain pulled around her bed and a representative from the hospice facility in the room. While my brother and sisters huddled with the hospice worker opposite the curtain, I stood shakily by my mother's bedside looking at her beautiful face cupped in silver curls, touching her hand, and telling her I loved her. I told her I did not want her to go. But she smiled and said calmly, "Betty Lou, dying is a part of living." I believe at that moment she accepted her coming passing and even looked forward to it, to seeing Daddy, Roger and Kelly, her parents, and countless other loved ones again. I told her yet again, "I am so sorry for all the pain I have ever caused you." And I asked her again to please forgive me. She looked up at me and tenderly replied, "Don't think your sisters haven't caused pain, too. Yes, I forgive you."

I thought back on times that now seemed ages ago when my mother had said to me, "Why can't you be more like your sisters?" It was a question I found silly and unrealistic. The simple answer and truth was, is, and would forever be, I am not like my sisters. I am different. And finally she realized it. Mama ultimately saw and valued who I was, and was not.

And then my mother asked for the black house slippers I bought her. Right then, Debbie walked around the curtain to her bedside. I told her Mama had asked for her slippers and asked whether she knew their whereabouts. She replied she had taken them home with Mama's clothes. I asked if she would bring them to Mama, and she replied, "No," and walked away. I told Mama not to worry, I'd get them for her and leaned down and kissed her forehead, and she said, "Thank you."

I joined my siblings near the window across the room from Mama's bed in their hospice dialog, and there I shared I'd buy Mama a new pair of black house slippers if it was a problem to retrieve the originals. At this, Jo Ann asked why, since Mama had a pair. I explained Debbie had them but had said she would not return them. When she asked Debbie why not, she replied, "Well, I guess I could." I repeated that I would be happy to buy a new pair. At this, Jo Ann raised her voice, told me to "Get out!" and threatened police force if I did not. I told her calmly, "I am Mama's daughter, she is my mother, I will not be leaving."

She then marched to the foot of Mama's bed, told her she had to leave or she "would hurt someone," pointing to me, and left the room. Mary, Debbie and Lynn followed her out saying nothing to me or to Mama. I was hurt by their behavior toward me but even more saddened at the insensitivity showed our mother, that they all had left without speaking to her. A nurse named Nick who had been standing behind Mama's bed giving her oxygen and heard and saw it all told me it is common to see adult children behave like high schoolers when a parent is sick and dying and lash out for no reason. He and I saw clearly Mama was upset. I held her hand, kissed her cheek and forehead, and told her it was OK. Nick said to me in a tender, soft voice, "You have a gentle heart and your Mama knows it."

I had grown to love my mother like a mother loves her only child. We had blessed each other especially over the past year with an intimacy words cannot describe. We had talked of God, Christ, heaven, life and death. Only two months prior, we had sat in her apartment when I asked if she had given her life to Christ, to which she replied she had not, so together we prayed: "Jesus, forgive me my sins, come into my heart, You are my Lord and Savior."

Lynn returned to retrieve papers and asked me whether I was coming outside to talk with them, and I replied, simply, No. He walked out and I wondered what I would do next. Lynn returned home to Florida.

When I returned to Mama's bedside, I told her I had to finish packing for the move in two days but I didn't want to leave her. She asked, "When will you be back?" I replied, "Tomorrow." She asked, "When tomorrow?" I told her, "Late morning or early afternoon." She said, "OK." I told her not to fear, she was safe, and I loved her. She said, "I love you, too." Before leaving, I gave her three soft kisses on her left cheek. At the third kiss, she said, "Now, I'm scared." I told her, "Don't be scared. Simply giving you kisses." But I knew I was afraid those kisses might be my last. And she sensed my fear. I drove home to Boerne deeply unsettled. I thought of the times I had said, I love you, when Mama had said in sweet reply, "I love you more." I didn't know when I left that there would be no more words with my mother come morning.

Once home I phoned Caye, and afterward, another friend. I needed to talk about what had happened at the hospital and restaurant. To get it off my heart, to feel comfort and support. They both told me the same thing in different words, that my calm conduct is no longer the angry way of my siblings, who likely interpreted my calmness as condescension because they are not used to it. And that I was light in the darkness in what was happening, calling it spiritual war. I also phoned Don, who told me the hard work I had done in recovery over the past eight years had enabled me to stay calm despite horrible conditions. I felt more grounded at hearing their affirming words.

Late that night Mama was transported by ambulance to a hospice facility not far from the townhome I was moving to in two days. At 1:40 a.m. I received a text from Jo Ann advising Mama was in hospice and given "24 hours." I dressed fast and drove back to San Antonio to be at my mother's side. By the time I arrived, Mama had begun her quiet leaving. Her green eyes shut, her breath labored and shallow. In the tiny private room where she lay, my sisters and some of my adult nieces and nephews sat in folding chairs or on a sofa bed or stood along walls.

Through the night, some took turns dozing on the sofa bed. But I sat by my mother, held her hand, kissed her forehead, told her, "I love you" and "Thank you" and "It's OK. You will be OK. I will be OK." I whispered prayers into her ear I knew she liked, the Our Father, Hail Mary and Psalm 23. Sometimes her index and middle fingers of the hand I held moved as if trying to hold mine. Sometimes her eyebrows raised as if she were trying to open her eyes, and her upper lip twitched as if she were trying to speak. But her blood pressure fell steadily, her lungs continued filling with fluid, her breathing became shallower. Sometimes her head turned slightly toward me and other times lifted slightly backward, her breaths in labored pants.

Before Noon the next day, a nurse advised that Mama could stay with us another 48 to 72 hours or leave by nightfall, but it was safe if we wanted to go home, shower, change and return. My sisters did so. I stepped into the lobby of the hospice facility to phone both the manager of the property in Boerne and the one in San Antonio of my current circumstances and request a delay on the planned move set for Aug. 17, the next day. The manager in Boerne told me to take my time. The manager in San Antonio was uncompassionate. She coldly told me my lease commenced the 17th and I had to pay the money, collect the keys, or lose the apartment. I next phoned Mary Frances who agreed to pick up a check from me and deliver it there. I called and canceled the movers. It was a most terrible predicament.

I drove home with my insides feeling full of bees, showered fast, packed an overnight bag in equal haste, and returned to Mama within the hour. I had prayed she wait till I returned and I thanked God she had. Everyone else who had left by then also had returned. Mary sat at Mama's left holding her left hand. Jo Ann and Debbie sat on her right, Debbie holding Mama's hand. I walked to where Mary sat, bent and kissed Mama's forehead and whispered, "Mama, it's Betty Lou. I love you. I'm here." And then I took a seat next to Mary. The vigil had begun.

A while later, when Mary stood and stepped outside I took her seat nearest Mama's face. A nurse arrived soon, asking us all to leave so they could freshen Mama and her bedclothes and informed us she was in her final one or two hours. Upon return, I then watched and heard disturbing things.

When Mary returned she told me I could keep my seat and sat down next to me. In the tiny crowded room, my mother lay extremely still on her back with her eyes closed and beneath a thin blanket. It was a reverent and solemn moment. One of my adult nephews sat near the foot of her bed with his shoes perched on the bedpost and accidentally shook it. Startled, I asked, "What was that?" when he apologized and lowered his feet. My eldest sister began talking openly and within earshot of Mama about her funeral, flowers and music, and others joined in. I wondered, did they not know Mama heard every word?

I wanted to ask them all to stop. I did not. Instead, I held my mother's hand and kissed her forehead, eyebrows and cheeks. I stroked her silver curls. I tried to drown out all talk of burial by whispering into her ear prayers she liked and other reassuring words: Our Father… Hail Mary… The Lord is my Shepard… You have been a good mom… You can fly away… Be with Daddy, Roger, Kelly, Grandma and Grandpa… I'm going to be OK… We all will be OK… It's alright for you to go… I will love you and honor you forever….

The first hour passed, and then the second, and we all hovered over each advancing minute. Suddenly, Jo Ann exclaimed, "What's ya waitin' on Mama! You always said you'd be late for your own funeral!" I said nothing, staying my focus even more intently on Mama, being present with her as she was taking leave of this world and us.

I learned later from hospice staff, of all the senses hearing is the last to go when someone dies. Mama most certainly had heard my whispered I love you's and prayers. She had heard the talk of her burial and insensitive words. And I knew, Mama being Mama, forgave it all.

I fixated on her breathing. The hospice nurse had administrated morphine when Mama had arrived but we were told there had been none since. There were no wires, tubes, machines or medicines. Only blood pressure monitoring.

Despite Mama's congestive heart failure, tumors pressing into her lungs, and kidney failure, she seemed comfortable and at peace. Either more morphine had been administered or God was nestling Mama in His infinite grace.

I watched as the skin around her eyes and lips began to turn lavender and she took fewer breaths. I continued holding her hand, kissing her forehead, which now felt cooler than before and I noticed she was perspiring. A minister arrived and prayed over her. I kept thinking, Mama's waiting for Lynn, who was absent. When the minister said, "In Jesus's name, Amen," my mother took a noticeably deeper breath, and then one more, less labored, to which I clung, suspended, waiting for yet another. But there were no more. I heard the hushed subduing words escape my mouth as if someone else had said them, "She's gone. Mama's gone. She's gone." It was a minute past 4.

And then I sobbed uncontrollably. I hurt so deep inside there seemed no bottom and no rebound, like taking a deep breath and being unable to exhale. I free-fell into my own soul and there was no end to the fall. Someone, I didn't know who, wrapped herself around me as I sat and wept loud, sobbing with me and holding on to me the whole time. I later learned it was Mary. I heard others repeat "She's gone. Mama's gone." And I heard their cries.

Very soon afterward, my sobs turned to quiet tears and I turned to thank Mary. Then, everyone left the room headed for the restaurant next door. Not me. They said, Come with us. I did not want to. I alone stayed. I lingered next to my mother, this woman who had carried me inside her body nine months and given me life. My eyes soaked her in, impressing detail into my heart. Her hands. Her face. Her hair. Her arms. The length of her body. I had watched the life that was my mother take its leave. Her neck now was not warm. Her head now leaned and rested to the left toward me. There was no pulse. The prominent blood vessel on the top right side of her forehead that stretched from her hairline to her right eye had disappeared. Her face held a tranquil countenance. I lay my hand gently on her chest. I kissed her cool forehead. I touched her soft silver curls for the last time. I carefully lay my upper body from where I sat across hers. Her former fullness had left and I could feel the difference.

My Mama had flown away and now her body could not live minus the life that had left it. I told myself, You better go while you still can remember her as she was. I held her hand the final time and looked at the rose-colored fingernails I had polished only days before and sat with the memory a meditative minute.

I thought of the mother she had been to all us little ones. The wife she had been to Daddy. The daughter she had been to Grandma Floy and Grandpa Tedo. The only sister she had been to my uncles. The meals, temperature checks, laundry and endless work. I thought of the aunt, cousin, granddaughter, grandmother, great-grandmother, friend and Christian she had been. How her one life touched countless others. The notes, cards and letters she wrote and mailed. The calls she made. The birthday cakes she baked. The hell she endured. The times she said, "We each have only one mother," reminding me of the sanctity of the mother-child bond. And now, this far-reaching life, my mother who gave me mine, had tranquilly given up hers and slipped into eternity right beside me. It was as intimate and spellbinding as a birth but in reverse. I told my mother again I loved her. I thanked her for "everything!" I asked her please to visit me in my dreams. Death was a beautiful new beginning for Mama. But it was not for me.

It was very, very hard to get up and walk away from her. My body was heavy stone. She as I had known her was no longer there, but I believed her spirit lingered and so I stayed until I was told I must go. But I did not want to go. Going meant she was gone and I would never ever again feel her hug or hear her laughter or share a meal with her or take her for a drive or bring her chocolate or polish her nails or look upon her face. Not in this world. I missed her reminders to wash my hands, her reassuring words when I was scared or lonely, and her sincere "I love you more."

My mother's last request of her daughters was to get along with each other. But I knew, as did she, getting along took equal effort and sometimes would happen only at a distance. So I joined my family at the restaurant but could not weather the storm of laughter and after a while excused myself after declining to write Mama's obituary. Everyone knew I was in the midst of moving yet no one offered a hand. I drove to Mary Frances's home where there we talked a long while and then I spent the night. If it were not for her warmth and company, I would have lost my mind.

Two days later on the anniversary of Roger's birthday I relocated from Boerne to San Antonio. On the very early morning that day of Aug. 18, God sent me Lori who I knew from recovery. She showed up in Boerne with her wide smile and widespread heart, asking to clean my apartment for me before the movers arrived that day. She said, "An angel sent me." As tears welled in my eyes, I handed her the keys to the apartment and to my heart all at once. In sweltering summer heat Lori cleaned without air-conditioning. I would never forget her extraordinary kindness.

Among my belongings was Mama's beautiful Ansonia wall clock Daddy had purchased for her. The clock was designed with mechanical gears. It chimed every quarter-hour and required hand winding weekly. I had not wound it for weeks, and had removed the pendulum and wrapped it in a cloth and laid it inside the clock cabinet. As a result, there had been no chiming. In my new apartment I had the movers, one of whom was named Roger, lay the clock on its backside on a wide open shelf. On Aug. 19, the day after my move, three days after Mama's passing on the date of my parent's wedding anniversary, as the clock lay untouched and unwound, it randomly chimed. And it chimed again. And again. And again.

My mother's viewing and rosary ritual was held at St. Benedict Aug. 20. In advance, I provided 22 handwritten pages of remembrances about my mother to Fr. Eddie to draw from as he chose. He had officiated Daddy's funeral and would solemnize Mama's. The rosary was truly beautiful; Father paused periodically to impart bits of Mama into it. The following day, Aug. 21, a Wednesday, the middle day of the week on which Mama had given me birth, we attended Mama's open-casket funeral. Unsurprisingly, she had pre-ordered a limo for us and it was lovely.

Before the Mass began, Fr. Eddie stood in the front of the church at the head of her casket with Lynn at the foot and my sisters and I on both sides. Father knew our family's history. Seeing Mama lying in a coffer was hard enough. But when the lid was closed, as we unfolded a soft blanket across it and then filed away to return to our seats, I froze. It seemed I watched myself from outside my own body put my arms across the top of the casket and linger. It was just like that long ago day in Victoria when I was 8 and Mama stayed at a hospital there and Daddy drove us all to a park where we picnicked with her and I clung to my absent Mama.

So I clung to her casket, until Lynn came for me and escorted me to a seat next to his in the front pew, where our line of eight had sat through hundreds of Masses in the past. From my seat, I silently told myself I would see her in the twinkling stars and glowing moon, in the blazing sun, raindrops and leaves twirling in the breeze. I told myself I would be alright, that she would make sure of it.

During the eulogy, Fr. Eddie spoke of Mama's hardships, of her loss of a baby stillborn, of her illness when a young mother of six, of Roger's untimely taking, of the wounds she endured in the deaths of her husband and parents. Through it all, he said, she was strong and held to her faith. And he spoke sternly of stopping hatred and gossip. When it came time to offer each other a sign of peace, I turned and hugged Mary and felt a hand on my back from the opposite side. But by the time I turned around the hand had been withdrawn and the service moved forward. I turned to Debbie, presuming it had been her, and whispered, "I wish you only good things in life" and hugged her. Returning the hug, she said only, "Thank you."

When the service concluded we trailed the casket toward the front doors with Debbie and I arm-in-arm. After the burial and meal, I went home feeling deeply deserted. I was grateful to have three weeks off work to mourn and get settled in my apartment. And I promised myself to surround myself with people unafraid to show feelings of love or talk of meaningful matters or pray with me.

On the day of Mama's funeral, the clock that had chimed for three days chimed no more. The mysterious bells ceased. Her spirit had stayed with me three days. One day soon afterward, my friend Ronny arrived at my apartment to hang the clock on the wall. He will never know what a gift that was. After it was secured, I attached the pendulum, wound the clock, and welcomed the heavenly chiming and with it, my parents' comforting presence and memories that filled the minutes.

Three days later, I drove to St. Jerome's Cemetery at sunrise to water grass at four gravesites: Mama's, Daddy's, Roger's and William's, Lynn's infant son. And I wept a river. I missed Mama's voice. I was reinventing my life without her in it. Life felt sadly temporary and tenuous. It was hard work, living. Back home, I grieved, felt whatever moved on the inside. I put my apartment in order. I watched the film "Rocky" and the ones that came after it, five in all, one after the other, over and over again. Sly Stallone wrote the first Rocky in 20 straight hours and it was nominated for 10 Academy Awards winning 3. Rocky kept me company and filled my emptiness with hope.

When I returned to work, grief came with me; I could no longer phone Mama as often I had done. I wondered how long I would mourn. But the love I shared with her while she was within reach deserved its time of my grieving the loss of all that was her and all she had poured into me. Life does not simply go on after a beloved's passing. Grief takes its own sweet time and to fight or deny it is futile. Mama's leaving left a gaping vacuum in me. It was extremely hard living with that.

Sometimes, it felt as if she was not gone but up the road in C-18 at Morningside. For days and days after Mama passed, I kept thinking, I need to call her. She'll want to know what colors I am using in my bathroom and where I put this or that and how big my kitchen is. And then I would remember. Her death seemed a vivid stain on the rest of my existence. It does not help the bereaved to tell them, She is in a better place, or, You must get on with your life, or, She would not want you to be sad, or any other well-intended but unwitting inanity. The only words to speak to the bereaved, if words must be spoken at all, are those that affirm the depth of loss. And that is all and that is enough.

Life resumed. I rose at 4 workdays to exercise, pray and put in a full day's work. I kept watching the Rocky series in the evenings. I listened to CDs I'd purchased at pow wows of Indian drumming and singing. I appreciated Mama had taken keen interest in my interest in Indian people and pow wows. I missed her and Daddy especially on Sundays. One twinkle in their eye, one hug, was missed magic.

I went camping in November and had a long cry alone. Often, I did not want to be around anyone. I wanted to be left to my sadness and anger, until I was done with it. I did not want to wear a happy face. Please don't ask me what's wrong if I'm not smiling. Please don't tell me what to do with it. I know what to do… live with it until it is no more. But it's hard and it hurts and she was worth the missing and the hurting. My mother's death also breathed into me a sense of urgency for major change, call it advancement perhaps. I cannot speak for everyone but for me there comes a time in life when I know there's more to it than how I'm doing it. I asked God for crystal clear direction.

In early December, following Mama's birthdate, I awoke from my first dream about her. In it, I walked through the back gate on the side of our old house to get a towel off the clothesline to dry Cristi who had been lying in a water puddle. It was a cloudy gray day and must have rained earlier. As I stepped onto the back porch, I saw Mama inside through the kitchen window. She was wearing one of her thin snap-up housecoats. This one was pale pink with tiny yellow flowers on it. She was in a rush, looking flustered, trying to open a can of ground coffee. And Cristi did not seem happy either. I wondered why. And then I woke up. When Roger had died, he had come to me in a dream in which he looked at peace and was happy and told me so. I was bothered Mama was unhappy in my dream. I wondered whether it was because I was holding on to her too hard. Or was it because her last wish was not kept? She had wanted her girls to get along.

Unfortunate episodes of division would continue to indelibly stain our family story, tarnishing even more the one I once had known, the one Mama and Daddy had given birth to, loved, and raised in faith and unity. Despite multiple illnesses and deaths our family had suffered already, familial dysfunction often would overrule mutual compassion. But I thanked God for my recovery and faith. I knew no matter the circumstances I could live in peace within myself, knowing it is God who loves all and ultimately is in control of all. I was reminded of God's empowering promise: "Now may the God of hope fill you with all joy and peace in believing, that you may abound in hope by the power of the Holy Spirit" (Romans 15:13 NKJV).

After Mama's passing, I reflected on all I'd learned and worked on so very hard in recovery and counseling over the prior eight years; on detaching with love; on respecting myself by setting healthy protective boundaries; on protecting my heart, mind, and spirit by steering clear of people, places and things that caused me harm or harbored clear potential. I had learned to live by recovery and God's words.

The first Mother's Day without Mama, I put yellow daffodils on her grave and then sat in my camp chair next to her tombstone eating a salad and drinking iced tea from Bill Miller Bar-B-Q. I shed sad tears, asked her and Daddy to help me take life in stride, and asked for a sign they'd heard me. As I sat quietly in the sunny breeze, a tiny yellow butterfly flew in front of me quickly trailed by a second, and when I left, two white birds flew overhead.

A year after Mama's passing I canceled my TV subscription in a newfound aim to simplify and improve my life. I pledged to read more and use my TV for recorded movies, documentaries and concerts. I made other changes. I was learning I did not want or need to spend precious time on people, places or things without a shared meaningful connection, and on meaningful connection is where I would focus my time and energy.

It took me a full year to mourn. I knew the sadness and anger had taken their rightful places in my personal history when I began noticing random feelings of joy. And I noticed and appreciated small but uplifting messages that came my way unexpectedly. Something as small as a lady in the car next to mine at a traffic light who exclaimed through a shining smile, "I love your truck! It's beautiful!"

And there were much bigger, obvious traces, too. Like the day I was on my usual lunch-hour walk in fresh air at the Army base where I worked. As I approached a trimmed field encircled by a paved trail, I saw a string of six tall black horses with riders galloping across the turf. One horse and rider broke from the rest and came fast and straight toward me. I stood still where I was, feeling curiously content, as the coming horse and rider slowed to a walk and then stopped, with the tall steed's nostrils within inches of mine.

I was captivated by the animal's enormity; it was taller than any I had ever seen. Neither I nor the rider spoke at first. Slowly I looked up fully at the horse's face and then asked his rider, "May I?" He replied, "Sure." I raised the palm of my hand gingerly toward the massive nostrils, let him sniff it, then laid it flat on his massive cheek. He received it fine. I then moved my hand softly and slowly down his long neck and he let me. I heard myself softly say, "Hey, baby." His coat was damp. Then, as quickly as they had arrived, horse and rider inched backward and then galloped away. I raised my hand to my nose; there was no scent to speak of. Not like a dog or a boy who has a sweaty smell after running. There was none, and I thought, those horses are clean and well-cared for.

I asked myself, Why did that one horse break from the rest toward me? Why was I not afraid the massive animal would step on me or knock me down? And this is the conclusion I came to. My spirit was wide open, happy, light and grateful. That horse sensed it and wanted to be near it and so came to me. And then, he left, leaving both of us content.

Mama and Kelly's passings after Roger and Daddy's repainted and reordered my world. It was at once a bigger scarier place and a most alluring adventure. Their leaving left me pondering mine. But after I had driven alone from Texas to Georgia and back again for Kelly's funeral, I learned something about myself. I liked the road and was unafraid to be on it alone for stretches of time. And once the four people I loved most in this world no longer walked the earth with me, I decided the road would be my new love. I would strike out across America's far-reaching highways and byways to discover its diverse and natural beauty. I now would take up this most worthy quest. But before I roamed, a ghostly encounter seized my complete attention.

Angels and Ghosts

Scripture speaks more than 100 times of angels and ghosts, including of the Holy Ghost nearly two dozen times. I believe Scripture, and I have seen both. Other words for ghost are spirit, apparition, specter or phantom.

Six months after Mama passed, in February 2014, I awoke to the annoying buzz of my alarm clock from a charming dream.

In it, I was in an unusually beautiful place, sitting outside on a stoop. My gaze ahead was fixed upon a colorful landscape that stretched to the horizon and abounded in row after pretty row of vibrant blossoms of every color and shape. Suddenly, a pleasingly handsome and enchanting man appeared. In utter silence, he sauntered easily by me to step into the flowering sea and cut a single bloom. He then drew near, smiling quietly, and handed me the fresh-cut flower. His soft features were soothing to see and sense. He had hair of yellow and eyes of blue and wore a ball cap. The flower he gave me was periwinkle blue and looked like a hybrid of a gladiola and a bluebonnet with petite bell-shaped petals. I awoke feeling very calm. I believe this gentle "man" was an angel sent to comfort me. This vision has not recurred, but its impression is tattooed lastingly in my memory like ink in my skin. The day before, a biopsy had been performed after a mammogram revealed "abnormal." The radiologist who performed the biopsy reviewed the benign result with astonishment. Before the biopsy, she had been "very concerned," but at seeing the benign result asked the pathologist, "Are you sure?" I wondered, had I been touched by the angel who handed me a flower of health?

Two months after the amiable angel dream, I had a different encounter while awake. At the time, I dealt daily with a workplace turned toxic. We had endured two mass layoffs and a merger that brought with it ambiguity and frustration. My job and bosses changed three times in two weeks. On this particular night, I was in bed lying on my back, covered to my chin in blankets, listening to the hum of the air-conditioner and whir of the overhead ceiling fan. The clock on my nightstand showed 10 minutes had passed since I'd climbed into bed. I shut my eyes.

Suddenly my eyes broke open as wide as they could go when I sensed and there appeared—yes, appeared—a man inside my bedroom doorway, the door to which I had pulled nearly shut before reclining. His body was abnormally tall and oddly elongated and he wore oversized clothing that draped a thin frame. Atop his head was a floppy khaki fishing hat beneath which showed silvery hair that touched his shirt collar. He wore a long-sleeved pale plaid shirt with unbuttoned cuffs and khaki slacks. Immediately and quietly, he began to float, not walk, around the foot of the bed till he came alongside me nearest my face. From where I lay, I could not see the ends of his legs or feet. His face was indistinguishably opaque and a filmy mist surrounded his body. I wanted to scream but nothing came out. It happened very fast and left me trembling beneath the covers. Finally, I cried out, "My God!" And immediately, the man disappeared. My heart beat so hard I thought it would burst from my chest and left me scared I was having a heart attack. I thought, I have no will prepared, no trip to Yellowstone in August, I'm dying. I lay frozen and prayed, scared the man would return. Scared it was real. But it was real, and I knew it. I had not dreamt it. I had watched, and felt, him appear and disappear. Two days later, I drew a picture of the apparition that came calling on me that night. And I wondered, do angels wear khaki? Do angels arouse fear?

The next day, I phoned the Lipan Apache Christian pastor whose drum circle I attended to ask his thoughts on what I'd encountered. He believed an apparition had visited me and he would purge my home if I wanted. Yes, I wanted. When he and three others arrived three days later, they walked throughout my home while burning sage and humming soothing songs of prayer as I trailed behind them. He ordered evil spirits to leave and welcomed good spirits to stay. When he entered my bedroom, he lingered in the corner near a portrait of my mother as an 18-month-old. He hummed and waved his eagle feather across rising smoke, fanning it toward the portrait, and then blessed it with the feather. He then smudged me and prayed over me, softly patting my shoulders with soothing touches of his feather.

After the purging, the pastor confided that upon entering my bedroom near Mama's childhood portrait he had sensed confusion. I flashed back to my dream four months earlier about Mama in her kitchen, where she was in a rush, looking flustered and unhappy. I was bothered by that and now the pastor's report troubled me. Yet he reassured me he sensed no evil in my home, which he described as very peaceful. He said the visiting spirit was a friendly apparition I need not fear. My fear, he suggested, stemmed from being startled at its appearance, something I'd never encountered before, except in a dream. And should it reappear, he said to simply ask it, What is it you want? The pastor and his entourage had seen and spoken with spirits, and, in fact, multiple reappearances of them. I wondered if mine had been Roger or Daddy or even Mama or Kelly, or an angel dressed like Norman from "On Golden Pond" come to comfort me during a trying time.

Whoever it was, the pastor believed the fishing hat was a gesture of good nature and fun, not harm. Even so, I left a nightlight on for a full week following the encounter. To this day, that spirit has not returned. But its visit left me believing even more in physical manifestations of the spiritual realm, and the more I believe it, the more apt I am to experience it.

4,000 Miles

Trains have captured my fancy since I was little. Their haunting whistles carried by the night air through the open screened window captivated and carried me with them. I yearned to hold onto every one, even as the elusive pull of the beckoning blow faded. Likewise, the bellowing rumble of a motorcycle thundering toward someplace after nightfall.

Ever since the SIR cycle ride in Montana, I hungered for more of the mountains and even more of the life-giving stimulations I found there. This indescribable mystery I have found mostly in only two places: God's magnificent natural handiwork and that which throbs within my own breast.

When Daddy's time above-ground ended, it was rough on me. But when Mama followed—and Kelly before her, and all three after Roger who went before them all—I in that moment became an orphan. The year before Mama's last breath, I had contemplated a grand excursion, partly borne of Montana and partly snared by the reality of loss and the certainty of death coming for us all. I wanted to see and sense breathtaking scenic beauty while I could, while it existed preserved and undeveloped. It was time.

At 59, when most people are settled as domiciled grandparents, I dared do something some said was unthinkable for a woman alone. I aimed to road trip solo to see all 58 original national parks, tent-camping along the way. With rare exception, I watched eyebrows rise and jaws fall when I spoke of my colossal quest with family and friends. But I was not to be dissuaded by their well-meaning skepticism. Well-intentioned individuals afraid to do a thing sometimes try to talk adventuresome others out of it.

Choosing the first one from among 58 was easy. Yellowstone National Park was America's first, so to Yellowstone I would go. I aimed to experience all four diverse regions of its 2.2 million acres and also head west to Montana to visit friends. Lured by the prospect of seeing firsthand the park's preserved parklands and wildlife, I poured over pictures of the park beforehand, but nothing would prepare me for its immense astonishing grandeur.

A 4,000-mile road trip would be strenuous enough in its planning but compounding plans was traveling unaccompanied. Attending to the fine details was crucial for my safety's sake. So I joined the Automobile Association of America (AAA) and Kampgrounds of America (KOA) and purchased an

America the Beautiful national park pass. I planned to tent-camp overnight at KOAs or state parks I judged safe while enroute to primary destinations, where most of the time I'd splurge on deluxe lodging and fine dining while striking out from these base camps to site-see. There were innumerable aspects of preparing for traveling alone I enjoyed learning and the mounting anticipation of my first extended road trip was exhilarating.

I also traded my 4-cylinder 2002 Tacoma for a larger v-6 2012 with a double cab. I invested in a high-grade tent and mattress from REI so I could sleep comfortably and make and break camp in under 10 minutes, particularly welcome should it rain. I bought all-weather clothing and new hiking shoes and trekking poles, a sturdy multi-pouch lightweight backpack and a Sunday Afternoon polyester sunhat I could fold and stow. I inventoried my gear, counting a Coleman stove, lantern, coffee pot and mug essential. I bought a small portable potty to stow inside my tent to avert restroom ventures outside after dark and an 800-kilovolt shock taser to keep with me at all times. I phoned friends in Montana to let them know I'd be heading their way.

Five months ahead of departure, I mapped my route intending to drive no more than 400 miles a day but conceding to a cap of 500, and cited lodging locations for the entire round trip. I called visitor centers where I planned to stay to talk with folks who lived there. Happily, they took ample time telling me about weather, terrain and other useful tidbits not else noted in websites, maps or tour books and mailed me helpful brochures.

I next nailed down all lodging, beginning with Yellowstone, and in so doing ordered a "Yellowstone Expedition Guide" to learn about the park's terrain and wildlife. I secured multiple lodgings in three different areas of the park instead of dwelling in one quadrant the whole time—Grant Village and Old Faithfull in the south, Mammoth Hot Springs in the north, and Yellowstone Lake in the east—and made dinner reservations with fine restaurants located in the poshest lodges. Reserving economy quarters, I treated myself to exquisite evening meals and breathtaking tours, beginning the morning after arrival.

Yellowstone in a Day was a 10-hour, 60-passenger motor coach expedition through the entire park to see its iconic natural wonders that included stops along the way to gaze, grab a snack and snap pictures. I also reserved the less-frequented Wake Up to Wildlife sunrise tour seating only 12 in a vintage 1930s restored bus and booked a two-hour horseback ride.

My trip would not begin till mid-August but by early July I had stowed my camping gear in the back seat of my truck, savoring the smokey smell of it whenever I drove anywhere. On the 16th of August 2014, the first anniversary of Mama's passing, I climbed into my Tacoma, turned the key, and headed for points northwest. I had jam-packed every inch of the cab and truck bed with gear, clothing, nonperishable food, water, maps, itinerary, travel guidebooks and CDs. I had done all I could do to prepare and so began the solo sojourn with a prayer on my lips and a wide smile on my face.

I drove first through flat West Texas wind farms that stretched for miles, gawking at the monster blades spinning and cattle grazing while listening to Bob Marley and George Thorogood. Passing Happy, Texas, I arrived at Palo Duro Canyon's panoramic orange gorges and there it rained while I made camp. The next day, on a long stretch of lonely road, I ducked unnoticed and in need into a church's restroom in rural Dalhart, but before I rushed away I asked two friendly looking ladies to pray for me on my trip.

Soon after crossing the New Mexico border, rising red earth gifted me with pleasing scenery. Taking in the Sierra Grande along Highway 87, I welcomed Colorado's pristine Fort Collins Lake Resort KOA where I made camp on the sanctum banks of the tree-draped crystal-blue water. I sat in my tent at its open flap looking across the lake and darkening night, with all five senses absorbing the animate masterpiece like sponges. What with the sun setting across the water and nary a bug, the scene made for a palliating visual nightcap beneath an increasing starlit sky. I fell asleep to the soft wind wafting the sides of my tent and native calls of night. The following morning was abustle with a brisk hike around the lake after a chuckwagon breakfast of pancakes, bacon and coffee, and then onward went I.

I stopped for fuel in Lander, Wyoming in advance of traversing the expansive Wind River Reservation. The road through it held neither town nor fuel station for 80 miles, only rising hills lined with snow fences. Dusk arrived on the anniversary of Roger's birthday as I pulled into Yellowstone's south entrance where an elk crossed the road ahead of me. I drove past it a few miles more to Grant Village Lodge. There I found my upstairs room outfitted with a full coffee bar, pretty view of towering lodgepole pines, and stuffed bison greeting me from the foot of my bed.

After a few anxious hours' sleep I arose before 6, donned multiple layers, grabbed my backpack, trekking poles and camera, and drove west past steaming vapors rising on both roadsides to the Old Faithful Lodge. There I would board the all-day tour bus by 8 and spend the night in an original rustic cabin built in the early 1900s. But before boarding, we all counted down the minutes on the clock to 45 to watch Old Faithful Geyser blow.

Passing Kepler Cascades, we rode northeast and parallel along the vast 136-square-mile Yellowstone Lake before heading north to Hayden Valley. There we deboarded to look through scopes set toward a distant hillside where a bear fed on a bison carcass. A favorite of my Yellowstone visit was here, where I stood in the foreground thigh-high in what I guessed Idaho Fresco grass backdropped by rolling green hills, and behind the grasslands and hills, lush green forests lining the horizon, and above it all, blue-white sky. Far and wide, dense forests, rising cliffs, stunning green valleys dotted with buffalo and infinite skies surveilling the landscape outdid each other at every new bend in the road. With each breathtaking view for which I could not fathom another surpassing in beauty, again and again yet a new breathless site dispelled that illusion.

We next wound through mountain passes and past thick forests to the Upper and Lower Falls of the Grand Canyon of the Yellowstone, where the Yellowstone River first plummets more than 100 feet before plunging over 300 feet more in mighty, resounding, ear-deafening roars. It was on this road we saw a terrifying scene. As our bus entered a long curve along a slender 2-lane pass, thousands of feet high with no guard rails, we saw in the distance up ahead a pickup truck stretched across the road at a 90-degree angle with its towed RV hanging off the ledge. Vehicles were backed up in both directions patiently waiting for this frightening scene to ease. Emergency vehicles rescued both the truck and its towed load and I heard no news of anyone being lost down the mountainside.

Midday, we stopped for lunch in the center of the park at Canyon Village where I savored a chocolate-vanilla-huckleberry frozen yogurt and then meandered about with nothing particular in mind. Arriving next at Lamar Valley, this stunningly beautiful vale reminded me of a scene from the movie

"Dances With Wolves" where buffalo thundered across a prairie and winding stream. We paused for pictures. I hiked a short way into open grass to catch a better glimpse of an elk herd grazing afar. A bit later, we strolled through sprawling meadows in which nestled the park's first ranger station. We next headed north through the most mountainous parts to Mammoth Hot Springs. There I meandered along boardwalks built on sloping terraces stained chalky white and yellow from shifting limestone, over dried springs, and past streaming fountains. Elk were abundant, descending from encircling hillsides to graze on lush green grasses below.

On the return trip southmost through Yellowstone, steaming vaporous basins abounded across the volcanic caldera, which reportedly erupted hundreds of thousands of years ago and is overdue. I was treated to closeup walk-through views of multiple geyser basins where across the panorama blistering steam pushed and hissed its lively way out of the earth in loud whistles, spraying the air with steamy white vapor. I walked on raised boardwalks through the basins to see the eerily beautiful and blue-hued pools, gigantic Steamboat Geyser, and stunning Emerald Spring. My eyes feasted on the many-colored acidic Artists Paint Pots and Fountain Paint Pots of bubbling muddy iron-rich reds, browns, blues and yellows.

Near sunset, we returned to Old Faithful Lodge. I had reveled up close herds of buffalo, and spotted pronghorn on forested ridges and marmots sunning themselves lakeside. I had been astonished at seeing dozens of mammoth elk among us. Never before had I had a day like this day; I was sated with wonder and sweetly spent. After wolfing down a delectable dinner at the inn's dining room I slept peacefully in my comfy cabin.

I awoke the next morning to a crisp 37 degrees to head north in my Tacoma on the two-hour drive through the park to Mammoth Hot Springs. There I would lodge two nights in a bungalow with hardwood floors, a queen-size bed, a covered porch and the Mammoth Hot Springs Hotel dining room within a short walk. The road north took me past Nez Perce Creek when I thought of the infamous Chief Joseph who, in his military genius, outsmarted the U.S. Cavalry for 1,500 miles as the tribe advanced toward Canada.

Along the first leg of my morning drive, I spotted a big bison afar off in a meadow surrounded by lodgepole pines, those tall lean trees used by Plains Indians for tipis. As the road continued northward, Yellowstone's terrain became deeply steep, largely unguarded and winding, though which I experienced only one spine-tingling curve along a slim 2-lane pass aside an unfathomably steep crest. When I arrived, the air was cool and drizzly. After settling into my cabin, I walked to the dining room, sat inside by windowed walls and ate lunch while people-watching and mountain-gazing.

I was up the next morning at 5, eager for the Wake Up to Wildlife tour. Arriving early to climb inside the restored 1930s bus, Montana native, Cody, our driver, asked me to ride shotgun. We first encountered a buffalo herd meandering across the road, with red-hued calves trailing the bulls and cows, which we watched and waited to pass. We next drove to Lamar Valley where I saw through a scope a pair of wolves, one black and one gray, near their den in the hills. We saw more elk grazing. And then from the safety of our bus we watched where a few yards into the grass a bison row began, as two colossal muscular males butted heads for mating rights. Cody next steered southeast to Yellowstone Lake, offering sitings of mule deer, pronghorn and large boisterous black ravens along the way.

That afternoon, as I meandered to the stables for my horseback ride, I strolled past a babbling brook that cut through verdant grassland and came upon a sign that read, "Rides are cancelled." And another, "Bear Frequenting Area. There is no guarantee of your safety while hiking or camping in bear country." I popped into the nearby ranger station where I learned a rain forecast had forestalled the ride, and on the wall was a prominent display I found particularly helpful. A Scat Board displayed pictures of wild animal scat, the word for wildlife poop, including for bears, wolves and mountain lions. From then on, wherever I hiked, I took keen interest in scat.

It never ceases to amaze me how senseless some human beings can be in wild environments. Throughout Yellowstone signs are posted warning people not to approach, touch or feed wildlife. Yet, I watched a man snap a picture at dawn using a flash in the face of an elk, which reared up on her hind legs in a threatening posture. Believe it or not, as soon as she receded he took a second photo. I also heard of a man who in the 1970s when pets were allowed in the park brought along a small dog that jumped into an acidic paint pot and the man followed. The outcome was grossly predictable. Both succumbed to deadly acidic conditions in the pool as their skin stripped quickly and gruesomely from their bones.

I went to sleep praying for no rain the next day, when I would exit Yellowstone through its northernmost Roosevelt Junction that led to Gardiner, Montana. This 4-mile stretch was a blind, winding, narrow 2-lane mountain pass. I had been forewarned it was precarious and to pay close attention. Rain would only compound the daring drive. Sure enough, I awoke to a drizzling dawn. I gulped deep breaths and drove it, rolling along at 15 miles per hour. The road was slick from drizzle, as slick as my perspiring palms. Elated cannot begin to describe my happy heartbeat when finally I caught glimpse of Roosevelt Arch. It marks the north exit from the park and through it I drove vowing I'd never traverse that daring road again.

In Montana nearly immediately, I was eager to see Indian friends in St. Ignatius and Elmo but paused to rest along the banks of the Yellowstone River. As I continued west toward Missoula, I laughed at a sign that read "Used Cows." When finally arriving at the perimeter of the Flathead Indian Reservation there rose the spectacular Mission Range of the Rocky Mountains. I continued west past the National Bison Range to pull into the St. Ignatius Community Center where Frank and his bride-to-be were making ready for their wedding. I later attended the nuptials where Francis introduced me to his father who at 86 still was dancing, and Emery offered lodging at his house for two nights and I accepted.

The next day I drove past the Elmo Community and Wellness Center where I had met Francis in 2010 and then a few miles more to visit him and Deanna at their home on the Flathead Lake. She served me a plate of slow-cooked venison and gifted me with homemade huckleberry jam from berries she had picked. From there, I returned to Emery's, and treated us to steaks at the Old Timer Cafe when he gifted me with CDs of Indian drumming and singing. When I had first arrived at his home, I had seen bear scat in his yard, when he told me black bears regularly came looking for food on his front deck. The next morning as I readied to leave and Emery was leaving for work, I asked what I should do if a bear turned up. "Feed him," he cajoled, and laughing boisterously jumped in his truck and drove off. I packed fast and hit the road, returning to West Yellowstone for a grand finale.

The allure of the open road is intoxicating. I passed vast golden fields dotted with spools of harvested hay, drove parallel to the lively West Yellowstone River and stared at stunning mountain views the whole way. I drove past where the 1992 movie "A River Runs Through It" was filmed. Once in the park again, I drove to its eastern quadrant to spend two nights in a 1920s one-room pioneer cabin. Modestly furnished, it had two double beds, a full bathroom with shower, and a small basin and imposing 50-gallon water heater both situated directly across from the beds. On the wall was a framed painting of a bison that kept me company. The security door lock of this tiniest of abodes consisted of an elastic band fixed to the doorframe that looped around a wobbly dead bolt. It was delightful. And the view from my itty bitty front stoop faced the forest-flanked river bordered by a rustic cedar fence. After settling in, I walked the short path to the eloquent Yellowstone Lake Hotel and Restaurant to dine. Its architecture resembles an historic 4-story plantation with an equally elegant interior, complete with shining wood flooring and plush carpets. As I was ushered to a small linen-clothed table, I passed a Steinway piano at which sat a pianist performing a Chopin nocturne.

The next morning, I walked to Indian Lake where there I met up with Ranger Rick for a hike through the dense pine, spruce and fir forests that surround Yellowstone Lake. We hiked along Indian Pond, a crater formed by volcanic eruption, and Storm Point, where easterly storms crash lake waters against the rocky shore. We trailed through the forests tall and thick with lodgepoles dotted with squawking ravens and along the lakeshore where a marmot relaxed atop a boulder. We walked through grasslands where we spotted purple flax flowers blooming and volcanic glass, or obsidian, Indians used to craft arrows and spears. After the hike, I was duly hungry and downed a bowl of bison chili and ice cream for desert at the Lake Lodge Cafe. And then I struck out on my own, discovering wild strawberries and a desire to stay. I then headed to the Fishing Bridge above the crystal clear waters of the Yellowstone River where cutthroat trout once abounded.

Back at my cabin, I sat quietly on the front stoop revisiting a mental image of the past 11 days. I thought about the jaws that dropped when I said I was going alone. About the breaks I'd had. The friendly people I'd met who before this trip were strangers, and old friends and joyful tears. And then I went to bed. I awoke warm and toasty inside my cabin but outside it was 33 degrees and frost covered the windshield of my Tacoma. But because the air that high is dry, the cold temperature felt wonderfully invigorating. I packed and then walked to the cafe for breakfast before taking a farewell stroll around the place.

It was distinctly inked into my heart's memory now, the unforgettable vistas, the pine-perfumed air, the restful lodgings.

Upon exiting the south entrance, despite knowing it would add unplanned drive time to my drive back to Fort Collins, I obeyed my urge to veer east to Jackson Hole to see Grand Teton National Park and was glad I did. The Tetons are unlike other mountains I had seen. Snow-topped and grandiose, they stand as stately as celestial giant kings. Jackson Hole was a visual treat, with its taxidermized full-size elk herd in prance inside its visitor center, diverse and colorful landscape, horsedrawn stage coach, and delectable huckleberry lemonade. Motorcycles lined every sidewalk curb while cyclists peddled the Grand Loop bicycle route that parallels the Tetons. How I longed to stay a while longer.

I next traveled southeast through Laramie, Wyoming beneath dusk's burning orange skies, and by the time I arrived at Fort Collins I had driven 12 hours, the last two of which in spotty rain, and was exhausted. Instead of pitching my tent I upgraded to a tiny cabin with a white wooden bunny above its door. After a restful sleep and a chuckwagon breakfast and seeing actual bunnies hopping about, I hiked the lush trail around the lake and then headed toward New Mexico for home. As soon as I crossed the Texas border, I baptized myself in Stevie Ray Vaughan's greatest hits, noted the 90-degree temperature on my vehicle's thermometer, sighed, and then stopped at the first Dairy Queen I came to for ice cream.

Along the road home were trains of every imaginable size, shape, color and length with many of their cars delightfully vandalized by graffiti artists. How I fancy the whistling, clinking and clanking of trains heading down a track going someplace. Again I drove through the West Texas Plains, past oil rigs, windmills, cattle ranches and cotton farms. While camping in Lubbock, I met Nadja and Pascal, an adventuresome Swedish couple in their 30s who had quit their jobs to take off on bicycles to see the world. Each bike was loaded with 100 pounds of gear. But with ample muscular thighs and tanned oiled skin, off they rolled at dawn to strike another 70 miles that day headed north, and I headed south for home.

After a salad in Sweetwater and a break in Ballinger, I drove into rain-laden Eden, where above the puddle-lined neglected streets and banty shacks shone a brightly hued rainbow arcing the length of the tiny town, and inside it a cloud shaped like a howling wolf. And I knew. There it was. My confirmation, my affirmation, and my jubilation. The wolf, my guide, showed up to welcome me home and remind me of where I had been.

The memories I had made were all mine to keep. The new friends I had made and the old friends I had seen again. The everchanging landscapes that kept me in awe nearly every minute. The untamed. The beauty of pink dawns and orange sunsets across a valley, lake or river or atop a mountain. The campsites, hotel rooms and log cabins. The food. The wind. The sweet-smelling air. The trains… oh, the trains! They are going somewhere. The rush of mighty waterfalls and hissing steam escaping from the ground and still, starry nights. The sharp call of ravens. The shapes and sizes of wispy, puffy, overshadowing clouds. The blue skies and gray skies, and flushed and violet and ginger skies. The frightful, steep, narrow, winding, unguarded mountain passes. The ice in August. The ambiguous sweep of Colorado pavement I drove for miles in darkness. The kind people who answered questions for directions and the best local places to eat and how far it was to here or there. Friends and family back home who stayed interested in my trek. The inner knowing I now possessed that said, Lou, You did it! You dared do the joy, excitement, fear and faith. You did the uncertain, ever-unfolding, adventuresome road. I knew, and nobody could ever take from me what I knew, the immeasurable evolution that had happened on the road while moving through magnificence.

I had driven 4,003 miles across five states and back in 15 days and once home again I began planning my next big adventure. But Yellowstone would remain my definitive and unforgettable road trip.

The finishing of this benchmark journey produced in me a confidence growth spurt. And because I dared do it, I learned a heap of things: Sometimes road maps digital or printed are wrong. AAA does not have all the answers; in fact, the people supposed to help plan road trips have not road-tripped cross-country and know little about it. Traveling alone creates an environment for making new friends. I could do something amazing, scary, wonderful and daring alone and be stronger for it. I could count on ingenuity, determination and God especially when something did not go as planned, but my planning was so meticulous little went wrong. Grown men told me upon hearing of my solo sojourn they wished they could do likewise. My response, So, why don't you?

When home from Yellowstone it seemed a fitting time to free my spirit of certain things past. I ceremonially burned the previous nine years of journaling I had done in recovery and when the flames had smoldered to ash, I ate pie. And then I set plans in motion for my next road trip.

Over the ensuing decade, I met with unexpected setbacks including two spine surgeries and a spinal cord injury that interrupted my road trips some years yet still I discovered 15 of America's national parks. I drove distances of 2,500 to 5,000 miles per foray for a total of more than 24,000 wondrous and exciting miles, and would neither sell nor trade for money nor fame the indelible memories and sensations these expeditions deposited inside me. I would remember where I had been, what I had seen, the people I had met and the indescribable joy and pleasure I had felt, together with the surprising delights that unfolded during these cross-country adventures I have lived.

In 2015, I drove across Texas, New Mexico, Colorado, Montana, Idaho, Utah and home again. While in Montana, I walked the greasy grass of the Little Bighorn Battlefield on the Crow Indian Reservation in smoldering midsummer sun, surrounded by strong spirits and rattlers. I lodged several days in the Rose Room of the charming Blue Mountain Bed & Breakfast nestled on a mountainside in Missoula from where each day I ventured out: to watch the 125th Arlee Pow Wow; visit with Aggie, a Pend d'Oreille Indian of the Confederated Salish, Kootenai and Pend d'Oreille people of the Flathead Reservation; and share barbecue with Francis and Deanna across from Sacajawea Park. I hiked the Bitterroot National Forest bordering Idaho past stacked masses of red and brown boulders overlain in mighty sculptures and along smooth earthen paths that meandered uphill toward black bear hideouts. The trail was caressed on both sides by all kinds and colors of avocado, jade, olive and emerald greens, bright sunny yellow and blushing pink flowers, wild red raspberries, fallen logs inhabited by untold tiny life, and crystal-clear waters swirling and rushing stridently downhill over moss-covered rocks. At the trail's end, a large white moth landed inside my backpack, as if to say, "Take me with you," or perhaps, "Stay," and lingered a while. That night I slept soundly till softly awakened at twilight by a gentle voice whispering "Lou…" and wondered whether the silky speech and white moth were joined.

After Montana, in a single day, I drove across Robert Redford country first through Utah's northernmost mountain passes in a thunderstorm, thrilled and frightened by winding, twisting, downhill switchbacks before arriving with relief at the foothills. But there the flattened road opened to dessert, where a giant sand gale erupted and lasted for miles, rendering driving sight nearly blind. In a short span of time, I was humbled and challenged by towering mountains and a sandstorm, and astounded and silenced by incomparable breathtaking views.

At Arches National Park, I was dwarfed by colossal rock formations spectacularly shaped by water, weather and time. I drove through dramatic Moab, and past picturesque Canyonlands National Park with its aqua hillsides, and above them, a cloud in the shape of an eagle.

I stayed for days in a cozy room at the historic Strater Hotel in downtown Durango, Colorado, surrounded by the San Juan Mountains, through which I rode the Durango-to-Silverton Narrow Gauge Railroad 48 miles and back. It was my first train ride ever, my first conductor to ask, "Ticket please," my first coal-covered train engineer in just-as-soiled coveralls and cap. I rode in the Vista caboose because of its 360-degree view thanks to open windows and see-through roof. I rocked with the locomotive as it clickety-clacked along tracks, sometimes by rock walls close enough to touch with my outstretched fingertips, sometimes over cliffhanger rails at the sheer edge of a deep, steep ridge.

Back in New Mexico, I dared descend 740 feet, more than twice the length of a football field, into Carlsbad Caverns National Park's belowground marvel. There, I walked carefully along skinny boardwalks within blackened caves lit sparsely by spotlights aimed at blues, whites, yellows and oranges of indescribable shapes and mounds, some fat, some slim, that rose from the earth or hung aloft. After 30 minutes beneath the surface, my heart raced as did I, up the elevator. And finally in Pecos, Texas, at the West of the Pecos Museum there stood a giant red "Howdy" sign in the shape of a boot and a tall good-looking cowboy from Odessa named Sean who with a wide pearly smile greeted me with, "Girl, git own in this house!"

In 2018, I traveled to the Rocky Mountain National Park in northern Colorado. There I base-camped in a cabin at the Estes Park KOA enveloped in aromatic gigantic blue spruce, Douglas fir and ponderosa pine. I first acclimated my body to the height of Rocky trailheads and summits topping 10,000 feet by tooling around the town's 7,500-foot altitude for two days, walking several miles a day from my cabin to town and back along the pristine banks of the lively Big Thompson River. Inside Rocky, I hiked the flat paved trail that encircles alpine-lined Bear Lake at 9,450 feet and then struck for Emerald Lake ascending natural trails to 10,100 feet. At points along the hike, I trekked gingerly across snow-covered ground and carefully watched my step along several spoors, as a misstep would have sent me plummeting over a rocky ledge. I hiked past Dream Lake, Nymph Lake, Alberta Falls and Glacier Gorge. I walked pleasingly among natural boulder formations that flanked footpaths, thick foliage and pretty flowers. By the time I descended, I had hiked nearly 10 miles through the heart of Rocky.

On another morning, I fell in with Ranger Will who led a small troupe into the thick forests behind Bear Lake. And that afternoon, I caught the shuttle north to Moraine Valley where I was surprised by a mammoth elk with colossal velvet antlers that ran in front of me then headed for higher ground. I wept the day I left Estes Park. Strangers said, perhaps I belonged there. I wondered.

In 2021, I raised my tent-camping habit, trading ground gear for a custom camper shell affixed to the bed of my Tacoma, and outfitted it with a bed, carpeted floor, and curtains. The next summer, in 2022, I headed west into the deserts and canyons of New Mexico, Colorado, Utah and Arizona to see places I had learned about in western movies, to the birthplace of Old West folklore. I visited the grave of Billy the Kid, when my excitement rose at the prospect of soon being in the midst of John Ford country. I slept in Navajo land in Utah across from Monument Valley at a wide-open KOA engulfed by windy red swirling gusts. It was wonderfully raw. In the wee hours that night, I looked through the window of my camper to see a thick heavenly blanket of stars. The next morning, I traversed the rugged, craggy floor of Monument Valley. It is a mystical place, where sensations flowed through me the entire two-hour drive through it, past towering red mesas, buttes and spires. With every new vista, I kept wondering how one country could contain so many unique and wondrous scenic places.

From there I headed to Zion National Park, entering it along 6 miles of Utah 9's streaming switchbacks finished by a 3-mile stretch of blind curves rising in altitude, some guarded, some not. And along this scary stretch were hikers and cyclists hugging the shoulders of rising cliffs as vehicles, RVs and motorcycles passed them, all sharing the same strip of curvy asphalt. Meanwhile, drivers in the opposite-directed lane encroached on mine, as if afraid of falling over the ledge next to which they steered. I believe I held my breath the entire 3 miles. Fright aside, Utah 9 was picturesque and I did not regret driving it. My rustic cabin was in a valley dwarfed by the towering canyons of Zion and a short walk from the lodge with its sprawling lavish lawn, perfectly flowered and dotted with mule deer.

I struck out afoot at sunrise on lower trails past skyscraping rock constructions named Angels Landing, Altar of Sacrifice and Great White Throne. They had been carved by time and the Virgin River, and at their walls and bases were opulent valleys replete with murmuring streams and waterfalls. I climbed aboard an open-air shuttle in the evening to see more, including Court of the Patriarchs (Abraham, Isaac, Jacob) and Angel Peak, over which hikers dared trek close to the edge thousands of feet above ground; from below, they looked like bugs. I chatted with another passenger about the scary Utah 9 switchbacks I'd navigated when he told me how brave I was to have done it. Perhaps. Or perhaps I had known no better at the time.

From Zion, I day-tripped to Bryce Canyon National Park but took an alternate route to Utah 9, this time through Springdale. The town led to easy straightaways and twists through the Dixie National Forest that ascends to 9,900 feet. I learned driving through forests meant slow going through tiny wooded towns. I hiked up and gazed down and across Bryce Canyon's depth and width from four vantage points, absorbing its red rock creations called Hoodoos, "the ancient Legend People turned into stone," according to Native Paiutes. I braved Utah 9 a second time on my return to Zion and yet a third when I left it. I drove through Paiute and Navajo country and Kaibab and Coconino National Forests to finally camp in Flagstaff, where I fell blissfully asleep to raindrops on the roof of my camper.

On my way to Tucson, I rested at Jacob Lake to take in the Grand Staircase, where Zion and Grand Canyon meet, and upon arriving in Tucson was met by a sudden monsoon and flooded streets. As cars sat stalled like a waiting train, a policeman told me to scale the median and head back in the opposite direction. He said, "You can do it, you have a Tacoma!" Well, he was right. I later drove the 8-mile loop of Saguaro National Park where I saw up close and across sprawling landscape a thick imposing community of saguaro cactus giants. From there, I made my way to Tombstone along stretches of land gripped and haunted by ghosts of the fearless men and their women who braved harsh country to experience the West when it was wild. I visited the infamous Boot Hill where I read humorous and sad epitaphs. I walked the town's unpaved streets and visited Wyatt Earp's Oriental Saloon, Crystal Palace Saloon and the Birdcage Theater, and had my picture taken with Doc Holliday, and Wyatt and Virgil Earp. All gentlemen, they offered a raised arm bent in escort and called me ma'am. I observed the shootout at OK Corral depicted and narrated as in the movie, "Tombstone," and a working blacksmith toiling over buggies and surreys. It was such fun walking those dusty streets of history with the ghosts who live there.

The spring of 2023 took me past the Continental Divide exclusively into Arizona, where first I ambled through the fallen fossils of Petrified Forest National Park before next driving Route 66 to Williams. There I lodged at the Grand Canyon Railway Hotel. Its Old West charm, towering lobby ceilings, titanic chandeliers, cush carpet, and inviting vestibule furnished with soft leather couches and grand canvases hung above a great flagstone fireplace were as welcoming as the view from my second-story room. Its enlarged picture windows opened to a pristine airy atrium graced by life-size granite sculptures and tree-underlined sky.

Early the first morning, I boarded the train to Grand Canyon South Rim and thereon was entertained during the two-hour ride by a crooning troubadour. Inside the park, I hiked the upper Rim trail, taking in the grand vista from atop its mighty fringe, while braver ones ventured down the deeply steep narrow switchbacks a mile to the canyon floor afoot or on muleback. In flabbergasted awe I watched how alarmingly close mules' hooves came to the ledge's edge. On the return ride, the Cataract Gang galloped alongside and stopped the train, boarded, robbed us and then galloped away again into the rolling horizon. On my final two nights in Williams, I camped in 40-degree overnight frost near Kaibab National Forest where from the banks of Kaibab Lake I fished for trout beneath a blue sky dotted white, while listening to the lake's waves lapping against the quiet shoreline.

In 2024, I headed to the sensational Dakotas. Leaving Texas for Colorado's Kit Carson country, I traced the Santa Fe and Oregon trails and Comanche National Grasslands till reaching the Sand Creek Massacre National Historic site. There I happened upon an oration by a Cheyenne elder and relative of those massacred, and pulled by strong spirits, lingered a while. With others, I climbed the rising trail that overlooks the camp where the Indians were killed by the U.S. Cavalry in 1864 and was overcome by sorrow. I touched the prayer wall laden with memorial ribbons, in silent petition for those buried and those left to remember. I next drove along the Pony Express Trail north through vast unceasing plains.

In South Dakota, an Oglala Lakota elder of the beautiful and tragic Pine Ridge Reservation escorted me through landscapes that took my breath. I prayed at the Wounded Knee Massacre site, tied a red tobacco flag to the chain link fence encasing the mass grave where some 300 men, women and children were massacred and mass-buried by the 7th Cavalry in 1890. I walked to the execution site from which the people had fled in all directions from uniformed madmen. I left this place of senseless slaughter inspired yet again by the enduring and endearing spirit of Native people. I learned firsthand of the raw beauty and majesty of the Black Hills and stirring disturbing never-forgotten histories of Native people.

In North Dakota, I hiked Teddy Roosevelt National Park along trails with indefinite twists and rises where buffalo roam free. In South Dakota, I breakfasted with Presidents Washington, Jefferson, Roosevelt and Lincoln at Mount Rushmore. Traversing the thick Black Hills National Forest, I crawled along the 18-mile Wildlife Loop within Custer State Park where everyone stopped their cars frequently to reverently gaze at bison grazing roadside, friendly donkeys inviting petting, and barking prairie dogs emerging from their underground abodes. It was there I hiked the Prairie Trail that rose steadily by 400 feet. At Wind Cave National Park, an elk herd startled me as the animals crossed the road in front of my truck and then nimbly scaled a flanking slope from where they looked back at me.

One full day I devoted to Badlands National Park. Once past the Buffalo Gap Grasslands, I drove a 24-mile stretch of the 39-mile loop, stopping to watch pronghorn and bighorn sheep and stare at the buffalo herds. I walked a causeway constructed across a never-ending sea of tall grass where I found myself nervously in hidden company of coiled rattlers. Inside the Badlands, I beheld impossibly rugged beauty all its own, became absorbed, and lost all track of time. Another day's drive was careful and slow along a 19-mile skinny, winding, scenic roadway through Spearfish Canyon north of Deadwood to discover spectacular waterfalls plummeting from skyscraper-height rock canyon walls 1,000 feet tall. The drive began beneath clear skies then darkened quickly as ominous clouds pelted rain, and just as suddenly, temperatures plunged turning rain to hail that blanketed the road.

The grand finale that year was Great Sand Dunes National Park in the desert region of southern Colorado. To get there, I drove the 8-mile wind-carved pass through the Sangre de Cristo (Blood of Christ) Mountains, where peaks reach 14,000 feet and introduce and influence the park's enduring formation. When through the pass there appeared the vast, lofty mounds that looked from a distance like gigantic melting heaps of sculpted butter. There, I washed my soul in cold melted snow streaming down from the highlands and rippling across the sandy foothills. It felt like a welcome, affording an oasis of the purest and simplest joy, God's silky sandy playground.

As I end this chapter nearing the end of this book, plans are etched for certain returns to the road, as I add to my memorable collection of never-before-experiences that contour the woman I am and am becoming.

Mama and me, 2011

Me with Daddy on his 79th birthday, 2002

Outside Club 12, 2008

Me and SIR Redroad, Montana, 2010

Heading out on a Hill Country ride on Red Spirit, 2012

Daddy and Mama, my Befores

Lynn and Angus aside his RV at my home in Texas, 2020

Me about to board the tour bus at Yellowstone National Park, 2014

Lynn

My Big Brother crossed into eternity at the age of 78 but not without leaving lasting love in my heart and remembered words to live by. On the morning of the third day after he passed, while on a walk I spotted a swarm of dragonflies. A large one flew toward me and hovered overhead when suddenly I heard myself utter: Hello, Lynn. And a moment later, it rejoined the others in heavenly flight.

Lynn left home when I was little but the memories of my time with him, with my Big Brother, have stuck sweetly with me. The day he wore his full dress blues uniform and "dixie cup" hat to St. Benedict to walk us home from school; he towered above us all and I was so proud. That fall day in October when he made a stuffed man and hung him from a tree Old West style in the empty lot next door, and boiled grass in water over a small open fire, pretending for us it was stew. And those precious few afternoons when he played ball with me in our backyard wearing his Navy white bell-bottom trousers, tee-shirt and dixie cup.

A retired U.S. Navy Master Chief and an enterprise owner of Aquarius Marine Systems, Patrick Lynn Guckian was known to others as Pat but to family he was Lynn. Despite the decades that passed as we lived separate lives, our brother-sister bond stayed and in fact marked a special reconnected friendship later in life that held lasting joy, and for that, I will love Lynn forever.

When he entered mid-life, Lynn survived cancer and lived with and through it a robust life. He kept moving forward. In retirement, after his wife Judy bore a debilitating stroke that left her an invalid, Lynn cared for her till she died, and kept moving forward. That same year, in 2020, he motor-coached with his dog Angus from where he lived in Florida to spend Thanksgiving with me in Texas, and the following year at his invitation I drove to Florida to spend Thanksgiving with him. Lynn grabbed life by the horns. He paid service to his church, relished time with cherished friends, rode his motorcycle, road-tripped even completing a solo 6,600-mile round-trip RV road trip from southeastern Florida to Tacoma, Washington and home again, and cared for his pets.

Lynn was gruff at times but also tender, generous and funny. He gave quirky names to things, like "rain locker" for the shower, and called various meats by "oink, cluck or moo" and tagged fish "fin." In 2023, my Big Brother handwrote me these words: "Dear Sis, What folks see in me is what they get, bark and all, and I am happy and satisfied with that. That said, and like you, our reconnection and relationship was and is special and heartwarming. In the meantime, take care, stay safe and healthy, and remember, I love you, too, Lou! Love, Bro."

After Daddy died, Lynn was the one I'd call to ask about, oh, everything. How to barbecue chicken, rig a fishing line, adapt an electrical cord at an RV campsite, or change parts in the toilet tank. And after Judy died, we spoke often and at length about our shared resurrected and sealed faith in Jesus Christ, and our relatives, road trips, westerns, military history, music and food, and the life-sustaining and enriching gift of friendship for independent characters like us.

Despite his private struggles and longstanding health hurdles, even up until those difficult final few days before his final breath, my Big Brother kept moving forward. When I'd ask how to pray for him, he'd say, "that I can keep moving forward." I did. And he did. And I will keep moving forward, too, Lynn, I promise.

Debbie

My little sister at the age of 69 began her new beginning in winter. She had fought a brave battle against illness and life's rigors for a long time, but from her bedroom at home surrounded by love and peace flew away to be with four others of our family of eight who had gone before her. They surely welcomed her home.

In the early morning that day, as I heard the news, I also heard the soft and soothing pitter-patter of rain drops outside. And as I pushed aside the curtains covering my large bedroom window, I beheld a beautiful gray winter sky brushed with soft cloud cover and sketched with bare treetops.

For the previous three days, I'd seen many happy birds of all shapes, sizes and colors visit the bare tree limbs and birdbath in my backyard. The day before she left this earthbound life, a great bright red cardinal perched a very long time in a tree in the greenbelt immediately behind my backyard fence line and faced me. I had welcomed it with warm hellos and asked what message it held for me. The next day, my sister made her heavenly flight.

Since childhood, Debbie possessed a lasting and endearing sense of humor. At the drop of a hat, she could spill out the funniest remarks with silly facial expressions to go with each one. Throughout her lifetime, my little sister's clowning comedy was her crowning gift that offset a tough facade. And she is well-loved and well-remembered by everyone, including me, for her love of laughter.

Over the years, I wished so very much to be best friends with Debbie, my little sister. Only 13 months apart in our ages, I had hoped to chat casually by phone, to meet and visit over coffee, to break bread together, to take walks and hikes, to go camping and fishing, to share our secrets and recipes. I even imagined a road trip together. But as much as I yearned for these things they would not come to pass.

I loved my little sister, as I love all my family. And nothing in this world or the next would ever change the depth and truth of the affection I held and will hold in my heart and thoughts for Deborah Jean. Rest in peace, Debbie. I know you're sharing wide smiles and endearing comedy with heavenly hosts. And I will always remember you this way.

Confident Humility in Self-Validity

It took me a half century to learn confidence is not arrogance, just as a whisper is not a shout. And humility is not pathetic humiliation but poised power that comes from within. Humility stems from an infinite knowing I have overcome, and the confidence that permeates this knowing requires no further justification, not to anyone, not even to myself. From such confidence springs power to keep moving forward when I want to lie down and quit, patience to keep my mouth shut when I want to scream, courage to speak when it is my duty to do so.

Confident humility is the matter of moral courage, a brand of bravery that validates oneself through belief in God. Validating myself came not without a battle, one fought with my unbelieving self. For ages I lived in the opposite of confident humility, in arrogance, which kept me caged inside a hard shell that blocked God's goodness, tenderness and joy. Somewhere along the way of life, I lost my moral compass. Finding it again brought my battle nearly to its end.

Insecurity and jealousy cannot coexist with confident humility, I learned. The insecure and jealous are like perpetual foals trailing their dams' udders forever; they do not mature beyond juvenile dependence. Only after I saw myself through the eyes of God did I let go of insecurity and jealousy. Only then did I behold my beauty and specialness. This awareness filled me with surety in who I am, a woman of heart, spirit, intelligence, compassion and creativity. A person who lives through confident humility carries within herself immense yet subtle power, no less than the energy that moves a river or ignites a thunderstorm or brings forth a newborn.

Confident humility is also a standard of living through which my thoughts, words and actions are filtered. It is the cool audacity to be God's work of art in this world. It is praying boldly expecting results. It is saying No. That little word, No, carries gargantuan might. Sometimes I must say No to you to say Yes to a healthy me. A No does not have to be crude or brash. But No it sometimes must be.

Finally, possessing confident humility is appreciating myself as seen through the eyes of God. And because God is pure good and love itself, and I am God's creation, I make no excuse or apology for the infinite good in me.

"For thus says the high and lofty One, who inhabits eternity, whose name is Holy. 'I dwell in the high and holy place, with him who has a contrite and humble spirit, to revive the spirit of the humble, and to revive the heart of the contrite ones' " (Isaiah 57:15 NKJV).

Divine Accounting

In my youth, I did not give so much as a fleeting thought to biblical significance of the numbers that collectively informed my life, or for that matter, the biblical etymology that informed my name, but I have come round to the verity of these significances. My first name, Betty, in Hebrew stems from Elizabeth, or Elisheba, meaning "oath of God," and in English translates to "my God is bountiful" and "God of plenty."

I am not a scientist or theologian. But I see plainly the numeric connotations sewn throughout the fabric of my life and experiences. This awareness leaves me believing people and events are spiritually, that is, divinely, connected, and these connections are traced to numbers, to which some refer as biblical numerology. Because it is God who created the universe and everything in it, it is easy for me to believe what we call numbers are symbolic bits and pieces of God's imperial design for a very ordered universe, including everything and everyone in it. Examples of numbers bearing out in my life over time are endless. Too many to note here. But I'll offer a few examples to show tangible evidence.

Daddy's birth date was Jan. 12 and Mama's was Dec. 1. Thus: 1-12. 12-1. Scripturally, 12 represents God's power and authority. Twelve is a prominent number in the Bible, appearing nearly 190 times. My parents' first names, Eugene and Margie, contain 6 letters each for a total of 12 letters. They married and raised 6 children (the number of letters in their names and one-half of 12). My parents' ages were 4 years apart; Mama survived Daddy by 8 years, double the disparity in their ages. And 4 plus 8 equals 12.

I am convinced the supernatural summations, divisions or combinations of numbers have natural, or material, relevance and consequence. My birth date includes the numbers 3, 9 and 55. Biblically, 3 means completeness, 9 the fruit of the Holy Spirit (love, joy, peace, patience, goodness, kindness, gentleness, faithfulness, self-control), and 5 grace, so 55 is grace doubled. And 3 plus 9 equals 12, again, a key number in both my parents' birthdates. My parents' marriage was preordained by God as was my birth.

I was 23 when I fell in with the irresistible guiles of alcohol and 32 when I curbed it. Between 32 and 23 is a 9-year distance and the number 9 is my birth day. Coincidentally, there are 9 fruits of the Spirit.

On a pivotal day only days after Daddy passed, I placed seven phone calls to begin the process of changing my life course. Biblically, the number 7 signifies perfection. Other words for perfection are precision, rightness and aptness. Dialing seven numbers for help was precise, right and apt. The perfect action at the perfect time. Also in light of the number 7, my first bylined article in a major daily newspaper was published in 1997, note the 7 in the year, and seven years later, in 2004, I published the Father's Day story about my father, not knowing he would be gone the following year. Those articles materialized precisely, rightly, aptly.

When I experienced my first spiritual cleansing by a shaman in Hunt, Texas, in 2011 it dawned on me the last time, which was the first time, I had been in Hunt was on my senior class picnic when I was 18 (1 plus 8 equals 9). In 2011, I was 56, and 5 plus 6 totals 11 (consider 2011).

Mama passed into the spirit world on the 16th of August, Daddy on the 13th of October. Those two dates 16 and 13 are 3 days apart, 3 signifying completeness. My parents had completed their assigned purposes on Earth. And together they live eternally in completeness of that purpose. Mama's wall clock chimed 3 days after her burial without its pendulum connected or having been wound for months.

As I pen the end of this book, its release now is slated for Nov. 8, 2025, on a month and day unplanned in advance. Twenty years ago on Nov. 8, 2005, I entered the rooms of recovery. Happenstance? I think not.

"Your eyes saw my substance, being yet unformed. And in your book they all were written, the days fashioned for me, when as yet there were none of them" (Psalm 139:16 NKJV).

God is the sole Creator of life and authority over death, and all life and death are by God's design and in His divine timing. It therefore and conclusively is God, the one and only Divine Authority, Who created supernatural or unearthly law. Supernatural law reveals itself in natural or earthly law. And numbers often are present, even relevant, in those revelations—in all life, in me, and in you.

Down River

Through unbridled youth and decades of run-ins with self-destruction, economic hardship, illness and tragedy, the death of people I loved deeply, and the loathing and leaving of people I thought loved me, through it all, there remained microscopic dabs of something special and bright. And as it turned out, those tiny dabs were more than enough for God to work with. Which leaves me pondering, What's down river? What will I summon, dismiss or meet by surprise?

On this particular day, as I finish penning this book, I sit in a comfy green straight-back armchair that belonged to my parents. I gaze longingly across the room at a montage of vintage photographs arranged thoughtfully within framed glass years ago by my mother for my father. In its upper left corner is a monochrome snapshot taken in 1943 toward the end of WWII. It is of Sergeant Eugene P. Guckian in a war-worn, dusty U.S. Army uniform, and behind him, a dismal backdrop of Naples, Italy in rubble. Daddy was 21 then but looked older, austere, Spartan. Central to the photo album is a black-and-white portrait of him as an infant in a dressing gown. Holding a rattle, he is seated on a cushion sitting atop an ornate wicker chair, eyes widely gazing upward. As my eyes wander across the infant, soldier, newlywed, father of six and working man traveling abroad, to my parents at home in their retired 60s, it occurs to me, I, like Daddy, like he and Mama, have lived numerous lives. And through those lives I am becoming my parents, and yet, I am still me.

I have lived as an infant, and a toddler, teen and reckless young woman, a studious graduate, working professional, published writer and road-tripper. I have been a daughter, sister, cousin, friend, granddaughter, niece, wife, divorcee, partner, business owner, and an aunt and great aunt. With each phase and facet of life, with each depiction at each transforming phase, the former one has given way to a new one, but not without carrying with it some residue of the earlier self. And so it goes, until we arrive at an accumulated finish. The infant who comes in filled with wonder hopefully will go out as a wise old person swathed in silver scars, some sweet, some sour. And within this old person will live multiple persons, some existing in parallel, some standing on the shoulders of another in a progressive march, but all embodied in the one. Will anyone remember "us?" Will anyone gain from our contributions?

So as I reflect on these photos, I think of my mother and father and all the lives they lived and arrive at a conclusion. My "nexts" are built upon my "befores" and my befores inform who I am becoming. Before me were my parents. Mama and Daddy were instrumental in forming the foundation of my being, in who I have become, who I am at my core, every bit of which always was within and whispering to me even and especially when I strayed. I remember far less their words and far more their example of abiding the unremitting changes and challenges of everyday living. They, are my befores.

My befores also are formed in the waves of circumstances I myself have lived through and tell of. Nothing I have overcome or accomplished or will has meaning except in the light and grace of God, all splendidly orchestrated, and finally, at long last, with me in agreement. Me and God, we have formed an alliance, with Him at the helm.

With each new day, I embrace my befores, embodying my parents' character. For me, it has been and will be a process of evolving, of being willing to change, to grow, to grow up. To look at the ugly in me, and like spring after winter produce through it something pretty. More maybes and somedays await me down river along with the what-ifs. But two things I know for certain: Life is not easy but it is easier with God. And, if we are lucky, our lives are very long stories with very short endings—and each ending gives birth to a new beginning.

Wherever I go, the sky is above me, and with it, stretching perpetually, way up high, are whimsical clouds. In the clouds, I can see a stallion, a dog, a roadrunner, a dragon, a whale, the ants that go marching, an angel, a turtle, a king. There, as in the river, are secrets of bygone befores and the mystery of what's next. I hope when I am 100, on this side of the grass or beneath it, when all my nexts, save the final one, have become befores, my life down river will be a place where I am remembered for something of merit. I hope when you look up you will see me in a cloud winking back at you, or when you stroll alongside a river you will sense I am there, too, in the drifting ripples. I hope you will remember a time you shared with me and smile in the remembering. And that you will carry within your heart the best parts of me, which is God, as the One heart of us all knocks on yours.

About the Author

B. Lou Guckian is a native Texan who resides in San Antonio. Lou is a three-time Bronze Quill award winner and nationally published writer. She holds post-secondary degrees in communication and communication arts from Southwest Texas State University and the University of the Incarnate Word. Following a 25-year career in both the federal government and corporate business world, including owning and operating a communication consulting enterprise, she wrote two nationally published exposes, one on pervasive elder abuse and neglect and another on medical hypnoanalysis. Lou attributes the goodness and hope in life to the one Creator—and willingness to believe.

Reader Reviews

"What a ride! Lou's story is mankind's story of trying again and again to get it right but failing. I cheered her on, and I cried with her. This book shows all of us there is a better way and Lou found it."

"Lou has a lyrical and relaxing way of describing situations and places in detail; it's like I'm there, seeing things firsthand. Everything she's written is based on truth and experience and it should be heard."

"This book is engrossing, impossible to put down. It touched my heart about what matters to me in life."

"Were I still in private psychotherapy practice, Lou's book would be required reading for my clients. It is insightful, honest, and directive, as well as spiritually and emotionally challenging."

"I loved reading it! Lou's book is emotionally stimulating and educational. Her recovery showed me how to concentrate on improving myself instead of focusing on others' faults."

"I'm not a big reader, but this book grabbed me and kept me reading."

"The chapter, The River, sets the tone for this book. Betty Lou's courage to tell her unvarnished truth is admirable and inspiring."

www.ingramcontent.com/pod-product-compliance
Lightning Source LLC
Chambersburg PA
CBHW050849160426
43194CB00011B/2090